THE GUGGENHEIM MUSEUM COLLECTION: PAINTINGS 1880-1945

THE GUGGENHEIM MUSEUM COLLECTION

PAINTINGS 1880-1945

Volume I

by Angelica Zander Rudenstine

The Solomon R. Guggenheim Museum, New York

Published by
The Solomon R. Guggenheim Foundation
New York, 1976

International Standard Book Numbers
Complete Set—ISBN 0-89207-002-1
Volume I   ISBN 0-89207-003-x
Volume II   ISBN 0-89207-004-8

Library of Congress
Card Catalogue Number 75-37356

Published with the partial assistance of a
grant from The Ford Foundation, and supported by a grant from the National Endowment for the Arts in Washington, D.C.,
a Federal Agency.

CONTENTS

Dedicated to

HARRY FRANK GUGGENHEIM
1890-1971

whose deep interest in the Museum
and whose service as third president
of The Solomon R. Guggenheim Foundation
will always be remembered

The publication of the first two volumes of a catalogue that will eventually encompass the entire collection of The Solomon R. Guggenheim Museum affords a welcome opportunity to summarize, in broad outline, this institution's now almost forty-year history. For it is obvious that the accumulation of paintings and other works of art is the result of a systematic effort that has involved, through the past decades, Presidents, Boards of Trustees, Directors, and Staff. The Collection now in our custody, and subject to further development, may therefore be regarded as the Guggenheim's most tangible monument as well as its greatest asset.

From our present vantage point, the history of The Solomon R. Guggenheim Foundation, the parent body of the Museum itself, falls into three clearly separable phases. The first of these—1937 to 1949—begins with the creation, by my grandfather, Solomon R. Guggenheim, of the Foundation that bears his name, and ends with his death. It coincides approximately with the lifetime of the Museum of Non-Objective Painting and the term of its first Curator and Director, the late Baroness Hilla Rebay von Ehrenwiesen.

The Museum's second phase—1952 to 1959—followed a brief transition under the Presidency of Earl Castle Stewart and may be said to begin with its renaming as The Solomon R. Guggenheim Museum. It ends with the move to our present and permanent quarters—the spiral dome on Fifth Avenue, constructed by the great American architect Frank Lloyd Wright. This stage was guided by my now deceased cousin, Harry F. Guggenheim, and coincides with the tenure of the second Director, James Johnson Sweeney.

Harry Guggenheim's Presidency extended well into the current, third phase —1959 to the present. This period, in turn, coincides roughly with the services rendered to date by the Guggenheim's third Director, Thomas M. Messer, and has continued since 1970 under my Presidency.

The Guggenheim Museum Collection was formed, on the one hand, through the piecemeal gathering of individual works and, on the other, through massive acquisitions that took place from time to time in the form of purchases, donations, and bequests of large groups of works. The first category consists of purchases, gifts, or exchanges, proposed successively by each of the three Directors, and approved by the appropriate Committee of the Foundation's Board of Trustees. However, the rarer collective acquisition moves have their own history which, in brief, is as follows:

> By far the largest benefaction in the Museum's history resulted from the series of transfers of my grandfather's private collection of twentieth-century art that followed the creation of The Solomon R. Guggenheim Foundation in 1937. These were the works bought throughout the late 1920's and much of the 1930's under the guidance of Hilla Rebay which, even now, constitute the backbone of the Collection. Besides hundreds of works by Kandinsky, Bauer, and by Rebay herself, the gifts and bequests included many of the great names of Cubism and of its successor movements.

> The next move of prime importance, still under the aegis of the Baroness in 1948, was the purchase of the Karl Nierendorf estate which followed the sudden death of this German-born New York dealer. Additions that came to the Collection from this source strengthened, in the main, the earlier choices of Hilla Rebay, but also included figurative works by Kokoschka, Kirchner, Klee, and Chagall that stood somewhat apart from the more typically "non-objective" examples she had sought out.

> A smaller but qualitatively very important gift came to the Museum through the Katherine S. Dreier bequest, which was consummated in 1953 early in the Directorship of James Johnson Sweeney. Paintings by Mondrian and Gris, as well as sculptures by Brancusi, Archipenko, Duchamp-Villon, and Calder thus enriched a Collection that had previously excluded sculptors from its scope.

> Upon Mr. Sweeney's recommendation, the Foundation's trustees also approved the purchase of a number of Brancusis, bringing the total holdings of this pioneer of modern art's rare work to eleven, thus establishing the Guggenheim as one among a very few institutions with comparable concentrations.

> The Justin K. Thannhauser Collection of Impressionist and twentieth-century art came to the Guggenheim Museum as a result of initiatives taken by the present Director, Thomas M. Messer. The seventy-five works that constitute this priceless group, which includes thirty-four paintings and drawings by Pablo Picasso, have been on loan to the Museum from the Justin K. Thannhauser Foundation since 1965. They were confirmed by the donor and Harry F. Guggenheim as a bequest after his lifetime to The Solomon R. Guggenheim Foundation.

> Harry F. Guggenheim also executed an agreement with our cousin Peggy Guggenheim concerning her Foundation's collection of twentieth-century art and the palazzo in Venice which houses it. According to this agreement, the Peggy Guggenheim Foundation is eventually to be administered in Peggy Guggenheim's name in the Venetian palazzo by The Solomon R. Guggen-

heim Foundation. It recently became my privilege to sign papers setting into motion the legal transfer of Peggy Guggenheim's palazzo and collection under these terms.

Before this, I also presided over a settlement with the estate of the Hilla Rebay Foundation which returned to The Solomon R. Guggenheim Foundation a portion of the first Director's private collection and subsequently placed the remainder of her holdings under this Foundation's auspices.

Finally, the Board of Trustees approved Mr. Messer's recent recommendation resulting in the purchase of six key works by Jean Dubuffet from the Baron Elie de Rothschild's collection in Paris. Together with an equal number of works previously acquired by Mr. Messer in piecemeal fashion, this major purchase establishes the Guggenheim Museum as a prime repository of Dubuffet's art.

While throughout the history of the Guggenheim Museum its directors provided the lead in the development of the Collection, trustees and staff must be credited with often decisive supporting roles. In this connection, the part played by art professionals serving on the Foundation's Art and Museum Committee, aiding presidents and directors in various important ways, requires special mention. In the period covered here, these were Carl Zigrosser, whose Committee membership extended from 1952 to 1974; H. Harvard Arnason, who chaired the Committee while he held the position of Vice President for Art Administration from 1960 to 1970, and Daniel Catton Rich, who subsequently assumed that Chairmanship and holds it at present. Staff members who have aided directors through research, negotiation, and administration in the complex purchase procedures, and who, through their exhibitions, have often brought valuable works within our purchase range, include Margit Rowell and Louise Averill Svendsen, who have served in various curatorial capacities during one and two administrations respectively. Other curators have performed similar functions in areas to be covered in future volumes.

The Guggenheim Museum Collection continues to stand, as it always has, at the very center of our institutional purpose. We hope, therefore, that even under less favorable conditions than those that prevailed at the Foundation's inception, the Collection's growth and its qualitative improvement will retain a significant momentum.

PETER LAWSON-JOHNSTON, *President*
The Solomon R. Guggenheim Foundation

The surveying of a museum collection is an immense undertaking and that of The Solomon R. Guggenheim Museum is no exception to this rule. Despite a half-decade of research, the two volumes here published cover only the medium of painting and that only within the dates 1880 to 1945; they, therefore, constitute no more than a beginning toward a comprehensive treatment of all the accumulations that make up this Museum's permanent Collection.

As far as can be determined in advance, subsequent volumes of this catalogue will be devoted to the Justin K. Thannhauser Collection, to the Peggy Guggenheim Collection, to Sculpture and Works on Paper, 1880-1945, and to Works of the Post-World War II Era. The volume devoted to the Thannhauser Collection is now in preparation, and initial research on the Peggy Guggenheim Collection in Venice is under way. Since we have been humbled by the scope of the current effort, no publication dates are being advanced for the remainder of this lengthy task. Volumes I and II, then, restrict themselves to the area indicated by the title of the book: *The Guggenheim Museum Collection: Paintings, 1880-1945*.

I made the choice of works included in this catalogue in consultation with concerned members of the curatorial staff and in keeping with considerations briefly mentioned in the following paragraph. Research, documentation, and authorship of the catalogue became the responsibility of Angelica Zander Rudenstine, the Guggenheim's Research Curator, who was aided in this complex task by virtually every department in the Museum. The product of Mrs. Rudenstine's labors speaks for itself, but the diligence and effort required for its completion, and the rigor and precision underlying its conception and execution cannot but evoke my deepest appreciation and gratitude.

Ideally, everything under an art museum's roof should be part of its catalogue. Ideally, also, every object should enter a museum collection as the result of a deliberately exercised and, in principle, irreversible qualitative judgment. As the historical sketch given by the Guggenheim's President indicates, such methodical and systematic acquisition practices existed only in part. The original bequest from Solomon R. Guggenheim, for example, included a sizeable and valuable group of old master paintings which stood outside the Collection's range, as did examples of Oriental and Pre-Columbian art that came to us through the purchase of the entire Karl Nierendorf estate. Such works were sold and proceeds were applied to new acquisitions. But even within the twentieth century and within categories of stated institutional interest, lesser examples by major artists or accumulations of works that have in decades past remained marginal to the Collection as a whole would have, in our view, diluted the substance of this catalogue. They were therefore excluded from this publication if not previously eliminated from the Collection altogether. Volumes I and II of *The Guggenheim Museum Collection: Paintings, 1880-1945* thus contain that part of our institutional holdings that conforms to the indicated medium and timespan and that has been confirmed in our assessment as a permanent component of the Guggenheim's Collection. A few works of importance have also been omitted for technical reasons, either because they were acquired after the deadline for completion of research had passed, or because problems of attribution, condition, or quality could not be conclusively resolved. These remain under consideration for possible inclusion in future editions.

The financing of these volumes through their stages of preparation and production required extraordinary efforts even after the Museum's own resources were strained to the limit. It is therefore distinctly more than a figure of speech if we insist here that publication of *The Guggenheim Museum Collection: Paintings, 1880-1945* would not have been possible without the generous aid provided by the Ford Foundation and by the National Endowment for the Arts, whose combined resources were added to those made available by The Solomon R. Guggenheim Foundation. The willingness of the two outside foundations to support this publication so effectively is deeply appreciated by the Guggenheim's trustees and staff.

It may be stated without making too large a claim that these two volumes document and present one of the finest modern painting collections in the world. At times it has been called the greatest among unseen modern collections — a half truth, perhaps, since various parts of it surface with regularity and some frequency. Nonetheless, if these volumes will lead to greater familiarity with the remarkable concentrations of painting acquired since the Museum's founding in 1937, and if, beyond this, their publication should lead to greater permanence of presentation, the effort will have been fully worthwhile.

THOMAS M. MESSER, *Director*
The Solomon R. Guggenheim Museum

This catalogue is intended primarily as a resource for scholars and students of nineteenth- and twentieth-century art. The format has therefore been developed to convey as completely as possible the relevant factual information concerning each painting in the collection.

Since monographic studies now exist on virtually every artist included, biographical data has been limited to the date and place of an artist's birth and death, or, in the case of a living artist, to the date and place of birth and present whereabouts. Individual entries begin with technical information on medium, support, dimensions, signature, inscriptions, and condition. Provenance and exhibition history are given in considerable detail. This detail is important not so much to clarify issues of attribution and authenticity, but rather to establish facts about a painting's availability at various points in time to influence other artists, as well as to illuminate the history both of collecting and of taste.

The actual text for each entry is limited to a discussion of objective, factual issues and problems. A particular entry may contain, for example, a discussion of dating, of iconography, of the identification of a portrait's subject, or of the preparatory studies and their relationship to the final work. Matters of style, comments of a more general critical nature, and attempts to place a given picture within the overall context of a painter's oeuvre are touched upon only insofar as they shed light upon the specific issues mentioned above.

The demands of this format have necessarily led to considerable variation in the length of the entries, and this variation is only sometimes a direct reflection of the relative importance of the works of art in question. A major painting which poses few unresolved factual problems may thus receive relatively brief discussion, whereas a work of less significance, which poses a difficult dating problem, may be the subject of considerable analysis.

Naturally many questions remain unresolved, and some of the proposed solutions are presented in only tentative terms. The primary aim throughout has been to raise as many relevant questions as possible and to distinguish rigorously — as Sir John Pope-Hennessy has phrased it — "between what is possible, what is probable, and what is fact."

By its very nature, a collection catalogue is a collaborative undertaking, and without the participation of a great many people, its realization would be impossible. In the course of the research for the present two volumes, I have benefited from the assistance of several people on the staff of the Guggenheim Museum. Notable among these were Alfred Vondermuhll, Research Fellow, my chief assistant during the first three years, and Linda Shearer, Assistant Curator, my chief assistant during the last three years. Both undertook independent research and helped with bibliographical problems; Mr. Vondermuhll worked extensively on the preparation of condition reports; Ms. Shearer obtained reproduction permissions, compiled the list of photographic credits, and helped to prepare the final manuscript. Both also contributed in innumerable other ways, and I am deeply indebted to them.

Others who have assisted with exhibition histories and with bibliographical and research problems are William Hennessey, who also worked on the preparation of condition reports; Mimi Poser, who was involved with certain aspects of the project from beginning to end; Susan Ferleger, and many of the Museum's part-time student volunteers.

The detailed condition statements on each painting would not have been possible without the technical assistance and expert advice of Orrin Riley, Conservator, Lucy Belloli, Dana Cranmer, and Museum Preparator Saul Fuerstein. Photography for the catalogue was undertaken by Robert E. Mates and his staff. The task of editing the entries was shared by Carol Fuerstein and Joanne Greenspun, who succeeded in introducing consistency into the manuscript while also making many suggestions for its improvement.

Louise Averill Svendsen, Curator, shared her extensive knowledge of the Guggenheim Museum's history and collection. Daniel Catton Rich, Chairman of the Trustees' Art and Museum Committee, offered important guidance, especially at the outset when many decisions concerning the nature and format of the catalogue had to be made. Finally, Thomas M. Messer, Director, has generously made his knowledge and judgment available at every stage and has supported from the beginning the detailed conception of the catalogue which I had in mind. His commitment to the entire enterprise is clearly reflected in the scope of the present volumes.

The research was carried out in many different libraries. I am indebted to Mary Joan Hall and Marion Wolf of The Solomon R. Guggenheim Museum library for their innumerable efforts on my behalf. Inge Vorslund of The Museum of Modern Art library provided kind help with a whole range of bibliographical problems. Frederica Oldach of The Princeton University Library generously provided me with working space and made the resources of The Marquand Library available. My thanks are also due to Mildred Steinbach, Librarian of the Frick Art Reference Library, to members of the staff of The New York Public Library, the Thomas J. Watson Library of The Metropolitan Museum of Art, the Witt Library, Courtauld Institute of Art in London, the Bibliothèque Nationale, the Bibliothèque Doucet, and the library of the Musée National d'Art Moderne in Paris.

I have also benefited from the specialized knowledge of many scholars in various fields. For opinions and for answers to specific questions I am indebted to Ronald Alley, The Tate Gallery, London; Troels Andersen, University of Copenhagen; Max Bill, Zurich; Sarah Bodine, New York; John E. Bowlt, The University of Texas at Austin; William A. Camfield, Rice University, Houston; Henry Certigny, Paris; Mary Chamot, London; Alessandra Comini, Southern Methodist University, Dallas; Douglas Cooper, Argilliers; Pierre Daix, Paris; Edward F. Fry, New York; Jürgen Glaesemer, Paul Klee Stiftung, Bern; John Golding, The Courtauld Institute of Art, London University; Donald Gordon, University of Pittsburgh; Christopher Green, The Courtauld Institute of Art, London University; Peggy Guggenheim, Venice; Peter Hahn, Bauhaus-Archiv, Berlin; Erika Hanfstaengl, Städtische Galerie im Lenbachhaus, Munich; Robert L. Herbert, Yale University, New Haven; William I. Homer, University of Delaware, Newark; Michel Hoog, Musée du Jeu de Paume, Paris; Maurice Jardot, Galerie Louise Leiris, Paris; J. M. Joosten, Stedelijk Museum, Amsterdam; Daniel-Henry Kahnweiler, Paris; Florian Karsch, Galerie Nierendorf, Berlin; Hans Klihm, Munich; Klaus Lankheit, University of Karlsruhe; Kenneth C. Lindsay, State University of New York at Binghamton; Rose-Carol Washton Long, Queens College of the City University of New York; Joan M. Lukach, New York; Marianne Martin, New York University; Evan Maurer, The Art Institute of Chicago; Sir Roland Penrose, London; Margaret Potter, New York; John Rewald, New York; Michèle Richet, Musée National d'Art Moderne, Paris; Daniel Robbins, Braintree, Vermont; Hans K. Röthel, Princeton, New Jersey; Robert Rosenblum, Institute of Fine Arts, New York University; John Russell, New York; Merle Schipper, University of California at Los Angeles; Virginia Spate, Cambridge University; Otto Stangl, Munich; Clemens Weiler, Wiesbaden; Peg Weiss, Everson Museum of Art, Syracuse; Robert P. Welsh, University of Toronto.

Several private collectors have kindly invited me to study specific works in their collections which are related to those in the Guggenheim Museum: Christabel Lady Aberconway, London; Clara Binswanger, New York; the late Harry Bakwin, New York; Alexander Lewyt, New York; Mr. and Mrs. Paul Mellon, Upperville, Virginia; Mr. and Mrs. I. David Orr, New York; Mr. and Mrs. Burton Tremaine, New York.

Last, but by no means least, is my debt to the artists, and the relatives of artists whose generous cooperation has added greatly to my knowledge and hence to the ultimate usefulness of the catalogue. They are Marc Chagall and his daughter Ida Chagall; Sonia Delaunay; Max Ernst; T. Lux Feininger; Juliette Roche Gleizes; Esther Gottlieb; Jean Hélion; Andreas Jawlensky; Nina Kandinsky; André Masson; Joan Miró; Arlette Seligmann; Maria Helena Vieira da Silva, and Ilse Vordemberge-Leda. To all of these I extend my gratitude.

ANGELICA ZANDER RUDENSTINE, *Research Curator*
The Solomon R. Guggenheim Museum

EXPLANATORY NOTES

Measurements:

These are given in inches followed by centimeters in parentheses. Height precedes width. The dimensions of the painted surface, not the supporting canvas or panel, are given. In cases where the edges have been taped, only the visible painted surface is included in the dimensions.

Inscriptions:

The artist's inscriptions and signatures on the stretcher or reverse of a work are recorded in the entry; they are reproduced when clearly legible. Inscriptions not in the artist's hand are recorded but not reproduced.

Right and left:

Unless otherwise stated these terms indicate the spectator's right and left.

Medium:

The works included in these two volumes are defined as paintings either by virtue of their medium (oil, oil and tempera, oil and gouache, oil and watercolor) and/or by virtue of their support (canvas, panel, canvasboard or paperboard, all varieties of the latter being designated here as board). Works on paper are not included, even if they contain some oil in their medium. Some pure watercolors on canvas or board are included in the present volumes on the grounds that their supports and their scale bring them into closer relationship with the paintings in the collection than with the works on paper. (See Gleizes, cat. nos. 52 and 53; and Klee, cat. nos. 147 and 148.)

Exhibitions:

The exhibition histories are, as far as possible, complete. In these exhibition listings the state in which an institution is located is not included if the city is a major one, e.g., Boston, Museum of Fine Arts. The city is not listed if it forms part of the name of the institution, e.g., The Los Angeles County Museum. The English spelling is given for names of foreign cities, unless those cities form part of an institution's name. Thus, Zurich, but Kunsthaus Zürich.

Since the permanent collection of the Guggenheim Museum is not regularly on exhibition, and since the choice of works to be shown thus involves a constant process of selection comparable to that involved in the creation of an exhibition, the exhibitions of the Museum's own collection are included. A chronological list containing detailed information of all exhibitions organized by The Solomon R. Guggenheim Museum appears on pp. 700-721 of this catalogue. In the exhibition histories for individual entries, references to these exhibitions are abbreviated. Exhibitions drawn entirely from the Guggenheim collection and shown only on the premises are designated by the initials of the Museum and an arabic numeral, e.g., SRGM 84. Exhibitions drawn from the collection and shown elsewhere (and sometimes at the Guggenheim as well) are designated by an arabic numeral followed by the letter "T" and preceded by the city in which the exhibition was first shown, e.g., "London, SRGM 104-T." The fact that this exhibition then traveled to The Hague, Helsinki, Rome, Cologne, and Paris is not recorded in the catalogue entry but is indicated in the chronological list, pp. 700-721. The titles of these two categories of collection exhibitions are not listed in the entry. However, where the exhibition is organized by the Guggenheim but includes paintings from other collections as well as its own, an abbreviated title is given, e.g., SRGM 233, *Picabia*. Thus a Kandinsky exhibition shown only in New York and drawn solely from the Guggenheim's holdings is cited simply as SRGM 43, while a traveling Kandinsky exhibition drawn from other collections as well as its own is listed as Pasadena, 146-T, *Kandinsky*.

Pagination for catalogue numbers and reproductions is given only when necessary. A question mark following an exhibition entry indicates that definite proof of the painting's identification with that entry has not been found.

References:

The references are selective rather than comprehensive. In general the entries include only early publications, *catalogues raisonnés*, and sources, including exhibition catalogues, that contribute something new to the understanding of the work of art. At least one color reproduction of the work is included where possible. If the reader's attention is being drawn to a reproduction, the reference is given as: repr. p. 115. If the reader's attention is being drawn to the text, which may include a reproduction, the reference is given as: p. 115, repr.

Condition:

Although a comprehensive account of the condition of each work has not been attempted, all important factors are included. If the painting has been cleaned, lined, or placed on a new stretcher, this is noted. Areas of damage, repair, and repaint are indicated in order to establish which sections of the picture might now be considered unreliable. Treatment, if any, is described first; this is followed by a general statement on the present condition. Qualitative evaluations of the condition as "good," "poor," etc., are to be understood in relation to the painting's probable original condition when completed by the artist and not as descriptive of the work's current state of fragility or stability. Thus, for example, a work which has suffered considerable

losses, but which is presently stable, would be described as in "fair" or "fair to poor" condition; a work which has not suffered losses, but which shows signs of incipient cleavage of the paint film, would be described as in "good but fragile" condition. Many of the initial condition studies were prepared either by Alfred Vondermuhll or William Hennessey. The final statements have been written by the author after examination of every work in consultation with the Conservation staff of the Museum.

Titles:

The artist's title, where known, is given first in English. Following in parentheses are the artist's title in its original language (if other than English) and other titles by which the picture has been known. In cases where the original title is not known, this fact and the source of the present title is noted.

Russian titles and names:

Russian titles are given, where known, in the original Cyrillic, in transliteration, and in translation, with commas between each form. This applies not only to titles of paintings, but to titles of exhibitions in which Guggenheim paintings have been shown. The Russian is given only where the original source has been seen by the author.

The system of transliteration is that of the Library of Congress. In the case of certain proper names, however, the spelling given is that adopted by the Russians themselves during their sojourn in the West (i.e., Exter, Wassily Kandinsky, Werefkin, Alexej Jawlensky, Chroustchoff, Chroustchova, etc.).

Certain apparent inconsistencies in transliteration are due to discrepancies in linguistic systems. Thus "Goncharova," when occurring in the title of a French bibliographical reference, will appear as "Gontcharova."

I am much indebted to John Simmons, All Soul's College, Oxford, who has provided invaluable assistance with problems of transliteration and correct Cyrillic orthography.

ABBREVIATIONS

Art of Tomorrow, 1939:

Art of Tomorrow, Fifth Catalogue of the Solomon R. Guggenheim Collection of Non-Objective Paintings, part of which is temporarily exhibited at 24 East 54th Street, New York City, New York, 1939.

Briefwechsel, 1964:

August Macke-Franz Marc Briefwechsel, Cologne, 1964.

Brisch, 1955:

K. Brisch, *Wassily Kandinsky: Untersuchungen zur Entstehung der gegenstandlosen Malerei an seinem Werk von 1900-1921,* unpublished doctoral dissertation, Rheinische Friedrich-Wilhelm-Universität, Bonn, 1955.

Centennial Catalogue, 1971:

M. Bill, N. van Doesburg, J. M. Joosten, T. M. Messer, M. Rowell, R. P. Welsh, C. von Wiegand, L. J. F. Wijsenbeek, *Piet Mondrian: Centennial Exhibition,* exhibition catalogue, New York, The Solomon R. Guggenheim Museum, 1971.

Cooper, *Cubist Epoch,* 1970:

D. Cooper, *The Cubist Epoch,* New York, 1970.

Delaunay, Album:

Robert Delaunay, Album, published in Paris [1912] in connection with Der Sturm exhibition in Berlin. Contains first edition of G. Apollinaire's poem "Les Fenêtres." For a full bibliographical account of this rare book see Hoog, 1967, p. 21.

Eichner [1957]:

J. Eichner, *Kandinsky und Gabriele Münter,* Munich [1957].

Francastel, 1957:	See Habasque, 1957.
GM, 1968:	*Mondriaan in de collectie van het Haags Gemeentemuseum*, 2nd ed., The Hague, 1968 (first published 1964). Catalogue by C. Blok.
GMS:	Gabriele Münter Stiftung, Städtische Galerie im Lenbachhaus, Munich.
Golding, *Cubism*, 1968:	J. Golding, *Cubism: A History and Analysis/1907-1914,* revised ed., Boston, 1968 (first published London, 1959).
Grohmann, 1924:	W. Grohmann, *Wassily Kandinsky,* Leipzig, 1924 (*Junge Kunst,* Band 42).
Grohmann, 1930:	_____, *Kandinsky,* Paris, 1930 (ed. Cahiers d'Art).
Grohmann, 1933:	_____, *Wassily Kandinsky,* Cahier 14, Editions Sélection, Antwerp, 1933.
Grohmann, 1956:	_____, *W. Kandinsky: Farben und Klänge,* Baden-Baden, 1956.
Grohmann, 1959:	_____, *Wassily Kandinsky: Life and Work,* trans. from German by N. Guterman, London, 1959 (first published in English, New York, 1958, and in German, Cologne, 1958).
Habasque, 1957:	G. Habasque, *Catalogue de l'oeuvre de Robert Delaunay* in *Du Cubisme à l'art abstrait,* ed. P. Francastel, Paris, 1957. Habasque's information is in large part taken from the family archives of Sonia Delaunay.
Hoog, 1967:	M. Hoog, *Robert et Sonia Delaunay,* Inventaire des collections publiques françaises, no. 15, Musée National d'Art Moderne, Paris, 1967.
IBM:	Isobutylmethacrylate (re. Condition).

Kandinsky 1901-1913, 1913:	W. Kandinsky, *Kandinsky 1901-1913*, Berlin, Der Sturm, 1913. Contains "Rückblicke," "Notizen," "Komposition 4," "Komposition 6," "Das Bild mit weissem Rand."
Lankheit, 1970:	K. Lankheit, *Franz Marc, Katalog der Werke*, Cologne, 1970.
Lindsay, 1951:	K. C. E. Lindsay, *An Examination of the Fundamental Theories of Wassily Kandinsky*, unpublished Ph.D. dissertation, University of Wisconsin at Madison, 1951.
MOMA:	The Museum of Modern Art, New York.
PBM:	Polybutylmethacrylate (re. Condition).
PVA:	Polyvinylacetate (re. Condition).
Robbins, 1964:	D. Robbins, *Albert Gleizes, 1881-1953: A Retrospective Exhibition*, exhibition catalogue, New York, The Solomon R. Guggenheim Museum, 1964.
Robbins, 1975:	_____, *Albert Gleizes*, unpublished Ph.D. dissertation, Institute of Fine Arts, New York University, 1975.
Röthel, *Gr. W.*, 1970:	H. K. Röthel, *Kandinsky: Das Graphische Werk*, Cologne, 1970.
Schardt, 1936:	A. Schardt, *Franz Marc*, Berlin, 1936.
Seuphor [1956]:	M. Seuphor [pseud. F. L. Berckelaers], *Piet Mondrian: Life and Work*, New York [1956]. cc refers to the Classified Catalogue, pp. 353-395.
Spate, 1970:	V. Spate, *'Orphism, pure painting, simultaneity:' the development of non-figurative painting in Paris, 1908-1914*, unpublished Ph.D. dissertation, Bryn Mawr College, 1970.
SRGM:	The Solomon R. Guggenheim Museum.

SRGM *Handbook,* 1959:   *A Handbook to the Solomon R. Guggen-heim Museum Collection,* New York, 1959.

SRGM *Handbook,* 1970:   *Selections from The Guggenheim Museum Collection: 1900-1970,* New York, 1970.

Vriesen and Imdahl, 1969:   G. Vriesen and M. Imdahl, *Robert Delaunay: Light and Color,* trans. from German by G. Pelikan, New York, 1969 (first published Cologne, 1967).

V. V. Kandinsky, 1918:   В. В. Кандинский, Текст художника, Moscow, 1918. This Russian edition of *Kandinsky 1901-1913,* Berlin, 1913, differs in some respects from the German edition.

Washton, 1968:   R. C. Washton [Long], *Vasily Kandinsky 1909-1913, Painting and Theory,* unpublished Ph.D. dissertation, Yale University, 1968.

Weiss, 1973:   P. Weiss, *Wassily Kandinsky: The Formative Munich Years (1896-1914). From Jugendstil to Abstraction,* unpublished Ph.D. dissertation, Syracuse University, 1973.

Welsh, *TM,* 1966:   R. P. Welsh, *Piet Mondrian: 1872-1944,* exhibition catalogue, Toronto, The Art Gallery of Toronto, February 12-March 20, 1966.

CATALOGUE: NUMBERS 1-144

Josef Albers

Born March 1888, Bottrop, Ruhr district, Germany.
Lives in Orange, Connecticut.

1   b and p. 1937.

48.1172 x264

Oil on Masonite, 23⅞ x 23¾ (60.6 x 60.2)

Signed and dated l.r.: *A 37*; inscribed by the
artist on reverse: *"b and p" / (B + P)*
(transcribed but not photographed before
being covered by stretcher): *Albers '37.*

PROVENANCE:

Collection J. B. Neumann, New York, by
1945 (New Art Circle exhibition catalogue);[1] Karl Nierendorf, New York, by
1946 (City Art Museum of St. Louis exhibition catalogue); acquired with the Estate
of Karl Nierendorf, 1948.

CONDITION:

The work has received no treatment since
its acquisition.

The white areas have been unevenly varnished and the varnish has discolored to
some extent. The condition is excellent.
(May 1974.)

The work is technically unique in Albers' oeuvre in that it is painted directly
onto the support without a ground. Large areas of the brown Masonite board
are left unpainted and function coloristically and texturally as part of the
composition. The use of lettering is reminiscent of Albers' experiments with
such designs in his 1934 woodcut (poster) *BPOE* and his extensive work with
alphabets while at the Bauhaus. (See, for example, his 1926 and 1931 *Kombi-
nationsschrift.*)

   Finkelstein points out that *b and p* marks an important turning point in
Albers' work in that it reintroduces the notion of the "paired image," which
became a central preoccupation in the works of the 1940's.

EXHIBITIONS:

Minneapolis, University Gallery, U. of Minnesota, *Josef Albers,* Jan. 7-28, 1938 (no cat.),
traveled to Northfield, Minn., Carleton College, St. Paul, Minn., The St. Paul Gallery and
School of Art;[2] New York, American Fine Arts Society, *American Abstract Artists,* Feb. 15-28,
1938, no. 1 (for sale $200), traveled to Seattle, San Francisco, Kansas City, Milwaukee, Beloit,
Wisc.;[3] New York, New Art Circle, *Josef Albers,* Jan. 2-17, 1945 (checklist); Cincinnati,
Loring-Andrews Gallery, *From Realism to Abstraction,* Feb. 26-Mar. 17, 1945 (checklist),
repr. on cover; City Art Museum of St. Louis, *39th Exhibition, American Painting,* Feb. 16-
Mar. 19, 1946, no. 1 (lent by Nierendorf Gallery); New York, SRGM 64 (no cat.); New Paltz,
N.Y., SRGM 76-T (no cat.); New Haven, Yale University Art Gallery, *Josef Albers: Paintings,
Prints, Projects,* Apr. 25-June 18, 1956, no. 17; New York, SRGM 118 (checklist); New
Rochelle, N.Y., Spellman Hall, Iona College, Creative Arts Festival, Mar. 31-Apr. 4, 1964 (no

1. A label on the reverse identifies the picture as "collection J. B. Neumann," but it has not
been possible (from Albers' records) to establish when Neumann acquired it, or when it
was sold or transferred to Nierendorf.

2. Information from Albers' own annotated exhibition list preserved in the archives of The
Museum of Modern Art. Correspondence with the University Gallery, U. of Minnesota confirmed that the exhibition took place and that the 18 works were lent by the artist.

3. Specific details about the itinerary of this exhibition have yet to be established.

cat.); New York, SRGM 151, 153 (checklists); Washington, D.C., The Washington Gallery of Modern Art, *Josef Albers: The American Years,* Oct. 30-Dec. 31, 1965, no. 14, traveled to New Orleans, Isaac Delgado Museum of Art, Jan. 23-Feb. 27, 1966, San Francisco Museum of Art, June 2-26, 1966, Santa Barbara, The Art Galleries, University of California, July 8-Sept. 7, 1966, Waltham, Mass., Rose Art Museum, Brandeis University, Sept. 23-Oct. 29, 1966; New York, SRGM 195 (no cat.); 196 (checklist); 227 (no cat.); 232, pp. 12-13 repr.; Princeton, N.J., The Art Museum, Princeton University, *Josef Albers,* Jan. 4-25, 1971 (checklist); New York, Zabriskie Gallery, *American Geometric Abstraction of the 1930's,* June 1-July 14, 1972 (checklist); Dallas Museum of Fine Arts, *Geometric Abstraction: 1926-1942,* Oct. 7-Nov. 19, 1972, no. 3, repr.; St. Petersburg, Museum of Fine Arts of St. Petersburg, Florida, Inc., *The City and the Machine,* Oct. 6-Nov. 4, 1973, no. 9, traveled to Orlando, Fla., Loch Haven Art Center, Inc., Nov. 15-Dec. 30, 1973, Jacksonville, Fla., Cummer Gallery of Art, Jan. 15-Feb. 10, 1974.

REFERENCES:

I. Finkelstein, *The Life and Art of Josef Albers,* unpublished Ph.D. dissertation, Institute of Fine Arts, New York University, 1967, pp. 123-125; M. Rowell, "On Albers' Color," *Artforum,* vol. x, Jan. 1972, p. 37, repr. p. 36.

2

2   Open (B). December 1940.

48.1172 x263

Oil on Masonite,[1] 19⅞ x 19⅝
(50.7 x 49.8)

Signed and dated l.r.: *A⁴⁰*; on reverse:
Open (B) / Albers 1940.

PROVENANCE:

Gift of the artist to Karl Nierendorf, New
York, 1942;[2] acquired with the Estate of
Karl Nierendorf, 1948.

CONDITION:

In 1953 surface dirt was removed with 1½%
Soilax solution and spirits of petroleum. In
1958 the original frame was replaced (at the
artist's request). Pencil marks and smudges
on the edges were removed with water, and
some extremely small losses at the top and
bottom edges were inpainted with watercolor.

Some rabbeting along the right and bottom
edges has resulted in paint loss and soil.
Some abrasions in the paint film are probably the result of the palette knife technique.
Apart from considerable surface dirt, the
overall condition is good. (Feb. 1973.)

Open, a study for *Open (B),* is in the collection of Hollins College, Virginia
(fig. a). The colors in the two works are almost identical. Although the title
suggests that this was the second of two versions, it has hitherto not been possible to establish whether there was an *Open (A),* and it is conceivable that the
Hollins College study is in fact *Open (A).*

1. Albers' description of the media and technique (inscribed on the reverse) is as follows:
   GROUND [XII '40]
   Front: 4 coats of Texolite (Amer. Gypsum Co.), sprayed on, sandpapered
        after 2. and 4. coat.
   Back: 2 coats of Texolite / 2 coats of Oil paint (Sears Roebuck).

   Margin:—brushed / Zincwhite (pretested) Permalba (Weber) + Dike [?] *Yellow Ochre
   light (pretested).*

   PAINTING [XII '40]
   Cadmium Yellow Pale (Pretested)

   Yellow Ochre Light (pretested) + permalba (Weber)

   Terre Verte (Winsor and Newton) + permalba

   Permanent Blue (Talens) + permalba

   Pure Yellow Ochre Light

   Ultraton [?] *Red (Permanent pigment) with Linseed Oil*

   *Without painting
   medium. put on
   with spatula.*

   *Without
   painting
   medium.*

   *put on with
   spatula.*

   *Ultramarin Red painted over (brushed) with Cobalt Violet (Winsor and Newton) + Cobalt
   Violet Dark (Winsor and Newton) + Alizarin purple (Winsor and Newton) + Alizarin
   Crimson (pretested)*

2. The artist's records include the notation "Hahn Bros. informed me Jan. 24, 1942 sent to
   Nierendorf (Open B) Present to K. N. for exhibition." The picture appears in Nierendorf's
   1942 inventory.

As Finkelstein has pointed out, the uneven, ragged edges of the color planes in *Open (B)* and the textured, mottled quality of the color itself are unusual in Albers' works of 1940, which are generally characterized by a more precisely defined sense of form.

fig. a.
Albers, *Open,* 1940, oil on paper, 12½ x 13½ in.,
31.8 x 34.3 cm., Collection Hollins College, Virginia.

EXHIBITIONS:

New York, Nierendorf Gallery, *Josef Albers,* Feb. 10-Mar. 1, 1941 (no cat.; picture mentioned in *The New York Times* review, Feb. 16, 1941); Andover, Mass., Addison Gallery of American Art, *European Artists Teaching in America,* Oct.-Nov. 1941 (not in cat., but an exhibition label appears on the reverse); New York, Helena Rubinstein's New Art Center, *Masters of Abstract Art,* Apr. 1-May 15, 1942, no. 1; Williamstown, Mass., SRGM 103-T (no cat.); Raleigh, North Carolina Museum of Art, *Josef Albers,* Feb. 3-Mar. 11, 1962, no. 6, repr.; New York, SRGM 151, 153 (checklists); 195 (no cat.); 196 (checklist); New York, Zabriskie Gallery, *American Geometric Abstraction of the 1930's,* June 1-July 14, 1972, no. 1; New York, SRGM 266 (no cat.); St. Petersburg, Museum of Fine Arts of St. Petersburg, Florida, Inc., *The City and the Machine,* Oct. 6-Nov. 4, 1973, p. 31, traveled to Orlando, Fla., Loch Haven Art Center, Nov. 15-Dec. 30, 1973, Jacksonville, Fla., Cummer Gallery of Art, Jan. 15-Feb. 10, 1974.

REFERENCE:

I. Finkelstein, *The Life and Art of Josef Albers,* unpublished Ph.D. dissertation, Institute of Fine Arts, New York University, 1967, p. 125.

3   Memento. 1943.

48.1172 x262

Oil on Masonite.[1] Visible surface, delimited
by artist's pencil outline: 17⅝ x 20
(45.8 x 50.8); total support: 18½ x 20⅝
(47.1 x 52.4)

Signed and dated l.r.: *A*[43]; inscribed by the
artist on reverse: *"Memento"/Albers '43.*

PROVENANCE:

Karl Nierendorf, New York;[2] acquired with
the Estate of Karl Nierendorf, 1948.

CONDITION:

In 1954 some slight retouching in the white
border top and right and some retouching
of the buff border on the right side apparently occurred. These are not visible under
UV or with the naked eye.

Apart from a faint abrasion with transfer
material in the buff area lower right and
some general surface soil, the condition
is good. (Feb. 1973.)

1. Albers' description of the media and technique (inscribed on the reverse) is as follows:
   Panel: Masonite / Ground: 3 x white ground, wet on wet.
   Paint: Alizarin (pretested) Cobalt Violet (Winsor & Newton) Cadmium Red Light
   (permanent) permanent Green Light (Pretested) Light Red (Winsor & Newton) all these
   [...] and without painting medium
   Ultramarine Red (permanent) with oil + turpentine
   Pink (partly wet upon Ultramarine Red) Alizarin (pretested) + permalba (Weber)
   all applied with knife.

2. It has not been possible to establish from Albers' records when Nierendorf acquired the
   picture.

For a similar range of colors and a discussion of their effects, see J. Albers, *Interaction of Color,* London and New Haven, 1963, text, pp. 52-55, pls. XVIII:7 right, 9 left, 10 left. None of these plates contains the precise range of colors used in *Memento,* but several similar juxtapositions occur.

EXHIBITION:
New York, SRGM 266 (no. cat.).

---

4   Penetrating (B). 1943.

48.1172 x261

Oil, casein, and tempera on Masonite,[1]
21⅜ x 24⅞ (54.3 x 63.2)

Signed and dated l.r.: *A⁴³*; inscribed by the artist on reverse: *"Penetrating" (B) / Albers '43.*

PROVENANCE:
Karl Nierendorf, New York, by 1946 (Albers' annotated exhibition list, entry for

Egan Gallery exhibition); acquired with the Estate of Karl Nierendorf, 1948.

CONDITION:

In 1953 surface dirt was removed with 1½% Soilax solution. Although not recorded, some retouching of the extreme edges appears to have been done at this time. The surface was sprayed with PBM.

There are some scattered tiny losses in the umber areas and a few scattered elsewhere. Apart from 3 abrasions, the condition of the paint film is excellent. (Feb. 1973.)

Between 1936 and 1943 Albers produced a series of works in which a central form of intersecting and interpenetrating planes, constructed out of one continuous white line, is placed against a uniform or—in the single case of the Guggenheim picture—a textured background. (Three other paintings in the series are in the collection of the artist: *Untitled,* 1936; *Penetrating Gray,* 1937-43; *Equal and Unequal,* 1939.) The crucial ingredient in these apparently

---

1. Albers' description of the media and technique (inscribed on the reverse) is as follows:
    Ground front: 4 coats of texolite sprayed on, sandpapered
    back: 2 coats of texolite, oilpaint.

   Painting: Center of Figure: Reilly's Grey 4, Raw Siena (both Weber)
       Sides of Figure: Illustrators Gray III with IV (Schmincke) [?] Burned Siena (pretested)
       Around Figure: Caputmootum (Neish) with [?] Zinc White (pretested)

   Raw Umber (pretested) with Yellow Ochre Light (pretested)
   all applied with knife without painting medium.

   Lines of Figur [sic] Casein Zinc White (Skira) with Tempera Duckalacker (Neish) [?]
   Brim: Reilly's Gray 7 (Weber) with Dutch Dryer.

4

simple constructions is the complex spatial ambiguity created by their method of intersection.

As Finkelstein observes in relation to *Equal and Unequal,* "the overlapping planes seem to bend refractively at the . . . point of overlap . . ." (p. 148), but the nature of their changing interrelationship is not clarified by the reading of this point. The diagonals of the left-hand plane thrust it clearly into perspective; the right-hand plane is apparently parallel to the picture plane except at the point and to the left of intersection, where the crucial ambiguity is introduced. The combination of overlapping, intersecting, and transparency work to obscure perception of which of the planes is in front of and which behind the other.

The treatment of interlocking and intersecting planes in the *Penetrating* series leads directly into the *Biconjugates* of 1943-45. A related set of problems in linear construction based on four parallel white lines is later posed in *Formulation: articulation,* 1972, II: 10. Some related issues of perceptual ambiguity are raised by Albers in connection with *Formulation: articulation,* II: 25, 26.

EXHIBITIONS:

New York, New Art Circle, *Josef Albers,* Jan. 2-17, 1945 (checklist); New York, Egan Gallery, *12 Works of Distinction,* May 20-June 8, 1946 (no. cat.; Albers' own records state that the picture was included and lent by Nierendorf); New York, SRGM 64 (no cat.).

REFERENCE:

I. Finkelstein, *The Life and Art of Josef Albers,* unpublished Ph.D. dissertation, Institute of Fine Arts, New York University, 1967, pp. 146-151.

---

5 Bent Dark Gray. 1943.

48.1172 x260

Oil on Masonite,[1] 19 x 14 (48.2 x 35.5)

Signed and dated l.r.: *A⁴³*; inscribed by the artist on reverse: *"Bent Dark Gray"* / *Albers 1943.*

PROVENANCE:

Karl Nierendorf, New York, by 1946 (Albright-Knox exhibition catalogue); acquired with the Estate of Karl Nierendorf, 1948.

CONDITION:

In 1953 the picture was given a surface cleaning with 1½% Soilax. In 1958 the work was removed from its original frame; Lucite 46 was applied to all edges and Elmer's Glue to the corners which were damaged. All corners and some minor losses along the edges were inpainted with dry pigment, Lucite 46, and watercolor. A new frame was constructed. In 1959 some chips and losses at the edges were filled and inpainted with PBM. The picture was lightly surfaced with PBM.

Apart from some pinpoint losses scattered over the surface, some rubs and scratches, and general surface soil, the condition is good. (Jan. 1974.)

Bent Dark Gray is the third version of a composition first painted by Albers in 1940 when he produced *Bent Black A* (Addison Gallery of American Art, Andover, Massachusetts, 37¾ x 28 in., 95.9 x 71.1 cm.) and *Bent Black,* which presents the same image in reverse (The Hirshhorn Museum and Sculpture Garden, Smithsonian Institution, Washington, D.C., 26½ x 19¾ in., 67.3 x 50.1 cm.). The Andover picture differs from the Guggenheim one in the tone of its outer border, which consists of a darker inner band and a light outer one, instead of two barely distinguishable pale grays. All three works are painted

1. Albers' description of the media and technique (inscribed on the reverse) is as follows:
   Panel: Masonite. former painting sanded off.
   Ground: 3 x Texolite, sandpapered.
   Paint: Illustrators permanent Gray I, II, III (Schmincke) [?] *White: permalba (Weber) with*
   yellow ochre light (pretested)
   all applied with knife without painting medium.
   Back: Several blue-whiting and white. [?] *Ground / Enamel / Flat paint.*

in similar combinations of grays, black, and white, and though they differ markedly in size, the internal proportions are exactly the same.

The basic conception itself may be traced back to *Composure* of 1937 (Collection Mr. and Mrs. T. C. Adler, Cincinnati, 31½ x 36½ in., 80 x 92.7 cm.). In that work, also painted in grays, black, and white, the basic geometric structure of right-angled planes is interrupted by two forty-five degree diagonals, which project one of the planes forward into the picture plane.

In the 1940-43 *Bent Black* and *Bent Dark Gray* compositions, this plane projects with far greater force. As Finkelstein observed of *Bent Black A:*

The black figure touches the light grey frame at the left, apparently having to be on the same spatial level, but below, it is tangential to a box-like form whose corner and point of tangency is depicted as considerably behind the picture plane. In a vigorous counter-movement, the parallelogram, whose vertical and lower diagonal edges are highlighted by a thin white line, shoots forward [from] the picture plane, seeming to overlap it above (p. 130).

The forms alternately recede and advance, and the perceptual ambiguities and contradictions are similar in kind to those subsequently explored by Albers in the 1943 *Biconjugate* series. (For a discussion of that composition and its spatial ambiguities, see G. H. Hamilton, *Josef Albers,* exhibition catalogue, Yale University Art Gallery, New Haven, Connecticut, 1956, pp. 27-28.)

The illusion of transparency created by the overlapping triangle at the top of the composition is achieved, as always in Albers' work, by the juxtaposition of individual opaque colors, rather than the use of thin transparent washes or glazes. Albers' own analysis of the perception of opacity as translucence is published in *Interaction of Color,* London and New Haven, 1963, text, pp. 32-33, 74.

Formulation: articulation (1972, I: 25) contains a pair of complementary prints based on the Andover and the Hirshhorn pictures. The interrelationship between tonal values is almost identical in the prints and the paintings. Albers' comment on the composition is: "On tiptoe and pendant between points" *(Formulation: articulation,* Commentary, I: 25).

EXHIBITIONS:
Buffalo, N.Y., Albright-Knox Art Gallery, *Eighty New Paintings,* Apr. 5-May 5, 1946, no. 1 (lent by the Nierendorf Gallery); Laguna Beach, Cal., SRGM 143-T (no cat.); Richmond, Va., SRGM 188-T (no cat.); New York, SRGM 195 (no cat.); 196 (checklist); Rochester, N.Y., SRGM 263-T (no cat.).

REFERENCE:
I. Finkelstein, *The Life and Art of Josef Albers,* unpublished Ph.D. dissertation, Institute of Fine Arts, New York University, 1967, pp. 128-130, 141-142.

Rudolf Bauer

Born February 1889, Lindenwald, German Poland.
Died November 1953, Deal, New Jersey.

6   Sinfonie 16. 1915.[1]
(Improvisation).

40.1

Oil on canvas, 35½ x 47¼ (90.1 x 119.1)

Signed l.r.: *Rudolf Bauer*; inscribed by the
artist on reverse: *Rudolf Bauer Sinfonie 16*;
on stretcher: *Sinfonie 16*. Not dated.

PROVENANCE:

Purchased from the artist by Solomon R.
Guggenheim under the terms of the agree-
ment of December 1939; Gift of Solomon R.
Guggenheim, February 1940.

CONDITION:

The work has received no treatment.

The edges are slightly worn, the corners
more severely so. Minor traction cracks are
scattered over most of the surface. There are
a few scattered abrasions and a ¼ inch loss
of paint and ground at the lower right edge.
The overall condition is good. (June 1974.)

EXHIBITIONS:

Berlin, Der Sturm, 57. *Ausstellung: Rudolf Bauer,* Nov. 1917, no. 30 *(Sinfonie 16);* New York,
Hutton-Hutschnecker Gallery, *Rudolf Bauer,* Oct. 23-Dec. 19, 1970, no. 24 *(Improvisation).*

REFERENCE:

Art of Tomorrow, 1939, no. 1, repr. *(Improvisation).*

1. Few of Bauer's works are dated, and no satisfactory chronology of his oeuvre has hitherto
   been established. The problem is compounded by the fact that he apparently worked on
   many of his paintings over a period of several years. The provisional dates given in the
   following entries are taken from *Art of Tomorrow,* the 5th catalogue of The Solomon R.
   Guggenheim Foundation, which was compiled with Bauer's collaboration in 1939.

7   Sinfonie 18. 1917-1923.
    (Bisinfonie 16[1]).

40.11

Oil on canvas, 53⅜ x 69 (135.5 x 175.3)

Signed l.r.: *Rudolf Bauer*; on reverse:
Rudolf Bauer; on stretcher (not reproduced): *Bauer / Rudolf Bauer*. Not dated.

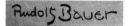

PROVENANCE:

Purchased from the artist by Solomon R.
Guggenheim under the terms of the agree-
ment of December 1939; Gift of Solomon
R. Guggenheim, February 1940.

CONDITION:

The work has received no treatment.

There are scattered drying cracks over the
surface. Apart from some minor abrasions
the condition is good. (July 1974.)

EXHIBITIONS:

Berlin, Der Sturm, *57. Ausstellung: Rudolf Bauer*, Nov. 1917, no. 62 *(Sinfonie 18)*; Berlin,
Der Sturm, *86. Ausstellung: Rudolf Bauer*, May 1920, no. 22 *(Sinfonie 18)*; Berlin, Der Sturm,
98. Ausstellung: Rudolf Bauer, Vjera Biller, Gesamtschau, May 1921, no. 13 *(Sinfonie 18)*;
Berlin, *Grosser Berliner Kunstausstellung*, summer 1926;[2] Berlin, Das Geistreich, 1937;[3]
Indianapolis, John Herron Art Museum, *Cubist and Non-Objective Paintings*, Dec. 29, 1946-
Feb. 2, 1947, no. 2 *(Sinfonie 18)*.

REFERENCE:

Art of Tomorrow, 1939, no. 11, repr. color *("Sinfonie 18, 1917-23")*.

1. This is given as a former title in the 1939 Guggenheim Collection inventory.
2. The work bears a label on the reverse from this exhibition with the number 1430. This does
   not correspond with the catalogue number of any of the Bauer paintings listed. One must
   assume that the work was exhibited but not listed in the catalogue.
3. The work is visible in a dated installation photograph preserved in the files of the SRGM.
   It is not clear whether this photograph records a special exhibition or merely the current
   installation of the gallery.

8   White Fugue. 1923-1937.
(*Weisse Fuge*).

37·73

Oil on canvas, 52¾ x 76¼ (133.9 x 193.6)

Signed l.r.: *R. Bauer*; inscribed by the artist
on stretcher: *Weisse Fugue Bauer*; on turned
edge of the canvas (not reproduced): *Rudolf
Bauer*. Not dated.

PROVENANCE:
Purchased from the artist by Solomon R.
Guggenheim at an unknown date; Gift of
Solomon R. Guggenheim, June 1937.

CONDITION:
The work has received no treatment.

The surface is considerably soiled. There are
areas of scattered drying cracks and some
scattered minor losses of paint and ground.
The condition in general is fair to good.
(June 1974.)

EXHIBITIONS:
Charleston, S.C., SRGM 1-T, no. 4, repr.; Berlin, Das Geistreich, 1937;[1] Philadelphia, SRGM
3-T, no. 4, repr.; Charleston, S.C., SRGM 4-T, no. 19, repr.; Baltimore, SRGM 5-T (not in
cat.).[2]

REFERENCES:
Les Nouvelles des expositions, 3ᵉ année, Sept. 1, 1937, repr. p. 4 (*Fugue blanche*); *Art of
Tomorrow*, 1939, no. 73, repr.

1. The work is visible in a dated installation photo preserved in the files of the SRGM.

2. The catalogue for this exhibition included only an incomplete set of illustrations and no
   checklist. This work appears in an installation photograph preserved in the SRGM files.

9   Fugue. 1927.

40.112

Oil on canvas, 51¼ x 51¼ (130.2 x 130.2)

Signed on reverse: *R. Bauer*; on stretcher
(not reproduced): *Bauer*. Not dated.

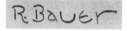

PROVENANCE:

Purchased from the artist by Solomon R.
Guggenheim under the terms of the agree-
ment of December 1939; Gift of Solomon
R. Guggenheim, February 1940.

CONDITION:

The green circle and parts of the green
rectangle at the lower left were reworked
at an unrecorded date, probably not by the
artist.

The edges and corners, especially the lower
edge, are worn with scattered losses. There
are heavy drying cracks with incipient
cleavage in the large circle at the right, and
there are scattered losses of paint and
ground elsewhere on the surface. Drips of
varnish appear throughout the left side of
the picture. The condition in general is fair
to good. (June 1974.)

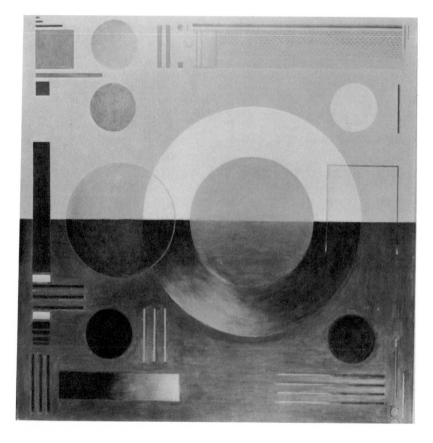

EXHIBITION:

Berlin, Das Geistreich, 1937.[1]

REFERENCE:

Art of Tomorrow, 1939, no. 112, repr. (*Fugue,* 1927).

1. See above cat. no. 7, fn. 3.

10   Invention. 1933.
      (Composition 31[1]).

41.149

Oil on canvas, 51⅜ x 51⅜ (130.5 x 130.5)

Signed l.r.: *Bauer*; on reverse: *Rudolf Bauer.*
Not dated.

PROVENANCE:

Purchased from the artist by Solomon R.
Guggenheim, 1938; Gift of Solomon R.
Guggenheim, November 1941.

CONDITION:

The work has received no treatment.

The work is very slightly worn and soiled at
the edges, and there are scattered drying
cracks in the black areas. Underdrawing is
visible at the lower left center. The overall
condition is good. (June 1974.)

EXHIBITIONS:

Baltimore, SRGM 5-T (not in cat.);[2] Summit, N.J., SRGM 31-T (no cat.); Cazenovia, N.Y.,
SRGM 33-T (no cat.); New York, SRGM 195 (no cat.); 196 (checklist); Columbus, Ohio,
SRGM 207-T, p. 33, repr.

REFERENCE:

Art of Tomorrow, 1939, no. 149, repr. color.

1. This is given as a former title in the 1939 Guggenheim Collection inventory.
2. See above cat. no. 8, fn. 2.

11   Blue Triangle. 1934.

40.153

Oil on canvas, 51⅜ x 51¼ (130.2 x 130.0)

Signed l.r.: *Bauer*; on reverse: *Rudolf Bauer.*
Not dated.

PROVENANCE:

Purchased from the artist by Solomon R.
Guggenheim under the terms of the agree-
ment of December 1939; Gift of Solomon R.
Guggenheim, February 1940.

CONDITION:

The work has received no treatment.

There is a rabbet impression on all margins
and the edges are slightly worn. There are
scattered stains in the center of the work
and minor cracks in the central white circle.
The overall condition is good. (June 1974.)

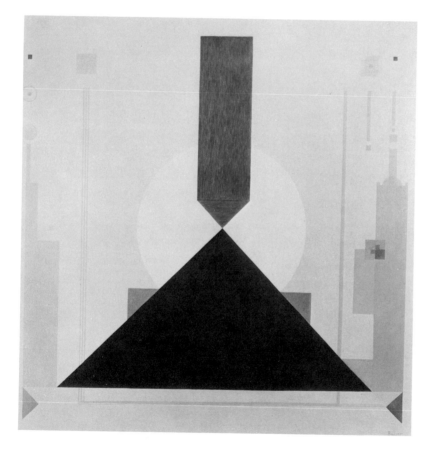

EXHIBITIONS:

Berlin, Das Geistreich, 1936;[1] Baltimore, SRGM 5-T (not in cat.);[2] Norton, Mass., SRGM
21-T (no cat.); New York, Hutton-Hutschnecker Gallery, *Rudolf Bauer,* Oct. 23-Dec. 19,
1970, no. 44, repr.

REFERENCE:

Art of Tomorrow, 1939, no. 153, repr.

1. The painting is visible in a dated installation photograph preserved in the Guggenheim
   Museum files.
2. See above cat. no. 8, fn. 2.

12   The Holy One. 1936.
      (Red Point).

37.170

Oil on canvas, 51⅜ x 51⅜ (130.4 x 130.4)

Signed l.r.: *Rudolf Bauer*; on reverse: *Bauer*;
on stretcher (not reproduced): *Rudolf
Bauer*. Not dated.

PROVENANCE:
Purchased from the artist by Solomon R.
Guggenheim at an unknown date; Gift of
Solomon R. Guggenheim, June 1937.

CONDITION:
The work has received no treatment.

Ground cracks are scattered over most of
the surface, especially in the upper half.
Drips and stains appear in a 3 in. margin
along the lower edge. There are also scattered varnish stains in the upper portion
of the large circle. Many, but not all, of the
forms show pencil underdrawing. The overall condition is good. (June 1974.)

In her catalogue entry for this picture in *Art of Tomorrow,* Rebay states that
the Trylon and Perisphere, designed by Harrison and Fouilhoux for the 1939
New York World's Fair, were inspired by *The Holy One.* The assertion is
questioned by S. Ringbom, who illustrates both the painting and the actual
building and quotes Harrison to the effect that paintings and former designs
"had little to do with the actual project" (*The Sounding Cosmos,* Abo, 1970,
pp. 204 ff., pls. 119-120). Until further evidence emerges, the question remains
unresolved.

EXHIBITIONS:

Philadelphia, SRGM 3-T, no. 66, repr. *(Red Point)*; Charleston, S.C., SRGM 4-T, no. 87, repr. color *(The Holy One)*; Baltimore, SRGM 5-T, repr. color; New York, Hutton-Hutschnecker Gallery, *Rudolf Bauer,* Oct. 23-Dec. 19, 1970, no. 51, repr. color *(The Holy One)*.

REFERENCES:

H. Rebay, *Innovation: une nouvelle ère artistique,* Paris, 1937, repr. n.p. *(Point Rouge)*; *Art of Tomorrow,* 1939, no. 170, repr. color *(The Holy One)*.

---

13   Tetraptychon II No. 1. 1936.

40.179

Oil on canvas, 51⅜ x 19⅞ (130.3 x 50.4)

Signed l.r.: *Bauer*; on reverse: *Rudolf Bauer*; inscribed by the artist on stretcher: *Tetraptychon II 1*. Not dated.

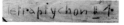

PROVENANCE:

Purchased from the artist by Solomon R. Guggenheim under the terms of the agreement of December 1939; Gift of Solomon R. Guggenheim, February 1940.

CONDITION:

The work has received no treatment.

The edges are soiled with some abrasion. Losses of paint and ground are scattered on the right edge and at all corners. There is a wide, but minor, abrasion at the lower center. The overall condition is good. (July 1974.)

13-16

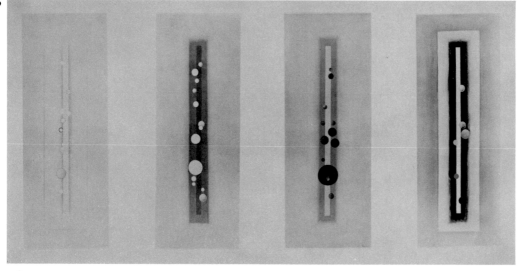

EXHIBITIONS:

Savannah, Ga., SRGM 50-T (no cat.); New York, SRGM 202, repr. p. 56; New York, SRGM 266 (no cat.); New York, Hutton-Hutschnecker Gallery, *Rudolf Bauer,* Oct. 23-Dec. 19, 1970, no. 50; Dallas Museum of Fine Arts, *Geometric Abstraction: 1926-42,* Oct. 7-Nov. 19, 1972, no. 4, repr.

REFERENCE:

Art of Tomorrow, 1939, no. 179, repr.

14 Tetraptychon II No. 2. 1936.

40.177

Oil on canvas, 51⅜ x 19⅞ (130.2 x 50.6)

Signed l.r.: *Bauer*; on reverse: *Rudolf Bauer*; inscribed by the artist on stretcher: *Tetraptychon II 2*. Not dated.

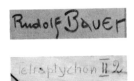

PROVENANCE:

Purchased from the artist by Solomon R. Guggenheim under the terms of the agreement of December 1939; Gift of Solomon R. Guggenheim, February 1940.

CONDITION:

The work has received no treatment.

All edges and particularly the corners are slightly abraded. There is a faint rabbet mark on all margins and slight overall soil. The condition overall is good. (July 1974.)

EXHIBITIONS:

Savannah, Ga., SRGM 50-T (no cat.); New York, SRGM 202, repr. p. 56; New York, SRGM 266 (no cat.); New York, Hutton-Hutschnecker Gallery, *Rudolf Bauer*, Oct. 23-Dec. 19, 1970, no. 48; Dallas Museum of Fine Arts, *Geometric Abstraction: 1926-42*, Oct. 7-Nov. 19, 1972, no. 4, repr.

REFERENCE:

Art of Tomorrow, 1939, no. 177, repr.

15 Tetraptychon II No. 3. 1936.

40.176

Oil on canvas, 51⅜ x 19⅞ (130.2 x 50.4)

Signed l.r.: *Bauer*; on reverse: *Rudolf Bauer*; inscribed by the artist on stretcher: *Tetraptychon II 3*. Not dated.

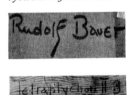

PROVENANCE:

Purchased from the artist by Solomon R. Guggenheim under the terms of the agreement of December 1939; Gift of Solomon R. Guggenheim, February 1940.

CONDITION:

The top right corner and scattered areas on the lower edge were inpainted at an unknown date.

There are scattered minor losses of paint and ground on the top edge, scattered transfers on the right edge, and scattered abrasions on the right and lower edges. The varnish is unevenly applied. There are traction cracks in the black circle and some scattered fingerprints and stains elsewhere. The overall condition is fair to good. (July 1974.)

EXHIBITIONS:

Savannah, Ga., SRGM 50-T (no cat.); New York, SRGM 202, repr. p. 57; New York, SRGM 266 (no cat.); Dallas Museum of Fine Arts, *Geometric Abstraction, 1926-42*, Oct. 7-Nov. 19, 1972, no. 4, repr.

REFERENCE:

Art of Tomorrow, 1939, no. 176, repr.

16   Tetraptychon II No. 4. 1936.

40.178

Oil on canvas, 51⅜ x 19⅞ (130.2 x 50.4)

Signed l.r.: *Bauer*; on reverse: *Rudolf Bauer*; inscribed by the artist on stretcher: *Tetraptychon II 4.* Not dated.

PROVENANCE:

Purchased from the artist by Solomon R. Guggenheim under the terms of the agree-ment of December 1939; Gift of Solomon R. Guggenheim, February 1940.

CONDITION:

The upper corners, lower left corner, left edge at the center, and right edge at scattered locations were inpainted at an unknown date.

The edges and corners are slightly abraded with a rabbet mark visible on the top edge, lower right edge, and at scattered other locations. The overall condition is very good. (July 1974.)

EXHIBITIONS:

Savannah, Ga., SRGM 50-T (no cat.); New York, SRGM 202, repr. p. 57; New York, SRGM 266 (no cat.); New York, Hutton-Hutschnecker Gallery, *Rudolf Bauer*, Oct. 23-Dec. 19, 1970, no. 49; Dallas Museum of Fine Arts, *Geometric Abstraction: 1926-42*, Oct. 7-Nov. 19, 1972, no. 4, repr.

REFERENCE:

Art of Tomorrow, 1939, no. 178, repr.

---

17   Blue Balls II. 1938.

40.205

Oil on canvas, 51¼ x 51½ (130.2 x 130.6)

Signed l.r.: *R. Bauer.* Not dated.

PROVENANCE:

Purchased from the artist by Solomon R. Guggenheim under the terms of the agreement of December 1939; Gift of Solomon R. Guggenheim, February 1940.

CONDITION:

At an unknown date the work was infused with wax resin and placed on a new stretcher. The picture has been heavily inpainted in a 4 in. band around all sides of the work and in a vertical line 11 in. from the right. The fact that this inpainting is far more generalized than would have been essential to cover any losses, and the existence of a coat of varnish beneath the inpaint suggest that it is the work of Jean Xceron, who inpainted a number of the Museum's pictures in this manner in the late 1940's and early 1950's.

While the edges and corners of the work are in generally good condition, there is a ½ in. rabbet mark on all margins. There is a 7 in. curved abrasion in the paint layer at the lower left corner. The overall condition is fair to good. (June 1974.)

EXHIBITIONS:

New York, Hutton-Hutschnecker Gallery, *Rudolf Bauer,* Oct. 23-Dec. 19, 1970, no. 57; New York, SRGM 266 (no cat.).

REFERENCE:

Art of Tomorrow, 1939, no. 205, repr.

17

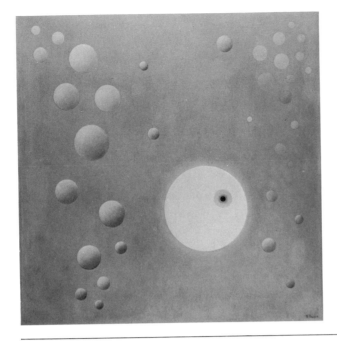

18   Purple Center. 1939.

40.215

Oil on canvas, 43⅜ x 43½ (110.2 x 110.7)

Signed l.r.: *Rudolf Bauer*. Not dated.

PROVENANCE:

Purchased from the artist by Solomon R. Guggenheim under the terms of the agreement of December 1939; Gift of Solomon R. Guggenheim, February 1940.

CONDITION:

The work has received no treatment.

There is very slight wear on all edges and corners with the lower corners more severely worn. There is a faint rabbet mark on the top edge, and slight rubs and transfers appear in a wide band at the top of the picture. The condition is otherwise good. (June 1974.)

REFERENCE:

Art of Tomorrow, 1939, no. 215, repr.

Ilya Bolotowsky

Born July 1907, St. Petersburg, Russia.
Lives in New York.

19   Upright in Gold and Violet. 1945.

46.1030

Oil on canvas, 41 x 21⅞ (104.1 x 55.7)

Signed and dated l.r.: *Ilya Bolotowsky 45*;
inscribed by the artist on stretcher: *"Upright in Gold and Violet"* / *Ilya Bolotowsky* /
69 Tiemann Place, NYC 27.

PROVENANCE:

Purchased from J. B. Neumann, New York, 1946.

CONDITION:

The work has received no treatment since its acquisition.

There are some large pigment cracks in various parts of the surface and some incipient cleavage. The lower edge and corners are chipped and abraded with loss of paint and ground. A few scattered abrasions are visible as is a 1 in. transfer of blue paint 4½ in. down from the top and ½ in. from the left side. There is considerable surface soil; the condition in general is fair. (Dec. 1973.)

EXHIBITIONS:

New York, New Art Circle (J. B. Neumann), *Ilya Bolotowsky,* Feb. 11-28, 1946 (checklist);
Zurich, SRGM 60-T, no. 4; New York, SRGM 277, *Ilya Bolotowsky,* no. 13, repr.

Pierre Bonnard

Born October 1867, Fontenay-aux-Roses, France.
Died January 1947, Le Cannet, France.

20   Dining Room on the Garden. 1934-1935.
*(Grande salle à manger sur le jardin; Salle à
manger de campagne).*

38.432

Oil on canvas, 50 x 53¼ (126.8 x 135.3)

Signed l.l.: *Bonnard*. Not dated.

PROVENANCE:

Purchased from the artist by Galerie Bernheim-Jeune, Paris, 1935 (information supplied by Bernheim-Jeune, correspondence
with the Museum, July 1961); purchased
from Bernheim-Jeune by Galerie Pierre
(Pierre Loeb), Paris, February 1937; purchased from Loeb, 1938.

CONDITION:

In 1969 the work was cleaned (with the exception of the left section of the window,
which was found to be soluble). In 1970 it
was lined with wax resin and placed on a
new stretcher.

The right edge is slightly worn, as are the
upper right and left corners. The lower corners show minor damage to the support. A
very few areas of surface crackle were closed
by the lining process. The condition is excellent. (Apr. 1974.)

A label formerly attached to the reverse of the painting (but now lost) evi-
dently carried the date 1933. The fact that the picture is dated "before 1933"
in all Guggenheim publications between 1953 and 1968 is based on this
apparently misleading evidence.

Terrasse (1967, and in correspondence with the Museum, May 1974) has
identified the room represented in this and another closely related painting
(Collection E. Bragaline, New York, M. Knoedler & Co., Inc., *Twentieth
Century Masters,* 1963, repr. color no. 1) as the dining room of a villa at
Bénerville-sur-Mer. Bonnard rented this villa only once, from June to September 1934, and although photographs of its interior do not exist, Terrasse
has argued convincingly that since the interiors of the other villas periodically
rented by Bonnard are well known, Bénerville-sur-Mer must, by process of
elimination, be the setting for the present two paintings. Thus the Guggenheim
picture cannot have been painted before summer 1934 and was certainly completed by autumn 1935 when it was submitted for exhibition in the *Salon
d'Automne.* Although it is likely that both the Guggenheim and the Bragaline
pictures were painted at Bénerville-sur-Mer itself, as Terrasse believes, it is
possible that one or the other of them was painted later. A date of 1934-35 is
therefore the most plausible.

A drawing in the Sapiro collection in Paris (fig. a) records the same scene.
Its vertical format, which cuts off the scene on either side of the window,
brings it into closer relationship with the Bragaline painting than with that of
the Guggenheim. Certain of the still-life elements from the drawing, however,
are incorporated into the Guggenheim painting but omitted from the Bragaline
version. (See, for example, the jug at the far left and the pot of jam resting on
the book.) Both paintings include the figure of Bonnard's wife, Marthe, which

20

does not appear in the drawing. In the Guggenheim picture she appears three-quarter length, full-face, while in the Bragaline painting only her head and hand appear in profile, cut off at the right edge of the canvas. The interrelationship of the drawing and the two paintings is hence somewhat complex.

It is difficult to establish which of the two paintings came first. The drawing and the two paintings probably date from approximately the same time, and the drawing, while strictly speaking more readily identifiable as a sketch for the Bragaline picture, was also clearly involved in the development of the Guggenheim work.

fig. a.
Bonnard, study for *Dining Room on the Garden,* pencil on paper, 6⅞ x 4⅞ in.,
17.5 x 12.5 cm., Collection Sapiro, Paris.

EXHIBITIONS:

Paris, *Salon d'Automne,* Nov. 1-Dec. 8, 1935, no. 159 *(Salle à manger de campagne)*; Paris,
Musée du Petit Palais, *Les Maîtres de l'art indépendant, 1895-1937,* June-Oct. 1937, no. 25;
New York, The Museum of Modern Art, *Art in Progress: 15th Anniversary Exhibition,* May
24-Oct. 15, 1944, repr. p. 35; Boston, Institute of Modern Art, *Bonnard-Vuillard,* Oct. 3-Nov.
11, 1944 (cat. not located); New York, SRGM 79 (checklist, dated "before 1933;" so dated in
all subsequent SRGM publications until SRGM 202, 1968); 83 (no cat.); 87 (checklist); San
Francisco Museum of Art, *Art in the Twentieth Century,* June 17-July 10, 1955, p. 11; New
York, SRGM 95 (checklist); Hartford, Conn., Wadsworth Atheneum, *Twentieth Century
Painting from Three Cities: New York, New Haven, Hartford,* Oct. 19-Dec. 4, 1955, no. 6,
repr.; New York, SRGM 97 (checklist); Palm Beach, Fla., The Society of the Four Arts,
Bonnard, Jan. 4-27, 1957, no. 22; London, Tate Gallery, SRGM 104-T, no. 2 (dated "before
1933" in London, Hague, Helsinki, Cologne cats. and 1925-34 in Paris and Rome cats.); New
York, SRGM 112, 118, 129 (checklists); Philadelphia, SRGM 134-T, no. 6, repr.; New York,
SRGM 144 (checklist); New York, The Museum of Modern Art, *Bonnard and his Environ-
ment,* Oct. 7-Nov. 29, 1964, no. 57, repr. (dated ca. 1933), traveled to The Art Institute of
Chicago, Jan. 8-Feb. 28, 1965, Los Angeles County Museum of Art, Mar. 31-May 30, 1965;
New York, SRGM 173, no. 61, repr. color; 187 (checklist); 202, p. 41, repr. (dated 1934); 216,
227 (no cats.); 232, 241, pp. 42-43, repr. color; 251, 260 (no cats.).

REFERENCES:

J. Guenne, "Le Salon d'Automne," *L'Art vivant,* no. 198, Nov. 1935, p. 247, repr.; *Verve,* vol. 1,
Dec. 1937, repr. color, p. 87; *Art of Tomorrow,* 1939, p. 171 (dated 1934); J. Rewald, *Bonnard,*
New York, 1948, p. 116, repr. (dated 1934); R. Melville, review of SRGM 104-T, *Architectural
Review,* vol. 122, July 1957, p. 76, repr.; SRGM *Handbook,* 1959, p. 24, repr. p. 25 (dated
"before 1933"); A. Terrasse, *Bonnard,* Geneva, 1964, p. 80, repr. color p. 74 (dated 1934);
A. Terrasse, *Pierre Bonnard,* Paris, 1967, pp. 144-145, repr. color p. 146 (dated 1934);
A. Fermigier, *Pierre Bonnard,* New York, 1969, repr. color p. 141 (dated ca. 1934); J. and H.
Dauberville, *Bonnard: catalogue raisonné de l'oeuvre peint 1920-1939,* Paris, 1973, no. 1524,
repr. (dated 1934).

Georges Braque

Born May 1882, Argenteuil.
Died September 1963, Paris.

21

22

21   Violin and Palette. 1909-1910.
       (Violon et palette; Violine).

54.1412

Oil on canvas, 36⅛ x 16⅞ (91.7 x 42.8)

Signed on reverse (visible through lining): *Braque.* Not dated.

PROVENANCE:

Purchased from the artist by D. H. Kahnweiler, Paris, 1910;[1] purchased from Kahnweiler by Wilhelm Uhde, Berlin, 1910;[1] Edwin Suermondt (d. 1923), Burg Drove, Die Eifel, Germany, ca. 1910-23;[1] Mrs. Edwin Suermondt, 1923-ca. 1926;[2] Alex Vömel, Dusseldorf, ca. 1926-53;[3] purchased from Vömel by Fine Arts Associates, New York, 1954; purchased from Fine Arts Associates, 1954.

CONDITION:

At some point prior to its acquisition by the Museum, the painting was lined with wax resin. Since the canvas had been sized with glue by the artist but not primed, the wax resin has, in certain thinly painted areas, penetrated to the surface as a mottled brown color. In 1955 the painting was cleaned and placed on a new stretcher. There are some minimal touches of repaint along the edges.

The overall condition is excellent, with some scattered minor losses and abrasions in the paint film. (Dec. 1971.)

Violin and Palette and *Piano and Mandola,* see below cat. no. 22, are closely related in style and subject matter to *Violin and Jug* in the Kunstmuseum Basel (Golding, pl. 33) and the Tate Gallery *Mandola* (Cooper, 1956, pl. 20b). Although opinions vary about the sequential development within this group, unanimity exists about the fact that all four date from the winter of 1909-10. (See Hope, who suggests that the Basel picture was begun at the end of 1909 but possibly not completed till the spring of 1910; Cooper, 1956 and 1970, Richardson, Russell, Leymarie, Golding, Rosenblum, and Mullins.)

All four pictures typify that moment in Braque's development when the principles of Cubism as he himself defined them reached their first full expression: faceting and fragmentation were used because

> *this was a means of getting as close to the objects as painting allowed. Fragmentation allowed me to establish a spatial element as well as a spatial movement and until this had been achieved I was not able to introduce objects into my pictures. Likewise at this period I painted musical instruments, in the first place because I was surrounded by them, secondly because by their very nature they appertained to my conception of a still-life and*

1. Information supplied by Kahnweiler, correspondence with the author, March 1971.
   W. George, in an article on Braque published in *L'Esprit nouveau,* no. 6 [1921?], p. 643, implies that in 1921 Kahnweiler still owned the picture. The caption (*"Coll. Simon,"* which refers to Kahnweiler's post-World War I gallery), carried by each reproduction in the article, is an error, except insofar as Kahnweiler still held reproduction rights to the works by Cubist artists he had acquired before 1914.

2. Suermondt's widow married Alex Vömel in 1926. Although it is not entirely clear whether all the pictures in her collection were thereafter jointly owned, some of them, including the present picture, were later lent to exhibitions either by the Galerie Flechtheim (of which Vömel was a partner; see also Rousseau, below cat. no. 222) or by Vömel himself.

3. Vömel was the lender to the 1953 Bern-Zurich *Braque* exhibition.

lastly because I was already working towards a tactile *space . . . and musical instruments have the advantage of being animated by one's touch. That is why I was attracted to them far more than to other objects or to human figures . . .*

(D. Vallier, "Braque, la peinture et nous," *Cahiers d'Art,* vol. xxix, October 1954, p. 16, trans. by Richardson, p. 10; for further analysis of this moment in Braque's development see Richardson, pp. 9-11; Cooper, 1956, nos. 19-23; Golding, pp. 80-85; Cooper, 1970, pp. 44-46).

In all four of these pictures the space is shallow though ambiguous. As Rosenblum has pointed out (1960, pp. 57-58), "the illusion of depth inferred [in the Basel picture] from the sharp cut of the wall and triple molding at the right is contradicted by the continuous oscillation of planes that seem to cling to the picture surface as if magnetized." A stark contrast to this ambiguity is provided by the *trompe l'oeil* realism of the nail projecting obliquely from the top center of the canvas in both the Basel picture and the Guggenheim *Violin and Palette.* Kahnweiler first drew attention to the significance of this device, in which the cast shadow deliberately draws attention to the differences between Cubist and traditional conceptions of both space and illusion. According to Cooper (1956, p. 31), this detail was the subject of extensive discussion immediately after the pictures were painted, and it has remained one. (See especially, Greenberg, p. 47, also Rosenblum, pp. 57-58.)

The development within this group of four pictures is discernable despite the fact that they are extremely close in time of execution. From the Basel *Still Life* to the *Violin and Palette,* the *Piano and Mandola,* and finally the Tate Gallery picture there is a progressive reduction in the spatial depth, an increased flattening out of the faceted forms, and a gradual disintegration of recognizable shapes into a structure of interlocking planes which blur the distinctions between objects and background.

EXHIBITIONS:
Cologne, *Internationale Kunstausstellung des Sonderbundes Westdeutschen Kunstfreunden und Künstler zu Köln,* May 25-Sept. 30, 1912, no. 231 *(Die Violine)*; Moscow, Бубновый валет (Bubnovyi valet, *Jack of Diamonds),* Mar. 3-Apr. 6, 1913, no. 11 ("Скрипка, 1909," Skripka, *Violin)*; Berlin, Galerie Flechtheim, *Matisse, Braque, Picasso: 60 Werke aus Deutschem Besitz,* Sept. 21-mid. Oct. 1930, no. 16 *(Die Violine,* dated 1911); Kunsthalle Basel, *Georges Braque,* Apr. 9-May 14, 1933, no. 22 *(Die Violine)*; Kunsthalle Bern, *Georges Braque,* Apr. 25-May 31, 1953, no. 22, traveled to Kunsthaus Zürich, June 7-July 19, 1953, no. 23; New York, SRGM 95 (checklist; withdrawn Sept. 12); The Arts Club of Chicago, *An Exhibition of Cubism on the Occasion of the Fortieth Anniversary of the Arts Club of Chicago,* Oct. 3-Nov. 4, 1955, no. 2; New York, SRGM 97 (checklist); Edinburgh, Royal Scottish Academy, *G. Braque,* Aug. 18-Sept. 15, 1956, p. 30, no. 21, pl. 14b, traveled to London, Tate Gallery, Sept. 28-Nov. 11, 1956; London, SRGM 104-T, no. 4; New York, SRGM 112, 118, 129 (checklists); Philadelphia, SRGM 134-T, no. 9; New York, SRGM 144 (checklist); Worcester, Mass., SRGM 148-T, no. 4, repr.; New York, SRGM 151 (checklist), 153 (checklist; commentary, repr. color); New York, Saidenberg Gallery, *Braque: An American Tribute, Fauvism and Cubism,* Apr. 7-May 2, 1964, no. 14, repr.; New York, SRGM 173, no. 16, repr. color; 196 (checklist); 198-T, 216, 221 (no cats.); 232, p. 47, repr. color p. 48; Los Angeles County Museum of Art, *The Cubist Epoch,* Dec. 15, 1970-Feb. 21, 1971, traveled to New York, The Metropolitan Museum of Art, Apr. 9-June 8, 1971, no. 19, color pl. 24, p. 43; New York,

SRGM 241, p. 47, repr. color p. 48; 251 (no cat.); Cleveland, SRGM 258-T, pl. 1; Paris, Orangerie, *Georges Braque,* Oct. 16, 1973-January 14, 1974, no. 29, repr. p. 77.

REFERENCES:

D. H. Kahnweiler, *Der Weg zum Cubismus,* Munich, 1920, p. 24; G. Isarlov, *Georges Braque,* Paris, 1932, no. 70 ("*La Palette,* 1910"); D. Cooper, *G. Braque,* exhibition catalogue, Edinburgh and London, 1956, no. 21, pp. 30-31, pl. 14b; C. Greenberg, "The Pasted Paper Revolution," *Art News,* vol. 57, Sept. 1958, p. 47, repr.; J. Russell, *Georges Braque,* Garden City, N.Y., 1959, p. 120; J. Richardson, *Braque,* Harmondsworth, Middx., 1959, pp. 9-10, color pl. 7a; R. Rosenblum, *Cubism and Twentieth-Century Art,* New York, 1960, revised ed., 1961, p. 58, pl. 30, p. 52; Golding, *Cubism,* 1968, p. 92, pl. 34; J. Leymarie, *Braque,* Lausanne, 1961, p. 48, repr. color p. 42; E. Mullins, *The Art of Georges Braque,* New York, 1968, pp. 56-58, 67, repr. p. 57; Cooper, *Cubist Epoch,* 1970, no. 19, pp. 44, 277, color pl. 24, p. 43.

22   Piano and Mandola. 1909-1910.
(*Piano et Mandore; Harmonium; Piano and Lute*).

54.1411

Oil on canvas, 36⅛ x 16⅞ (91.7 x 42.8)

Signed on reverse (visible through lining): *Braque.* Not dated.

PROVENANCE:
See above cat. no. 21 *Violin and Palette.*

CONDITION:

At some point prior to its acquisition by the Museum, the painting was lined with wax resin. Since the canvas had been sized with glue by the artist, but not primed, the wax resin has, in certain thinly painted areas, penetrated to the surface as a mottled brown color. In 1955 the painting was cleaned and placed on a new stretcher. A small tear center left was repaired and filled, and some scattered minor paint losses were retouched.

The overall condition is excellent with few losses or abrasions in the paint film. (Dec. 1971.)

The instruments represented in *Piano and Mandola* were identified by Kahnweiler in 1910 as "*mandola et piano*" (photographic archives, Paris, no. 1028), and a fragmentary handwritten label from the back of the painting, probably dating from the same time, carries the notation "*piano et man[dore] Kahn[weiler]*." Cooper has concurred with this title (1956, pl. 15b; 1970, no. 18) as has Richardson (pl. 7b). Furthermore, Cooper stated (in conversation with the author, New York, 1971) that Braque himself identified the painting by this title.

Various other titles have been suggested: the picture appeared in four exhibitions under the title *Harmonium* (Cologne, 1912, no. 232; Moscow, 1913, no. 12; Berlin, 1930, no. 15 [erroneously dated 1911]; Basel, 1933, no. 21). In 1958 the picture was exhibited as *Piano et guitare* (Paris, Musée des Arts Décoratifs, SRGM 104-T, no. 33) and in 1964 as *Piano and Mandolin* (Saidenberg Gallery). In all publications of the Guggenheim Museum, and in some others, the picture has been called *Piano and Lute.*

The Tate Gallery *Mandola,* which clearly depicts the same instrument as the Guggenheim picture and is therefore an important factor in any study of the latter's subject, has generally been identified in print as a mandola, although the Tate Gallery's photographs and a few published references carry the title *Mandolin.*

The mandola *(mandora, mandore)* is a rather rare instrument of the lute family; unlike the lute itself, which is characterized by a broken-off neck, the mandola has a rounded bent-back peg case. It also has an almond-shaped body and is usually half to three-quarters the size of a normal treble lute. (For descriptions and diagrams of various mandolas, lutes, and mandolins see C. Sachs, *Reallexikon der Musikinstrumente,* Berlin, 1913, pp. 251-252, and *Handbuch der Musikinstrumentkunde,* Leipzig, 1920, p. 229, pl. 94.)

Comparison of the Tate and Guggenheim instruments with illustrations of mandolas and lutes reproduced in Sachs and elsewhere is inconclusive.

Furthermore, none of the instruments visible in a ca. 1911 photograph of Braque's studio is clearly identifiable as a mandola, although one example shown in profile might conceivably qualify (E. Fry, *Cubism,* New York, 1966, fig. 58).

The keyboard instrument in the Guggenheim painting offers a set of similarly problematic alternatives. Whereas it is certainly readable as an upright piano (with the sheet music resting on the stand and a candle in its scrolled holder attached to the left side), the instrument may also be seen as a harmonium or indeed a harpsichord.

While Braque has reported that at this stage in his development he worked constantly with the musical instruments that surrounded him in his studio, it is also obvious that he was not working directly from objects as he perceived them, but rather—as he himself described the process—"towards objects" as he conceived them (D. Vallier, "Braque, la peinture et nous," *Cahiers d'Art,* vol. xxix, October 1954, p. 16, trans. by Richardson, p. 10). Thus, while the conception was undoubtedly specific, and the finished picture was as much as possible to be comprehended as such, the fragmented realization inevitably created ambiguities. (It was for this very reason that, as the language of Cubism became increasingly hard to read, Kahnweiler urged Picasso and Braque to provide titles for their pictures to help the spectator understand the subject matter.) In the case of the Guggenheim and Tate paintings, as well as in many other pictures of this phase in Braque's work, therefore, the inconclusive nature of the visual evidence necessitates dependence on the titles provided by the artist, or on contemporary witnesses such as Kahnweiler and Cooper for the identification of the subjects represented.

EXHIBITIONS:

Cologne, *Internationale Kunstausstellung des Sonderbundes Westdeutschen Kunstfreunden und Künstler zu Köln,* May 25-Sept. 30, 1912, no. 232 *(Harmonium)*; Moscow, Бубновый валет (Bubnovyi valet, *Jack of Diamonds*), Mar. 3-Apr. 6, 1913, no. 12 (фисгармония, Fisgarmoniya, *Harmonium)*; Berlin, Galerie Flechtheim, *Matisse, Braque, Picasso: 60 Werke aus Deutschem Besitz,* Sept. 21-mid. Oct. 1930, no. 15 *(Harmonium)*; Kunsthalle Basel, *Georges Braque,* Apr. 9-May 14, 1933, no. 21 *(Harmonium)*; Kunsthalle Bern, *Georges Braque,* Apr. 25-May 31, 1953, no. 21, traveled to Kunsthaus Zürich, June 7-July 19, 1953, no. 22; New York, SRGM 95 (checklist; withdrawn Sept. 12); The Arts Club of Chicago, *An Exhibition of Cubism on the Occasion of the Fortieth Anniversary of the Arts Club of Chicago,* Oct. 3-Nov. 4, 1955, no. 1; New York, SRGM 97 (checklist); Edinburgh, Royal Scottish Academy, *G. Braque,* Aug. 18-Sept. 15, 1956, p. 30, no. 20, pl. 15b, traveled to London, Tate Gallery, Sept. 28-Nov. 11, 1956; London, SRGM 104-T, no. 3; New York, SRGM 112, 118, 129 (checklists); Philadelphia, SRGM 134-T, no. 8, repr.; New York, SRGM 144 (checklist); Worcester, Mass., SRGM 148-T, no. 3, repr.; New York, SRGM 151, 153 (checklists); New York, Saidenberg Gallery, *Braque: An American Tribute, Fauvism and Cubism,* Apr. 7-May 2, 1964, no. 15, repr.; New York, SRGM 173, no. 15, repr.; 196 (checklist); 198-T, 216, 221 (no cats.); 232, p. 49, repr. color p. 48; Los Angeles County Museum of Art, *The Cubist Epoch,* Dec. 15, 1970-Feb. 21, 1971, traveled to New York, The Metropolitan Museum of Art, Apr. 9-June 8, 1971, no. 18, color pl. 23, p. 43; New York, SRGM 241, p. 49, repr. color p. 48; 251, 260 (no cats.); Paris, Orangerie, *Georges Braque,* Oct. 16, 1973-Jan. 14, 1974, no. 30, repr. color p. 4.

REFERENCES:

G. Isarlov, *Georges Braque,* Paris, 1932, no. 76 ("*L'Harmonium,* 1910"); D. Cooper, *G. Braque,* exhibition catalogue, Edinburgh and London, 1956, no. 20, pp. 30-31, pl. 15b; J. Russell, *Georges Braque,* Garden City, N.Y., 1959, pp. 14, 120; J. Richardson, *Braque,* Harmondsworth, Middx., 1959, pp. 9-10 color pl. 7b; J. Leymarie, *Braque,* Lausanne, 1961, p. 48, repr. color p. 43; E. Mullins, *The Art of Georges Braque,* New York, 1968, repr. p. 57; Cooper, *Cubist Epoch,* 1970, no. 18, pp. 44, 277, color pl. 23, p. 43.

Heinrich Campendonk

Born November 1899, Krefeld.
Died May 1957, Amsterdam.

23   Listening. 1920.
      (*The Lovers*? or *Russian Fairy Tale*?[1]).

53.1337

Oil on canvas, 49⅛ x 37¼ (124.7 x 94.6)

Signed and dated l.r.: *C. / 1920*.

PROVENANCE:

Purchased from the artist by Katherine S. Dreier, West Redding, Connecticut, by 1921 (*Annual Report of the Société Anonyme, 1921-31*, repr. p. 22)—52;[2] Gift of the Estate of Katherine S. Dreier, 1953.

CONDITION:

The work has received no treatment since its acquisition.

All corners are worn with loss of paint and ground, and the edges show scattered wear, with a 2 in. loss of support on the lower edge 2 in. from the right. A heavy coat of varnish covers several areas of minor cracks in the paint layer. The condition in general is very good. (Dec. 1973.)

EXHIBITIONS:

New York, Société Anonyme, *14th Exhibition: Campendonk, Klee, Molzahn, Donas, Stuckenberg, Schwitters*, Mar. 15-Apr. 12, 1921? (no cat.);[3] Mass., Worcester Art Museum, *Paintings by Members of the Société Anonyme*, Nov. 3-Dec. 5, 1921, no. 11 *(Russian Fairy Tale)* or no. 12 *(The Lovers)*;[1] Springfield, Mass., George Walter Vincent Smith Art Museum, *Mysticism in Art*, Oct. 5-26, 1936, no. 16; New Haven, Yale University Art Gallery, *In Memory of Katherine S. Dreier: Her Own Collection of Modern Art*, Dec. 15, 1952-Feb. 1, 1953, no. 13; New York, SRGM 79 (checklist; withdrawn Oct. 20); Toronto, SRGM 85-T, no. 1; Vancouver, SRGM 88-T, no. 4, repr.; Boston, SRGM 90-T (no cat.); Montreal, SRGM 93-T, no. 3; London, SRGM 104-T, no. 5; Boston, SRGM 119-T, no. 2; Lexington, Ky., SRGM 122-T, no. 1; New York, SRGM 144 (checklist); 205, *Rousseau, Redon and Fantasy* (checklist).

1. Only 2 Campendonks appeared in the Société Anonyme exhibition in 1921, and their titles were *Russian Fairy Tale* and *The Lovers*. (See above EXHIBITIONS.) The Guggenheim painting carries on its reverse a label for this exhibition, but without title, and although its box and entry numbers correspond to those in the Worcester records for that show, it is impossible to establish which of the 2 titles applies (information supplied by Stephen A. Jareckie, correspondence with the author, July 1972).

2. Dreier and Campendonk were friends by 1920 and, as the artist's son Herbert Campendonk has said (correspondence with the author, Jan. 1974), it is certain that she bought the picture directly from his father on a visit to the Seehaupt/Starnberger See atelier.

3. Since the picture belonged to Dreier by 1921, it would probably have been included in the March exhibition.

Paul Cézanne

Born January 1839, Aix-en-Provence.
Died October 1906, Aix-en-Provence.

24 Man with Crossed Arms. ca. 1899.
(Homme aux bras croisés; L'Horloger; The Clockmaker).

54.1387

Oil on canvas, 36¼ x 28⅝ (92 x 72.7)

Not signed or dated.

PROVENANCE:

Mrs. Martha Reuther, Heidelberg, ca. 1906(?)[1]—52; purchased from Reuther by Durand-Matthiesen Gallery, Geneva, 1952 (information supplied by J.-P. Durand, correspondence with the author, March 1971); purchased from Durand-Matthiesen by M. Knoedler & Co., Inc., New York, 1953; purchased from Knoedler, 1954.

CONDITION:

At some time prior to acquisition by the Museum, the canvas was lined with glue.

The edges of the original canvas were trimmed on all sides so as to coincide with the turn of the lining canvas; the edges were bound to the lining canvas and reinforced with paper tape. In 1954 the paper tape was removed and the edges were found to be unpainted; filling and inpainting approximately 5/16 in. in width along all edges was performed at this time. Some earlier inpainting, mostly of pinpoint losses, presumably dates from the time of lining. 4 larger areas of inpainting are concentrated along and slightly below the sitter's right arm; 1 is just above the sitter's left hand.

Apart from some areas of traction cracks concentrated in the sitter's jacket, especially the right arm, the condition is excellent. (Mar. 1973.)

Since its acquisition by the Guggenheim in 1954 the picture has been known as *The Clockmaker* and dated 1895-1900. Venturi, who lists the picture as *L'Homme aux bras croisés,* was the first author to allude to the alternative title, but he gave no source for the information *("Tableau dit aussi 'L'Horloger' ").* No substantiating evidence for this designation has been found in earlier literature, where the picture has been known only as *Man with Crossed Arms.*

A second portrait of the same unidentified sitter was formerly in the Tilla Durieux-Cassirer Collection, Berlin (35½ x 28 in., 90.2 x 71.2 cm., Collection Mrs. Carleton Mitchell, Annapolis, Maryland, Venturi no. 685). Although the two portraits are similar and probably date from approximately the same time, there are some notable differences between them.

The figure in the Mitchell picture is standing, facing full front, with his head turned slightly to the left, his eyes directed towards the upper left. He is leaning against a dark background wall broken only by a dado, and the picture space is reduced to an absolute minimum. As is frequently the case in Cézanne's work, the line of the dado, interrupted by the figure, is discontinuous; the right-hand side here is slightly lower than the left. (For a discussion of this and

1. Martha Reuther reported that her husband bought the picture in about 1906 in Paris, possibly from Vollard, or from Reber. She was not sure of the source, but was sure of the approximate date of purchase (telephone conversation between Martha Reuther and Georg Poensen, Director of the Kurpfäzisches Museum, Heidelberg, who forwarded the information to the SRGM, March 1954). It is possible that he purchased the picture from Vollard after the 1904 *Salon d'Automne* (see below fn. 2).

related elements of Cézanne's style see R. W. Ratcliffe, *Cézanne's Working Methods and their Theoretical Background*, unpublished Ph.D. dissertation, Courtauld Institute of Art, University of London, December 1960, pp. 184-208. Ratcliffe suggests that such discontinuities are almost always the result of reworkings.)

The figure in the Guggenheim painting is seated, facing three-quarters right, but his eyes—like those of the Mitchell figure—are directed towards the upper left. His seated position places him in a somewhat deeper space. A palette and easel are leaning against the wall to his right, and the discontinuity of the dado is even more pronounced here than in the companion portrait.

Although the colors in the two works appear to differ considerably, it is extremely difficult to compare the two since the varnish of the Mitchell picture appears to have darkened considerably with age. A photograph of the Mitchell picture in the 1962 edition of the original Cologne Sonderbund catalogue of 1912 (pl. 22) suggests that darkening of the varnish may have tended to blur Cézanne's strongly contrasting areas of light and shadow. Whereas the figure now appears to stand before a rather uniform dark background, the early photograph suggests that this background was originally very light and that the figure cast a strong shadow to the left. Similarly, this photograph indicates that there were considerable contrasts of light and dark in the man's clothing and highlights in his hair, none of which are visible at present. The problem is further complicated, however, by the fact that at least one example of the original 1912 catalogue (that owned by J. Rewald) contains an illustration which shows the background and the figure to be even more uniformly dark than they appear today. It has hitherto not been possible to establish the source or date of the photograph in the 1962 publication, and the question of its accuracy is thus presently unresolved. It remains true, however, that the apparent differences in palette between the two versions may be in large part attributable to condition, and a comparison between them in their present state might obscure rather than illuminate their relationship.

Ratcliffe's carefully documented chronology of Cézanne's movements between 1895 and 1900 establishes that he spent periods of time in Aix, Paris, Vichy, Talloires, and Montgeroult (op. cit., pp. 21-27). Rewald pointed out (in conversation with the author) that Cézanne almost certainly painted no oils in Vichy or Talloires, where he stayed in hotels and therefore had no studios. It has hitherto not been possible to identify the room in which these two portraits were painted with studios Cézanne might have occupied in Aix, Paris, or Montgeroult, an identification which might provide a firm basis for dating them.

Andersen has suggested, without any evidence, that the Mitchell version was shown in the 1895 exhibition at Vollard's gallery (p. 43, fn. 7). Rewald much more convincingly dates both pictures ca. 1899 on stylistic grounds (conversation with the author, June 1974). The rather thinly applied paint of the Guggenheim version as well as its palette brings the picture into close relationship with works such as *Self-Portrait with a Beret* (Museum of Fine

Arts, Boston, Venturi no. 693), which has traditionally been dated ca. 1900. Rewald originally accepted this date *(Cézanne: An Exhibition in Honor of the 50th Anniversary of the Phillips Collection,* Washington, D.C., Chicago, Boston, 1971, no. 30); he now inclines to date the picture 1898-1900. The Guggenheim painting is also closely related to works such as *The Drinker* (Barnes Collection, Merion, Pennsylvania, Venturi no. 690) and *Peasant* (Private Collection, California, Venturi no. 691), both of which Rewald also dates 1898-1900. The latter work shares with the Guggenheim painting the otherwise unknown compositional device of a still-life in the lower left corner. (I am indebted to Rewald for bringing this fact and the presence of the picture in America to my attention.)

EXHIBITIONS:
Paris, *Salon d'Automne,* Oct. 15-Nov. 15, 1904, no. 10 *(Portrait d'homme);*[2] New York, SRGM 84, 87 (checklists); The Art Institute of Chicago, *Great French Paintings: An Exhibition in Memory of Chauncey McCormick,* Jan. 20-Feb. 20, 1955, no. 5, repr.; New York, SRGM 89 (no cat.); 95, 97 (checklists); The Hague, Haags Gemeentemuseum, *Paul Cézanne,* June-July 1956, no. 43, repr.; Toronto, The Art Gallery of Toronto, *Comparisons,* Jan. 11-Feb. 3, 1957, no. 11; London, SRGM 104-T, no. 6, pl. 1; New York, SRGM 112, 118 (checklists); 127 (no cat.); 129, 144 (checklists); 153 (checklist; commentary, repr. color); 160 (no cat.); 173, no. 6, repr. color; 196 (checklist); 216, 221 (no cats.); 232, 241, pp. 64-65, repr. color; 251, 260 (no cats.).

REFERENCES:
A. Vollard, *Cézanne,* Paris, 1914, repr. foll. p. 136;[2] E. Bernard, "La Technique de Paul Cézanne," *L'Amour de l'art,* 1920, repr. p. 271 *(Portrait);* T. Klingsor, *Cézanne,* Paris, 1923, p. 55 *(Homme aux bras croisés);* L. Venturi, *Cézanne: son art, son oeuvre,* Paris, 1936, vol. 1, no. 689, vol. 2, pl. 224 ("*Homme aux bras croisés,* 1895-1900"); SRGM *Handbook,* 1959, p. 34, repr. p. 35 *(The Clockmaker);* D. Robbins, *Cézanne and Structure in Modern Painting,* New York, 1963, repr. color n.p.; K. Badt, *The Art of Cézanne,* Berkeley, 1965, p. 122; W. Andersen, *Cézanne's Portrait Drawings,* Cambridge, Mass., 1970, pp. 37, 43, fns. 2, 7.

2. The picture is clearly visible in the installation photograph published by Vollard. Venturi erroneously identifies this entry in the *Salon* catalogue and the installation photograph published by Vollard with the Mitchell version (no. 685). The palette and canvas at the lower left of the installation photograph, neither of which occur in the Mitchell picture, clearly establish the picture as the Guggenheim version.

Marc Chagall[1]

Born July 1887, Vitebsk.
Lives in St. Paul de Vence, France.

25   Portrait of the Artist's Sister Aniuta.
1910.

48.1172 X91

Oil on canvas, 36¼ x 27⅝ (92.3 x 70.3)

Signed and dated l.l.: *Chagall* / [1]*910.*

PROVENANCE:

Possibly Herwarth Walden, 1914-ca. 1935;[2]
Karl Nierendorf, New York, ca. 1935-48(?);[3]
acquired with the Estate of Karl Nierendorf,
1948.

CONDITION:

In 1957 the canvas was mounted on pressed
wood, and in 1960 some losses on the right
edge were retouched.

Apart from some extremely minor scratches
in the paint film, the condition is excellent.
(Jan. 1975.)

Chagall's oldest sister Aniuta was born in Vitebsk in 1890 and died during the
Siege of Leningrad. She was married to a tradesman and had one daughter.
The portrait was painted shortly before Chagall's departure for Paris in the
summer of 1910.

EXHIBITIONS:

Berlin, Der Sturm, *25. Ausstellung: Kubin-Chagall,* Apr.-May, 1914 (?);[4] Berlin, Der Sturm,
26. Ausstellung: Chagall, June 1914 (?);[4] Berlin, Der Sturm, *96. Ausstellung: Schwitters,*

1. In January-February 1974 M. Rowell, Curator of Special Exhibitions at the Guggenheim
Museum, visited Ida Chagall in Basel and Paris, and Marc Chagall himself in Nice, to pose
a series of detailed questions on the author's behalf concerning the works in the Guggenheim Collection. Information from their interviews is specifically cited in the course of the
individual entries which follow.

In 1944 J. J. Sweeney published a strong statement by Chagall which warned against the
restrictive nature of an artist's pronouncements on his work:

*A painter should never come between the work of art and the spectator. An intermediary
may explain the artist's work without any harm to it. But the artist's explanation of it
can only limit it. Better the understanding that grows from familiarity and the perspective that will come after the artist's death. After all, it is better to judge a painter by his
pictures. His words, I am afraid, do nothing but veil the vision (Partisan Review, vol. xi,
Winter 1944, p. 88).*

Though there is some wisdom in this warning, it nonetheless remains that Chagall's perspective on his own work, when available, is invariably illuminating, provocative, and
certainly to be taken into account.

2. Shortly before the outbreak of the First World War, Chagall met Herwarth Walden at one
of Apollinaire's weekly soirées in Paris. Apollinaire persuaded Walden to exhibit Chagall's
work in Berlin, and the first exhibition took place in April-May 1914, the second in June.
When the war broke out Chagall went back to Russia but the pictures remained with
Walden, and the artist never recovered them. Although it has not been possible to establish
whether the present picture appeared in either exhibition, Chagall believes that it was
among the works sent to Berlin (in answer to questions from the author, Feb. 1974).

3. Chagall suggested (Feb. 1974) that Nierendorf might have acquired this picture directly
from Walden. Shortly after Hitler came to power, Nierendorf apparently sent a large group
of works, including many from Der Sturm, to the U.S.A. It is possible that the present
picture was among them, but no documentation on this point has hitherto come to light.

4. Walden's exhibitions of 1914 apparently did not have catalogues. Since the painting probably was sent to Berlin, however, it almost certainly would have been shown in either the
first exhibition, the second, or both. Nell Walden (in conversation with M. Poser, Mar.
1974) said the picture definitely was included in the 1914 exhibition.

fig. a.
Chagall's family. Aniuta is standing in
the back row at the extreme left.

Gesamtschau, Apr. 1921, no. 75 *(Aniuta)*; New York, SRGM 95 (checklist); Pasadena Art
Museum, *Marc Chagall,* May 26-July 28, 1957, no. 2; Waltham, Mass., Goldfarb Library,
Brandeis University, *Marc Chagall,* May 15-June 15, 1960 (no cat.); Laguna Beach, Cal.,
SRGM 143-T (no cat.); New York, SRGM 266, 276 (no cats.).

REFERENCES:

SRGM *Handbook,* 1959, p. 36, repr.; F. Meyer, *Marc Chagall,* New York, 1963, repr. p. 746,
no. 25.

---

26 ## The Soldier Drinks. 1911-1912.
(Le Soldat boit; Trinkender Soldat).

49.1211

Oil on canvas, 43 x 37¼ (109.1 x 94.5)

Signed l.r.: *Chagall.* Not dated.

PROVENANCE:

Herwarth Walden, Berlin, 1914-24;[1] Nell
Urech-Walden, Ascona, Switzerland, 1924-
49; purchased from Nell Walden, 1949.

CONDITION:

In 1954 the surface was cleaned with 2%
Soilax, followed by a benzine rinse. It was
noted that the blues and reds were especially
sensitive to solvents. A ½ in. loss in the
yellow 16 in. from the left side and 18½ in.
from the bottom was inpainted. This has
since discolored. The surface was sprayed
with PBM. In 1957 the canvas was restretched, and some further losses in the
yellow paint were inpainted. In 1960 the
canvas was lined with wax resin and placed
on a new stretcher. Some inpainting in the
blue area at the lower left probably dates
from this time. In 1970 active cleavage of
paint in the white ring around the base of
the samovar and the gray/black area above
it was arrested. Cracks are now visible in
these areas, but no paint was lost.

There is some cracking along the edges with
some loss of pigment, ground, and even, in
a few places, support. There is also fairly
widespread cracking elsewhere in the paint
film, but this condition does not at present
seem to pose any threat of further cleavage.
(May 1972.)

1. See above cat. no. 25, fn. 2. The present picture was definitely among those sent to Berlin.

The picture has been dated 1912 except by Cassou, who dated it 1911. Chagall himself believes it to have been painted in 1911-12 (February 1974).

A gouache study for the work was formerly in the collection of Mrs. D. Ogden Stewart (Ella Winter), London (fig. a). (Ella Winter also formerly owned a sepia drawing which may have been a study for the Guggenheim painting too, but this work has not been traced and no photograph of it has been published. It is listed in the catalogue of her collection shown at the Stedelijk Museum, Amsterdam, December 22, 1961-January 29, 1962, no. 5.

However, the picture reproduced in that catalogue as no. 5 is actually the gouache here reproduced as fig. a and not the sepia drawing.) A second gouache of the composition, owned by the Guggenheim Museum, almost certainly dates from ca. 1923-24 (fig. b); both Ida Chagall, January 1974, and Marc Chagall, February 1974, identified this as a reprise dating from the early to mid 1920's. For a discussion of Chagall's 1923-26 replicas and variants of earlier compositions, see below cat. no. 30.

Chagall never served in the military. He has described this work, and others of soldiers painted during the years 1911 and 1912, as reminiscent of the Russo-Japanese war of 1904-05, when the Tsar billeted soldiers with private families. Chagall was seventeen at the time, and the experience of having soldiers living in his house apparently had a strong impact upon his imagination (February 1974).

The "41" on the soldier's epaulette (the same number is worn by the figures in *Soldiers* of 1912, Collection Eric Estorick, London, Meyer, repr. p. 188) may possibly be related to a regiment which Chagall actually encountered, but this seems unlikely. Several commentators (starting with George) have suggested that the soldier in the Guggenheim painting is drunk and that the small figures dancing in the foreground are either a physical expression of his suppressed desires, or else a nostalgic vision of his own past conjured up in his inebriated state.

fig. a.
Chagall, study for *The Soldier Drinks*, 1911-12, gouache on paper, 7⅞ x 6⅞ in., 20 x 17.5 cm., formerly Collection Mrs. D. Ogden Stewart (Ella Winter), London.

fig. b.
Chagall, *The Soldier Drinks*, ca. 1923-24, gouache on paper, 25 x 18 in., 63.5 x 45.7 cm., The Solomon R. Guggenheim Museum, New York.

Chagall himself has explicitly rejected these interpretations (February 1974). The soldier is drinking tea, not vodka, and represents an evocation of the artist's own memories. Similarly the dancing figures do not, in the artist's view, lend themselves to explicit interpretation, but are rather a more general expression of the painting's mood. Defining that mood, with its combination of whimsy, nostalgia, and intensity, is difficult. Nevertheless it should be borne in mind that Chagall's intention in this and other paintings was clearly to create such moods through essentially irrational and fantastic imagery rather than to forge an explicitly symbolic iconography.

EXHIBITIONS:

Berlin, Der Sturm, *25. Ausstellung: Kubin-Chagall,* April-May, 1914 (?);[2] Berlin, Der Sturm, *26. Ausstellung: Chagall,* June, 1914 (?);[2] Kunsthalle Basel, *Marc Chagall,* Nov. 4-Dec. 3, 1933, no. 15; Kunstmuseum Bern, *Sammlung Nell Walden aus den Jahren 1912-20,* Oct. 1944-Mar. 1945, no. 278; Kunsthalle Basel, *Francis Picabia: Sammlung Nell Walden,* Jan. 12-Feb. 13, 1946, no. 220; New York, The Museum of Modern Art, *Marc Chagall,* Apr. 9-June 23, 1946, p. 22, repr., traveled to The Art Institute of Chicago, Nov. 14, 1946-Jan. 12, 1947; Amsterdam, Stedelijk Museum, *Chagall,* Dec. 1947-Jan. 1948, no. 9 (not in Paris showing), traveled to London, Tate Gallery, Feb. 4-29, 1948; New York, SRGM 78 (checklist); 83 (no cat.); Minneapolis, Walker Art Center, *Reality and Fantasy: 1900-1954,* May 23-July 2, 1954, no. 30, repr.; New York, SRGM 87 (checklist); New York, SRGM 89 (no cat.); London, SRGM 104-T, no. 7; Boston, SRGM 119-T, no. 3; Lexington, Ky., SRGM 122-T, no. 2, repr.; New York, SRGM 129 (checklist); Philadelphia, SRGM 134-T, no. 13; New York, SRGM 144 (checklist); Worcester, Mass., SRGM 148-T, no. 6, repr.; Tokyo, National Museum of European Art, *Marc Chagall,* Oct. 1-Nov. 10, 1963, no. 18, repr.; Boston, Museum of Fine Arts, *Surrealist & Fantastic Art from the Collections of the Museum of Modern Art and the Guggenheim Museum,* Feb. 14-Mar. 15, 1964, no. 7; Kunsthaus Zürich, *Chagall,* May 6-July 30, 1967, no. 32, repr.; Cologne, Wallraf-Richartz-Museum, *Chagall,* Sept. 2-Oct. 31, 1967, no. 40, repr.; New York, SRGM 202, p. 121, repr. p. 120; 205, *Rousseau, Redon and Fantasy* (checklist); 221 (no cat.); Paris, Grand Palais, *Marc Chagall,* Dec. 13, 1969-Mar. 8, 1970, no. 31, repr.; New York, SRGM 232, 241, pp. 66-67, repr.; Cleveland, SRGM 258-T, pl. 9; New York, SRGM 276 (no cat.).

REFERENCES:

Th. Däubler, *Der neue Standpunkt,* Dresden, 1916, pp. 129-131;[3] H. Walden, *Expressionismus, Die Kunstwende,* Berlin, 1918, repr. p. 23; A. Efross and J. Tugendhold, *Die Kunst Marc Chagalls,* trans. F. Ichak-Rubiner, Potsdam, 1921, repr. p. 33; Th. Däubler, *Marc Chagall,* Rome, 1922, pp. 6-7, repr. [p. 9];[3] H. Walden, *Marc Chagall,* Sturm Bilderbücher No. 1, 2nd ed., Berlin, 1923, repr. p. 9; *Sélection,* no. 6, Marc Chagall issue, Antwerp, Apr. 1929, repr. p. 81; SRGM *Handbook,* 1959, p. 37, repr.; W. George, *Les Artistes juifs et l'école de Paris,* Algeria, 1959, p. 23; F. Meyer, *Marc Chagall,* New York, 1963, pp. 179-180, repr. p. 184; J. Cassou, *Chagall,* New York, 1965, p. 102, pl. 71; W. Haftmann, *Chagall,* New York, 1973, p. 86, repr. color.

2. Ibid., fn. 2. Däubler (1922) identifies the picture as having been exhibited at Der Sturm, although he does not say in which exhibition.

3. Däubler's lengthy description may refer in part to the gouache, which would in that case also probably have appeared in one of the Der Sturm exhibitions. Some of the details mentioned by him occur in the gouache but not in the painting. Ida Chagall excluded the possibility of a second version, but agreed that Däubler might have seen the gouache (in conversation with M. Rowell, Paris, Feb. 1975).

27 The Flying Carriage. 1913.
    *(La Calèche volante; Burning House; La
    Maison brûle; Landschaft).*

49.1212

Oil on canvas, 42 x 47¼ (106.7 x 120.1)

Signed and dated l.r.: *Chagall Paris 13.*

PROVENANCE:

Herwarth Walden, Berlin, 1914-24;[1] Nell
Urech-Walden, Ascona, Switzerland, 1924-
49; purchased from Nell Walden, 1949.

CONDITION:

In 1954 the picture was given a slight surface
cleaning with 3% Soilax and benzine and
surfaced with PBM. Owing to ready solu-
bility of the cadmiums, a thorough cleaning
has so far not been attempted.

All edges show some abrasion with moderate loss of paint and ground. There are
some drying cracks in the magenta area, and
a stretcher impression along the top margin.
There is some minor cracking and flaking
elsewhere; the condition in general is good
to fair. (Mar. 1974.)

1. See above cat. no. 25, fn. 2. The present picture was definitely among those sent to Berlin in
   1914. Däubler (1922) identifies the picture as having been exhibited at Der Sturm, although
   he does not say which exhibition.

The identification of the scene as depicting a "burning house" is difficult to trace, but it appears to postdate Nell Walden's acquisition of the painting in 1924. The work was published by Walden merely as *Landschaft* (Sturm Bilderbücher No. 1), and the Sturm label on the reverse of the painting bears this same title. By 1944 (Bern exhibition) the picture is firmly described as *Burning House,* and it is with few exceptions subsequently published under that title. Moreover, interpretations of the "burning house" imagery abound in the literature. Segui sees the fire as a symbol of the nightmares induced by Chagall's self-exile; Meyer interprets the picture as a cosmic representation of night and day, of astral powers, and of "the house of man forever burning yet never consumed;" Cassou (1965) suggests a connection with Chagall's deepest unconscious memories—presumably a reference to the fire that broke out in his house on the occasion of his own birth (Chagall, *Ma Vie,* Paris, 1931, p. 1). Haftmann suggests it may be seen as a "presentiment of oncoming war."

Chagall himself, on the other hand, has identified the scene as a peaceful one in which the predominant emotion is ecstasy, not panic or fear: *"C'est calme, mon tableau, Rien ne brûle. C'est la grande extase"* (February 1974). The inscription on the lintel of the typical Vitebsk timber house reads *LAV* for *LAVKA* ("boutique"). The "flying carriage" is an expression of joy, and the woman with raised arm in the background is, according to Chagall, expressing her ecstatic response to the scene.

Chagall's comments are consistent with the imagery itself, since no fire is visible. The vibrant yellow-orange of the sky, which has led critics to see the picture as depicting a fire, is presumably intended rather to express part of the "ecstasy" of which Chagall speaks.

In connection with this element of spiritual ecstasy, it cannot be ruled out that the motif of the flying carriage itself was inspired by a byzantine or medie-

fig. a.
12th-century bronze doors of the Cathedral in Novgorod
(photograph printed in reverse).

val representation of Elijah's Ascension into Heaven (II *Kings* ii, 11-13). The twelfth-century bronze door at Novgorod presents an obvious prototype (fig. a). Chagall had apparently not seen these doors, but he responded most positively to the suggestion that his painting might be associated in some way with this early theme (in conversation, February 1974). The possible existence of a local Vitebsk example, perhaps even closely dependent upon the Novgorod prototype, must be further explored. In the absence of such an example, it is conceivable that Chagall saw a reproduction of this or a related illustration of the theme. (I am indebted to M. Poser for drawing my attention to the specific example at Novgorod.)

A later version of the composition, which has been dated ca. 1914 and ca. 1917, actually derives (according to the artist, February 1974) from ca. 1923-24 when he returned to Paris after the war. (Oil on canvas, sold at Sotheby's, April 26, 1967, now in a private collection in Switzerland. For a discussion of Chagall's 1923-26 replicas and variants of earlier compositions, see below cat. no. 30.)

The 1933 Basel exhibition included a colored print *(Radierung aquarelliert)* entitled *La Calèche volante* (no. 166). No further information on this has thus far come to light.

EXHIBITIONS:

Berlin, Der Sturm, *25. Ausstellung: Kubin-Chagall,* Apr.-May, 1914 (?);[1] Berlin, Der Sturm, *26. Ausstellung: Chagall,* June 1914 (?);[1] Kunstmuseum Bern, *Sammlung Nell Walden aus den Jahren 1912-20,* Oct. 1944-Mar. 1945, no. 276 *(Brennendes Haus)*; Kunsthalle Basel, *Francis Picabia: Sammlung Nell Walden,* Jan. 12-Feb. 13, 1946, no. 218 *(Brennendes Haus)*; New York, The Museum of Modern Art, *Marc Chagall,* Apr. 9-June 23, 1946, p. 30 *(Burning House)*, traveled to The Art Institute of Chicago, Nov. 14, 1946-Jan. 12, 1947; Paris, Musée National d'Art Moderne, *Marc Chagall,* Oct.-Dec. 1947, no. 16 *(La Calèche volante)*, traveled to Amsterdam, Stedelijk Museum, Dec. 1947-Jan. 1948 *(De vliegende kar)*, London, Tate Gallery, Feb. 4-29, 1948 *(The Burning House)*; New York, SRGM 78 (checklist); Toronto, SRGM 85-T, no. 2; New York, SRGM 87 (checklist); Boston, SRGM 90-T (no cat.); Montreal, SRGM 93-T, no. 5, repr.; New York, SRGM 97 (checklist); London, SRGM 104-T, no. 8; Boston, Mass., SRGM 119-T, no. 4; Waltham, Mass., Goldfarb Library, Brandeis University, *Marc Chagall,* May 15-June 15, 1960 (no cat.); New York, SRGM 129, 144 (checklists); Tokyo, National Museum of European Art, *Marc Chagall,* Oct. 1-Nov. 10, 1963, no. 19; Boston, Museum of Fine Arts, *Surrealist & Fantastic Art from the Collections of the Museum of Modern Art and the Guggenheim Museum,* Feb. 14-Mar. 15, 1964, no. 8; New York, SRGM 173, no. 27; 187, *Gauguin and the Decorative Style* (checklist); Kunsthaus Zürich, *Chagall,* May 6-July 30, 1967, no. 38; New York, SRGM 202, p. 122, repr. p. 123; 205, *Rousseau, Redon and Fantasy* (checklist); 221 (no cat.); Paris, Grand Palais, *Marc Chagall,* Dec. 13, 1969-Mar. 8, 1970, no. 38, repr. color; New York, SRGM 232, 241, p. 71, repr. p. 70; 266, 276 (no cats.).

REFERENCES:

A. Efross and J. Tugendhold, *Die Kunst Marc Chagalls,* trans. F. Ichak-Rubiner, Potsdam, 1921, repr. p. 31 *(Landschaft)*; Th. Däubler, *Marc Chagall,* Rome, 1922, repr. [p. 27] *(Le Départ)*; H. Walden, *Marc Chagall,* Sturm Bilderbücher No. 1, 2nd ed., Berlin, 1923, repr. p. 11 *(Landschaft)*; J. Cassou, "Marc Chagall," *Art et décoration,* no. 24, 1930, repr. p. 74 *(L'Isba)*; SRGM *Handbook,* 1959, p. 38, repr. *(Burning House)*; F. Meyer, *Marc Chagall,* New York, 1963, p. 204, repr. p. 200 *(Burning House)*; S. Segui, "Marc Chagall au Japon," *XXe Siècle,* May 1964, *supplément,* n.p.; J. Cassou, *Chagall,* New York, 1965, p. 55 *(Burning House)*; W. Haftmann, *Chagall,* New York, 1973, p. 90, repr. color *(Burning House)*.

28   Paris Through the Window. 1913.
      (Paris par la fenêtre).

37.438

Oil on canvas, 53½ x 55¾ (135.8 x 141.4)

Signed and dated l.l.: *Chagall/1913.*

PROVENANCE:

Herwarth Walden, Berlin, 1914;[1] purchased by E. Kluxen, Berlin, 1914 (information supplied by Chagall, February 1974); purchased by Solomon R. Guggenheim by 1936 (source and exact date of purchase unknown); Gift of Solomon R. Guggenheim, 1937.

CONDITION:

In 1954 the work was cleaned with 1½% Soilax and water and lightly surfaced with PBM. In 1971 it was removed from the stretcher and lined with fiberglass (using the newly developed adhesive BEVA 371; for a discussion of the properties and advantages of this adhesive, as well as a description of the work performed on cat. no. 28, see O. H. Riley and G. A. Berger, "New Developments in the Conservation of Works of Art," *The Art Journal,* vol. 31, Fall 1971, pp. 37-40). The picture was then placed on a new stretcher, restoring 1 in. of the composition's lower edge and ¼ in. of each side. The artist had apparently tacked the unstretched canvas to a frame or wall to paint it; after the work was finished, he attached it to a stretcher which was slightly too small, forcing him to tack down portions of the composition, including the final "l" of his signature and a portion of the man's hand. Some early reproductions of the picture show the complete painting (Efross and Tugendhold, Moscow, 1918), others show it already cropped (Sturm Bilderbücher No. 1, 1923), and it is impossible to establish at what point in these early years the remounting took place.

There is a 1½ in. stain from an old patch 6 in. down from the top and 29½ in. from the left side. There are a few scattered areas of minor crackle, but the condition in general is excellent. (Mar. 1974.)

In spite of the fact that it has occasionally been published as dating from 1912 (see below REFERENCES), the 1913 date is probably correct (Ida Chagall, January 1974; Chagall himself concurred, although he thought the picture might have been started in 1912).

At least one preparatory gouache for the picture exists (fig. a), and there may have been others (Chagall, February 1974). A gouache version of the composition in a private collection (fig. b) may, according to Chagall, have been a preparatory study, but it may on the other hand have been done afterwards. A sketch for the work which was exhibited in Paris in 1935-36 (Galerie des Beaux-Arts et Gazette des Beaux-Arts, *Peintres instinctifs: naissance de l'expressionisme,* no. 12, "*Paris par la fenêtre,* esquisse, 1912, gouache, coll. particulière") has so far not been securely identified with either fig. a or b and may be a third version. The same is true of a gouache exhibited in the 1933 Basel exhibition, *Marc Chagall* (no. 125). Meyer refers to a "charmingly playful replica" of the Guggenheim painting (1963, p. 369, fn. 1), but this too has yet to be identified. It could perhaps be a version of 1930 which was exhibited in London at the Leicester Galleries in 1935 (*Paintings and Gouaches: Marc Chagall,* April-May, no. 9, "*Paris par la fenêtre 1930,*" not repr.).

The notion (frequently suggested in the literature) that Chagall's studio actually looked out on the Eiffel Tower is clearly false, since *La Ruche* (2, Passage de Dantzig) was across the Seine and over a mile away from the Champ

1. See above cat. no. 25, fn. 2.

de Mars. According to Chagall, the title for the painting was invented by Blaise Cendrars, and it must have been intended imaginatively rather than literally. The Eiffel Tower here, as in *Self-Portrait with Seven Fingers* (Stedelijk Museum, Amsterdam), and in many other works, is not intended to be seen as a physical object in an actual landscape, but rather as a metaphor for Paris, and for a host of experiences and associations symbolized by it. Attempts to explicate the imagery of the scene have produced widely differing interpretations. Däubler sees the double-headed Janus as Chagall, one face fixed upon the West, the other looking eastward towards Russia. Venturi described the picture as "the vision of a world on the brink of catastrophe, the expression of total panic." Erben, while emphasizing the picture's enigmatic, mysterious quality, suggests that the imagery evokes feelings of nostalgia and anxiety. Meyer suggests a connection not only between the literal indoor and outdoor worlds of the picture, but also between the inner spiritual and outer sensuous aspects of life. Rosenblum, while relating the picture to Cubist conventions, alludes to the overriding quality of fantasy and imagination that pervades the scene. Similarly, Cassou speaks of "poetic eccentricities . . . a capricious hand" and emphasizes the irrational humor of the work.

Rosenblum's and Cassou's responses to the imaginative element are perhaps most in tune with the artist's own sense that the painting must first and foremost be seen as a challenge to one's ordinary expectations concerning the nature of reality. His goal was to *"construire psychiquement un tableau,"* to break down the normal conceptions of physical "everyday" reality and substitute an illogical reality of his own (February 1974). The individual images are not susceptible to interpretation except in those terms. (For the artist's eloquent denial of anecdotal, symbolic, or fantasy content in his pictures, see J. J. Sweeney's interview with him published in *Partisan Review*, vol. xi, Winter 1944, pp. 89-91.) Blaise Cendrars, Chagall's close friend during these years, admiringly described the artist's work as "a series of senseless pictures" (*Prose du Transsibérien*, Paris, 1913).

> *J'ai peur*
> *Je ne sais pas aller jusqu'au bout*
> *Comme mon ami Chagall je pourrais faire une série de tableaux déments*
> *Mais je n'ai pas pris de notes en voyage.*

As Sweeney has pointed out (*Marc Chagall,* New York, 1946, p. 16), it was precisely the juxtaposition of contrasting images "and their untranslatable fusion in the whole" which made Cendrars so responsive to Chagall.

Chagall recalls that many of his contemporaries (Delaunay and Léger among them) failed to respond to the irrational element in works such as this, and that it was Breton who first grasped its significance. (*"Il fallait attendre Breton pour comprendre les fondements psychiques des choses."* February 1974.) Breton drew attention to Chagall's pioneering role in the establishment of a metaphorical visual language. *"C'est de cet instant que la métaphore, avec lui [Chagall] seul, marque son entrée triomphale dans la peinture."* *Le Surréalisme*

28

fig. a.
Chagall, study for *Paris Through the Window*, ca. 1912,
gouache on paper, 11⅞ x 10⅝ in., 30 x 27 cm., present
whereabouts unknown.

fig. b.
Chagall, *Paris Through the Window*, gouache, possibly
after the painting (?), dimensions unknown, Private
Collection, London.

et la peinture, New York, 1945, p. 89. ("It was with Chagall, and with him alone [that] metaphor celebrated its triumphal entry into painting.") The "liberation of the object from the laws of weight and gravity" was—as Breton saw—a crucial element in this development, and *Paris Through the Window* is thus perhaps Chagall's most profound statement in the "resolutely magical" language Breton so admired.

EXHIBITIONS:

Berlin, Der Sturm, *25. Ausstellung: Kubin-Chagall,* Apr.-May, 1914;[2] Berlin, Der Sturm, *26. Ausstellung: Chagall,* June 1914;[2] Charleston, S.C., SRGM 1-T, no. 110; New York, The Museum of Modern Art, *Fantastic Art, Dada, Surrealism,* Dec. 1936-Jan. 1937, p. 115, repr.; Philadelphia, SRGM 3-T, no. 142; New York, SRGM 4-T, no. 213; New York, Pierre Matisse Gallery, *Marc Chagall: Paintings and Gouaches 1910-1941,* Nov. 25-Dec. 13, 1941 (checklist); Boston, Institute of Modern Art, *Chagall and Soutine,* Jan. 22-Feb. 25, 1945, no. 5; New York, The Museum of Modern Art, *Marc Chagall,* Apr. 9-June 23, 1946, no. 13, traveled to The Art Institute of Chicago, Nov. 14, 1946-Jan. 12, 1947; Paris, Musée National d'Art Moderne, *Marc Chagall: Peintures 1908-1947,* Oct.-Dec. 1947, no. 14, traveled to Amsterdam, Stedelijk Museum, Dec. 1947-Jan. 1948, London, Tate Gallery, Feb. 4-29, 1948; New York, SRGM 78 (checklist); Toronto, SRGM 85-T, no. 3; New York, SRGM 87 (checklist); Buffalo, N.Y., Albright-Knox Art Gallery, *Fifty Paintings, 1905-1913,* May 14-June 12, 1955, no. 7, repr.; New York, SRGM 95, 97 (checklists); London, SRGM 104-T, no. 9; New York, SRGM 112, 118, 129, 144, 153 (checklists); 173, no. 28, repr; 202, p. 20, repr. color p. 21; 205, *Rousseau, Redon and Fantasy* (checklist; commentary, repr. color); 221 (no cat.), 232, 241, pp. 68-69, repr. color; 260, 266, 276 (no cats.).

REFERENCES:

G. Apollinaire, *Paris-Journal,* June 2, 1914 (review of Der Sturm exhibition); Th. Däubler, *Der neue Standpunkt,* Dresden, 1916, pp. 135-136; A. Efross and J. Tugendhold, Искусство Марка Шагала (Iskusstvo Marka Shagala, *The Art of Marc Chagall*), Moscow, 1918, repr. foll. p. 30; H. Walden, *Expressionismus, Die Kunstwende,* Berlin, 1918, repr. p. 24; A. Efross and J. Tugendhold, *Die Kunst Marc Chagalls,* trans. F. Ichak-Rubiner, Potsdam, 1921, pp. 52-55, repr. p. 43; Th. Däubler, *Marc Chagall* (French trans. of 1916 essay), Rome, 1922, p. 12, repr. [p. 26]; H. Walden, *Marc Chagall,* Sturm Bilderbücher No. 1, 2nd ed., Berlin, 1923, repr. p. 10; K. With, *Marc Chagall,* Leipzig, 1923, repr. n.p.; A. Salmon, *Chagall,* Paris, 1928, pl. 9 (dated 1912); *Sélection,* no. 6, Marc Chagall issue, Antwerp, Apr. 1929, repr. p. 79 (dated 1912); I. Kloomok, *Marc Chagall,* New York, 1951, pp. 32-33; L. Venturi, *Chagall,* Geneva, 1956, pp. 39-42; W. Erben, *Chagall,* New York, 1957, pp. 47-48; R. Rosenblum, *Cubism and Twentieth-Century Art,* New York, 1960, repr. p. 248; F. Meyer, *Marc Chagall,* New York, 1963, pp. 205-206, repr. color; J. Cassou, *Chagall,* New York, 1965, p. 134.

2. The picture was definitely among those sent to Berlin early in 1914 (Chagall, Feb. 1974). Its appearance in the Apr.-May and/or June exhibitions at Der Sturm is confirmed by Apollinaire, who specifically refers to it in his June 2 review (see REFERENCES). It is also reproduced in the announcement for the June exhibition.

29 Peasant Life.[1] 1917.
(Vie des paysans; The Stable; Night;
Man with Whip).

71.1936R 183

Oil on board, 8¼ x 8½ (21 x 21.7)

Signed and dated u.r.: *Chagall* / [1]*917;*
inscribed on reverse, not in the artist's hand
(photographed before mounting): *Marc*
Chagall / Vie dès [sic] *paysans / „der Stall"*
1917 / Hilla Rebay / Collection / The
Stable 1917 / Marc Chagall / Vie dès [sic]
paysans.

PROVENANCE:

Probably given by the artist to Hilla Rebay,
Greens Farms, Connecticut, 1936;[2] Estate of
Hilla Rebay, 1967-71; acquired from the
Estate of Hilla Rebay, 1971.

CONDITION:

In 1971 the work was mounted on a honeycomb panel, coated with Lucite 44 and then
with AYAF.

The ochre-colored areas, which appear both
under UV and to the naked eye as repaints,
are probably the work of the artist. The
scumbled area to the right of the male figure, for example, covers a pentimento, the
left arm apparently having originally extended to grasp the crook. It is difficult to
say whether the ochre retouching (probably
pigment mixed with varnish) was in all cases
to cover pentimenti or to strengthen certain
passages. X-rays of these areas have proved
inconclusive. Apart from 2 pinpoint losses,
the condition is excellent. (Jan. 1975.)

1. It has hitherto been impossible to establish Chagall's original title for this work. The
inscriptions on the reverse appear to be in Rebay's handwriting, but even they suggest 3
different titles. Ida Chagall (in conversation with M. Rowell, Feb. 1975) was unable to
clarify the problem. The present title must be regarded as tentative.

EXHIBITIONS:
Philadelphia, SRGM 3-T, no. 147 *(Night)*; Charleston, S.C., SRGM 4-T, no. 218 *(Night)*;
Bridgeport, Conn., Carlson Gallery, University of Bridgeport, *Homage to Hilla Rebay,*
Apr. 8-May 10, 1972, no. 7 *(The Stable)*; New York, SRGM 241 (addenda, *The Stable)*;
276 (no cat.).

REFERENCE:
F. Meyer, *Marc Chagall,* New York, 1963, repr. cc 298 *(Man with Whip).*

2. Ida Chagall is almost certain that the picture was given to Rebay at the time of the sale to
Solomon R. Guggenheim of *Green Violinist,* cat. no. 31, and *Birthday,* cat. no. 30.

---

30   Birthday. 1923.
      (Anniversaire).

37.443

Oil on canvas, 31⅞ x 39½ (80.8 x 100.3)

Signed l.r.: *Marc Chagall.* Not dated.

PROVENANCE:
Purchased from the artist by Solomon R.
Guggenheim, 1936; Gift of Solomon R.
Guggenheim, 1937.

CONDITION:
In 1953 the work was cleaned with Soilax
and surfaced with PBM. In 1960 it was
lined with wax resin and placed on a new
stretcher. There are minor touches of inpainting in the top right corner and along
the top edge.

The present signature, in white paint, has
been applied over an earlier one in Russian
script. This was almost certainly done by
the artist at the time of his sale of the work
to Guggenheim. Apart from some slight
abrasions at the edges, the condition is
excellent. (Apr. 1974.)

The first version of this composition (now owned by The Museum of Modern
Art, New York) was painted in Russia on or about July 7, 1915, Chagall's birthday, approximately two weeks before his July 25th marriage to Bella. In her
own book, *The First Meeting* (first published in Yiddish, *Di ershte bagegenish,*
New York, 1947, trans. Ida Chagall, *Lumières allumées,* Paris, 1973), Bella described the circumstances of the picture's creation. She arrived at Chagall's

30

room on his birthday bearing a bunch of flowers. As she opened the door, Chagall immediately seized a canvas and commanded her to stand still just as she was.

> *But what shall I do with the flowers? I cannot stay standing on the same spot. I want to put them in water or they will fade. But I soon forget them. You throw yourself upon the canvas which trembles under your hand. You snatch the brushes and squeeze out the paint—red, blue, white, black. You drag me into the stream of colors. Suddenly you lift me off the ground and push with your foot as if you felt too cramped in the little room. You leap, stretch out at full length, and fly up to the ceiling. Your head is turned and you turn mine too. You bend down behind my ear and whisper something to me. I listen to the melody of your soft, deep voice. I can even hear the song in your eyes. And together we rise to the ceiling of the gaily decked room and fly away. We reach the window and want to pass through. Through the window, clouds and blue sky beckon us. The walls, hung with my colored shawls, flutter about us and make our heads swim. Fields of flowers, houses, roofs, churches swim beneath us* (1973, pp. 258-259).

It is clear from this description that—as Meyer has suggested—Bella's memory of the exhilarating event has been fused with her memory of the painting itself.

In the interview in February 1974, Chagall explained the relationship between The Museum of Modern Art and the Guggenheim versions of this composition. The first version was sold not long after its creation to the Russian collector Kagan-Chabchaj. When Chagall was preparing to leave Russia in 1922, Kagan-Chabchaj (who feared that his entire collection might be confiscated by the State) gave Chagall two crates of paintings to take to Paris and deliver to the collector's brother for safe-keeping. Chagall did not in fact deliver the pictures until after 1923, and in the meantime they hung in his own apartment at 110, avenue d'Orléans. (See Meyer, p. 34, for a ca. 1923-24 photograph of the artist's studio, with The Museum of Modern Art version of *Birthday* clearly visible hanging on the wall.) Knowing that he would have to surrender these paintings before long, and that he would have nothing left from his earlier period (having lost approximately two hundred paintings in Berlin and having left many others behind in Russia), Chagall decided to make replicas of several of the works in Kagan-Chabchaj's collection. The second version of *Birthday* was made in 1923 at the specific request of Paul Guillaume, who subsequently decided not to buy it after all. It remained in the artist's collection until Guggenheim purchased it in 1936. (For an illuminating discussion of Chagall's attitude to variants, replicas, and new versions of earlier works, see Meyer, pp. 324, 333. He suggests that Chagall needed to have access to the imagery of his earlier works in order to create the new.)

A pencil sketch for The Museum of Modern Art version was presented to that museum by Chagall in 1949 (fig. a). A preparatory gouache for the Guggenheim painting dates from 1923 (Collection of the artist; information supplied by Ida Chagall and Marc Chagall, January-February 1974, but the study

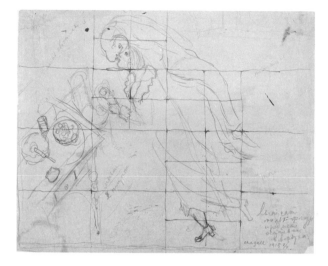

fig. a.
Chagall, study for *Birthday,* 1915, pencil on paper,
9 x 11½ in., 22.9 x 29.2 cm., The Museum of Modern
Art, New York. Gift of the artist.

itself has hitherto not been seen by the author). A third drawing (fig. b) was
done by Chagall specifically as an illustration for Bella's book and dates from
ca. 1942-44.

The differences between the two paintings are minor, although the fact that
The Museum of Modern Art version is painted on board does create a tighter
and harder surface effect. The decorative details in the wall hangings are handled with greater precision in the latter version, and the paint overall is more
thinly applied, with the board showing through in some places. The colors in
the two works are nearly identical, although the greens of Chagall's shirt are
slightly less blue in The Museum of Modern Art painting.

Only two compositional details distinguish the two versions from one
another. First, in The Museum of Modern Art version the handle of the window has a small circular ring at its base which is lacking in the Guggenheim
work. Second, in The Museum of Modern Art painting the three white clouds
(or puffs of smoke?) in the right-hand window pane (upper left) are set in the
blue sky; in the Guggenheim version one of these overlaps the church spire.
The view from the window included, as Bella related, the Ilytch church surrounded by a fence. This is clearly visible in the lower window pane and in the
background of the upper one.

EXHIBITIONS:

Philadelphia, SRGM 3-T, no. 146 (dated 1915); Charleston, S.C., SRGM 4-T, no. 217 (dated
1915, incorrect dimensions listed); Boston, Institute of Modern Art, *Chagall and Soutine,*
Jan. 22-Feb. 25, 1945, no. 6, repr. color cover (dated 1915); New York, The Museum of
Modern Art, *Marc Chagall,* Apr. 9-June 23, 1946, no. 28, repr. (dated 1915-23; so dated in
all subsequent publications), traveled to The Art Institute of Chicago, Nov. 14, 1946-Jan. 12,
1947; New York, SRGM 79 (checklist); Toronto, SRGM 85-T, no. 5, repr.; Vancouver,

fig. b.
Chagall, ink drawing, ca. 1942-44, present
whereabouts unknown.

SRGM 88-T, no. 5, repr.; Houston, The Museum of Fine Arts, *Chagall and de Chirico,*
Apr. 3-May 1, 1955, no. 41, repr.; Montreal, SRGM 93-T, no. 4; Hartford, Conn., Wads-
worth Atheneum, *Twentieth Century Painting from Three Cities: New York, New Haven,*
Hartford, Oct. 19-Dec. 4, 1955, no. 10; London, SRGM 104-T, no. 10; Paris, Musée des Arts
Décoratifs, *Marc Chagall,* June 12-Sept. 30, 1959, no. 92, repr.; Boston, SRGM 119-T, no. 5;
Lexington, Ky., SRGM 122-T, no. 3; New York, SRGM 129 (checklist); Philadelphia, SRGM
134-T, no. 16, repr.; Cal., Art Center in La Jolla, *Marc Chagall, 75th Anniversary Exhibition,*
Oct. 1-Nov. 11, 1962, no. 8, repr.; Worcester, Mass., SRGM 148-T, no. 7, repr.; Tokyo,
National Museum of Western Art, *Marc Chagall,* Oct. 1-Nov. 10, 1964, no. 31, repr.; Boston,
Museum of Fine Arts, *Surrealist & Fantastic Art from the Collections of the Museum of*
Modern Art and the Guggenheim Museum, Feb. 14-March 15, 1964 (checklist); New York,
SRGM 187, *Gauguin and the Decorative Style* (checklist); San Francisco Museum of Art,
Man: Glory, Jest and Riddle. A Survey of the Human Form through the Ages, Nov. 10, 1964-
Jan. 3, 1965, no. 239; Montreal, Expo 67, *Man and his World,* Apr. 28-Oct. 27, 1967, no. 74,
repr.; New York, SRGM 205, *Rousseau, Redon and Fantasy* (checklist); Columbus, Ohio,
SRGM 207-T, p. 18, repr. p. 19; Bogota, Colombia, Museo de Arte Moderno, *Inaugural*
Exhibition, Oct. 29-Dec. 15, 1970 (no cat.); New York, SRGM 276 (no cat.).

REFERENCES:

A. Efross and J. Tugendhold, Искусство Марка Шагала (Iskusstvo Marka Shagala, *The*
Art of Marc Chagall), Moscow, 1918, repr. foll. p. 46 (MOMA version); Idem, trans. F. Ichak-
Rubiner, Potsdam, 1921, repr. p. 68 (MOMA version); Th. Däubler, *Marc Chagall,* Rome,
1922, repr. n.p. (MOMA version); A. Levinson, "Chagall en Russie," *L'Amour de l'art,* Oct.
1923, p. 730, repr. p. 727 (MOMA version); W. George, "Chagall à Paris," *Sélection,* no. 3,
Antwerp, 1923-24, p. 262, repr. p. 390 (MOMA version); A. Levinson, "Divigation au sujet
d'une peinture de Chagall," *La Renaissance de l'art français,* vol. 10, Mar. 1927, p. 138, repr.
(MOMA version); W. George, *Marc Chagall,* Paris, 1928, p. 21 (MOMA version); *Sélection,*
no. 6, Marc Chagall issue, Antwerp, Apr. 1929, repr. p. 97 (MOMA version); W. Erben, *Marc*
Chagall, Munich, 1957, p. 60; F. Meyer, *Marc Chagall,* New York, 1963, pp. 237, 324, repr.
p. 259 (MOMA version); J. Cassou, *Chagall,* New York, 1965, p. 73, repr. (SRGM version,
attributed to MOMA collection).

31 Green Violinist. 1923-1924.
   (Violiniste).

37.446

Oil on canvas, 78 x 42¾ (198 x 108.6)

Signed l.r.: *Chagall / Marc*; inscribed on trouser cuff in Yiddish: אױ טאטע (Oh! Father). Not dated.

PROVENANCE:

Purchased from the artist by Solomon R. Guggenheim, 1936; Gift of Solomon R. Guggenheim, 1937.

CONDITION:

In 1953 2 tears at the lower left were patched; in 1954 nail holes top left were filled and inpainted, the surface cleaned and the edges taped. Cracking and cleavage of the paint film in some areas was noted. In 1970 extensive repairs were begun; reverse was coated with Lucite 44, worn edges were reinforced and inpainted, and the work was placed on a new stretcher. In 1973-74 cleaning with distilled water was completed on most of the surface (some of the white areas still remain to be cleaned). The reverse of the work was scraped, and the canvas lined with fiberglass and BEVA.

There is an area of traction cracks in the heavy white impasto center right. The thinly applied paint allows the canvas to show through in several places; there is some paint loss in the areas of the repaired tear below the figure's black boot. The overall condition of the paint film is excellent. (Jan. 1975.)

The picture has been variously dated 1917, 1918, 1920, 1923, 1923-26, 1924-25 (see below EXHIBITIONS and REFERENCES). Jouffroy first identified it as a replica of one of the murals for the State Jewish Kamerny Theater in Moscow, and he dated it after Chagall's return to Paris in 1923. Meyer concurred with this, as did Ida Chagall (January 1974) and Chagall himself (February 1974), both of whom placed it early in the second Paris period (1923-24).

Chagall's connections with the Kamerny Theater date from 1920 when the director Granovsky invited the artist to design the sets and costumes for the opening series of plays and later to paint murals for the auditorium. As Meyer has described (p. 296), the murals were painted in oil on canvas and attached to the walls. The largest, *Introduction to the Jewish Theater,* a horizontal panel, was intended for the left wall of the auditorium; the four smaller verticals were to be placed in the spaces between the windows on the facing wall. (All the murals, including one made for the frieze above the windows, one for the back wall, and one for the ceiling, are now stored in the State Tretiakov Gallery, Moscow.)

The four vertical panels were dedicated to the representation of those arts specifically identified in Chagall's mind with Jewish culture: Music, Drama, Dance, and Literature. These arts were personified by "a popular musician, a wedding jester, a buxom woman dancing, and a copyist of the Torah, the first poet dreamer" (Chagall, *Ma Vie,* Paris, 1931, p. 237). It is upon the figure of *Music* (fig. d) that *Green Violinist* is based. Like *Birthday* (see above cat. no. 30), the picture was among those replicas of earlier works which Chagall painted during his first three years back in Paris. His source in this case was not the original mural, but two of the studies which he had brought with him to Paris (figs. b and c).

Violinists appear again and again throughout Chagall's oeuvre. The particular form of the Moscow-Guggenheim figure goes back to an oil of 1912-13

fig. a.
Chagall, *The Violinist*, 1912-13, oil on canvas,
74 x 62¼ in., 188 x 158 cm., Stedelijk
Museum, Amsterdam.

fig. b.
Chagall, study for *The Violinist*, ca.
1918-19 (?), gouache on paper,
12⅝ x 8⅝ in., 32 x 22 cm., Collection
of the artist.

(fig. a, Stedelijk Museum, Amsterdam) in which many of the compositional elements are already present. A study usually associated with the Moscow mural (fig. b, Collection of the artist), although signed and dated 1917, was probably painted at least a year later. (Ida Chagall, January 1974, dates it ca. 1918-19.) If done in 1918-19, it would still predate Chagall's association with the Theater by over a year, indicating that the subject for the *Music* panel was not specifically conceived for the Theater series, but rather adapted from an existing work. The squarish format of this study, which brings it into close relationship with the 1912-13 Amsterdam oil and does not correspond to the proportions of the Moscow mural, would support this point.

A second study (fig. c) is signed and dated 1918, but probably dates from 1920. (It had not yet been dated when it was reproduced by B. Aronson in 1924 [*Marc Chagall*, Berlin, 1924, p. 20], and the date was probably added considerably later when Chagall no longer remembered precisely when he had done it.) This study is much more clearly relatable to the proportions and style of the mural and probably was made as a preparatory study, as soon as the dimensions for that work were established. The mural itself followed shortly afterwards.

At least two further versions of this theme were painted after the completion of the Guggenheim replica. The first, although considerably smaller, is otherwise almost identical to the Guggenheim's *Green Violinist* (Collection Joseph Randall Shapiro, Chicago, 35 x 20 in., 88.9 x 50.9 cm.); it was probably painted in about 1926 and may have been requested by a potential or actual buyer. Yet

fig. c.
Chagall, study for Moscow
mural (?), dimensions and
present whereabouts
unknown.

fig. d.
Chagall, mural for Kamerny
Theater, Moscow, 1919-20,
oil on canvas, 68⅞ x 35½ in.,
175 x 90 cm., State Tretiakov
Gallery, Moscow.

another reprise, squarer in format and more informal in style, probably dates from ca. 1928-29 (Collection Mrs. Benjamin K. Oko, New York, Meyer, repr. cc 364; for an illuminating discussion of the stylistic differences between the more "classical" conception of the earlier version and the freer character of the Oko picture, see Meyer, p. 333; the 1928-29 date for the latter was proposed by Ida Chagall, January 1974).

The significance of the violinist as represented in works such as the Amsterdam-Moscow-Guggenheim paintings has been described by Chagall (February 1974) as in some sense even broader than a personification of Music. In Russian villages, where there were no orchestras, no museums, and no paintings, the local country violinist personified everything—*"Tous les arts, tous les tableaux qu'on ne pouvait pas voir."* The violinist was forced to represent the arts as a whole, and for this reason he was of immense significance. Whether the violinist in Chagall's work also has a religious meaning, symbolizing—as some have suggested—the Hasidic aspirations of communion with God through music and dance, is not entirely clear. (See, for example, E. Genauer, *Chagall*, New York, 1956, pl. 13, who suggests such an interpretation for the Amsterdam picture.) Chagall's Uncle Neuch, who played the violin and indeed taught his nephew the instrument, was a member of the Hasidim, and it cannot be ruled out, therefore, that the figure carried some religious connotations.

The violinist in the Moscow and Guggenheim paintings wears clowns' checkered trousers—an allusion to Chagall's well-known passion for the circus and his conception of humanity as comprising in some sense a gigantic circus. (*"Le cirque pour moi c'est une énorme réalité. Nous sommes tous des personnages de cirque."* February 1974.) The ladder resting against the tree is seen by Chagall as an allusion on the one hand to the Biblical Jacob's ladder and on the other to memories of his own childhood, when he always wanted to be higher than the flat terrain allowed, to see more of the surrounding sky and landscape. (*"Il n'y avait pas de montagnes chez moi. Donc, il fallait monter dans les arbres ou sur le toit."* February 1974. This view is also reflected in a statement the artist made to L. Noel in a 1962 interview: "Up high one contemplates the world better than from below." *The Critic,* Chicago, vol. xxi, December 1962-January 1963, p. 35.)

Other elements in the composition, such as the violinist's green face—interpreted by some critics as a clear sign of his satanic nature—are described by Chagall as devoid of any meaning beyond one that is *"plastique, arbitraire, poétique"* (February 1974). As for the flying figure, already in 1947 J. J. Sweeney had stressed the essentially plastic compositional function of flying figures in Chagall's work, and the artist himself has consistently reaffirmed this. At the same time Chagall also suggests the degree to which normal expectations about the real world were intentionally undermined through the use of such devices. The flying figure could create a "psycho-plastic contrast," to "underline a new reality" by contrasting it with the old (Chagall to J. P. Hodin, in *The Dilemma of Being Modern,* London, 1956, p. 44).

EXHIBITIONS:

Kunsthalle Basel, *Marc Chagall,* Nov. 4-Dec. 3, 1933, no. 46 ("1923. *Violiniste*");[1] Philadelphia, SRGM 3-T, no. 149 (dated 1918; so dated in all subsequent SRGM publications until SRGM 202, 1968 when the date was changed to 1924-25); Charleston, S.C., SRGM 4-T, no. 220; New York, The Museum of Modern Art, *Marc Chagall,* Apr. 9-June 23, 1946, p. 43, repr. (dated 1918), traveled to The Art Institute of Chicago, Nov. 14, 1946-Jan. 12, 1947; New York, SRGM 78, 79 (checklists); Toronto, SRGM 85-T, no. 4; New York, SRGM 87 (checklist); 89 (no cat.); Kansas City, Mo., William Rockhill Nelson Gallery of Art, Atkins Museum of Fine Arts, *Contemporary American Painting in Honor of the American Jewish Tercentenary, 1654-1955,* Apr. 17- May 8, 1955 (checklist); Montreal, SRGM 93-T, no. 6; New York, SRGM 95, 97 (checklists); London, SRGM 104-T, no. 11, pl. 3; New York, SRGM 118 (checklist); 129, repr.; 144, 153 (checklists); 173, no. 46, repr. color; 196 (checklist); 202, p. 22, repr. color p. 23 (dated 1924-25); 205, *Rousseau, Redon and Fantasy* (checklist); 227 (no cat.); 232, 241, p. 72, repr. color p. 73; 266, 276 (no cats.).

REFERENCES:

W. George, *Marc Chagall,* Paris, 1928, p. 9, repr. p. 59; *Sélection,* no. 6, Marc Chagall issue, Antwerp, Apr. 1929, repr. p. 85 (dated 1913-20); I. Kloomok, *Marc Chagall: His Life and Work,* New York, 1951, pp. 52-53 (dated 1918); E. Debenedetti, "Saggio di interpretazione del violinista verde di Chagall," *Commentari,* vol. 9, Oct.-Dec. 1958, pp. 298-308, repr. (dated 1918); A. Jouffroy, "Les Aventures magiques des personnages de Chagall," *Connaissance des arts,* no. 72, Feb. 1958, repr. p. 27; F. Meyer, *Marc Chagall,* New York, 1963, p. 333, repr. color p. 295 (dated "between 1923 and 1926"); W. Erben, *Marc Chagall,* revised ed., New York, 1966, p. 69 (dated 1917).

1. A label on the reverse identifies the present work with the Basel exhibition of 1933.

Robert Delaunay

Born April 1885, Paris.
Died October 1941, Montpellier.

32   Saint-Séverin No. 3. 1909-1910.

41.462

Oil on canvas, 45 x 34⅞ (114.1 x 88.6)

Signed l.r.: *r. delaun*[ay]. Not dated.

PROVENANCE:

Purchased from the artist by Städtische Kunsthalle Mannheim, 1928;[1] banned by the German government as degenerate art, August 28, 1937 (F. Roh, *Entartete Kunst*, Hanover, 1962, p. 213, repr. foll. p. 248); purchased from Gutekunst und Klipstein, Bern, by Solomon R. Guggenheim, 1939; Gift of Solomon R. Guggenheim, 1941.

CONDITION:

At some point prior to its acquisition by the Museum, the painting underwent several repairs; 12 patches were attached to the reverse, apparently to repair breaks in the canvas, and filling and inpainting were per- formed on the front of the painting in some of these areas. Some scattered repaints, pre- sumably to compensate for paint loss, were also performed in areas where no patches had been attached. In 1954 the patches were removed; the canvas was lined with wax resin and placed on a new stretcher. The painting was cleaned and most of the old repaints were removed. Some new inpaint- ing was performed at this time. In 1957 the painting was slightly damaged in transit and suffered 3 punctures with paint loss in the lower right corner and 1 abrasion with paint loss at the upper left. These areas were filled with gesso and inpainted with PBM.

The edges of the canvas show considerable wear, especially the top and right edges where there are some deep cracks in the pig- ment and ground. Apart from the edges, the condition is in general good. (Aug. 1972.)

The Guggenheim picture is the third in a series of seven oils painted by Delau- nay of the church of Saint-Séverin. The church, located not far from Delaunay's studio, was started in the thirteenth century, although the choir depicted in the paintings dates from the fifteenth century. The original stained glass windows have recently been replaced by modern ones, so that it is no longer possible to see the interior under the particular conditions experienced by Delaunay.

The other six oil versions are: *Saint-Séverin No. 1* (Collection F. Meyer, Zurich, formerly Erbslöh Collection, signed and dated "R.D.09," Habasque, no. 43); *Saint-Séverin No. 2* (The Minneapolis Institute of Arts, signed and dated on reverse "2ᵉ étude Saint-Séverin 1909 r. delaunay, Paris," Habasque, no. 44); *Saint-Séverin No. 4* (Philadelphia Museum of Art, signed and dated "r. delaunay 1909," Habasque, no. 46); *Saint-Séverin No. 5* (Nationalmuseum, Stockholm, signed and dated on reverse "Nr. 5, époque du 'St-Séverin,' 1909- 1910. R. Delaunay, Paris. L'Arc-en-ciel," Habasque, no. 75); *Saint-Séverin No. 6* (Collection C. Giedion-Welcker, Zurich, not signed or dated, Habasque, no. 76); *Saint-Séverin No. 7* (formerly Collection Larapidie, Saint-Mandé, signed and dated "St-Séverin 1908 delaunay," Habasque, no. 150). In addition there are at least seven drawings associated with the subject (figs. a-f, h), as well as one watercolor (fig. g).

Although Delaunay himself occasionally cited 1907 as the origin of the Saint- Séverin series (ca. 1924, and in Raynal [1927]) and even dated the final work in the series 1908, there is considerable evidence for dating *Saint-Séverin No. 1*

1. A photograph of the Guggenheim picture in the artist's estate carries the notation *"Mme. Mannheim. Acheté 1928"* (see below REFERENCES: Delaunay, 1938-39). The picture was presumably purchased following its exhibition in Mannheim in 1927.

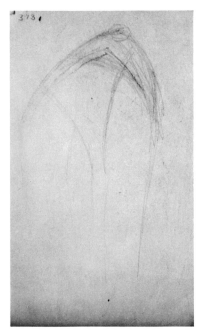

fig. a.
Delaunay, sketch of *Saint-Séverin,*
pencil, undated sketchbook page,
6⅞ x 4⅛ in., 17.5 x 10.5 cm.,
Habasque, no. 498, Collection
Sonia Delaunay, Paris.

fig. b.
Delaunay, sketch of *Saint-Séverin,*
pencil, undated sketchbook page,
6⅞ x 4⅛ in., 17.5 x 10.5 cm.,
Habasque, no. 498, Collection
Sonia Delaunay, Paris.

in mid 1909 and the others later. The first two works in the series are signed
and dated 1909; moreover, *Saint-Séverin No. 1* was dated 1909 when it appeared in the first *Blaue Reiter* exhibition in December 1911 and again when it
was published in late 1912 with the first edition of Apollinaire's "Les Fenêtres"
(Album [1912]). In the 1938-39 notes on Saint-Séverin and in the autobiographical outline published by Hoog (pp. 29-32) the series is again dated 1909.

All of this evidence would suggest that, although part of the series may have
been painted later than 1909, a date earlier than 1909 for its inception is extremely unlikely. The stylistic evidence substantiates this point. The influence
of Cézanne is often cited in connection with these works, and Delaunay himself
spoke of the series as a transition between Cézanne and Cubism (notes, 1938-
39).[2] However, in relation to *Saint-Séverin No. 1* and *No. 3*, it is impossible to
ignore the impact of Braque's paintings of early 1909 and those of his summer
visit to La Roche Guyon. Spate has argued convincingly (pp. 124-125) that
works such as Braque's *Harbor in Normandy* (The Art Institute of Chicago)
must have inspired Delaunay's handling in the first Saint-Séverin pictures, especially the method of faceting the floor. The *Harbor in Normandy* was almost
certainly exhibited in the March 1909 *Salon des Indépendants* (H. Hope,
Braque, New York, 1949, p. 37), an exhibition in which Delaunay also participated, and it is difficult to imagine that *Saint-Séverin No. 1* antedates this
exhibition. Furthermore, as Spate has suggested (p. 132), the unstable curving
and bulging of the Saint-Séverin interior, a quality that evoked for Apollinaire

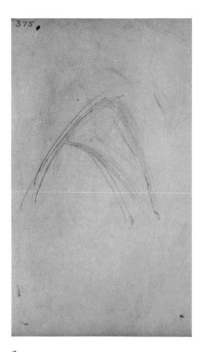

fig. c.
Delaunay, sketch of *Saint-Séverin*,
pencil, undated sketchbook page,
6⅞ x 4⅛ in., 17.5 x 10.5 cm.,
Habasque, no. 498, Collection
Sonia Delaunay, Paris.

fig. d.
Delaunay, sketch of *Saint-Séverin*,
pencil and charcoal, undated sketch-
book page, not in Habasque (?),
Collection Sonia Delaunay,
Paris.

the notion of an earthquake (see below cat. no. 35), does suggest the influence
of the La Roche Guyon and the Carrières Saint-Denis landscapes, which Delaunay could not have seen until the end of the summer.

The sequence of the series would thus probably run from summer 1909 to
some time in 1910. *No. 2* was, according to Delaunay's own records, exhibited
in the *Salon des Indépendants* in March-May 1910 (Habasque, no. 44) and
must therefore have been completed by then. The fact that Delaunay himself
described it as an *étude* might suggest that the Guggenheim picture *(No. 3)* was
by then not yet ready to exhibit. The Guggenheim picture may thus not have
been completed until spring 1910. This is further substantiated by the existence
of a drawing made from the finished painting and inscribed "*St. Séverin, 1909/
10, r. delaunay*" (fig. h). (Hoog, 1967, no. 17, first convincingly suggested that
this drawing might be a *reprise a posteriori* of the Guggenheim picture. Sonia
Delaunay, in conversation with the author, corroborated this view.) The Philadelphia picture *(No. 4)* is dated 1909, but the Stockholm version *(No. 5)* 1909-
10. The final version presents special problems since according to Habasque
(no. 150) it was reworked in wax in Madrid in 1915. Although Delaunay himself (presumably in 1915) added the date of 1908, F. G. de la Tourette dated
it 1910 (color pl. 6). The colors suggest Delaunay's work of 1912-15, and it is
thus impossible to know when the picture was actually started, though it was
probably not before 1910.

The six drawings for the series that have so far come to light (figs. a-f) cannot
with any degree of certainty be described as preparatory works for particular

fig. e.
Delaunay, sketch of *Saint-Séverin,* conté
crayon on paper, 16¾ x 12¼ in.,
42.5 x 31.1 cm., Habasque, no. 501,
formerly Collection Mr. and Mrs.
Richard S. Davis, Minneapolis.

fig. f.
Delaunay, sketch of *Saint-Séverin,*
crayon on paper, 12¼ x 9¼ in.,
31 x 23.5 cm., Musée National d'Art
Moderne, Paris.

versions of the theme, although they were probably all (with the exception of
fig. e) done in the church itself and were all preparatory to the series as a
whole. The four sketchbook drawings (figs. a-d) probably represent Delaunay's
earliest responses to the building and would date from 1909. A drawing formerly in the collection of Mr. and Mrs. Richard S. Davis, Minneapolis (fig. e)
is a more detailed study of the Gothic architecture and includes neither the
windows nor the floor. A drawing in the Musée National d'Art Moderne,
Paris (fig. f) is inscribed lower left "*St. Séverin / Musée de Mannheim,*" relating
it specifically to the painting now in the Guggenheim collection, but it is not
clear whether this is an accurate reflection of the drawing's original role or a
more general reference to the series as a whole exemplified by the third version.
The watercolor (fig. g) is extremely detailed and finished and was probably
conceived as a separate work of art, rather than as a study for any of the oils,
possibly after the completion of the series. It is closest to the Guggenheim picture, although its colors are more varied and generally brighter than those of
the oil.

EXHIBITIONS:
Städtische Kunsthalle Mannheim, *Wege und Richtungen der abstrakten Malerei,* Jan. 30-
Mar. 27, 1927, no. 32 (dated 1907); New York, SRGM 74, 78, 79, 87 (checklists); 89 (no cat.);
91, 95, 97 (checklists); Paris, Musée National d'Art Moderne, *Robert Delaunay,* May 25-
Sept. 30, 1957, no. 15, traveled in part to Amsterdam, Stedelijk Museum, Oct. 18-Dec. 1, 1957,
no. 9, Eindhoven, Stedelijk van Abbemuseum, Dec. 6-Jan. 11, 1958, London, Arts Council
Gallery, Jan. 25-Feb. 22, 1958, no. 8, repr. (listed as "*Saint Séverin No. 7*"); New York, SRGM

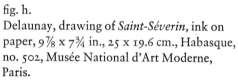

fig. g.
Delaunay, *Saint-Séverin,* watercolor on paper, 19 x 14 in., 48.2 x 35.5 cm., Private Collection, Massachusetts.

fig. h.
Delaunay, drawing of *Saint-Séverin,* ink on paper, 9⅞ x 7¾ in., 25 x 19.6 cm., Habasque, no. 502, Musée National d'Art Moderne, Paris.

118, 129 (checklists); Kunstverein in Hamburg, *Robert Delaunay,* Jan. 26-Mar. 11, 1962, traveled to Cologne, Wallraf-Richartz-Museum, Mar. 24-May 6, Frankfurt Kunstverein, May 18-June 24, 1962, no. 8, repr.; New York, SRGM 151, 153 (checklists); 173, no. 14, repr. color; Ottawa, National Gallery of Canada, *Robert and Sonia Delaunay,* Oct. 8-31, 1965, traveled to Montreal Museum of Fine Arts, Nov. 10-Dec. 5, 1965, no. 9, repr.; New York, SRGM 196 (checklist); 202, p. 62, repr. color p. 63; 221 (no cat.); 232, pp. 87-88, repr. p. 86; 240 (no cat.); 241, pp. 87-88, repr.; Cleveland, SRGM, 258-T, pl. 2; New York, SRGM 276 (no cat.).

REFERENCES:

R. Delaunay, notes written on *Saint-Séverin,* ca. 1924, in Francastel, 1957, p. 62; M. Raynal, *Anthologie de la peinture en France de 1906 à nos jours,* Paris [1927], pp. 114-116, repr.; A. Gleizes, *Kubismus: Bauhausbücher 13,* Munich [1928], pl. 5; R. Delaunay, notes written on reverse of a photograph of the Guggenheim *Saint-Séverin,* ca.1938-39,[2] in Francastel, 1957, pp. 86-87; Idem, lecture delivered Feb. 16, 1939, Ibid., pp. 227-228; *Art of Tomorrow,* 1939, no. 462; F. G. de la Tourette, *Robert Delaunay,* Paris, 1950, pp. 18-21; Habasque, 1957, no. 45; SRGM *Handbook,* 1959, p. 45, repr.; R. Rosenblum, *Cubism and Twentieth-Century Art,* New York, 1960, pp. 149-150; Hoog, 1967, p. 50; Vriesen and Imdahl, 1969, pp. 26-28, 74-75, fig. 10; Spate, 1970, pp. 121-125.

2. Spate suggests that this text may possibly date from somewhat earlier, e.g. ca. 1928-33 (correspondence with the author, Oct. 1973).

33   Eiffel Tower with Trees. Summer 1910.
      (*Tour Eiffel aux arbres; Eiffel Tower*).

46.1035

Oil on canvas, 49¾ x 36½ (126.4 x 92.8)

Signed and dated l.l.: *r. delaunay 09*.

PROVENANCE:

Purchased from Sonia Delaunay, Paris, 1946.

CONDITION:

In 1955 an old lining canvas was removed
and the picture was lined with wax resin on
natural linen, the reverse being sprayed with
PBM beforehand. In 1957 rubs and some

paint losses at the bottom center were inpainted with watercolor.

Some old tack holes with rust marks are
visible at the upper and lower edges, but the
edges otherwise show only minor wear. The
paint was thinly applied in most areas (on a
sized canvas, but without ground), and
much of the canvas remains unpainted.
There are 2 ½ in. repaints 3 in. from the
bottom and 2½ in. from the right side.
Apart from some scattered minor stains,
the condition is good. (Oct. 1973.)

Late in 1909, Delaunay began a series of works that were to occupy him for the
next two years—their subjects were the Eiffel Tower and the city of Paris itself.
The dates for these crucial works of 1909-11 have been difficult to establish
since many of the paintings in question were apparently antedated at a slightly
later time. (For a helpful note on this problem see Golding, *Cubism*, 1968,
p. 155, who does, however, erroneously record some information from the
Galerie Barbazanges exhibition catalogue and suggests that this catalogue is a
more reliable document than it has proved to be.)

   The earliest *Eiffel Tower* is the picture Delaunay apparently painted to celebrate his engagement to Sonia Terk (Sonia Delaunay in conversation with
the author, 1971; Collection Sonia Delaunay, Paris, Habasque, no. 69). Since
she was married to Wilhelm Uhde until the end of 1909 and did not marry
Delaunay until November 1910, it is likely that the picture dates from the very
end of 1909 or even early in 1910. This first canvas was probably followed by
three roughly contemporary works: the study for *The City* on the reverse of
The Minneapolis Institute of Arts *Saint-Séverin No. 2* (Habasque, no. 44), the
study for *The City* formerly in the collection of Sonia Delaunay (Kunstmuseum
Winterthur, Habasque, no. 73), and the *Eiffel Tower* on the reverse of the
Philadelphia Museum of Art *Saint-Séverin No. 4* (Habasque, no. 46). A study
for the tree in the latter *Tower* (Musée National d'Art Moderne, Paris, Habasque, no. 80; Hoog, 1967, no. 12) is inscribed on the reverse "*Etude St.-Cloud,
1910*," but both Habasque and Hoog date it 1909, Hoog placing it in the
summer of that year. The starkness of the silhouette in the Philadelphia *Tower*,
and the treatment of foliage in both the study and the painting are reminiscent
of Braque's 1908 L'Estaque landscapes rather than those painted at La Roche
Guyon the following year. It seems possible, therefore, that Delaunay painted
the Philadelphia picture late in 1909, although a date of early 1910 for it cannot be ruled out.

   Soon afterwards Delaunay must have painted the first full-scale conception
of *The City*, a picture which, although now lost, is reproduced in an article by
W. Bombe, "Franz Marc und der Expressionismus," *Das Kunstblatt*, I. Jg.,
March 1917, p. 75. This picture has been convincingly identified by J. Langner

33

as the work once owned by Jawlensky, Habasque, no. 72 ("Zu den Fenster-Bildern von Robert Delaunay," *Jahrbuch der Hamburger Kunstsammlungen,* Band 7, 1962, p. 70). It was first exhibited at the March 1910 *Salon des Indépendants* (as "*Ville*, n.d."); then at the first *Blaue Reiter* exhibition in Munich, December 1911-January 1912, where it was purchased by Jawlensky (no. 16, "*Die Stadt*, 1910,*" the asterisk correctly identifying it as the only *La Ville* by then sold); and later it was exhibited at the February-March 1912 Galerie Barbazanges exhibition, where it is dated 1909 (no. 7). Although many of the dates in the latter catalogue are accurate, some demonstrable errors and inconsistencies suggest that the publication as a whole must be treated with caution. *(The City No. 2 [study]* is dated 1910 in the catalogue list, 1909-11 in the caption to its illustration; *Saint-Séverin No. 1*, although correctly dated 1909, is reproduced in reverse; the Köhler *Eiffel Tower* [no. 4], which had been dated 1911 in Munich, is here dated 1910, etc.) Jawlensky purchased *The City* at the *Blaue Reiter* exhibition (not, as stated by Hoog, 1967, no. 16, at the 1912 Der Sturm exhibition in Berlin), and two letters from Kandinsky to Delaunay refer to the sale; the first is dated December 20, 1911, the second January 2, 1912 (Collection Sonia Delaunay, Paris; both unpublished, but the contents referred to by Vriesen, p. 36). This picture and a work which is probably a study for its lower half (Tate Gallery, London, Habasque, no. 71, not signed or dated), together with the Minneapolis and Winterthur studies for *The City* and the Philadelphia study for the *Eiffel Tower*, share certain stylistic characteristics. The tower in each case is shown as a simple silhouette, and the scene is depicted from a single vantage point. The houses of the city are solid, block-like forms, except in the lower right corner where they acquire some of the bulging, curving characteristics of the Saint-Séverin paintings. All of these works were probably painted in 1910, although a date of late 1909 for some of them cannot be ruled out.

With the Guggenheim's *Eiffel Tower with Trees*, Delaunay's style took a decisive turn. The solid forms of the Philadelphia study have been broken into a series of dynamic, fragmented lines and shapes. As Vriesen has pointed out, the most striking aspect of this development is the sudden introduction into the pictorial context of the element of time. The Tower is shown simultaneously from several different viewpoints as if in succession. It is the beginning of what Delaunay was to call his "destructive" phase, and it was to be much further developed in subsequent versions of the Eiffel Tower. The sudden change in style may be attributable partly to the publication of the *Technical Manifesto of Futurist Painting* on May 18, 1910, and the dissemination of various Futurist ideas, partly to Delaunay's understanding and absorption of the 1909-10 developments in Picasso and Braque. (For a detailed discussion of Futurist influence see Spate.) Sonia Delaunay herself recalled that two of the large *Eiffel Towers* were painted in Nantua during the summer of 1910 and that the rest were painted in their new studio at 3, rue des Grands Augustins which they did not move into until after their wedding in November 1910 (Vriesen and Imdahl, p. 32). The two works painted in Nantua would in that case probably have been the Guggenheim's *Eiffel Tower with Trees* and an *Eiffel Tower* now in a private collection in Krefeld (Habasque, no. 83, possibly exhibited at Galerie Barbazanges, "no. 18, *Etude pour la Tour*," Vriesen, fig. 53).

As a work of the summer of 1910, *Eiffel Tower with Trees* represents the starting point of Delaunay's major stylistic contributions of the coming years.

EXHIBITIONS:

New York, SRGM 78, 84, 91, 95 (checklists); Hartford, Conn., Wadsworth Atheneum, *Twentieth Century Painting from Three Cities,* Oct. 19-Dec. 4, 1955, no. 14; Paris, Musée National d'Art Moderne, *Robert Delaunay,* May 25-Sept. 30, 1957, no. 17, repr. (dated 1909), traveled in part to Amsterdam, Stedelijk Museum, Oct. 18-Dec. 1, 1957, no. 10, repr., Eindhoven, Stedelijk van Abbemuseum, Dec. 6-Jan. 11, 1958, London, Arts Council Gallery, Jan. 25-Feb. 22, 1958, no. 9, repr.; Boston, Mass., SRGM 119-T, no. 6; Palm Beach, Fla., The Society of the Four Arts, *The School of Paris,* Mar. 4-Apr. 5, 1960, no. 6, repr.; Kunstverein in Hamburg, *Robert Delaunay,* Jan. 26-Mar. 11, 1962, no. 11 (dated 1909), traveled to Cologne, Wallraf-Richartz-Museum, Mar. 24-May 6, 1962, Frankfurt Kunstverein, May 18-June 24, 1962; New York, SRGM 196 (checklist); 202, p. 91, repr. p. 90; 240, 266, 276 (no cats.).

REFERENCES:

M. Seuphor, *L'Art abstrait,* Paris, 1950, p. 285, repr. p. 151 (dated 1910), revised ed., 1971, repr. p. 157; F. G. de la Tourette, *Robert Delaunay,* Paris, 1950, pp. 26-28 (dated 1909), pl. 8 (dated 1910); *Aujourd'hui,* no. 11, Jan. 1957, p. 31 (dated 1910); Habasque, 1957, no. 70, color pl. III (dated 1909); Vriesen and Imdahl, 1969, p. 29, fig. 12 (dated 1909); Spate, 1970, pp. 127-128, pl. 10 (dated 1910).

34 Eiffel Tower. 1911.
(Tour Eiffel).

37.463

Oil on canvas, 79½ x 54½ (202 x 138.4)

Signed and dated l.r.: *r delaunay 1910*; inscribed by the artist l.l.: *la tour 1910*; on reverse (photographed before lining): *"la tour 1910" / salle 41 indépendants / 1911 / r. delaunay 19 / Bl. malesherbes.*

PROVENANCE:

Purchased from the artist by Solomon R. Guggenheim;[1] Gift of Solomon R. Guggenheim, 1937.

CONDITION:

In 1942 the work was strip lined with PVA adhesive. In 1955 the strip lining patches were removed. A new lining canvas was prepared by spraying with AYAF and Lucite 46 and was then attached by the Dutch method. In 1957 some rubs and losses were filled with gesso and inpainted: a 2 in. area at the top left corner; a rabbet mark and some other minor touches along the left edge; a 9 in. by ½ in. vertical line centered 12 in. from the left side and 30 in. from the top; a 2 in. area 14 in. from the right side and 9 in. from the bottom; a 1½ in. circle 4 in. from the top and 6 in. from the right side; several other very minor touches.

There are some scattered losses of paint, ground, and support at the extreme edges, which also show considerable abrasion from the rabbet of a previous frame. There is a line (drip of varnish?) running vertically down the center of the canvas approximately 23 in. from the right. Certain impasto areas, chiefly whites, show crackle and some loss from old cleavage, but the overall condition of the paint film is excellent.

Examination of the signature under strong magnification suggests that it was probably added some time after the completion of the picture but definitely at an early date. Whereas the signature and date appear to be applied over 1 or 2 cracks in the paint film, several other cracks go through them, and the writing clearly antedates the inpainting in the area. (Mar. 1974.)

Cooper first suggested that the present picture dates from 1911 (p. 79) and stated that Delaunay did not produce an *Eiffel Tower* until 1910. As has been suggested above (cat. no. 33), the picture now in a private collection in Krefeld (Habasque, no. 83) probably followed fairly soon after the Guggenheim's *Eiffel Tower with Trees,* during the summer of 1910. The fact that Habasque identifies the Krefeld work with no. 18 in the Galerie Barbazanges exhibition of 1912 (*"Etude pour la Tour, 1910"*) suggests that Delaunay himself saw it as a study for the Köhler *Eiffel Tower,* the major work that followed. In November 1910 the Delaunays moved into their new apartment (see above cat. no. 33), and between December 1910 and June 1911 Delaunay produced several major new paintings.

The Köhler *Eiffel Tower* was probably completed just in time for the opening of the *Salon des Indépendants* in April 1911 (see fn. 2). The Guggen-

1. The date of purchase is not recorded. The picture was for sale, but not sold, at the 1929 Zurich exhibition (information from Kunsthaus Zürich, correspondence with the author, Oct. 1971). Guggenheim might have purchased the picture on any of his visits to Paris between 1930 and 1936.

fig. a.
Delaunay, *Eiffel Tower,* 1911, pencil, pen,
and ink on brown board, 21¼ x 19¼ in.,
54 x 48.9 cm., Habasque, no. 509, The
Museum of Modern Art, New York.
Abby Aldrich Rockefeller Fund.

heim *Tower,* which represents a stylistic development beyond the Köhler one, was not exhibited before June 1911 in Brussels and could thus have been completed in April or May.

The external evidence for dating the Köhler and Guggenheim *Eiffel Towers* in 1911 rather than 1910 is substantial. The Köhler picture appeared in the first *Blaue Reiter* exhibition in December 1911 and was reproduced in the catalogue with the date 1911 (no. 17). Köhler purchased the picture shortly after the exhibition opened (Vriesen, pp. 36, 38, and unpublished letters in the collection of Sonia Delaunay). The Der Sturm volume (with its first edition of Apollinaire's "Les Fenêtres," Delaunay, Album [1912]) includes a reproduction of the Köhler picture with the date 1911 (no. 10). A drawing in The Museum of Modern Art, New York (fig. a), closely related to the Guggenheim and Köhler pictures, carried the date 1911 in the lower left corner; the final digit has somewhat clumsily been changed into an "0," but the inscription clearly originally read "1911." (Habasque identified this drawing [no. 509] as a preparatory study for the Guggenheim work. The drawing is, however, an extremely polished version of the composition and must have been made after, rather than before, the completion of the painting, perhaps combining elements from both the Köhler and the Guggenheim versions. Sonia Delaunay and M. Hoog [in conversations with the author, July 1971] concurred with this view. Delaunay's working method, which clearly involved painting directly on the canvas, precluded the need for such detailed preparatory drawings.) In addition, although Delaunay almost always referred to the *Eiffel Towers* as having been painted in 1909 or 1910, in his own "Cahier" of 1939-40 he dated the present Guggenheim picture 1911 (Francastel, p. 79, no. 18).

34

One further *Eiffel Tower* of the same period and scale as the Köhler and Guggenheim pictures is difficult to place exactly, but it was probably executed shortly after the Guggenheim painting in the early summer of 1911 (Kunstmuseum Basel, Habasque, no. 84).

A transfer lithograph of the Eiffel Tower was made by Delaunay in 1926 (titled and dated "*La Tour* 1910"). It is extremely close to the Köhler and Guggenheim versions of early 1911. An example is in the collection of The Museum of Modern Art, New York, another in the collection of Sonia Delaunay, Paris.

EXHIBITIONS:

[Erroneously recorded in SRGM *Handbook,* 1959, p. 46 and 1970, p. 88 as having appeared in the April 1911 *Salon des Indépendants*];[2] Brussels, *VIII Salon des Indépendants,* June 10-July 3, 1911, no. 54;[3] Paris, Grand Palais, *Trente ans d'art indépendant, 1884-1914,* Feb. 20-Mar. 21, 1926, no. 684;[4] Kunsthaus Zürich, *Abstrakte und Surrealistische Malerei und Plastik,* Oct. 6-Nov. 3, 1929, no. 21 (dated 1910);[5] Charleston, S.C., SRGM 1-T, no. 112 (dated 1910; so dated in all subsequent SRGM publications); Philadelphia, SRGM 3-T, no. 160; Charleston, S.C., SRGM 4-T, no. 231; New York, SRGM 78 (checklist); Toronto, SRGM 85-T, no. 7; New York, SRGM 87, 91 (checklists); 89 (no cat.); Paris, Musée National d'Art Moderne, *Robert Delaunay,* May 25-Sept. 30, 1957, no. 22, repr. (dated 1910), traveled in part to Amsterdam, Stedelijk Museum, Oct. 18-Dec. 1, 1957, no. 11, Eindhoven, Stedelijk van Abbemuseum, Dec. 6, 1957-Jan. 11, 1958, London, Arts Council Gallery, Jan. 25-Feb. 22, 1958, no. 10, repr.; Palais des Beaux-Arts de Bruxelles, *50 Ans d'art moderne,* Apr. 17-July 21, 1958, no. 69, repr.; New York, SRGM 118, 129, 144 (checklists); 221 (no cat.); 232, pp. 88-90, repr.; Los Angeles County Museum of Art, *The Cubist Epoch,* Dec. 15, 1970-Feb. 21, 1971, traveled to New York, The Metropolitan Museum of Art, Apr. 9-June 8, 1971, no. 61, color pl. 79, p. 81 (dated 1911?); New York, SRGM 241, pp. 88-90, repr.; 276 (no cat.).

REFERENCES:

R. Delaunay, lecture given on Feb. 16, 1939, Francastel, 1957, p. 227; Idem, "Cahier," ca. 1939-40, Ibid., p. 79, no. 18 (dated 1911); F. G. de la Tourette, *Robert Delaunay,* Paris, 1950, pl. 9 (dated 1910); Habasque, 1957, no. 78 (dated 1910); SRGM *Handbook,* 1959, p. 46, repr. p. 47 (dated 1910); R. Rosenblum, *Cubism and Twentieth-Century Art,* New York, 1960, pp. 149-150; Golding, *Cubism,* 1968, pp. 148-149, pl. 67 (dated 1910); M. Martin, *Futurist Art and Theory,* Oxford, 1968, pp. 106-107, pl. 74a (dated 1910); U. Laxner, "Robert Delaunay: Tour Eiffel," *Museum Folkwang, Essen, Mitteilungen,* 1969, 3. Band, no. 12 (dated 1910); Cooper, *Cubist Epoch,* 1970, no. 61, pp. 79-80, 282, color pl. 79, p. 81 (dated 1911?); Spate, 1970, pp. 129 ff. (dated 1910).

2. The picture has twice been identified with the 1911 *Salon* entry no. 1705 *"Paysage, Paris"* (SRGM *Handbook,* 1959, p. 46; 1970, p. 88). As Cooper correctly observed, however (p. 79), Habasque had already identified the picture exhibited in Paris as the *Eiffel Tower* formerly in the Köhler collection, Berlin (Habasque, no. 77, destroyed in the war). Further evidence for this point is provided by the fact that it is the Köhler version, rather than the Guggenheim picture, that is reproduced in R. Allard's article on the *Salon* ("Sur quelques peintres," *Les Marches du Sud-Ouest,* June 1911, pp. 57-64). The inscription on the reverse of the Guggenheim picture was added by Delaunay in the 1920's (when he moved to the Blvd. Malesherbes), and he perhaps no longer remembered which version had been sent to the Paris *Salon* (see fn. 3).

3. It is possible that the Basel Tower (Habasque, no. 84), rather than the present work, was lent to Brussels. Delaunay's inscription on the reverse of the present painting, referring to the Paris *Indépendants,* suggests, however, that he remembered sending the picture to 1 of the 2 *Indépendants* but forgot whether it was Paris or Brussels.

4. The entry reads *"La Tour—1910—Salle 41 des IND. 1911—Première manifestation collective d'un art nouveau."* Habasque identifies this entry with either the Köhler or the Guggenheim picture. It seems probable that Delaunay lent the present work to the 1926 show either to take the place of the Köhler picture, which was not available for loan, or because he genuinely forgot which of the 2 he had lent to the exhibition in Paris. He must have added the inscription on the reverse of the Guggenheim picture at about this time.

5. The dimensions of the Zurich catalogue entry (138 x 203) correspond with those of the present picture and with none of the other Eiffel Towers.

35 The City. 1911.
(La Ville; La Ville no. 2).

38.464

Oil on canvas, 57⅛ x 44½ (145 x 111.9)

Inscribed by the artist l.l.: *la ville 1911 r. delaunay*; on reverse (transcribed but not photographed before lining): *année 1909-10-11-12; 1er exposition / cubiste / Salle 41 aux indépendants / 1911.*[1]

PROVENANCE:

Purchased from the artist by Solomon R. Guggenheim, 1938; Gift of Solomon R. Guggenheim, 1938.

CONDITION:

In 1943 the work was cleaned. In 1953 it was cleaned and lined with wax resin, and the stretcher was replaced. The wax has penetrated the surface and is clearly visible in some areas, resulting in a considerable darkening of the background, especially in those places where the paint is thinly applied, where losses have occurred, or where the bare canvas has been left untouched. This is notably true of a large rectangular area in the lower left corner extending from the final digit of the *"1911"* approximately 25 in. up from the bottom. Inpainting of uncertain date is clearly visible under UV (fig. a) and is concentrated mainly in the center (7 areas varying from 1 to 2 in. in diameter) and near the lower right corner (3 areas varying in diameter from 2 to 4 in.). Extensive pentimenti in both the right and left curtains are visible under UV: those areas which are now painted in smoothly brushed color were originally covered with pointillist dots identical to those of the surrounding areas. One area along the left margin, which had originally been uniformly painted, was subsequently dotted by the artist.

There is a horizontal scratch extending across most of the surface 12 in. from the bottom; a second scratch, concentrated across the central area, 21½ in. from the bottom; a third, 8 in. long 18 in. from the bottom. There is crackle and scattered loss in most areas of white impasto, especially along the right edge and at the upper right. Crackle and chipping are present (perhaps with some incipient cleavage) in most areas of the pentimenti. Apart from the darkening caused by the wax lining, the condition in general is good. (Apr. 1974.)

Langner has, with the help of Sonia Delaunay, established the source of the *The City* composition as a photograph taken from the southwest corner of the top of the Arc de Triomphe looking across at the Eiffel Tower and the intervening buildings with the avenue Kléber on the right and the avenue Iéna on the left. The photograph (fig. b) was kindly provided by Sonia De-

1. Although the inscription on the reverse identifies the picture with this exhibition, Delaunay apparently added the inscriptions at a later date when he was no longer sure which pictures had been shown (see above cat. no. 34, fn. 3). Only 3 paintings by the artist—each called *Paysage, Paris*—appeared in the 1911 exhibition; one of these is securely documented as the Köhler *Eiffel Tower* (Habasque, no. 77), since it is reproduced in R. Allard's review of the exhibition (see above cat. no. 34, fn. 2). At least 3 additional works (and possibly more) bear inscriptions attesting to their appearance in the same exhibition (Habasque, nos. 78, 82, 87), indicating the problems raised by the inscriptions and suggesting that only in conjunction with other corroborating evidence can they be regarded as reliable. Of the latter 3, only 1 (Habasque, no. 82) is actually associated with the exhibition by Habasque, but it is not clear whether he had evidence other than the inscription at his disposal. The lack of further corroborating evidence and the vagueness of the titles makes it virtually impossible to establish which works were involved. On stylistic grounds, however, it would be most likely that by late March 1911 only the Jawlensky *The City* (Habasque, no. 72), the Mannheim *The City* (Habasque, no. 146), and conceivably, though not certainly, the Musée National d'Art Moderne version (Habasque, no. 82) would have been ready for exhibition.

fig. a.
The City. UV photograph.

launay. Langner argues that the earliest version of the theme is a study for *The City*, formerly in the collection of Sonia Delaunay (Kunstmuseum Winterthur, Habasque, no. 73), and that this was followed by the lost picture once owned by Jawlensky, reproduced by W. Bombe in *Das Kunstblatt*, 1. Jg., March 1917, p. 75 (for a discussion of the latter, see above cat. no. 33). Langner dates both works 1909.

As has already been stated (see cat. no. 33), the earliest conception of *The City* seems rather to be the study on the reverse of the Minneapolis *Saint-Séverin*, followed soon afterwards by the Winterthur version, and these probably both date from the end of 1909 or early in 1910. The *Kunstblatt*

fig. b.
Photograph taken from the southwest corner of the top of the Arc de Triomphe, Collection Sonia Delaunay, Paris.

picture represents a slightly later phase, but also dates from early in 1910 (the date it carried in the *Blaue Reiter* exhibition catalogue of December 1911). Similarly, the Tate Gallery's *City, First Study* (Habasque, no. 71), which is probably although not certainly a detailed study for the lower half of the *Kunstblatt* picture, must date from 1910. Both these pictures share, as Langner has stated (p. 70, fn. 6), many of the stylistic qualities of the Saint-Séverin series and are a logical extension of it. The buildings in the foreground, especially in the *Kunstblatt* picture, have lost the block-like stability of the first two studies and seem to be toppling over towards the picture plane. It was presumably to this detail—as well as to the curving, bulging quality of the interior of Delaunay's Saint-Séverin—that Apollinaire was referring when he described the artist's entries to the 1910 *Salon* as reminiscent of earthquakes (*L'Intransigeant,* March 18, 1910, reprinted in *Chroniques d'Art,* ed. L. C. Breunig, Paris, 1960, pp. 75-76).

Following the *Kunstblatt* picture is a version now in the Städtische Kunsthalle Mannheim (Habasque, no. 146), which presents some problems in dating since it was, according to Habasque's entry, started in 1910 and reworked in 1914; the painting certainly manifests, especially in its use of color, stylistic qualities typical of the later period. Nonetheless, the composition itself is clearly a slightly more abstract rendering of the *Kunstblatt* version and was probably painted soon after it. The motif of the curtains framing the composition, turning the picture into a view from a window, is introduced here for the first time. Both Langner (p. 72) and Hoog state that this element appears for the first time in the Paris version of *The City* (Habasque, no. 82). While it is clear that the Mannheim picture precedes the Paris one, it is not certain whether the curtains were part of the original 1910 conception or whether they were added later.

After the completion of the *Kunstblatt* and Mannheim pictures, there seems to have been a hiatus during which Delaunay must have worked on pictures such as the *Eiffel Tower with Trees* and the Krefeld *Eiffel Tower*. By the time he returned to the theme of *The City*, the "destructive" period which began in the late summer and fall of 1910 was well underway.

The first work in this second phase is the Musée National d'Art Moderne, Paris, *The City* (Habasque, no. 82, Hoog, 1967, no. 16, signed and dated 1910), for which the watercolor in the Philadelphia Museum of Art, A. E. Gallatin Collection (Habasque, no. 350) is probably the preparatory study. The Paris picture was possibly but not certainly exhibited at the April 1911 *Salon des Indépendants* ("*Paysage, Paris* n.d.," see above fn. 1) and definitely exhibited at the *Blaue Reiter* exhibition in Munich in December 1911 ("No. 18, *Die Stadt,* 1911"). Habasque erroneously identified this entry as the Guggenheim *The City,* and the exhibition's second entry for *Die Stadt* ("No. 16. *Die Stadt,* 1910*") as the Paris version. These identifications are unconvincing on two counts. First, the asterisk in the catalogue indicates that no. 16 had been sold between the opening of the exhibition and the publication of the catalogue a few weeks later. This could only apply to the *Kunstblatt* picture purchased by Jawlensky (see above cat. no. 33); the Paris picture was not sold until much later. Second, evidence for the appearance of the Paris rather than the Guggenheim picture as the second *City* is provided by another source. E. von Busse's article on Delaunay, which was published in the *Blaue Reiter Almanach* of 1912 (pp. 48-52), illustrates the Paris version of the picture (p. 52); he could only have seen it in the 1911-12 exhibition where it must, therefore, have been no. 18. The next time the picture was exhibited was at the Galerie Barbazanges, where it was dated 1910 in the catalogue list and 1909-11 in the caption to the illustration. The 1910 date inscribed on the picture is accepted by both Langner (p. 70) and Hoog, as well as by all other authors. As will be argued below, it seems more likely to have been painted in 1911.

The second work in this group is the present picture (hereafter cat. no. 35). This picture is signed and dated 1911 and is generally accepted as dating from that year; it was first exhibited at the Galerie Barbazanges exhibition (as "*La Ville No. 2*, 1911"). The third work is *Window on the City No. 3* (hereafter cat. no. 36), firmly dated on several occasions by Delaunay to December 1911 (for details on this point, see below cat. no. 36).

All three works are closely related in their use of dabbed, pointillist brushstrokes, which are used sparingly in the Paris version; they become an all-over screen through which the buildings are seen in cat. no. 35; and in cat. no. 36 they almost completely obliterate these buildings. All three pictures, in their use of the window motif, in the treatment of space, and in the gradual intensification and brightening of color from the first of them to the last, lead directly to the 1912 *Windows*.

Although it is conceivable that work on these three pictures could have extended over a long period of time—the Paris picture dating from late in 1910, cat. no. 36 from December 1911, and cat. no. 35 from somewhere in between—it is much more likely that all three works were painted within a relatively short period in the last six to nine months of 1911. The stylistic evidence points to this conclusion, and two external factors seem to reinforce it. First, the Paris picture, when it appeared in the Galerie Barbazanges catalogue of 1912, was described as a study for cat. no. 35, implying some proximity in time of execution; second, the Paris picture *was* dated 1911 when it appeared in the *Blaue Reiter* exhibition. If, as seems most likely, all three works do date from the second half of 1911, the Paris picture of course could not have appeared in the April 1911 *Salon des Indépendants*.

NOTE: As Langner has noted (p. 72, fn. 10), the numbering of the three versions of *The City* has presented problems. These derive from the fact that Delaunay was himself apparently uncertain whether to describe the Paris picture as a study for cat. no. 35 or as a version in its own right. In the Galerie Barbazanges catalogue he included *The City No. 1* (Jawlensky-*Kunstblatt*); *The City No. 2* (cat. no. 35); *The City No. 2 (Study)* (the Paris picture); *Window on the City No. 3* (cat. no. 36).

At the end of 1912, when cat. no. 36 was reproduced with the first edition of Apollinaire's "Les Fenêtres" (Delaunay, Album [1912], pl. 5), it still carried the title *Fenêtre sur la ville no. 3,* while the Paris version was reproduced with the title *La Ville no. 2* (pl. 11). By assigning the number "2" to the Paris version which had previously been called *"étude,"* Delaunay was technically forced to change the title of cat. no. 35 to *La Ville no. 3* and of cat. no. 36 to *Fenêtre sur la ville no. 4.* Although he did later so inscribe the latter picture on its reverse (which Langner did not realize), he did not do so in the case of the former, and he seems to have preferred to call it simply *La Ville.* Since the Paris picture and cat. no. 35 were thus both at different times entitled *La Ville no. 2,* it is not possible to establish with certainty whether the picture exhibited as *La Ville no. 2* in the April 1912 Der Sturm group exhibition was the Paris picture or cat. no. 35.

EXHIBITIONS:

[Erroneously recorded in SRGM *Handbook,* 1959, p. 49 and 1970, p. 91 as having appeared in 1911 *Salon des Indépendants*];[1] Paris, Galerie Barbazanges, *Robert Delaunay-Marie Laurencin,* Feb. 28-Mar. 13, 1912, no. 8 (*"La Ville—No. 2, 1911"*);[2] Berlin, Der Sturm, 2. *Ausstellung,* Apr. 12-May 15, 1912, no. 41? (*La Ville 2*);[3] Paris, Les Expositions de "Beaux Arts," *Les Etapes de l'art contemporain V,* Mar.-Apr. 1935, no. 27 (*"La Ville, 1911"*); New York, SRGM 78 (checklist); 83 (no cat.); 87 (checklist); 89 (no cat.); 91, 95 (checklists); Paris, Musée National d'Art Moderne, *Robert Delaunay,* May 25-Sept. 30, 1957, no. 26, repr., traveled in part to Amsterdam, Stedelijk Museum, Oct. 18-Dec. 1, 1957, no. 14, Eindhoven, Stedelijk van Abbemuseum, Dec. 6-Jan. 11, 1958, London, Arts Council Gallery, Jan. 25-Feb. 22, 1958, no. 13; Boston, SRGM 119-T, no. 7; Lexington, Ky., SRGM 122-T, no. 4; New York, SRGM 129 (checklist); Kunstverein in Hamburg, *Robert Delaunay,* Jan. 26-Mar. 11, 1962, traveled to Cologne, Wallraf-Richartz-Museum, Mar. 24-May 6, 1962, Frankfurt Kunstverein, May 18-June 24, 1962, no. 14, repr.; New York, Leonard Hutton Gallery, *Der Blaue Reiter,* Feb. 19-Mar. 30, 1963, no. 26, repr.; Ottawa, National Gallery of Canada, *Robert and Sonia Delaunay,* Oct. 8-31, 1965, traveled to Montreal Museum of Fine Arts, Nov. 10-Dec. 5, 1965, no. 14, repr.; New York, SRGM 196 (checklist); Buenos Aires, Museo Nacional de Bellas Artes, *De Cézanne à Miró,* May 15-June 5, 1968, traveled to Santiago, Museo de Arte Contemporaneo de la Universidad de Chile, June 16-July 17, 1968, Caracas, Museo de Bellas Arte, Aug. 4-25, 1968, p. 30, repr.; New York, SRGM 221 (no cat.); 232, p. 91, repr. p. 90; Los Angeles County Museum of Art, *The Cubist Epoch,* Dec. 15, 1970-Feb. 21, 1971, traveled to New York, The Metropolitan Museum of Art, Apr. 9-June 8, 1971, no. 62, color pl. 83, p. 85; New York, SRGM 241, p. 91, repr. p. 90; 266, 276 (no cats.).

REFERENCES:

R. Delaunay, "Le Petit cahier," ca. 1933, Francastel, p. 73, no. 9 (dated 1910); R. Delaunay, "Cahier," ca. 1939-40, Francastel, p. 79, no. 16 (dated 1911); Habasque, 1957, no. 87 (dated 1911); J. Langner, "Zu den Fenster-Bildern von Robert Delaunay," *Jahrbuch der Hamburger Kunstsammlungen,* Band 7, 1962, pp. 70-72; Hoog, 1967, no. 16; Golding, *Cubism,* 1968, pp. 155-156, pl. 68 (dated 1911); Cooper, *Cubist Epoch,* 1970, no. 62, pp. 80-81, 282, color pl. 83, p. 85.

1. See above, p. 93, fn. 1.

2. The Musée National d'Art Moderne *The City* appears as no. 9 in the catalogue of the Galerie Barbazanges exhibition: *"La Ville—no. 2 (étude), 1910."* In the caption to the illustration it is dated 1909-11.

3. For a discussion of whether this entry refers to the Paris version or to the present picture, see above NOTE.

36 Window on the City No. 3. 1911-1912.
(La Fenêtre sur la ville no. 3; Fenêtre sur la ville).

47.878

Oil on canvas, 44¾ x 51½ (113.5 x 130.7)

Signed and dated l.r.: *r. delaunay 1910-11*; inscribed by the artist on reverse: *r. delaunay / 19[. . .]—1910—Paris—1911—1[. . .] / fen[. . .]e sur La Ville nº 4.*

PROVENANCE:

Initial transaction with the artist, 1941; acquired from Sonia Delaunay, 1947.

CONDITION:

In 1954 the work was strip lined with wax resin and cleaned with detergent. Some inpainting of losses was done with PBM and the work surfaced with IBM. In 1967 it was noted that the painted image on the reverse (not legible) makes an effective lining impossible. Inpaint of 2 distinct dates is clearly discernible under UV (fig. a). This is extensive along the edges and extends as much as 3 in. into the canvas in places; it is also scattered over the upper right quarter of the picture. Inpaint of a later date is visible along the entire top edge and in the lower right corner.

The early inpaint is almost certainly the work of the artist himself. The signature and date were added over inpaint and cracks in the original paint layer. This retouching and the signature and date were probably added at the time of the picture's sale to the Museum. The more recent inpainting probably dates from 1954.

The canvas at the edges is generally in good condition except for extensive inpaint losses. The presence of a painting on the reverse (probably painted 1-4 years prior to the work on the obverse) may have contributed to some of the losses because of the different drying rates of the 2 works. The overall condition is good. (Mar. 1974.)

Delaunay himself variously dated the present work December 1911 (Album [1912], pl. 5; Francastel, p. 107 no. 5, 108 no. 6), December 1911-January 1912 (Ibid., p. 110, no. 8), and 1910-11 (on the canvas itself). It is not clear when the latter date was added to the canvas, but it was certainly no earlier than 1913, since the reproduction in Apollinaire's Der Sturm Album, published

fig. a.
Window on the City No. 3.
UV photograph.

36

at the very end of 1912, does not include the date. Indeed, the addition may well have been substantially later when Delaunay no longer precisely remembered the picture's date.

The December 1911 date, accepted by Langner, Vriesen, and Spate, is entirely compatible with Delaunay's stylistic development at the end of that year (see above cat. no. 35), although one cannot rule out the possibility that he continued to work on the picture into the beginning of January, just before departing for Laon. The brilliant hues used in this final version of *The City* lead directly into Delaunay's pure colors of Laon and into the development of Orphism during 1912.

EXHIBITIONS:

Berlin, Der Sturm, *12. Ausstellung: R. Delaunay,* Jan. 27-Feb. 20, 1913, no. 15 *(La Fenêtre sur la Ville, no. 3);*[1] New York, World's Fair, French Pavilion, *L'Art français contemporain,* 1939, no. 42 ("*Ville,* 1911-12"); New York, SRGM 78 (checklist, "*Window on the City, No. 4,* 1910-11;" so dated in all subsequent SRGM publications); Toronto, SRGM 85-T, no. 8; New York, SRGM 91 (checklist); London, SRGM 104-T, no. 13; New York, SRGM 118 (checklist); Cleveland Museum of Art, *Paths of Abstract Art,* Oct. 4-Nov. 13, 1960, no. 27, repr.; Philadelphia, SRGM 134-T, no. 20; New York, SRGM 144 (checklist); Utica, N.Y., Munson Williams Proctor Institute, *1913 Armory Show 50th Anniversary Exhibition 1963,* Feb. 17-Mar. 31, 1963, traveled to New York, Armory of the 69th Regiment, Apr. 6-28, 1963, no. 256, repr.;[2] New York, SRGM 151, 153 (checklists); Bordeaux, Musée de Bordeaux, *La Peinture française dans les collections américaines,* May 13-Sept. 15, 1966, no. 91; New York, SRGM 198-T (no cat.); 199, *Neo-Impressionism,* no. 170, repr. color (erroneously described as having appeared in the 1911 *Salon des Indépendants*); 240 (no cat.); Cal., Fine Arts Gallery of San Diego, *Color and Form 1909-1914,* Nov. 20, 1971-Jan. 2, 1972, traveled to Cal., The Oakland Museum, Jan. 26-Mar. 5, 1972, Seattle Art Museum, Mar. 24-May 7, 1972, no. 9, repr. color; New York, SRGM 266, 276 (no cats.).

REFERENCES:

Delaunay, Album [1912], no. 15, pl. 5 (dated "Dec. 1911"); R. Delaunay, notes of Oct. 1913, Francastel, 1957, p. 110 (dated Dec. 1911-Jan. 1912); Idem, notes of ca. 1918-19, Ibid., p. 107 no. 5, p. 108 no. 6 (dated "Dec. 1911");[3] Idem, ca. 1924, Ibid., p. 62; W. Haftmann, *Malerei im 20. Jahrhundert,* Munich, 1955, repr. color p. 139; Habasque, no. 86 (dated 1910-11); H. B. Chipp, "Orphism and Color Theory," *The Art Bulletin,* vol. xl, Mar. 1958, pp. 59-61, repr. (dated 1910-11); J. Langner, "Zu den Fenster-Bildern von Robert Delaunay," *Jahrbuch der Hamburger Kunstsammlungen,* Band 7, 1962, pp. 70 ff., repr. (dated "Dec. 1911"); Vriesen and Imdahl, 1969, p. 42, fig. 17 (dated "Dec. 1911"); Spate, 1970, p. 135, fn. 27 (dated "Dec. 1911-Jan. 1912").

1. For a discussion of the confusion in the numbering of the 4 versions of *The City,* see above cat. no. 35. The present picture was reproduced as *La Fenêtre sur la ville, no. 3* in the 1912 Album on Delaunay, which was published in connection with the Der Sturm exhibition. This clearly suggests that the identical entry in the Der Sturm catalogue refers to the present picture and not to cat. no. 35. According to Delaunay's own notes (Francastel, p. 107), this picture was included in the group of works which traveled from Der Sturm to Cologne (Feb. 1913) and Budapest (May 1913).

2. The picture that appeared as No. 256 in the original 1913 Armory Show ("*Les Fenêtres sur la ville,* lent by M. K., Paris") was not the present work.

3. Spate (in correspondence with the author, Oct. 1973) convincingly dates this text 1918-19 on the grounds that it refers to the 1917 exhibition held in Stockholm as well as to an exhibition in Barcelona which must have taken place while the Delaunays were staying there during the war. The fact that there is no reference to the 3rd version of the *Manège électrique* would indicate that the text definitely dates from before 1922.

37 Red Eiffel Tower. 1911-1912.
(La Tour rouge, Eiffel Tower).

46.1036

Oil on canvas, 49¼ x 35⅜ (125 x 90.3)[1]

Signed l.r.: *r. delaun*[ay]. Not dated.

PROVENANCE:
Purchased from Sonia Delaunay, Paris, 1946.

CONDITION:
According to a condition report of 1955, the canvas was lined with wax resin sometime in the 1940's. In 1955 the surface was cleaned and some resin removed. Some "larger and deeper lacunae" were filled with wax gesso and inpainted; the surface was then sprayed with PBM. Examination of the painting under UV in 1972 revealed extensive inpainting throughout the entire surface, some of recent origin (presumably 1955), but most of it apparently dated from much earlier. (See fig. a.) It would seem that at some point the artist himself, possibly having had the canvas rolled up for a considerable period, substantially reworked the entire surface.

The present cracking and paint loss throughout the surface is possibly due to poor bonding between the layers of paint. (Sept. 1972.)

The picture was dated 1914 by J. J. Sweeney, but without discussion (SRGM exhibition catalogues from 1952-68 and *Handbook,* 1959). It has otherwise been assigned to 1911, a date which is consistent with Delaunay's development during that year.

Late in 1911, possibly not until after the visit to Paris of Boccioni and Carrà in October, Delaunay returned to the Eiffel Tower theme and began a series of four works in which the Tower itself is rendered in a more stylized, more rigid form than that of the versions painted between the summer of 1910 and

fig. a.
Red Eiffel Tower. UV photograph.

1. As the canvas is stretched at present, the painted surface extends beyond the turn of the canvas at the top, right, and bottom edges. Exactly how much painted surface has been lost cannot be established since all edges are taped just beyond the turn of the canvas. The dimensions given are those of the visible painted surface.

37

May 1911. As G. Vriesen has pointed out in relation to one of these works (Vriesen and Imdahl, 1969, p. 30), the multiplicity of viewpoints is gradually reduced at this stage and the focus is more and more strongly on the effects of light on the outer contours of the structure.

The first two works in the group were probably the present picture (hereafter cat. no. 37) and an unfinished painting dedicated to Apollinaire, now in the collection of the Museum Folkwang, Essen (Habasque, no. 85, repr. color; Laxner, 1969, no. 7). Laxner has argued that a hitherto unpublished pencil sketch in Munich (GMS 675, fig. b) is the preparatory study for the Essen picture and that the latter is in turn preparatory to the present picture. She places the three works after the Krefeld and Köhler pictures, but before SRGM cat. no. 34 and the Basel version, and dates the Essen picture late 1910.

Her chronology presents several problems. However, her association of the Munich pencil sketch with both the Essen and the Guggenheim *Towers* is

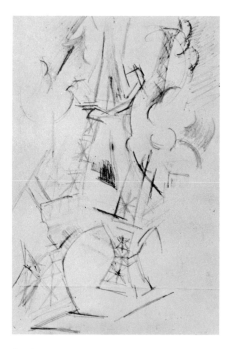

fig. b.
Delaunay, study for *Eiffel Tower,* pencil
on paper, 9⅞ x 6⅜ in., 24.6 x 16.2 cm.,
signed and dated on reverse: *"r. delaunay,
paris 1911,"* Städtische Galerie im Lenbachhaus, Munich.

fig. c.
Delaunay, reverse of fig. b.

convincing, and these three works must indeed be extremely close in date.
Whether they actually follow the sequence suggested by Laxner is rather less
clear. The greater freedom and vitality of the Essen version might indicate
that it was a rapid reprise of the somewhat stiffer Guggenheim picture, rather
than a study for it. Similarly it is not certain that the Munich drawing can be
described simply as a study for the Essen or the Guggenheim painting. Two
factors suggest that it might have served a more general preparatory function
within this group. Firstly, it contains the motif of the top of the Tower broken
off and depicted alongside the rest of the structure—a detail which does not
appear in either the Guggenheim or Essen pictures, but does occur in the next
two, the Chicago *Eiffel Tower* (formerly Collection Tarsila do Amaral, now
The Art Institute of Chicago, Habasque, no. 88) and *The City of Paris* (Musée
National d'Art Moderne, Paris, Habasque, no. 100). Secondly, the verso of
the drawing (fig. c) appears to contain some extremely fragmentary preliminary ideas for the rectangular and triangular areas of color that make up the
background of *The City of Paris.* It cannot be ruled out, therefore, that the
Munich drawing was being used by Delaunay not only as a preparatory study
for the Essen and Guggenheim pictures, but also at a slightly later moment
for those in Chicago and Paris.

Following the Guggenheim and Essen pictures, the Chicago *Tower* represents a dramatic development within this later group. Delaunay abandoned
the picture before it was finished, probably in order to take up work on *The
City of Paris,* and he may not have completed it until much later. (It is repro-

fig. d.
Delaunay, study for *Eiffel Tower,* here dated
1913, ink on paper, 16 x 12¾ in., 40.5 x 32.4
cm., not signed or dated, Habasque, no. 507,
Collection Sonia Delaunay, Paris.

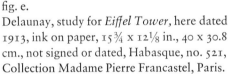

fig. e.
Delaunay, study for *Eiffel Tower,* here dated
1913, ink on paper, 15¾ x 12⅛ in., 40 x 30.8
cm., not signed or dated, Habasque, no. 521,
Collection Madame Pierre Francastel, Paris.

duced in its incomplete state both in the February 1912 catalogue for the
Galerie Barbazanges exhibition [no. 5] and with the first edition of Apollinaire's "Les Fenêtres," which was published in Paris in December 1912 [p. 3].)
It is thus the incomplete version that one must consider in analyzing the
relationship of the work to its two predecessors.

Delaunay has in part reverted in the Chicago composition to the *Towers*
of early 1911. He has reintroduced the framing buildings as well as those
beneath the arch of the Tower. In every other respect, however, he has pursued
the path he embarked upon in the Essen and Guggenheim works. The Tower
is seen from the same vantage point as in these latter works. The cascading
bright white light that surrounds the Tower in both the Essen and Guggenheim pictures, beginning to encroach on and obliterate its contours at the right
side, becomes in the Chicago picture an even more powerful force. The jagged
fragmentation of the light and space around the Tower here overlaps and
obscures the structure on all sides, a process that is repeated in the Tower of
The City of Paris. It is in relation to these pictures above all that Delaunay's
own phrase of ca. 1924 "Light deforms all, breaks all—" (Francastel, 1957,
p. 62) seems most apt.

The unfinished Chicago picture is extremely closely related to the right side
of *The City of Paris.* However, in the lower portion of the later composition
Delaunay reverts to the overlapping ovals of the Essen and Guggenheim pictures, suggesting once again the close connection between all four of these
works.

fig. f.
Delaunay, study for *Eiffel Tower,* here
dated 1913, ink on paper, 11⅜ x 7⅞
in., 29 x 20 cm., signed and dated l.r.:
"*La Tour. Delaunay. 1910,*" Habasque,
no. 508, formerly Collection Léon Degand,
Paris, present whereabouts unknown.

fig. g.
Delaunay, study for *Eiffel Tower,* here
dated 1913, ink on paper, 24⅞ x 18½ in.,
63 x 47 cm., signed and dated l.r.: "*r.d.
1910,*" Habasque, no. 510, Musée National
d'Art Moderne, Paris.

The City of Paris was certainly completed by the middle of March 1912 in
time to be submitted to the March *Salon.* It may have been completed by early
January before Delaunay left Paris to spend some weeks at Laon. Alternatively
it could have been started before the journey to Laon and completed at the
beginning of February when he returned (M. Hoog, *Revue du Louvre,* 1965,
no. 1, p. 34); or else it was painted in its entirety after the opening of the
Futurist exhibition of February 1912 (J. Langner, *Jahrbuch der Hamburger
Kunstsammlungen,* Band 7, 1962, p. 74, fn. 11; Vriesen and Imdahl, 1969,
p. 40; Spate, 1970, pp. 139 ff.). Whether the picture as a whole shows the
influence of the Futurist exhibition is debatable. What is certain, however, is
that the right-hand third of the painting, with its close dependence upon the
immediately preceding Chicago picture and, more notably, upon the Essen
and Guggenheim pictures, is independent of any direct Futurist influence. All
four of these pictures must have been painted within a few months of one
another between the autumn of 1911 and March 1912; together, they conclude
what Delaunay described as the "destructive" phase of his career. With the
completion of *The City of Paris,* Delaunay embarked upon a new phase.

Finally, it is important to place a group of six large, closely related ink drawings of the *Eiffel Tower* (figs. d-i). One of these has been specifically described
by Habasque and by Cooper (*Cubist Epoch,* 1970, pl. 76, p. 80) as a study for
SRGM cat. no. 37; another has been characterized by Hoog as preparatory to
the whole 1910-11 series of *Towers* (1967, no. 15).

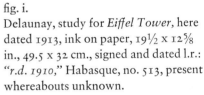

fig. h.
Delaunay, study for *Eiffel Tower,* here dated
1913, ink on paper, 25½ x 19½ in., 64.8 x 49.5
cm., dated u.l.: "*1910,*" l.l.: "*delaunay—Paris
1909-1910 la Tour et la Roue,*" Habasque,
no. 514, The Museum of Modern Art, New
York. Abby Aldrich Rockefeller Fund.

fig. i.
Delaunay, study for *Eiffel Tower,* here
dated 1913, ink on paper, 19½ x 12⅝
in., 49.5 x 32 cm., signed and dated l.r.:
"*r.d. 1910,*" Habasque, no. 513, present
whereabouts unknown.

Two of the six (figs. d and e) are undated; the other four are dated 1910,
but like many of the other works from this stage in Delaunay's career, these
dates are difficult to accept. The drawings represent a striking development
beyond Delaunay's treatment of the Tower theme in the four works discussed
above. The Tower itself is seen from the same vantage point as that of cat. no.
37, Essen, Chicago, and *The City of Paris,* but it is even further destroyed by
the imposition of a highly articulated structure of intersecting lines and planes,
sweeping arcs, and dramatic shading. The cumulus clouds to the right of the
Tower in the few earlier works have been replaced here by a forceful representation of the ferris wheel which had appeared in extremely understated form in
cat. no. 37 (but not at all in the other three works) and which was not to emerge
as a prominent element until 1913.

It is to the works of 1913 that one must turn to explain these drawings.
In *Sun, Tower, Airplane* (Albright-Knox Art Gallery, Buffalo, Habasque, no.
123) the richness of color of the 1912 *Windows* is incorporated into a composition of circular forms, propellor shapes, squares, rectangles, and arcs. The
six drawings, omitting the color, provide all of the structural ingredients for the
right side of this painting, although their peculiarly vital linear dynamism is
transposed into a pure coloristic dynamism in the final painting. It is interesting
to note that two of the six were published for the first time in 1913: Habasque,
no. 514 was published in *Montjoie!* March 18, 1913, suppl. to no. 3, p. 2;
Habasque, no. 513 was published in *Der Sturm,* August 1913, Jg. IV, no. 173-
174, p. 81. Figs. d-g, which are among Delaunay's most dramatic works on the

Eiffel Tower theme, almost certainly date from 1913. Fig. h, and especially fig. i (which is the least dynamic of the group), were probably conceived specifically for reproduction purposes and submitted to the periodicals shortly before publication.

EXHIBITIONS:

Paris, Galerie Barbazanges, *Robert Delaunay-Marie Laurencin,* Feb. 28-Mar. 13, 1912, no. 24 ("*La Tour rouge,* 1911");[2] Berlin, Der Sturm, *Robert Delaunay,* Jan.-Feb. 1913, no. 17 ("*La Tour rouge,* 1911");[2] [Paris, Galerie Louis Carré, *Robert Delaunay,* Dec. 1946-Jan. 1947, pl. 3[3]]; Paris, Musée National d'Art Moderne, *L'Oeuvre du XXe siècle,* May-June, 1952, no. 21, traveled to London, Tate Gallery, July 15-Aug. 17, 1952, no. 17 ("*Red Eiffel Tower,* 1914;*"* so dated in all subsequent SRGM publications until SRGM 202, 1968); The Arts Club of Chicago, *Robert Delaunay,* Oct. 24-Nov. 21, 1952, no. 11, repr. cover (dated 1914); New York, SRGM 78, 79 (checklists); 81, 88, 89 (no cats.); 91, 97 (checklists); London, SRGM 104-T, no. 16; New York, 112 (checklist); New York, Fine Arts Associates, *Robert Delaunay,* Jan. 13-31, 1959 (dated 1914); New York, SRGM 118 (checklist); Kunstverein in Hamburg, *Robert Delaunay,* Jan. 26-Mar. 11, 1962, traveled to Cologne, Wallraf-Richartz-Museum, Mar. 24-May 6, 1962, Frankfurt Kunstverein, May 18-June 24, 1962, no. 15, repr. color (dated 1911); Worcester, Mass., SRGM 148-T, no. 8, repr.; Rotterdam, Museum Boymans-van Beuningen, *Franse Landschappen van Cézanne tot Heden,* Oct. 4-Nov. 17, 1963, no. 32, repr. (dated 1911); The Baltimore Museum of Art, *1914,* Oct. 6-Nov. 15, 1964, no. 40, repr.; New York, SRGM 173, no. 38, repr.; Houston, Museum of Fine Arts, *The Heroic Years: Paris 1908-1914,* Oct. 21-Dec. 8, 1965 (no cat.); New York, SRGM 202, p. 92, repr. p. 93 (dated 1911); New York, The Museum of Modern Art, *The Machine as Seen at the End of the Mechanical Age,* Nov. 25, 1968-Feb. 9, 1969, traveled to Houston, University of St. Thomas, Mar. 25-May 18, 1969, San Francisco Museum of Art, June 23-Aug. 24, 1969, p. 72, repr. (dated 1911); New York, SRGM 240 (no cat.); 241 (addenda); Cleveland, SRGM 258-T, pl. 7; New York, SRGM 276 (no cat.).

REFERENCES:

Habasque, 1957, no. 89 (dated 1911); SRGM *Handbook,* 1959, p. 51, repr. (dated 1914); U. Laxner, "Robert Delaunay: Tour Eiffel," *Museum Folkwang, Essen, Mitteilungen,* 1969, 3. Band, no. 8, repr. (dated 1911).

2. Information from Habasque, no. 89.

3. Although the picture is illustrated in the catalogue, it is not on the list of works exhibited, and according to Carré (correspondence with the author, June 1971), it was not included.

38   Simultaneous Windows (2nd Motif,
      1st Part). 1912.
      (Les Fenêtres simultané [2ᵉ
      motif, 1ʳᵉ partie]; Les Fenêtres; Windows
      [Simultaneous composition 2nd motif, 1st
      part]).

41.464A

Oil on canvas, 21⅝ x 18¼ (55.2 x 46.3)

Inscribed by the artist l.l.: *les fenêtres
simultané / r. delaunay 12*; on reverse
(transcribed but not photographed before
lining): *'les fenêtres' 2ᵐ motif 1ʳ partie
(1912) r.d. Paris.*

PROVENANCE:

Purchased from the artist by Hilla Rebay,
Greens Farms, Connecticut, by 1937 (Phil-
adelphia exhibition catalogue); acquired by
Solomon R. Guggenheim in the Greens
Farms transaction of July 1938; Gift of
Solomon R. Guggenheim, 1941.

CONDITION:

In 1953 the work was cleaned with 1%
Soilax. Losses and chipping were set down
with wax resin using an infra-red lamp. The
surface was cleaned with naptha to remove
excess wax; extensive losses in the margin
areas were filled with gesso and inpainted
with PVA; the surface was sprayed with
PBM. In 1957 the work was lined with wax
resin on raw linen and restretched on the
original stretcher.

Since 1953 further losses on all edges have
occurred and have not been inpainted.
Scattered losses elsewhere on the surface
vary in size from ¼ in. to ½ in. The greater
part of the surface is covered with an irregular crackle pattern which becomes severe
in 2 or 3 places. Although the paint layer is
considerably damaged in parts, its condition
is stable, and there appears to be no im-
mediate danger of further cleavage or flaking. The condition in general is fair.
(Oct. 1973.)

Shortly after the opening of the March 1912 *Indépendants,* Delaunay embarked on the series of *Windows* which were to occupy him from at least
April to December 1912 and which represented the beginning of what he
called the "constructive" phase of his career. Habasque records seventeen oils
on this theme (nos. 90, 102, 104-112, 116-118, 743, *oeuvres à retrouver* no. 13
[now Basel, galerie d'art moderne, apparently painted in October 1914], and
p. 398, V, 2 [now Kunstsammlung Nordrhein-Westfalen, Dusseldorf]). In addition there is one large watercolor (no. 351). One oil unrecorded by Habasque
is in the Tate Gallery, London (18 x 14¾ in., 46 x 37.5 cm.). *The Window on
the City* (Habasque, no. 146, Städtische Kunsthalle Mannheim), which is
treated by Langner as part of this series and dated 1914 (p. 77, fn. 17), belongs
thematically to the 1911 *City* series, even though it was completed later (see
above cat. no. 35).

The first of the *Windows* were painted in April 1912. (For the establishment
of this date, as opposed to Francastel's and Habasque's 1911 for the Hamburg
picture, no. 90, see Langner, pp. 81 ff. et passim.) Whether Delaunay started
the series in Paris, or not until he reached La Madeleine in the Chevreuse Valley
where he and Sonia spent the summer, is not clear. Klee, who visited Delaunay's studio on April 11, 1912, does not record what he saw there (*The
Diaries of Paul Klee,* ed. F. Klee, Berkeley and Los Angeles, 1964, p. 268).
Although he is often reported to have seen the *Windows* on this visit—and he
may have done so—there is no actual evidence to prove that he saw the

pictures before July (see below). Three of the known versions date from April 1912 (Habasque, no. 90, Hamburg Kunsthalle; no. 104, Collection Sonia Delaunay, Paris; no. 105, Collection Neumann, Chicago). Two are dated June 1912 (Habasque, no. 351, Collection Chenu, Florence; no. 112, Philadelphia Museum of Art, A. E. Gallatin Collection, so dated in Delaunay, Album [1912], pl. 7). One is dated December 1912 (Habasque, no. 117, Collection Mr. and Mrs. W. Burden, New York; see Francastel, 1957, p. 139, no. 3). The study for the latter probably also dates from the end of the year (Habasque, no. 116, dated on the reverse 1912-1913, Musée National d'Art Moderne, Paris). Langner's contention that the series was completed between April and December is plausible, although it cannot be ruled out that one or two examples were completed early in 1913. It is difficult to establish a sequence for the remaining twelve works, although the Guggenheim picture, with its pale blues, greens, and pinks, is probably one of the earlier versions.

The numerical subtitles of the *Windows* do not correspond to any discernible chronological or thematic sequence. Delaunay's habitual use of the plural noun with a singular adjective *("fenêtres simultané")* has been explained by Langner as a contraction of the term *"contraste simultané"* (p. 77, fn. 16). The implied reference to Chevreul's theory of simultaneous contrasts, which Delaunay himself referred to in connection with his own theories of color (Francastel, pp. 81, 110, 113, 155-156, 159), is clearly intended, although Delaunay did not himself apply the theory systematically. Spate (in conversation with the author, March 1975) drew attention to two of Delaunay's statements regarding the word *simultané*. On the one hand, he used the word in a grammatically invariable form to emphasize that it was a technical term; on the other, he did so in order to avoid the metaphysical connotations of the word Simultanism (Francastel, p. 184 [1913] and p. 130 [1917]. For a discussion of Delaunay's use of Chevreul's theory see Vriesen, pp. 44, 46, and Imdahl, pp. 79 ff., who do, however, perhaps ascribe more importance to the theory's influence than is justified by the paintings themselves. For a discussion of Delaunay's response at this juncture in his career to a reading of da Vinci's theories of Simultanism and the role of the eye as window, see Spate, pp. 151-153; see also Spate's discussion of the influence of Delaunay's 1912 paintings on Apollinaire, as well as her analysis of the role of Simultanism in the theory and practice of Orphism, pp. 451 ff.).

The use of the term *"simultané"* in the titles of the *Windows* probably refers in part to Chevreul, in part to a preoccupation with the simultaneous "states of mind" of the Futurists (as well as with Delaunay's clear desire to set himself apart from them), and in part to the more general principles of Simultanism with which Delaunay was at this point so much concerned.

Two of the *Windows* were first exhibited at the Moderner Bund, Zurich, in July 1912, and Paul Klee wrote an enthusiastic and by now famous review in *Die Alpen* (Bern, vol. vi, August 1912). In October 1912 Macke and Marc came from Germany to visit Delaunay and were also struck by the paintings. (For a discussion of the impact of this visit see Vriesen, pp. 50-52.) In January

38

1913 twelve of the *Windows* appeared in Delaunay's one-man show in Berlin. Meanwhile Apollinaire, who had stayed with the Delaunays for six weeks in November-December 1912, had written his poem "Les Fenêtres," which was included in the deluxe volume printed on the occasion of the 1913 Der Sturm exhibition (Delaunay, Album [1912]).

EXHIBITIONS:

Philadelphia, SRGM 3-T, no. 161; Charleston, S.C., SRGM 4-T, no. 232; The Arts Club of Chicago, *Robert Delaunay*, Oct. 24-Nov. 21, 1952, no. 12; New York, SRGM 79, 91, 95, 97 (checklists); London, SRGM 104-T, no. 14; New York, SRGM 118, 129 (checklists); Philadelphia, SRGM 134-T, no. 21; New York, SRGM 144 (checklist); 173, no. 25, repr.; 187, *Gauguin and the Decorative Style*, 196 (checklists); 202, p. 65, repr. color p. 64; 221 (no cat.); 232, pp. 92-93, repr. color; Buffalo, N.Y., Albright-Knox Art Gallery, *Color and Field: 1890-1970*, Sept. 15-Nov. 1, 1970, traveled to Ohio, The Dayton Art Institute, Nov. 20, 1970-Jan. 10, 1971, Cleveland Museum of Art, Feb. 4-Mar. 28, 1971, no. 25, repr.; New York, SRGM 240 (no cat.); 241, pp. 92-93, repr. color; 266, 276 (no cats.).

REFERENCES:

R. Delaunay, notes of ca. 1918-19, Francastel, 1957, p. 108, no. 7;[1] Idem, "Fenêtres sur la ville 1911 et 1912," ca. 1924; Ibid., p. 63; Idem, "Notes historiques sur la peinture," 1924; Ibid., pp. 170-172;[2] Idem, letter to André Lhote, Ibid., pp. 97-98 (erroneously identified as a 1924 letter to Sam Halpert; see Vriesen, p. 69, fn. 29); Idem, "Petit Cahier," ca. 1933, Ibid., p. 75, no. 23; Idem, notes written on *Les Fenêtres*, ca. 1938-39, Ibid., p. 87; Idem, lecture delivered Feb. 16, 1939, Ibid., pp. 229-230; Idem, "Notes sur le développement de la peinture de R.D.," ca. 1939-40, Ibid., pp. 66-67; Habasque, 1957, no. 106; Golding, *Cubism*, 1968, pp. 172-176; J. Langner, "Zu den Fenster-Bildern von Robert Delaunay," *Jahrbuch der Hamburger Kunstsammlungen*, Band 7, 1962, pp. 76 ff.; Vriesen and Imdahl, 1969, pp. 42 ff.; Spate, 1970, pp. 150 ff.

1. For the dating of this text see above cat. no. 36, fn. 3.

2. This passage is dated 1928-30 by Francastel. Spate, however, points out (p. 152, fn. 66) that part of it was published in *Nouvelles littéraires*, Oct. 25, 1924.

39   Circular Forms. 1930.
      (Formes circulaires).

49.1184

Oil on canvas, 50¾ x 76¾ (128.9 x 194.9)

Signed c.l.: *r. delaunay*. Not dated.

PROVENANCE:

Purchased from Sonia Delaunay, 1949.

CONDITION:

In 1955 the work was lined with wax resin on natural linen, placed on a new stretcher, and cleaned with 2% Soilax and rinsed with a solution of xylene and benzine. Small voids were filled with gesso and inpainted with PBM. The inpainting is concentrated along the edges, especially the right. The work was surfaced with IBM. In 1957 it was restretched and the margins waxed.

The canvas appears once to have been stretched about ¾ in. smaller on the top and left edges; a line of severe crackle and some losses remains along these former edges. Certain areas of crackle scattered over the surface were set down in the lining process. Some additional deep pigment cracks, limited in number, have since developed. These are chiefly in the heavy impasto areas, especially at the right side of the picture. There is some cupping at the edges of the wide cracks. There is some distortion of the surface due to cold flow of the wax used in lining. The condition in general, with the exception of the deep pigment cracks, is good. (Apr. 1974.)

In 1930-31 Delaunay returned to the totally abstract circular forms which he had first explored in the Sun and Moon pictures of 1913. (For a convincing discussion of the dates of these pictures, most of which carry the date 1912 or 1912-13, see Spate, 1970, p. 184.) Whereas the earlier group is characterized by a fluid handling of color which is usually thinly brushed, the paintings in the later group, of which this is clearly an example, are painted in thick impasto (often applied with a palette knife) and with the outlines of the forms clearly articulated.

Typical examples of the earlier conception are *Circular Forms* (Stedelijk Museum, Amsterdam, Habasque, no. 119, dated 1912-13, but probably not painted before 1913); or *Circular Forms Sun No. 2* (Musée National d'Art Moderne, Paris, Habasque, no. 121; Hoog, 1967, no. 23, dated 1912-13, but also probably belonging to 1913); and *Disc* (Collection Mr. and Mrs. Burton Tremaine, New York, Habasque, no. 113, dated 1912, but probably not painted until 1913). Examples painted in the late period are *Rhythm, joie de vivre* (Musée National d'Art Moderne, Paris, Habasque, no. 273; Hoog, 1967, no. 37), or the *Circular Forms* (Private Collection, Zurich, on loan to the Kunsthaus Zürich, Habasque, no. 271). The stylistic difference between the handling of form and color in these later examples and that of the initial exploration almost twenty years earlier sets the two groups of works clearly apart from one another, in spite of their thematic similarity.

EXHIBITIONS:

New York, SRGM 74 (checklist, dated 1937); The Arts Club of Chicago, *Robert Delaunay,* Oct. 24-Nov. 21, 1952, no. 3 (dated 1930); New York, SRGM 78 (checklist); Toronto, SRGM 85-T, no. 9 (dated 1912?; so dated in all subsequent SRGM publications); Leverkusen, Städtisches Museum Leverkusen Schloss Morsbroich, *Robert Delaunay,* June 7-July 15, 1956, traveled to Kunstverein Freiburg, July 22-Aug. 19, 1956, no. 37, repr. (dated 1912/30); New York, SRGM 91 (checklist); London, SRGM 104-T, no. 15, pl. 12 (dated 1912?); New York, SRGM 118, 129 (checklists); Philadelphia, SRGM 134-T, no. 22; New York, SRGM 144 (checklist); 173, no. 26, repr.; 187, 196 (checklists); 198-T, 221 (no cat.); 232, p. 95, repr. p. 94; 240 (no cat.); 241, p. 95, repr. p. 94; 266 (no cat.).

REFERENCES:

H. Arp, *Onze Peintres,* Zurich, 1949, repr. p. 23 ("*Soleils,* n.d."); Habasque, 1957, no. 270 (dated 1930); SRGM *Handbook,* 1959, p. 51, repr. p. 50 (dated 1912?); SRGM *Handbook,* 1970, p. 95, repr. (dated 1912?); M. Seuphor, *L'Art abstrait,* Paris, 1971, repr. color, p. 148 (dated 1912).

40 Circular Rhythm. 1937.
(*Rythme circulaire*).

37.221

Oil on canvas, 100 x 118¼ (253.9 x 300.8)

Not signed or dated.

PROVENANCE:

Purchased from the artist by Solomon R. Guggenheim, 1937; Gift of Solomon R. Guggenheim, 1937.

CONDITION:

In 1955 the work was cleaned with water, and some old retouchings of uncertain date were found to be insoluble. Chipped and cleaved areas were waxed with a heat lamp, losses were filled with gesso and then inpainted. PVA was applied over repaired areas. At some time in the late 1950's the work was removed from its stretcher and

rolled. In 1971 it was unrolled and restretched. The condition of the support was judged to be precarious, and lining is planned but has not yet taken place.

The support is brittle, and there are numerous cracks and tears at the turn of the canvas. Cracks, some of which show cleavage and loss, are scattered over the surface, but large areas are totally free of such cracks. There are approximately 18 smallish areas of inpainting scattered over the surface, most of which have discolored and are visible with the naked eye. Some of these may have been the work of the artist. Some soil and stains are visible, but the condition of the paint film is in general very good, and the colors apparently well-preserved. (Apr. 1974.)

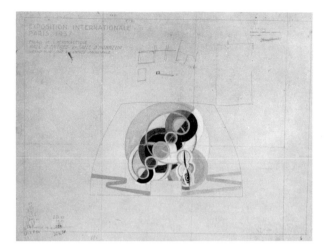

fig. a.
Delaunay, study for mural in the Palais de l'Air, ca.
1936-37, gouache on paper mounted on board,
21⅜ x 28⅛ in., 54.2 x 71.5 cm., Habasque, no. 455,
Collection Sonia Delaunay, Paris.

fig. b.
Delaunay, watercolor after the artist's project for the
Palais de l'Air, 28⅜ x 32⅜ in., 72 x 82.3 cm., Habasque,
no. 332, Musée National d'Art Moderne, Paris.

fig. c.
Architect's rendering of the interior of the Palais de l'Air,
ca. 1937, gouache, colored by Sonia Delaunay, 39 x 53⅝
in., 99 x 136 cm., Museum of Sketches, Lund, Sweden.

As M. Hoog has stated (1967, p. 91), Delaunay was commissioned in 1935 to take part in the planning for the 1937 international exhibition. He conceived and directed the execution of the decorations for the Pavillon des Chemins de fer and the Pavillon de l'Air, projects in which many other artists participated. The present painting was the final study for the mural on the end wall of the Palais de l'Air. The building, designed by the architects Audoul, Hartwig, and Gerodias, was 544 feet long, 118 feet wide, and 72 feet high (166 m. x 36 m. x 22 m.). The mural, which almost filled the end wall, thus occupied a space of approximately 65 x 98 feet (20 x 30 m.).

Several drawings and watercolors connected with the project survive. A study for the placing of the painting on the wall is in the collection of Sonia Delaunay (fig. a). A related watercolor in the Musée National d'Art Moderne, Paris, has been convincingly identified by Hoog (1967, no. 59) as a view of the entire ensemble after its completion rather than a study for the project (fig. b). A gouache rendering of the interior of the building, with the painting just visible on the end wall, is in the Museum of Sketches, Lund (fig. c). Some other preparatory sketches related to the mural are in the collection of Sonia Delaunay, but have not been studied by the present author.

EXHIBITIONS:

Charleston, S.C., SRGM 4-T, no. 96, repr.; New York, SRGM 74, 91 (checklists; installation photos of the latter show the painting hanging upside down); 276 (no cat.).

REFERENCES:

M. Asie, in *Les Nouvelles des expositions,* 3ᵉ année, Sept. 1, 1937, p. 2, repr. p. 3; F. G. de la Tourette, *Robert Delaunay,* Paris, 1950, pl. 25 (upside down); Habasque, 1957, no. 339.

Theo van Doesburg

(pseud. of Christian E. M. Küpper).

Born August 1883, Utrecht.
Died March 1931, Davos, Switzerland.

41
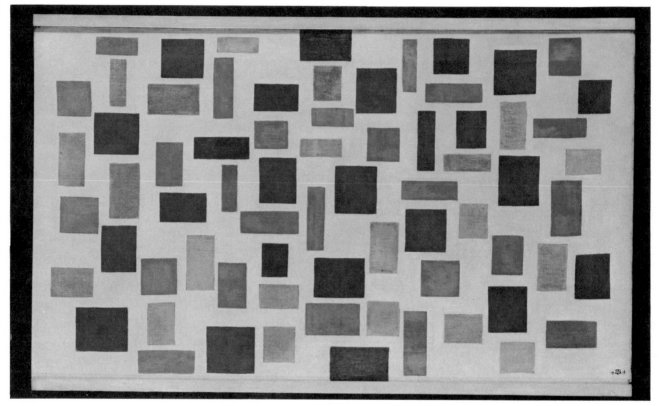

fig. a.
Reverse of *Composition XI.*

41   Composition XI.[1] 1918.

54.1360

Oil on canvas, mounted in artist's painted frame. Outer dimensions of frame: 25⅜ x 42⅞ (65.6 x 109); inner dimensions of frame: 23⅞ x 41⅜ (60.7 x 105.2); sight dimensions of canvas: 23⅜ x 39⅞ (56.9 x 101.3)

Signed and dated with monogram l.r.: *1918 VD*; with monogram on reverse: *1918 VD*.

PROVENANCE:

Gift of the artist to Evert Rinsema, Drachten (information supplied by J. Leering, correspondence with the author, August 1970); Jan Meijer, Amsterdam, 1947-53 (information supplied by Meijer, correspondence with the author, October 1970; he acquired the painting from Rinsema in exchange for some of his own paintings); purchased from Meijer by Mrs. Theo van Doesburg, Meudon, 1953; purchased from Mrs. van Doesburg, 1954.

CONDITION:

In 1953 the surface was cleaned with Soilax, benzine, and acetone and sprayed with PBM. In 1954 removal of some minor earlier inpaint in the upper and lower right corners was attempted, but the original paint layer beneath was in a stained and cracked condition so removal was interrupted. In 1955 some minor scratches were retouched, and the work was lined with wax resin and placed on a new stretcher. The artist's original frame, which forms a part of the composition, was retained.

All margins are slightly rubbed with scat-tered minor losses. There are some minor cracks in the paint, mostly in the ochre areas, but these were closed by the lining process. There is scattered minor crackle elsewhere, but the overall condition is good.

A 1954 photograph of the reverse (fig. a) reveals some pentimenti, most of which are not discernible on the recto. Contrary to his usual practice, which involved a thinly applied *alla prima* technique, van Doesburg appears in this instance to have made extensive changes in the size and placement of several of the colored planes; it also seems probable that he repainted the entire background after he had finally settled upon the distribution of these planes. Examination of the painting with the aid of high magnification, UV, infra-red, and x-ray has failed to satisfactorily establish the precise sequence of steps the artist followed, but the following tentative conclusions were reached. The colored planes were originally arranged upon a white background (probably zinc white); the work was then varnished with a natural resin which has discolored to some extent and has given several of the colored planes a mottled appearance. The off-white or cream colored background was applied over the coat of varnish and over several pentimenti in the colored planes. Some of the colored areas may have been retouched at this stage.

Since the conclusions reached here remain tentative and represent a considerable departure from what is known of the artist's normal practice, further technical study of the picture is planned. (Aug. 1974.)

fig. b.
Label formerly on reverse of *Composition XI*.

1. A De Stijl label formerly on the reverse (fig. b) carries the title in van Doesburg's hand: *Kompositie 11 (1918)*, the numeral clearly legible as an arabic 11, rather than a roman 2. Van Doesburg's system of numbering remains something of an enigma, but the series of works beginning with *Composition VII: The Three Graces* of 1917 (Washington University Gallery of Art, St. Louis) and ending with *Composition XXII*, 1920 (Stedelijk van Abbemuseum, Eindhoven), do seem to follow in sequence, only the use of arabic or roman numerals being somewhat inconsistent. During the period 1917-20 van Doesburg did, however, also produce several paintings to which he gave no numerical designation (e.g., *Russian Dance*, The Museum of Modern Art, New York).

During the course of 1917 and 1918, coinciding almost exactly with the publication of the first issues of *De Stijl*, van Doesburg painted a series of pictures in which color planes are distributed upon a monochrome background. None of these works bears any discernible relationship to motifs drawn from nature, but in almost every case preparatory drawings or other clues exist to establish the representational origin of the composition. Of eight such works painted between early summer of 1917 and the summer of the following year, only one—the Guggenheim picture—totally lacks evidence of a representational source. Whether such a source actually existed cannot for the present be established; but the combined evidence of van Doesburg's other paintings of this period and of some of his contemporary theoretical writings make it necessary to give serious consideration to such a possibility.

Probably the earliest in this group of numbered compositions is *Composition VII: The Three Graces* (Washington University Gallery of Art, St. Louis, Welsh, fig. 12; this article provides a detailed and illuminating analysis of van Doesburg's development, especially as this relates to Van der Leck's influence). Welsh has documented the appearance of this picture in an exhibition in Zeeland in July 1917 where it was specifically identified in the catalogue as having been derived from a particular source ("motif: The Three Graces;" Welsh, fn. 32). Preparatory drawings for this composition have hitherto not come to light, but the Zeeland catalogue entry clearly suggests a representational origin. The black background of this work (unusual, but not unique in van Doesburg's oeuvre) is convincingly cited by Welsh as a sign of Van der Leck's influence; but it is conceivable that it also reveals a relationship with the reproduction of J. B. Carpeaux's *Three Graces* photographed against a black ground, which van Doesburg included in his 1919 publication *Drie Voordrachten over de Nieuwe Beeldende Kunst*, Amsterdam (p. 96). The relationship with Carpeaux's sculpture cannot, however, be established without additional corroborating evidence.

In the case of the six remaining works in this group, the relationship between painting and representational source is much clearer. At least eleven studies survive for *Composition VIII: The Cow*, 1917 (The Museum of Modern Art, New York); they illustrate van Doesburg's progress from a realistic sketch of a cow to a series of apparently unrelated colored planes upon a white ground. *Composition IX: Abstract Transformation of the Card Players*, late 1917 (Haags Gemeentemuseum, The Hague, *Theo van Doesburg*, exhibition catalogue, Eindhoven, 1968, repr. A14), is explicitly derived from van Doesburg's own representational painting *Card Players* of about a year earlier. *Composition X* (Private Collection, Basel, *De Stijl*, 11.6.1919, repr. before p. 63, dated 1918) is preceded by at least one study of an interior dated 1917 (Stedelijk Museum, Amsterdam, oil on canvas). The compositional process behind *Russian Dance*, 1918 (The Museum of Modern Art, New York, *Theo van Doesburg*, 1968, repr. A23), is clearly and fully documented through a series of thirteen surviving studies. *Composition XII* (Kunstmuseum Basel) was derived, according to van Doesburg's own publication of it, from a sketch of a landscape with houses (*Grundbegriffe der neuen Gestaltenden Kunst,* Frankfurt am Main, 1925, figs. 16, 17, cited by Welsh, fn. 45). And the origin of *Composition XIII,* 1918 (Private Collection, Wassenaar), was also explained by van Doesburg himself when he published the original still-life source and one of the seven intermediary studies which followed it *(Drie Voordrachten over de Nieuwe Beeldende Kunst,* 1919, p. 93).

In the face of this essentially unbroken sequence in 1917-18 of abstract compositions based on representational subjects, it is difficult to exclude the possibility that the Guggenheim picture had such a source. As Welsh has demonstrated, moreover, van Doesburg's final abandonment of representational sources for his abstract works apparently did not come until at least 1919 and possibly even later. At the end of 1918 or early the following year, he produced *Composition XVI: In Dissonances* (Collection Marguerite Arp-Hagenbach, *De Hollandsche Revue,* vol. xxiv, no. 8, 1919, repr. p. 475), a square composition divided into sixteen modules horizontally and sixteen vertically. The picture's development from a photograph (entitled *Girl in the Studio*) is traced in detail through six intermediary stages by van Doesburg in his 1919 article entitled "Van 'Natuur' tot 'Kompositie' " (Ibid., pp. 470-476). In this article, and in at least one other (*De Stijl,* VII. 73/74. 1926, p. 17), van Doesburg characterizes *Composition XVI* as the final chapter in this phase of his own development from "nature" to "composition."

The origin of *Composition XI* is further complicated by its extremely close relationship to Mondrian's color plane pictures of 1917, a relationship that has been repeatedly noted in the literature on both artists. As J. Joosten has demonstrated, several of Mondrian's 1917 pictures were exhibited at the *Hollandsche Kunstenaarskring* in March 1918 ("Abstraction and Compositional Innovation," *Artforum,* vol. xi, April 1973, p. 55); moreover, some at least were known to van Doesburg in photograph form by no later than December of the previous year, since in the January 1918 issue of *De Stijl* (foll. p. 34) he reproduced Mondrian's *Composition with Colored Planes on White Ground* (Collection B. H. Friedman, New York, Joosten, loc. cit., repr. color, p. 54).

In considering the relationship between these 1917 paintings by Mondrian and *Composition XI* by van Doesburg, the latter's unusual technique must be borne in mind. As has been noted above (see CONDITION), this picture was not painted in the artist's habitually clear, premeditated *alla prima* technique, but was instead reworked to some extent after an initial application of varnish. The final effect, with its pentimenti and its painterly qualities, is a little closer to that of Mondrian's 1917 colored plane pictures than to van Doesburg's own earlier works. It seems possible, therefore, that after seeing Mondrian's actual paintings at the March 1918 exhibition, van Doesburg might have decided to introduce some of the same qualities into his own picture. Such an explanation of the technical questions raised by van Doesburg's process of composition in this work must for the time being be regarded as highly tentative. Further light may possibly be thrown on the subject by the entries in van Doesburg's diary (presently not available for study) or by other documentary sources, such as the artist's unpublished correspondence.

Van Doesburg's use in *Composition XI* of a painted frame which plays a role in the painting itself has precedents in his own earlier work as well as in that of Mondrian. In Mondrian's case, the use of a comparable device occurs for the first time in *Composition 1916* (see below cat. no. 204). In van Doesburg's oeuvre, the incorporation of the frame into the composition occurs for the first time in the Winston Collection *Still Life* also of 1916 (*Futurism: A Modern Focus,* exhibition catalogue, New York, 1973, repr. p. 84). In that picture, van Doesburg's exploitation of the ambiguous spatial relationships between background and planes, and background and frame, is even more complex than in the Guggenheim painting of two years later. It is interesting to note that van Doesburg apparently discussed the frame for *Composition XI,* referring specifically to its importance and function, in a letter to Evert Rinsema, the first owner of the picture (correspondence with Jan Meijer, October 1970, who acquired this letter with the painting and subsequently passed it on to the artist's widow. It has hitherto not been possible to trace this letter which may, however, be among the archives at Meudon, presently unavailable for study).

Although it is conceivable that van Doesburg's 1916 experiments with such framing devices might have been in part stimulated by the Mondrian *Composition 1916* (which he certainly saw exhibited in Amsterdam in March 1916), his own exploration of the issue as exemplified in the Winston *Still Life* and elsewhere is so strikingly original as to suggest a largely independent development. Moreover, as Welsh has pointed out, van Doesburg's article on Huszár in the January 1918 issue of *De Stijl* (1.3.1918, p. 35) explicitly draws attention to his preoccupation at this time with the interaction of color planes and their spatial ambient—a preoccupation which is clearly further demonstrated in his exploitation of the relationship between canvas and frame. Indeed, it is possible that his concern to maximize the interaction between background and planes even played some role in his decision to repaint the background of *Composition XI* after its completion, thus introducing the possibility that the spatial ambient existed in front of and around the planes rather than simply behind them. (For an illuminating discussion of the question of positive-negative space in van Doesburg, and of his exploitation of the notion of spatial ambiguity in the works of 1918 and later, see Welsh.)

EXHIBITIONS:[2]

Amsterdam, Stedelijk Museum, *De Stijl,* July 6-Sept. 25, 1951 (no checklist in cat.); XXVI Biennale Internazionale d'Arte Venezia, *De Stijl,* June 14-Oct. 19, 1952, no. 26; New York, The Museum of Modern Art, *De Stijl: 1917-1928,* Dec. 16, 1952-Feb. 15, 1953 (no cat.); New York, SRGM 81 (no cat.); 84, 87 (checklists); 89 (no cat.); Montreal, SRGM 93-T, no. 7; New York, SRGM 95, 196 (checklists); Eindhoven, Stedelijk van Abbemuseum, *Theo van Doesburg,* Dec. 13, 1968-Jan. 26, 1969, no. A17, repr., traveled to The Hague, Haags Gemeentemuseum, Feb. 7-March 24, 1969, Kunsthalle Nürnberg, Apr. 16-May 15, 1969, Kunsthalle Basel, Aug. 9-Sept. 7, 1969; New York, SRGM 227 (no cat.); 232, pp. 98-99, repr.; 236 (no cat.); 241, pp. 98-99, repr.; 260 (no cat.).

REFERENCES:

H. L. C. Jaffe, *De Stijl, 1917-1931: the Dutch Contribution to Modern Art,* Amsterdam, 1956, p. 48, pl. 13; SRGM *Handbook,* 1959, p. 54, repr.; [M. Rowell], SRGM *Handbook,* 1970, pp. 98-99, repr.; R. P. Welsh, "Theo van Doesburg and Geometric Abstraction," unpublished manuscript, 1974, fn. 34.

2. The label mentioned in fn. 1 was almost certainly an exhibition label since it carries a price ("f.450") and an address to which the work was to be returned. This address, Morschweg 20, Leiden, is identifiable from the *De Stijl* periodical headings as van Doesburg's address between Nov. 1918 and Mar. 1920. The hitherto untraced exhibition must have taken place within those 2 years.

Max Ernst

Born April 1891, Brühl, near Cologne.
Lives in Seillans, France.

42   Landscape. ca. 1914-1916(?).
      (Landscape Fantasy).[1]

48.1172 x280

Oil on burlap, 26¼ x 24½ (66.6 x 62.3)

Signed l.l.: *Max ERNST*. Not dated.

PROVENANCE:

Early history unknown; Karl Nierendorf, New York, by 1948; acquired with the Estate of Karl Nierendorf, 1948.

CONDITION:

In 1953 the work was lined with wax resin, placed on a new stretcher, and cleaned with a 3% Soilax solution and petroleum thinner. Approximately 10 small losses (varying from pinpoints to ½ in.) were inpainted at this time.

The corners are considerably worn and edges show some wear. There is some irregular crackle in the paint film concentrated in the heavy impasto, but no apparent cleavage. The condition in general is good. (Oct. 1973.)

The dating of Ernst's pre-1920 oeuvre poses certain problems. Very few of the paintings were dated at the time of execution, and the artist himself cannot always precisely reconstruct the history of this early period. The present picture was tentatively dated ca. 1916 at the time of its acquisition by the Museum. Lippard dates it 1919 and relates it to Dada principles of disrespect for traditional modes of painting. W. Spies also inclines towards a date of ca. 1919 (in conversation with D. Waldman, summer 1974, and with the author, February 1975). Ernst's more securely dated works of 1919, however (such as *Fruit of a Long Experience,* Private Collection, Geneva, or *Aquis Submersus,* Penrose Collection, London), demonstrate Ernst's wholly new post-war preoccupation on the one hand with Picabia and Zurich Dada, on the other with the work of de Chirico. Even by 1917, when he produced the dated watercolor *Battle of the Fish,* his personal style was notably more developed and established than it appears in *Landscape.*

Ernst himself remembers painting the picture shortly before the outbreak of the First World War (conversation with John Russell at the request of the author, November 1973, and with the author, February 1975). The pre-war paintings are almost all undated, but in general *Landscape* is stylistically somewhat more advanced than the works traditionally dated ca. 1913-14. In particular, *Hat in the Hand, Hat on the Head* (Penrose Collection, London), *Immortality* (Minami Gallery, Tokyo), and *Sunday Morning* (destroyed, formerly Hagen Collection, Cologne), while closely related iconographically to *Landscape,* are characterized by a treatment of space and form which is less developed and less ambitious in scale than that of the Guggenheim work, which would seem, therefore, to have been painted slightly later. A date of ca. 1914-16(?) seems for the time being the most plausible.

1. Ernst's original German title for the painting is not recorded. The title *Landscape Fantasy,* provided by Nierendorf, was apparently not based upon Ernst's original. The artist, when recently questioned on the subject, found the title *Landscape* the most satisfactory (conversation with the author, Feb. 1975).

A common iconography links many of the works of the 1913-16 era. Like *Landscape* they contain indeterminate but shallow landscape space in which figures are piled up above tightly juxtaposed tilting houses. These latter are surely inspired by Delaunay's two 1911 paintings of *The City* (Musée National d'Art Moderne, Paris, and The Solomon R. Guggenheim Museum). Both pictures were exhibited in Germany during 1911 and 1912, but Ernst might also have seen them during his 1913 visit to Paris. (For information on the dates and exhibition histories of the Delaunay paintings involved, see above cat. no. 35.) A ca. 1912 pen and ink drawing of a group of such houses may well represent Ernst's initial response to the Delaunay paintings (U. M. Schneede, *Max Ernst*, New York and London, 1972, repr. p. 11).

The massive animals in the foreground of *Landscape* do not appear frequently in Ernst's oeuvre of this period. They are reminiscent in type on the one hand of Marc and Campendonk, on the other of Chagall. The tiny figure with moustache and bowler hat, however, appears repeatedly in these early works, diminutively in *Immortality* and *Sunday Morning*, prominently in *Hat in the Hand, Hat on the Head*. He appears again in a related, though probably earlier, painting entitled *Home Life* (Národní Galerie, Prague). Similarly, the bird, plunging in the Penrose and Guggenheim pictures, soaring in *Immortality* and elsewhere, occurs again and again.

Although the imagery of the Guggenheim and related paintings has hitherto not proved entirely susceptible of interpretation, E. Maurer has convincingly suggested (in correspondence with the author, March 1974) that both *Landscape* and *Hat in the Hand* may well be directly relatable to the well-known dream which opens Ernst's autobiographical history *Au dela de la peinture* (first published in *Cahiers d'Art*, 1936). In the dream Ernst sees a panel which "calls forth associations of organic forms (menacing eye, long nose, great head of a bird with thick black hair, etc.)." In front of the panel a man stands making gestures "slow, comical and, according to my memories of a very obscure epoch, joyously obscene. This rogue of a fellow wears the turned-up moustaches of my father." His father, the painter, then begins to work on the panel and "quickly imparts to it new forms, forms which are at once surprising and abject. He accentuates the resemblance to ferocious or viscous animals to such a point that he extracts from it living creatures that fill me with horror and anguish . . ." (trans. D. Tanning, *Beyond Painting*, Documents of Modern Art, New York, 1948, p. 3). The father's crayon is then transformed into a whip with which he causes a "top to whirl and leap," and Ernst later perceives the entire dream as somehow strangely illustrative of the night of his own conception.

On one level, the relationship between the imagery of *Landscape* or *Hat in the Hand, Hat on the Head* and the early dream is demonstrably clear. The animals in *Landscape* are haunting and ominous, if not ferocious. The figure with turned-up moustache and bowler hat is directly relatable to a photograph of Max's father Philippe, who wears both black bowler and moustache (P. Waldberg, *Max Ernst*, Paris, 1958, p. 23), and the likelihood that this ubiquitous figure represents the artist's father is strong. The presence of a woman in both paintings may also elliptically refer to the clearly sexual overtones of the remembered dream. The presence of the bird, an image which runs throughout Ernst's oeuvre as a leitmotif with multiple meanings, may also be obliquely related to early childhood experience. The oft-cited trauma of his cockatoo's death, which coincided with the birth of his youngest sister, resulted in what he himself has described as a tortured confusion between birds and men. ("I have an idée fixe, an obsession about them. I regard every living person as being a bird." *Art in America*, vol. 54, January-February 1966, p. 92.)

Spies notes that it was in 1913 that Ernst read Freud's *The Interpretation of Dreams* and *Wit and its Relation to the Unconscious* for the first time *(Max Ernst 1950-1970; The Return of La belle jardinière*, New York, 1971, p. 38). Both books profoundly influenced him, and as Spies suggests, it was probably in the light of this reading that he was able to clarify and control aspects of his own personal experience. His relationship with his father (which is known to have been a strained and hostile one) and his intensely experienced early dreams are among those aspects of his conscious and subconscious which Spies sees as having been subjected to a Freudian self-analysis. Thus, while it is important not to over-emphasize the Freudian implications of any individual image in these (or later) paintings, and while the intentionally elusive nature of Ernst's iconography makes attempts to arrive at programmatic interpretations of his paintings irrelevant and misleading, it should be borne in mind that *Landscape* and the other paintings under discussion may have been painted under the direct and undoubtedly powerful impact of Ernst's first contact with Freud. As such, their relationship to autobiographical experience may be both plausible and potentially illuminating.

EXHIBITIONS:

Berlin, Der Sturm, *37. Ausstellung: Max Ernst, Georg Muche* [Jan. 1916], no. 17 *(Landschaft)?;*[2] New York, SRGM 107, 132 (checklists); Laguna Beach, Cal., SRGM 143-T (no cat.); Richmond, Va., SRGM 188-T (no cat.); New York, SRGM 205, *Rousseau, Redon and Fantasy* (checklist); 282, *Max Ernst,* no. 17, repr.

REFERENCE:

L. R. Lippard, "Dada into Surrealism," *Artforum,* vol. v, Sept. 1966, p. 13, repr. p. 14.

2. The picture's appearance in this exhibition has not been definitely established and is presently conjectural. Of the 19 items in the catalogue, 5 are listed merely as *"Bild."* If the Guggenheim picture did appear, it might have been one of these.

Lyonel Feininger

Born July 1871, New York.
Died January 1956, New York.

43 Gelmeroda IV. 1915.

54.1410

Oil on canvas, 39½ x 31⅜ (100 x 79.7)

Signed l.r.: *Feininger / 15*; inscribed by the artist twice on the reverse: *Gelmeroda*.

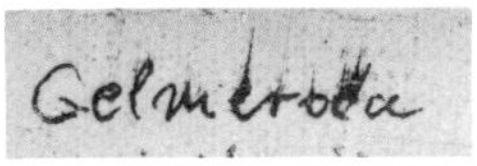

Gelmeroda [handwritten signature]

PROVENANCE:

Purchased from the artist by Erich Mendelsohn (1887-1953), Berlin and San Francisco, before 1928;[1] Mrs. Eric [sic] Mendelsohn, San Francisco, 1953-54; purchased from Mrs. Mendelsohn, 1954.

CONDITION:

The original natural varnish had already considerably yellowed by 1955; an attempt was made to remove it, but this could not be done without dissolving the paint layer. A superficial cleaning with 2% Soilax was completed and the painting coated with PBM. In 1966 the canvas was lined with a double thickness of natural white linen and placed on a new stretcher. Inpainting near the top left corner may date from this time.

Rabbet marks from a previous frame are visible at edges and there are some losses in these areas. Penciled right angles drawn at each of the 4 corners coincide approximately with the inside of these rabbet marks and possibly reflect Feininger's originally intended framing edge. Drying cracks are visible in the black areas, and there are some abrasions, especially in the thinly painted areas. The condition in general is fair to good. (Feb. 1973.)

Feininger's representations of the church at Gelmeroda form a leitmotif throughout his career, the earliest example—a pencil sketch dating from July 1906—and the latest—a lithograph from 1955. During those years he produced innumerable sketches and finished drawings of the church, at least three watercolors, eleven paintings, eight woodcuts, and one lithograph. The first three paintings were completed in 1913, the fourth in 1915; Nos. V and VI were executed only in charcoal; No. VII dates from 1917, No. VIII from 1921, No. IX from 1926, Nos. X and XI from 1928, No. XII from 1929, and No. XIII from 1936. All eleven are approximately the same size (39½ x 31⅜ in., 99.7 x 79.7 cm.), and each was preceded by a carefully worked out charcoal drawing; the composition was then redrawn in charcoal on the canvas before color work began. (For comments on this technique, see Feininger's letters to Julia Feininger of May 31, 1913, April 11 and June 9, 1914, Feininger Archives, Houghton Library, Harvard University, Cambridge, Massachusetts.)

The church itself, situated in a small Thuringian village near Weimar, dates originally from the Romanesque period, but most of what survived into the twentieth century was built between 1717 and 1830. The tower, which figured

1. It has hitherto been impossible to establish Mendelsohn's date of acquisition, although a letter from Mrs. Mendelsohn's agent to J. J. Sweeney in 1954 states that the picture had been in the family since it was painted. The picture was the focal point of the dining room in Mendelsohn's model house which he built for himself on the outskirts of Berlin in 1930 (see *Neues Haus, neue Welt* [p. 38]). Mendelsohn's caption for the photograph of the dining room reads: "It is not until the dining room beyond the hall is reached that there is a change in the color scheme. The room takes its coloring from the brown, white, violet and light green of the dominating point: Feininger's 'Gelmeroda IV.' Walls, light green enamel paint. Sideboard, vitreous, like the sky in the picture, transparent, leaving the right hand corner of the room undisturbed."

so prominently in almost all of Feininger's representations, dates from the end of this period (Krieger, p. 89). No written record apparently survives of Feininger's initial impressions of the church, but Julia Feininger has indicated that his fascination with the building dated from this very first encounter: *"Meines Mannes Verbundenheit mit 'Gelmeroda' stammt vom ersten Tage dieser Begegnung an, sie übersteigt bei weitem den Eindruck irgendeines 'Motifs'—Gelmeroda wurde im Laufe seines Lebens zu einem 'Begriff.'"* Letter to Krieger, October 5, 1966, cited by him, p. 89. ("My husband's attachment to Gelmeroda goes back to his very first encounter with it. It goes far beyond the impression made by some 'Motif.' In the course of his life, Gelmeroda became a symbol.")

One pencil sketch inscribed *"Gelmeroda / Sont. d.15 Juli 06"* records the earliest visit (formerly Collection Julia Feininger, Krieger, fig. 2), and he does not appear to have returned to the subject for seven years. But in April 1913 Feininger went back to Weimar for a visit of almost six months, and it was during this time that his preoccupation with the church became especially intense. Again and again he was drawn back to sketch the building from different viewpoints, and many of these sketches survive, both in the Feininger Archives at Harvard University and in the Archives of American Art in Detroit. In addition, Feininger's letters to Julia make repeated reference to the village of Gelmeroda and its church, as well as to his pictures of it. On April 3, for example, he wrote: *"Nachmittags krabbelte ich los mit'm Regenschirm und einem Block, nach Gelmeroda, ich habe dort 1½ Stunden herumgezeichnet, immer an der Kirche, die Wundervoll ist . . . und wie ich endlich mich aufmachte nach den Heimweg, war ich, statt müde und zerschlagen zu sein, angeregt und elastisch . . ."*[2] Feininger Archives, Houghton Library, Harvard University, Cambridge, Massachusetts. ("In the afternoon, armed with my umbrella and sketchpad, I took off for Gelmeroda. For an hour and a half I sketched all around the church, which is just wonderful. When I finally started on my way home, instead of being tired and worn out, I felt refreshed and resilient . . .") On May 31 he wrote: *"Seit 10 Tagen grinst mich ein aufgezeichnetes Bild, Kohle auf Leinwand, 80 x 100 [cm] an, zu dem ich immer sehnsuchtsverzehrtere Blicke hinüber sende—die Gelmeroda Kirche. . . ."* Feininger Archives, Houghton Library, Harvard University, Cambridge, Massachusetts. ("For ten days an outstanding picture has been grinning at me, while I look with consuming longing at it—charcoal on canvas, 80 x 100 [cm]—the Church of Gelmeroda. . . .")

The latter clearly refers to *Gelmeroda I,* for which the charcoal study was finished on May 22, but it is impossible to know when the oil version was completed. Apart from the May 31 letter, he makes few references to his work on the series, and when he does comment on it, he almost never indicates which version is involved. (See, for example, a letter of August 19, where he informs

---

2. The quotation from this letter and all other passages from Feininger's correspondence are by permission of T. Lux Feininger, Cambridge, Mass. and Harvard College Library, Cambridge, Mass. and the Estate of Julia Feininger.

Julia that he has almost finished the Gelmeroda picture, but gives no clue as to which of the three he refers to.) *Gelmeroda II* and *III*, both of which show the church from very different points of view, are also dated 1913, and the August 19 letter probably concerns one of them, but it is difficult to establish whether all three were indeed completed by the end of the year.

On June 15, 1914, he wrote to Julia in English: "I have a very fine new 'Gelmeroda Kirche.'" Since the first three pictures were completed during 1913, this letter must refer to Feininger's initial work on the fourth version—the Guggenheim painting. When war broke out in August 1914, he returned to Berlin, and he did not revisit the Weimar village until 1919. Thus the fourth version of the Gelmeroda theme was completed while Feininger was far away, but the June 15 letter would suggest that he had conceived the composition while he was still in daily contact with the church itself.

As Hess first noted, Feininger's single most powerful influence in *Gelmeroda IV* is the composition of *Gelmeroda I*. The vantage point is identical in the two works and they are clearly very closely related, even though the 1915 picture is much more obviously Cubist in style. Several of the 1913 drawings must also have served as inspirations for the Guggenheim painting, and a drawing of May 20, 1913 (fig. a), which clearly played a role in the development of *Gelmeroda I*, may also have served as a partial point of departure in this later

fig. a.
Feininger, study of Gelmeroda church, black crayon on paper, 8 x 6½ in., 20.3 x 16.5 cm., Busch-Reisinger Museum, Harvard University, Cambridge, Massachusetts.

fig. b.
Feininger, study of Gelmeroda church, black
crayon on paper, 7⅞ x 6½ in., 20 x 16.5 cm.,
Busch-Reisinger Museum, Harvard University,
Cambridge, Massachusetts.

work. Much more important, however, is a June 11, 1913, drawing (fig. b)
which is certainly a direct study for the Guggenheim painting. In particular its
flattened, planar tree on the left is the model for the even more faceted but
closely related form in the oil version. Other studies specifically for this version
were clearly made sometime between June 1914 and the completion of the picture in 1915, but these have not so far been located by the present author. (For
example, a pen drawing, present whereabouts unknown, appeared as no. 138
[*Gelmeroda IV*] in the 1919 Feininger exhibition in Dresden; this may be the
drawing which appears on an undated typed list of works in Julia Feininger's
collection preserved in the Busch-Reisinger Museum, Cambridge, Massachusetts [*"101 gelmeroda IV, 1916, federzeichnung"*].) The final charcoal study
for this version has also so far not come to light.

For a discussion of the development of style within the Gelmeroda series, see
especially Krieger, pp. 90-102; also Hess, pp. 61, 81; and Gluhman, pp. 216-
220, 302.

EXHIBITIONS:

Berlin, Der Sturm, *42. Ausstellung: Lyonel Feininger, Paul Kother, Felix Müller,* June 1916,
no. 3; Munich, Galerie Neue Kunst Hans Goltz, *Lyonel Feininger,* Oct. 1918, no. 20 (cat. lists
no lenders and does not indicate which of the works are for sale); Berlin, Nationalgalerie,

Neuerer Deutscher Kunst aus Berliner Privatbesitz, Apr. 1928, no. 11 *("Bes. Erich Mendel-
sohn, Westend");* New York, The Museum of Modern Art, *Lyonel Feininger, Marsden
Hartley,* Oct. 24, 1944-Jan. 14, 1945, p. 46, repr.; Stanford, Cal., Stanford Art Gallery,
Collector's Choice, Apr. 25-May 16, 1954, no. 21; New York, SRGM 87 (checklist); Boston,
SRGM 90-T (no cat.); Montreal, SRGM 93-T, no. 8; New York, SRGM 95 (checklist; withdrawn Aug. 27); Milwaukee Art Center, *55 Americans '55,* Sept. 9-Oct. 23, 1955 (no cat.);
New York, SRGM 97 (checklist); London, SRGM 104-T, no. 19; New York, SRGM 118
(checklist); 127 (no cat.); 129 (checklist); Philadelphia, SRGM 134-T, no. 24, repr.; New York,
SRGM 144 (checklist); Worcester, Mass., SRGM 148-T, no. 10, repr.; New York, SRGM 151,
153 (checklists); Detroit Institute of Arts, *Lyonel Feininger: The Formative Years,* Sept. 8-27,
1964, no. 137; Pasadena Art Museum, *Lyonel Feininger: A Memorial Exhibition,* Apr. 26-
May 29, 1966, no. 13, traveled to Milwaukee Art Center, July 10-Aug. 11, 1966, The Baltimore
Museum of Art, Sept. 7-Oct. 23, 1966; New York, SRGM 196 (checklist); 227 (no cat.); 232,
pp. 116-117, repr.; Los Angeles County Museum of Art, *The Cubist Epoch,* Dec. 15, 1970-
Feb. 21, 1971, no. 83, repr. color, traveled to New York, The Metropolitan Museum of Art,
Apr. 9-June 8, 1971; New York, SRGM 241, pp. 116-117, repr.; 260 (no cat.); Munich, Haus
der Kunst, *Lyonel Feininger,* Mar. 24-May 13, 1973, no. 88, repr., traveled to Kunsthaus
Zürich, May 25-July 22, 1973.

REFERENCES:

L. Feininger, letter to Julia Feininger, June 15, 1914, Feininger Archives, Houghton Library,
Harvard University, Cambridge, Mass.; E. Mendelsohn, *Neues Haus, neue Welt,* Berlin, 1932
[p. 38, repr.]; H. Hess, *Lyonel Feininger,* New York, 1961, pp. 74, 261, no. 146, repr. p. 184;
P. Krieger, "Lyonel Feiningers Variationen über das Gelmeroda-Motiv," *Zeitschrift des
deutschen Vereins für Kunstwissenschaft,* vol. 21, no. 1/2, 1967, pp. 89-102; J. W. Gluhman,
Lyonel Feininger: The Early Paintings, unpublished Ph.D. dissertation, Harvard University,
1969, pp. 275-276.

44 Cloud (Picture with Light Form). 1936.
(Bild mit heller Form; Abstract Light Form).

48.1172 x295

Oil on canvas, 18⅝ x 15¾ (47.3 x 40.1)

Signed u.l.: *Feininger*; inscribed by the artist on reverse (photographed before replacement of stretcher): *Lyonel Feininger. «CLOUD.» i936.*

PROVENANCE:

With Galerie Nierendorf, Berlin (probably on consignment), June 1936;[1] given on consignment to E. Galka Scheyer, Pasadena, 1938;[2] purchased from the artist by Karl Nierendorf, New York, February 1940 (?);[3] acquired with the Estate of Karl Nierendorf, 1948.

CONDITION:

In 1953 a 2⅝ in. tear in the canvas (sky area, upper right) was patched from the reverse with wax resin and the loss inpainted. In 1966 the patch was removed and the entire canvas lined with wax resin on natural linen; the work was placed on a new stretcher.

The condition is excellent. (Oct. 1972.)

EXHIBITIONS:
Berlin, Galerie Nierendorf, *Lyonel Feininger,* Apr. 1936, no. 21 (*"Bild mit heller Form, 1935"*);[4] Oakland, Cal., Mills College Art Gallery, *Lyonel Feininger,* June-July 1936 (checklist, *"Abstract Light Form, 1936"*), traveled to San Francisco Museum of Art, Aug.-Sept. 1936; Minneapolis, University Gallery, University of Minnesota, *Lyonel Feininger,* Apr. 1938, no. 21 (*Picture with Light Form*); New York, exhibition organized by Mrs. Cornelius J. Sullivan and Karl Nierendorf, *Lyonel Feininger,* Nov. 7-26, 1938, no. 15 (*"Cloud, 1936"*); New York, Nierendorf Gallery, *Feininger,* Nov. 1943, no. 25 (*"White Cloud, 1936, Oil"*); New York, SRGM 78 (checklist, *Cloud;* the title by which the picture has been known since its acquisition); 83 (no cat.); 87 (checklist); Boston, SRGM 90-T (no cat.); Montreal, SRGM 93-T, no. 10; New York, SRGM 95, 97 (checklists); London, SRGM 104-T, no. 20, pl. 11; New York, SRGM 112, 118, 129 (checklists); Philadelphia, SRGM 134-T, no. 30; Dallas Museum for Contemporary Arts, *Lyonel Feininger,* Apr. 10-May 5, 1963, no. 34; Tulsa, Okla., SRGM 159-T (no cat.); Pasadena Art Museum, *Lyonel Feininger: A Memorial Exhibition,* Apr. 26-May 29, 1966, no. 45, traveled to Milwaukee Art Center, July 10-Aug. 11, 1966, The Baltimore Museum of Art, Sept. 7-Oct. 23, 1966; New York, SRGM 195 (no cat.); 196 (checklist); Rochester, N.Y., SRGM 263-T (no cat.).

REFERENCES:
SRGM *Handbook,* 1959, p. 59, repr.; H. Hess, *Lyonel Feininger,* New York, 1961, p. 218, no. 373, pl. 46 (*"Cloud [Bild mit Heller Form], 1936"*).

1. The picture appeared in an exhibition at Mills College, Oakland, Cal., in June 1936 (*Abstract Light Form*); the works had been shipped to Mills from Galerie Nierendorf in Berlin, and the April bill of lading lists the picture as *"Bild mit heller Form, 1936, 48 x 40. 650 DM."*

2. In Jan. 1938 Feininger wrote to E. Galka Scheyer asking her to send the picture to the University Gallery, University of Minnesota in Minneapolis for their April exhibition (letter preserved in the Feininger Archives, Busch-Reisinger Museum, Harvard University, Cambridge, Mass).

3. The picture still belonged to Feininger in June 1939 when it was returned to him by Mrs. Cornelius Sullivan after her New York exhibition (receipt in the Feininger Archives, Busch-Reisinger Museum, Harvard University, Cambridge, Mass., entitled "Received from Mrs. Cornelius J. Sullivan 22 pictures by and belonging to Mr. Feininger"). No. 15 on the list was *"Cloud 1936."*

   The Feininger Archives at Harvard also contain a list of works purchased by Nierendorf in Feb. 1940, among which is *"Weisse Form,* oil." Although this information is too inconclusive to serve as positive identification, it may refer to the present work, and no other painting by this or a similar title has hitherto come to light. The picture belonged to Nierendorf by 1942 (July Inventory, no. 757).

4. The picture is dated 1936 on the reverse, and Julia Feininger's oeuvre catalogue (Hess) concurs with this date, as do all references to the picture in the Feininger Archives, Busch-Reisinger Museum, Harvard University, Cambridge, Mass., and subsequent exhibitions to which the artist submitted the work. It seems likely, therefore, that the Nierendorf catalogue is in error, although the possibility that the picture was completed at the end of 1935 cannot be ruled out.

Albert Gleizes

Born December 1881, Paris.
Died June 1953, Avignon.

45 Landscape in the Pyrenees

1908.

(Paysage dans les Pyrénées; Paysage à la couleur simplifiée; Paysage cadencé; Paysage précubiste).

63.1667

Oil on canvas, 21¼ x 25½ (54 x 64.6)

Signed and dated l.r.: *Alb gleizes 1908.*

PROVENANCE:

Juliette Roche Gleizes (Madame Albert Gleizes), Paris, 1953-63; Gift of Madame Albert Gleizes, Paris, 1963.

CONDITION:

In 1964 the canvas was lined with wax resin. It was not cleaned, and the original natural varnish is considerably discolored. The signature was painted in the present pale green over an illegible earlier inscription in brown.

Apart from some wear at the edges and corners, and a few scattered minor losses, the condition is good. (Dec. 1973.)

As Robbins has pointed out, Gleizes spent several summers in Gascony near Bagnères de Bigorre, where the present work was painted. (Confirmed by Juliette Roche Gleizes in conversation with the author, October 1971.)

EXHIBITIONS:

New York, Galerie René Gimpel, *Albert Gleizes,* Dec. 15, 1936-Jan. 15, 1937, no. 3 (*Paysage a la couleur simplifiée*);[1] Lyon, Chapelle du Lycée Ampère, *Albert Gleizes: 50 Ans de Peinture,* Nov. 15-Dec. 14, 1947, no. 3 ("*Paysage cadencé,* 1908");[2] [recorded in Robbins, 1964, as having appeared in Aix-en-Provence, 1960]; Avignon, Musée Calvet, *Albert Gleizes,* spring-summer 1962, no. 7 ("*Paysage précubiste* 1908");[2] Grenoble, Musée de Grenoble, *Albert Gleizes et tempête dans les salons, 1910-1914,* June 19-Aug. 31, 1963, no. 3; New York, SRGM 163, *Albert Gleizes,* no. 10, repr. color p. 34; 187 (checklist).

REFERENCES:

Robbins, 1964, p. 27, no. 10, repr. color p. 34; Idem, 1975, chapter IV.

1. Robbins (1964) identifies the present picture as no. 2 in the Gimpel catalogue (*"Paysage impressioniste,* 1903") but gives it the title of no. 3 ("*Paysage à la couleur simplifiée,* 1908"). The latter identification is the correct one and is based on photographic records in Juliette Roche Gleizes' possession. Robbins made the interesting suggestion (1975, chapter IV, fn. 6) that the title used in the Gimpel catalogue may "represent an effort in titling an early work to make its characteristics conform to what had crystallized as a mainstream development for cubism where, as in Picasso and Braque canvases, color use was very restricted." The fact that he included it in the Gimpel exhibition suggests that he attached considerable importance to it.

2. Robbins' identification of this entry with the present painting is based on photographic records in Juliette Roche Gleizes' possession (conversation with the author, May 1974).

46 Landscape. 1912.
(Paysage).

38.474

Oil on board, 14¾ x 17⅛ (37.5 x 43.3)

Signed and dated l.l.: *Alb Gleizes / 12.*

PROVENANCE:
Purchased from the artist, 1938.

CONDITION:

In 1953 the work was mounted on Masonite with PVA emulsion under pressure, and the Masonite reinforced with a pine frame. At this time and again in 1957, the corners were partly filled and retouched; the work was cleaned and surfaced with PBM. In 1963 further losses on the right and bottom edges were inpainted with PBM. Inpaint is visible at all corners and scattered along edges.

The support is moderately crushed at all edges and corners. Near the top left corner the paper veneer of the board has been torn in a diagonal line with substantial damage to the paint layer. There are approximately 15 long, straight, deep cracks in the surface running horizontally, vertically, and diagonally. These were probably caused by knife cuts present in the board before the artist began to paint (suggesting, for example, that he may have used this support as a cutting board). As the paint has aged, these cracks in the support have caused cracks in the ground and paint layers to open. There is, however, no apparent present danger of cleavage. Apart from this, the overall condition is fair to good. (Apr. 1974.)

During the summer of 1912 Gleizes was in Normandy, Puteaux, and various other places in the vicinity of Paris. It has so far not been possible to establish the precise location of the present scene, which has a river as its central subject.

EXHIBITIONS:

Amsterdam, *Moderne Kunstkring,* Oct. 6-Nov. 7, 1912, no. 114? (*Paysage,* 1912");[1] New York, SRGM 84 (checklist); Vancouver, SRGM 88-T, no. 10, repr.; Buffalo, Albright-Knox Art Gallery, *Fifty Paintings 1905-1913,* May 14-June 12, 1955, no. 18; New York, SRGM 95 (checklist; withdrawn Sept. 12); The Arts Club of Chicago, *Cubism,* Oct. 2-Nov. 4, 1955, no. 36, repr.; New York, SRGM 97 (checklist); London, SRGM 104-T, no. 22; Boston, SRGM 119-T, no. 11; New York, SRGM 129, 151, 153 (checklists); San Francisco, SRGM 164-T, no. 38, repr. p. 51.

REFERENCE:
Robbins, 1964, p. 31, no. 38, repr. p. 51.

1. The identification of the present work with this entry was tentatively made by Robbins (1964).

47 Harvest Threshing. 1912.
(Le Dépiquage des moissons).

38.727

Oil on canvas, 106½ x 139½ (270.3 x 354.3)

Signed and dated l.r.: *Albert Gleizes / 1912*;
inscribed on reverse, probably by the artist
(transcribed but not photographed before
lining): *Alb Gleizes Le Depiquage des
moissons 1912.*

PROVENANCE:

Purchased from the artist by Solomon R.
Guggenheim, 1938; Gift of Solomon R.
Guggenheim, 1938.

CONDITION:

In 1949 the painting, which had been rolled,
was stretched and a considerable amount of
mildew and paint loss was noted. The condition photograph (fig. a) indicates the
extent of losses which were then treated and
partially inpainted with oil. In 1953 the
work was apparently lined with wax resin
(the records are not entirely clear about
this date), and the inpainting, which had
been started in 1949, was completed with
watercolor. The work was coated with synthetic varnish. A horizontal seam 45 in.
from the top marks the join between 2
pieces of canvas.

There are minor losses scattered over the
surface and some abrasions. There are 4
tears in the canvas near the edges; 1 at the
right edge, 2 at the lower edge, and 1 at
the lower left corner, and a line of tack
holes along the entire left edge. The overall
condition is fair to good. (June 1974.)

fig. a.
Gleizes, *Harvest Threshing,* condition in 1949 before
treatment.

Gleizes worked on the studies for this painting during the summer of 1912
while staying with cousins in the Pyrenees, and the picture itself was painted in
Courbevoie (Juliette Roche Gleizes in conversation with the author, October
1971). Only one of these studies survives (fig. b, Robbins, 1964, repr. color,
p. 46), the others having been destroyed during the war. The remaining study
shows an advanced, but not yet final, stage in the development of the central
section of the composition. The central figure, which faces full-front in the
final painting, is seen in this study from the rear; the striking diagonal form of
his bending neighbor, whose body continues the line of the farmer's rake, is
missing altogether in the study. The highly analytic profile of the man left of

47

center in the painting is rendered here as a simple silhouette, and many other
details of structure and execution are lacking at this earlier stage. However,
the basic construction, as well as most of the colors and highlights are already
clearly worked out. Robbins has noted that the picture is in one respect a sum-
mary of Gleizes' intense interest at this period in the notion of man in harmony
with nature and presents an "epic panorama of mountains, valleys, clouds and
smoke, towns, workers and wheat" (1964). As such it reflects the principles of
the Abbaye de Créteil, a community of artists and writers which Gleizes had
helped found in 1906-07 and which had as its underlying principle the integra-
tion of art and life. (For an informative discussion of the Abbaye, see Robbins,
"From Symbolism to Cubism: the Abbaye of Créteil," *Art Journal*, vol. 23,
Winter 1963-64, pp. 111-116; also Idem, 1975, chapters II and III.)

Robbins suggests further that the specific source for Gleizes' painting might
be *La Terrestre tragédie* by Henri Martin [Barzun], which the Abbaye had
printed in 1907. The epic deals with various themes, some modern and related
to the city, others more explicitly universal and related to nature. Barzun himself described the poem as a vision "of all men simultaneously voicing their

fig. b.
Gleizes, study for *Harvest Threshing,* oil on board,
20¼ x 24⅝ in., 51.5 x 62.5 cm., Collection Paul
Josefowitz, Switzerland.

sorrows, hopes, ideals, in a vast multiple chorus, encircling the planet" (*Orpheus: Modern Culture and the 1913 Renaissance,* New Rochelle, 1960, cited by Robbins, 1975, chapter I). The second edition of the poem, which deals with the archetypal story of a pair of ill-fated young lovers misunderstood and ultimately ruined by their convention-bound parents, unfolds against the background of a haunting harvest chorus. Whether Gleizes intended his painting to evoke the universal symbols of love, pain, and suffering expressed by the poem (as Robbins implied) is not clear. Rather he seems to have been more directly concerned to depict a moment in the earth's cycle and man's harmonious involvement with and dependence upon nature. It is interesting in this context to note that Hourcade, in his 1912 review of the *Section d'Or,* described the impression made by the picture as one of a *"puissance* NATURISTE."

EXHIBITIONS:

Paris, Galerie de la Boëtie, *Salon de la Section d'Or,* Oct. 10-30, 1912, no. 43; Paris, Grand Palais, *Trente ans d'art indépendant,* Feb. 20-Mar. 21, 1926, no. 1058 *(Le Dépiquage [description perspective, multiplicité des points perspectifs]);* New York, SRGM 78, 79 (checklists); 163, *Albert Gleizes,* no. 34, repr. color p. 47; 222 (no cats.); Los Angeles County Museum of Art, *The Cubist Epoch,* Dec. 15, 1970-Feb. 21, 1971, traveled to New York, The Metropolitan Museum of Art, Apr. 9-June 8, 1971, no. 96, color pl. 65, p. 73.

REFERENCES:

O. Hourcade, "Courier des Arts," *Paris-Journal,* Oct. 23, 1912; *Les Beaux-Arts,* Aug. 1938, repr. p. 2; C. Gray, "Gleizes," *Magazine of Art,* Oct. 1950, p. 208, repr.; Golding, *Cubism,* 1968, p. 161, repr.; W. C. Camfield, *The Section d'Or,* unpublished M.A. thesis, Yale University, 1961, pp. 53-54; Robbins, 1964, pp. 17, 30, no. 34, repr. color, p. 47; Cooper, *Cubist Epoch,* 1970, no. 96, pp. 72, 74, 286, color pl. 65, p. 73; Robbins, 1975, pp. 49-50.

48   Portrait. 1912-1913.
      (Head in a Landscape).

71.1936 R 151

Oil on canvas, 14⅞ x 19⅞ (37.6 x 50.4)

Signed and dated l.r.: *Alb Gleizes 1/13*;
inscribed by the artist on reverse (photographed before lining): *To the Baroness* [?]
Rebay / en toute amitié / Alb Gleizes; not
in the artist's hand (partially obscured by
label and abrasion): *Gleizes /* (clearly
visible): *Portrait-1912.*

PROVENANCE:

Gift of the artist to Hilla Rebay, 1936,
Greens Farms, Connecticut; Estate of Hilla
Rebay, 1967-71; acquired from the Estate of
Hilla Rebay, 1971.

CONDITION:

In 1971 the work was removed from its
stretcher; its uneven topography was flattened under heat and pressure, and a double
lining of fiberglass was applied with BEVA.
The surface was then cleaned and some
inpaint removed. Some small losses were
filled with gesso and inpainted with poster
colors. The surface was sprayed with AYAF.

Under magnification it becomes clear that
the signature and date were applied in 2
different colors and possibly at 2 different
times. A grayish-toned pigment is under-
neath and a dark and more glossy brown on
top. It is difficult to tell whether any significant period of time elapsed between the
application of the 2 layers of paint. It does
seem that the "1/," applied only in the dark
brown, might have been squeezed in later.
The artist at that point may have then
strengthened some of the other letters in
order to give a uniform appearance. It is
impossible to say with certainty whether
the "3" was altered at that time from a "2."

There is a 3 in. line of almost continuous
inpainting 4 in. up from the bottom and
4½ to 7½ in. from the left side; other minor
touches of inpaint are scattered. Apart from
some minor surface cracks in the whites,
the overall condition is good. (Oct. 1973.)

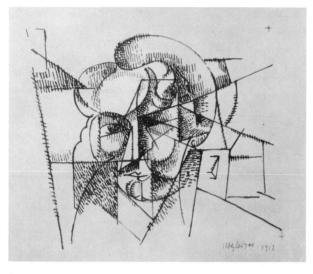

fig. a.
Gleizes, drawing for *Portrait,* 1913, sepia ink on paper,
4¾ x 5⅞ in., 11.4 x 14.9 cm., The Solomon R. Guggenheim Museum, New York.

Robbins dates the work 1913. The stylistic connections with works of 1912
such as *Man on the Balcony* (Philadelphia Museum of Art, Louise and Walter
Arensberg Collection) and even with *Harvest Threshing* (see above cat. no. 47),
where the treatment of form and the structure of overlapping planes is similar,
suggests that the work may well date from the previous year. On the other
hand, the treatment of the face is closely related to that of the *Man in a Ham-
mock* (Albright-Knox Art Gallery, Buffalo) and those of the *Women Sewing*
(Rijksmuseum Kröller-Müller, Otterlo), both of 1913. Since the work is dated
1912 on the reverse, and the 1913 date on the obverse may have been altered
some time after the completion of the picture (see above CONDITION), it would
seem advisable to treat both with some caution. Until further evidence emerges
for the establishment of a detailed chronology during these years, a date of
1912-13 seems most appropriate.

Robbins suggests that the picture is probably a self-portrait. This identification was confirmed in conversation with Robbins by Juliette Roche Gleizes
and also by Hilla Rebay (Robbins in conversation with the author, May 1974).

A detailed preparatory study for the picture is in the Guggenheim Museum
collection (fig. a).

EXHIBITIONS:

Munich, Galerie Hans Goltz, *Gesamtausstellung neue Kunst,* Aug.-Sept. 1913, no. 31 (*Kopf
eines Mannes*);[1] New York, SRGM 74, no. 49; San Francisco, SRGM 164-T, *Albert Gleizes,*
no. 51, repr. p. 59; New York, SRGM 241 (addenda), 266 (no cat.).

REFERENCE:

Robbins, 1964, no. 51, repr. p. 59.

1. The identification of the present work with this entry was made by Robbins (1964).

49   Portrait of an Army Doctor. 1914-1915.

37.473

Oil on canvas, 47¼ x 37⅜ (119.8 x 95.1)

Signed and dated l.r.: *Alb Gleizes / Toul 1914*; inscribed by the artist on reverse: *Alb Gleizes / Toul 1914 / exposition de la Triennale* [?] */ 1915*.[1]

PROVENANCE:

Purchased from the artist by Galerie René Gimpel, New York, 1937; purchased from Gimpel by Solomon R. Guggenheim, 1937; Gift of Solomon R. Guggenheim, 1937.

CONDITION:

In 1954 the work was cleaned with 10% diacetone alcohol, 10% alcohol, 88% benzine, and also with 3% Soilax solution; it was surfaced with PBM.

The edges, especially the top and right, show abrasion with some loss of paint. (There is no ground.) There is a ½ in. tear at the right edge, and there are 2 scratches elsewhere in the paint. There is a 10 in. line of fishbone crackle centered 12 in. from the left side and 14 in. from the top; additional crackle with some cupping in the pink and white dotted area, in the dark blue, and in the black 4½ in. from the top and 19 in. from the right side. The entire signature area is slightly abraded, but examination under UV and with the naked eye does not reveal any reworking or repainting of this area. Photographic evidence, however, suggests the contrary. The picture was published in Ozenfant and Jeanneret's *La Peinture moderne* in 1924, and the date, clearly visible in the reproduction, is "1914-15." The word *"Toul"* in this reproduction is painted in script with linked letters, and the crossing of the *"T"* was curved downwards. The *"Toul"* is now written with separate letters and the *"T"* curved upwards. It is impossible to establish when the artist reworked the signature and date in this way and difficult to know why such reworking remains totally undetectable to all forms of examination. The overall condition of the picture is good. (Mar. 1974.)

Early in August 1914 Gleizes was posted to Toul, an important arsenal southeast of Verdun, where he remained for approximately one year. The officer in charge of his unit, who knew and admired Gleizes' work, arranged his military assignments so that he could paint, and he found the space to do so in the hospitable house of the regimental surgeon, Dr. Lambert. Lambert, who had previously been a professor of medicine at the University of Nancy, became a close friend of Juliette Roche and Albert Gleizes during the year 1914-15 (information provided by Juliette Roche Gleizes in conversation with the author, October 1971. The doctor is identified as "Dr. Lourbet" in Robbins, 1964).

Eight studies for the portrait survive (figs. a-h). They are numbered by Gleizes himself, but as Robbins has pointed out (in conversation with the author, November 1971), the handwriting is of the 1930's, and he probably added the signatures, dates, and numbering at the time of Guggenheim's purchase of seven of the studies in July 1938. (The eighth—a gouache—is not numbered.) Gleizes' numbering should thus be treated with some caution.

The reordering of the sequence tentatively proposed here takes into consideration two major elements in the artist's gradual resolution of his composi-

1. It has so far proved impossible to identify an exhibition to which this inscription might refer.

fig. a.
Gleizes, study no. 1 for *Portrait of an Army Doctor,* ink on paper, 7¾ x 6 in., 19.7 x 15.2 cm., The Solomon R. Guggenheim Museum, New York.

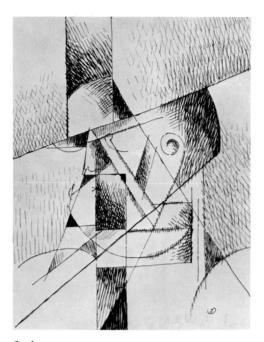
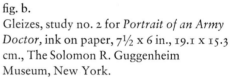

fig. b.
Gleizes, study no. 2 for *Portrait of an Army Doctor,* ink on paper, 7½ x 6 in., 19.1 x 15.3 cm., The Solomon R. Guggenheim Museum, New York.

fig. c.
Gleizes, study no. 3 for *Portrait of an Army Doctor,* pencil on paper, 8⅜ x 6½ in., 21.3 x 16.5 cm., The Solomon R. Guggenheim Museum, New York.

fig. d.
Gleizes, study no. 4 (?) for *Portrait of an Army Doctor,* pencil on paper, 9⅝ x 7⅜ in., 24.5 x 18.8 cm., The Solomon R. Guggenheim Museum, New York.

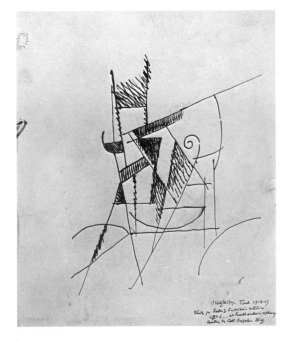

fig. e.
Gleizes, study no. 5 (?) for *Portrait of an Army Doctor,* ink with crayon on paper mounted on board, 9½ x 7¾ in., 24.1 x 19.7 cm., The Solomon R. Guggenheim Museum, New York.

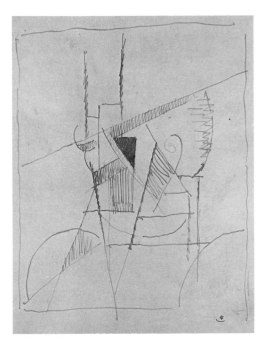

fig. f.
Gleizes, study no. 6 (?) for *Portrait of an Army Doctor,* ink on paper, 8⅜ x 7⅛ in., 21.3 x 18.1 cm., The Solomon R. Guggenheim Museum, New York.

fig. g.
Gleizes, study no. 7 for *Portrait of an Army Doctor,* ink with crayon on paper, 9¾ x 7⅞ in., 24.8 x 20 cm., The Solomon R. Guggenheim Museum, New York.

fig. h.
Gleizes, study no. 8 for *Portrait of an Army Doctor,* gouache on paper, 7½ x 6 in., 19.1 x 15.3 cm., Collection Mr. and Mrs. Andrew P. Fuller, New York.

49

tional problems: first, the highly complex structuring of planes that constitutes the sitter's head; and second, the proportions of the figure as a whole.

In nos. 1, 2, 3, and 4 (of the present sequence), the reversed apostrophe of the doctor's left eye is still a prominent feature; in the following two studies, however, it has given way to the forceful black triangle of the final work, thereby reducing the central area of the face entirely to a series of interlocking rectilinear planes. The uninterrupted curved outline of the head is abandoned by study no. 2. The strong diagonal below the nose, presumably a moustache, absent in nos. 1 and 2, is forcefully established by no. 3. The progression from detailed work on the head in nos. 1, 2, and 3, to a fully detailed study of the whole figure (no. 4) is entirely logical. The fact that even after this the head still apparently did not satisfy Gleizes gave rise to further versions of it: the first (no. 5) represents a resolution of the problem of the left eye, which is now converted into a forceful triangle. This was followed by a rapid sketch (no. 6) in which the prominent dark rectangle below the "moustache"—omitted experimentally in no. 5—was restored. The problem was now fully resolved and Gleizes proceeded to an overall study squared for transfer (no. 7) and a study of color (no. 8). Apart from the prominent pink triangle in the upper right section of the head, which is rejected in the final painting in favor of a bright, dark blue, the colors of the gouache closely approximate those of the final work.

The extremely graphic and finished nature of the first two studies suggests that Gleizes may initially have conceived the portrait purely as a head, and perhaps even as a drawing or a print rather than a painting. By no. 3, which is considerably more painterly in style, he had perhaps decided to turn the portrait into a painting, and only in no. 4 did he develop the notion of a full-length seated figure. Although this suggestion must remain in the realm of speculation, it would to some extent explain the curiously graphic quality of nos. 1 and 2 and the lack of compositional progress from no. 2 to no. 3.

The date of the painting, as well as of the studies for it, is difficult to establish with certainty. As has already been noted (see above CONDITION) the picture was originally dated 1914-15, and only later was the 1914 date substituted. Most of the studies are dated 1915, some are undated, and one is dated 1914-15. It seems likely that Gleizes worked on the picture during the winter of 1914-15.

EXHIBITIONS:

New York, Galerie René Gimpel, *Albert Gleizes,* Dec. 15, 1936-Jan. 15, 1937, no. 8; Philadelphia, SRGM 3-T, no. 166; Charleston, S.C., SRGM 4-T, no. 238; New York, SRGM 74, no. 51; 78 (checklist); Toronto, SRGM 85-T, no. 15; New York, SRGM 87 (checklist); 89 (no cat.); Boston, SRGM 90-T (no cat.); Montreal, SRGM 93-T, no. 12; New York, SRGM 97 (checklist); London, SRGM 104-T, no. 23; New York, SRGM 118 (checklist); 129 repr.; 144, 151, 153 (checklists); New York, SRGM 163, *Albert Gleizes,* no. 67, repr. color p. 63; New York, SRGM 196 (checklist); 202, p. 24, repr.; 221, 227 (no cats.); 232, pp. 136-137, repr.; 236, 240 (no cats.); 241, pp. 136-137, repr.; 266 (no cat.).

REFERENCES:

A. Ozenfant and C.-E. Jeanneret, *La Peinture moderne,* Paris, 1924, repr. p. 118; "Présence d'Albert Gleizes," *Zodiaque,* no. 6-7, Jan. 1952, pp. 32-33; Robbins, 1964, no. 67, repr. color p. 63; Idem, 1975, chapter II.

50   The Astor Cup Race (Flags). 1915.
      (Le Prix Astor Cup ou les drapeaux).

38.479

Oil and gouache on canvas, 39¼ x 29¼
(99.4 x 74.4)

Signed and dated l.l.: *Alb Gleizes 15 / N.Y.*

PROVENANCE:
Purchased from the artist, 1938.

CONDITION:
At an unknown date the work was mounted
on a honeycomb panel. Probably at this
time some minor inpainting in the corners
and along the edges was carried out.

The corners show wear, with some loss
of support, and there is slight wear on all
edges. There is a 6 in. diagonal tear at the
lower left corner and other minor tears at
the edges. The condition in general is
excellent. (Apr. 1974.)

The Astor Cup Race which must have inspired Gleizes' painting was held on
October 9, 1915, and was the opening event at the barely completed Sheeps-
head Bay Motor Speedway, Brooklyn, New York. Approximately one hundred
thousand people witnessed the race, which was apparently one of the great

fig. a.
Reproduction from an article
on the Astor Cup Race, *The
Automobile,* October 14, 1915,
p. 687.

social and racing occasions of the year. Albert and Juliette Gleizes, who had
arrived in New York less than a month before, were probably invited to attend
the race by some American friends.

Photographs of the cars lined up in front of the grandstand before the start
contain several clues to the sources of Gleizes' imagery (fig. a; I am indebted to
Jerry E. Gebby, Tucson, Arizona, for drawing the issue of the magazine in
which this photograph appeared to my attention). The bold numbers of
Gleizes' painting are clearly derived from those painted on the fronts and sides
of the participating cars (no. 1 in the first row, nos. 6 and 8 in the second). The
circular movement which dominates the surface of the painting may be partly
a reflection of the semi-circular draped flags, partly of the rhythmic repetition
of the lined-up wheels. The jumble of flags, numbers, wheels, and radiator
grills in Gleizes' painting conveys something of the speed, drama, and confusion of the event itself.

Robbins has suggested that the numbers 8 and 6 introduce a note of deep
irony into the picture, since 86 was the number of the French army regiment to
which his dead friend, Jacques Nayral, belonged. (Nayral was killed in action
December 9, 1914.) The three numbers which Gleizes used belonged to two
Peugeots and an American Stutz in the Astor Cup, none of which finished the
race. Whether a reference, conscious or unconscious, to Nayral was intended
here is impossible to say. What seems equally plausible, though still in the
realm of speculation, is that the numbers were those of two French cars and an
American one supported by the Gleizeses and their American host at the outset
of the race.

EXHIBITIONS:

New York, Montross Gallery, *Pictures by Crotti, Duchamp, Gleizes, Metzinger,* Apr. 4-22,
1916, no. 39; New York, SRGM 163, *Albert Gleizes,* no. 87, repr. p. 71.

REFERENCE:

Robbins, 1964, no. 87, repr. p. 71.

51   Chal Por. 1915.
      (Chal Post).

38.478

Oil and gouache on board, 40⅛ x 30⅛
(101.8 x 76.5)

Signed and dated l.l.: *Alb Gleizes / New
York 1915.*

PROVENANCE:
Purchased from the artist, 1938.

CONDITION:
At an unrecorded date the painting was
mounted on a honeycomb panel, and all
edges and corners were inpainted to cover
losses of the original support.

There is some abrasion along the lower
half of the left edge, the lower right edge,
and a few scattered areas elsewhere on the
surface. There are also some water stains
at the left end of the top edge, at the center
of the lower edge, and on the upper right
edge. A few of the impasto areas show some
crackle pattern, but there is no apparent
incipient cleavage. There is a 2½ in. vertical
tear at the top edge, and some minor tears
elsewhere along the edges. The overall condition is good. (Mar. 1974.)

fig. a.
Broadway at night, looking north from about Forty-
fourth Street (showing *Chalmers Porosknit Underwear*
sign), 1919, Museum of the City of New York.

Juliette Roche Gleizes' memoir of their first days in New York gives a striking
description of the impact of Broadway's orgy of colored lights on the newly
arrived couple (Robbins, 1975). Since Gleizes knew no English, the words
meant nothing to him, but the colors, lights, juxtapositions of typefaces, and
general confusion filled him with excitement.

Since its acquisition by the Guggenheim, the picture has been known as *Chal
Post*. The central lettering is, however, clearly taken from the Broadway adver-
tisement for *Chalmers Porosknit Underwear* which was displayed just north of
Forty-fourth Street at the time (fig. a). (The Gleizeses were staying barely a
block away at the Albemarle Hotel.) Gleizes' modification of the capitals of the
word "CHAL[MERS]" to match the script form of "Por[osknit]," and the juxtaposition of these apparently mobile words with the static capitals "VOTE" and
"FATI" from other (unidentified) signs, conveys something of the vitality and
confusion which had so impressed him.

EXHIBITIONS:

New York, Montross Gallery, *Pictures by Crotti, Duchamp, Gleizes, Metzinger*, Apr. 4-22,
1916, no. 36;[1] New York, SRGM 74, no. 52; San Francisco, SRGM 164-T, *Albert Gleizes*,
no. 80, repr. p. 70.

REFERENCES:

Robbins, 1964, no. 80, repr. p. 70; Idem, 1975, chapter XI.

1. Robbins (1964) identified the entry "*Broadway* (Gouache) 1915" with the present painting
   on the basis of photographic records in Juliette Roche Gleizes' possession.

52 Kelly Springfield. 1915.

38.496

Gouache on board,[1] 40⅛ x 30⅛ (102 x 76.5)

Signed and dated l.l.: *Alb Gleizes / N.Y. 15.*

PROVENANCE:

Purchased from the artist, 1938.

CONDITION:

At an unrecorded date the board was mounted on a honeycomb panel, and the support inpainted at all corners and at certain points along the edges.

The corners are crushed and the edges show some losses of paint layer and support. There are 4 tears in the paper veneer of the board varying in length from 2 to 6 in. There are some minor abrasions in the center, but the overall condition is excellent. (Apr. 1974.)

1. See below cat. no. 53, fn. 1.

fig. a.
Kelly Springfield illuminated sign on Broadway, *The Kant Slip*, 1915, p. 23.

As has already been noted above, cat. no. 51, Gleizes was fascinated by the advertising signs of Broadway. Since he knew no English, he was uninterested in content or legibility, but found the lettering, shapes, lights, and colors stimulating. The "Kelly Springfield" illuminated sign that clearly inspired Gleizes' painting was on Broadway at Fifty-fourth Street and faced west towards Times Square. It was erected in 1915 and dismantled some time the following year. (I am indebted for this information to Paul Henry, Editor of Publications, The Kelly Springfield Tire Company, Cumberland, Maryland.) A 1915 photograph from the Kelly Springfield company publication *The Kant Slip* illustrates the point (fig. a). Whether Gleizes actually saw the sign from north of Fifty-fourth Street (and hence in reverse), or whether he himself reversed the image to further express his sense of the animated confusion presented by Broadway is unknown.

EXHIBITIONS:
New York, Montross Gallery, *Pictures by Crotti, Duchamp, Gleizes, Metzinger,* Apr. 4-22, 1916, no. 37;[2] New York, SRGM 163, *Albert Gleizes,* no. 81, repr. p. 70; SRGM 266 (no cat.).

REFERENCES:
Art of Tomorrow, 1939, no. 496, p. 173("N.Y. City 1919"); Robbins, 1964, no. 81, repr. p. 70; Idem, 1975, chapter XI.

2. Robbins (1964) identified the entry *"Broadway* (Gouache) 1915" with the present painting on the basis of photographic records in Juliette Roche Gleizes' possession.

53   Composition (For "Jazz"). 1915.

38.817

Gouache on board,[1] 28¾ x 28¾
(73.0 x 73.0)

Signed and dated l.r.: *Albert Gleizes / 15
N.Y.*

PROVENANCE:

Purchased from Feragil Gallery, New York,
1938.[2]

CONDITION:

A number of areas of crackle, with some
loss through flaking, were treated in January 1974, and the process of flaking was
arrested.

There are many scattered abrasions and
scratches over the surface, and 2 tears in the
surface layer of the board near the upper
right corner. Some black transfer material is
clearly visible in the upper left quarter, and
a somewhat less severe area of transfer
material in the lower left quarter. The top
and right margins are somewhat soiled. The
condition in general is fair to good.
(Jan. 1974.)

1. Although this work and cat. no. 52 are technically watercolors, their scale and subject
   matter bring them into such close relationship with Gleizes' New York oils that their
   inclusion in this catalogue seems justified.

2. It has not been possible to establish whether the work was acquired directly from Gleizes,
   or whether there was an intermediate owner.

fig. a.
Gleizes, *Jazz,* 1915, oil on board,
39⅝ x 29½ in., 100.5 x 74.9 cm., Collection
René Deroudille, Lyon.

Juliette Roche Gleizes has provided a vivid description of the couple's first evening in New York and the dramatic experience which inspired the present work. (See Robbins, 1975.) They arrived in the late afternoon, drove to the Albemarle Hotel on Forty-fifth Street, and almost immediately set out for a long walk. After about two hours they entered a restaurant in Harlem where a black jazz group was performing with extraordinary vitality and force. It was an electrifying experience, comparable, they felt, to the discovery of Stravinsky. Within a few days Gleizes produced the present work, followed shortly afterwards by a full-scale oil entitled *Jazz* (fig. a). In spite of its title, the Guggenheim picture may represent a slightly different response to the same experience, rather than a specific study for the Deroudille work.

EXHIBITIONS:

Portland, Or., SRGM 19-T (no cat.); New York, SRGM 78 (checklist); Toronto, SRGM 85-T, no. 16; New York, SRGM 87 (checklist); 89 (no cat.); 95, 129, 144 (checklists); San Francisco, SRGM 164-T, *Albert Gleizes,* no. 78, repr. p. 68; New York, SRGM 196 (checklist); 202, p. 53, repr.

REFERENCES:

The Literary Digest, Nov. 27, 1915, repr. p. 1225 (Gleizes is at work on the painting); Robbins, 1964, no. 78, repr. p. 68; Idem, 1975, chapter XI.

54 Brooklyn Bridge. 1915.

44.942

Oil and gouache on canvas, 40⅛ x 40⅛
(102 x 102)

Signed and dated l.r.: *Brooklyn Bridge / Alb
Gleizes 15.*

PROVENANCE:

John Quinn (1870-1924), New York, 1916[1]-1924; purchased from the Quinn Collection
(American Art Association, New York, *The
Renowned Collection of Modern and Ultra-
Modern Art formed by the late John Quinn,*
Feb. 9-12, 1927, no. 263) by J. B. Neumann,
New York; purchased from Neumann, 1944.

CONDITION:

In 1953 the painting was given a very light
surface cleaning with benzine, and minor
losses in the red areas were inpainted. In
1958 the canvas was lined with wax resin
and placed on a new stretcher. A small loss
near the lower left corner was filled and inpainted, and the surface was coated with an
unidentified synthetic varnish.

Extensive flaking of the paint film has occurred in the red and brown areas, and this
condition has continued to develop since it
was first observed in 1953. It continues to
pose dangers. In the whitish-gray impasto
areas there is considerable crackle with
some minor loss. The canvas is torn in several places along the edges and in all corners
except for the upper left. These voids are
filled with wax resin, and residue from the
wax resin is visible in scattered places along
the edges. The surface is slightly abraded in
a number of areas, and the condition in general is fair. (Dec. 1973.)

As Robbins has noted, the Brooklyn Bridge made an indelible impression upon
Gleizes and inspired three major paintings during the New York years. Shortly
after his arrival in the States, he was interviewed by *The Literary Digest,* which
recorded some of his first impressions: "The genius who built the Brooklyn
Bridge is to be classed alongside the genius who built Notre Dame de Paris."

The present version was followed some months later by a much more abstract conception (Collection Madame P. de Gavardie, Paris, Robbins, 1964,
no. 85, repr. p. 73). The latter is signed and dated 1915, but was probably
painted early the following year. The final version (see below cat. no. 57) was
painted on Gleizes' second visit to New York in 1917.

EXHIBITIONS:

New York, Montross Gallery, *Pictures by Crotti, Duchamp, Gleizes, Metzinger,* Apr. 4-22,
1916, no. 40; New York, Rains Auction Rooms, Inc., *Modern Paintings . . . from the collec-
tion of J. B. Neumann,* New York, Jan. 19-24, 1936, no. 63, repr. (not sold); New York, The
Museum of Modern Art, *Cubism and Abstract Art,* Mar. 2-Apr. 19, 1936, no. 88, repr.; New
York, New Art Circle, *Documents of Modern Painting from the Collection of J. B. Neumann,*
Sept. 23-Nov. 30, 1940 (checklist); Ohio, The Toledo Museum of Art, *Contemporary Move-
ments in European Painting,* Nov. 6-Dec. 11, 1938, no. 40; New York, Buchholz Gallery,
Early Work by Contemporary Artists, Nov. 16-Dec. 4, 1943, no. 14; New York, SRGM 79
(checklist; withdrawn Oct. 20); 87 (checklist); 89 (no cat.); The Brooklyn Museum, *The
Brooklyn Bridge,* Apr. 28-July 27, 1958, repr.; Boston, SRGM 119-T (checklist); Lexington,
Ky., SRGM 122-T, no. 8; New York, SRGM 129, 144 (checklists); Worcester, Mass., SRGM

1. The catalogue of the 1927 Quinn sale indicates that the picture was purchased directly
   from the artist. This was confirmed by Juliette Roche Gleizes (in conversation with the
   author, Oct. 1971), who said that Quinn bought this and some other works out of the
   Apr. 1916 Montross exhibition.

148-T, no. 13, repr.; New York, SRGM 151, 153 (checklists); 163, *Albert Gleizes,* no. 84, repr. color p. 72; 196 (checklist); 202, p. 82, repr.; Columbus, Ohio, SRGM 207-T, p. 16, repr. p. 17; New York, SRGM 227 (no cat.); 232, p. 140, repr. p. 141; 240 (no cat.); 241, p. 140, repr. p. 141; 260, 266 (no cats.).

REFERENCES:

The Literary Digest, Nov. 27, 1915, repr. p. 1225 (barely visible at rear of room in photograph of Gleizes); R. Rosenblum, *Cubism and Twentieth-Century Art,* New York, 1960, p. 121, repr.; Robbins, 1964, no. 84, repr. color p. 72; Idem, 1975, chapter XI.

55 Equestrienne. 1916.
(Sur une écuyère de haute école [?];[1]
Abstraction of Equestrian).

37.494

Oil and sand on board, 39¾ x 30
(101 x 76.2)

Signed and dated l.r.: *Alb Gleizes. 16.*

PROVENANCE:

Probably purchased from Galerie René
Gimpel, New York, by Solomon R. Guggen-
heim, January 1937;[1] Gift of Solomon R.
Guggenheim, 1937.

CONDITION:

In 1942 a tear in the top right edge of the
support was set together; the painting was
cleaned and surfaced with Weber's Sala-
mander, then Winton varnish. In 1953 the
badly warped board was mounted on reinforced Masonite with PVA emulsion and
supported by a wooden frame; surface dirt
was removed with Soilax solution and the
painting coated with PBM. On this occasion, and again in 1957 and 1958, extensive losses in the corners and the margin
areas were filled and inpainted.

Some losses of paint and support are still
apparent along the top and bottom edges.
Apart from a 2 in. vertical paint crack starting near the center of the bottom edge, a 1
in. horizontal crack in the grayish-brown
arc at the upper left, and some fine cracks in
the white impasto of the horse's head, the
overall condition of the paint film is good.
(June 1972.)

According to Juliette Roche Gleizes (in conversation with the author, October
1971), Gleizes' visit to a circus in Courbevoie in 1914 inspired the first of his
circus compositions—a drawing of a female figure standing upon the back of
a horse (fig. a). As D. Robbins noted (1964, no. 119), this drawing was followed
in the same year by an etching (fig. c), although an ink drawing probably served
as the intermediate step (fig. b).

Gleizes' first painting of the subject is probably the present work. Early in
1916 the Gleizeses went to a circus in New York, and as a result, the artist was
once again inspired to treat the equestrian theme (conversation with Juliette
Roche Gleizes, October 1971). The Guggenheim painting is directly based on
the Firpo drawing (fig. b), although the decorative and pseudo-collage elements
of Gleizes' 1916 style have been added and many of the more legible elements
of the original composition suppressed. In at least two works of 1917, the
motif of a rider and horse (the latter now reduced to two circular forms) recurs,
and once again, the 1914 drawing (fig. a) provides the basic compositional
elements, though these are now more than ever transformed by decorative patterning (*On a Vaudeville Theme,* formerly SRGM, Robbins, 1964, no. 114,
repr. p. 86; *On a Circus Theme,* The Baltimore Museum of Art, D. Robbins,
"From Cubism to Abstract Art," *The Baltimore Museum of Art News,* vol.
xxv, Spring 1962, repr. p. 19).

1. A bill from René Gimpel to Guggenheim dated Jan. 1937 lists *Sur une écuyère de haute
école* as well as *Un médecin militaire* among the works purchased. No picture by the former
title is listed among the Museum's holdings, whereas the latter was definitely purchased by
Guggenheim at that time. Since no source for *Equestrienne* is recorded, and since it was,
like the *Army Doctor,* given by Guggenheim to the Foundation in June 1937, it is almost
certain that *Sur une écuyère de haute école* and *Equestrienne* are one and the same.

In 1919 Gleizes returned once more to the clearly legible female figure, poised with arms spread out, one foot resting on the horse's saddle (fig. d), and in 1920-21 he produced three final works on the theme. By this time the composition, though still formally linked to the 1914 drawing, was transformed into an almost total abstraction (figs. e, f, g).

EXHIBITIONS:

Paris, *Salon des Indépendants,* Jan. 28-Feb. 29, 1920, no. 1909 *(Cirque)*?;[2] New York, Galerie René Gimpel, *Albert Gleizes,* Dec. 15, 1936-Jan. 15, 1937, no. 15 *(Sur une écuyère de haute école)*;[3] Philadelphia, SRGM 3-T, no. 172 *(Abstraction of Equestrian)*; Charleston, S.C., SRGM 4-T, no. 246; Rochester, N.Y., SRGM 263-T (no cat.).

2. The reverse formerly carried the inscription (photographed before mounting of board): "*Exposé à Brooklin* [sic] *1918 / Indépendants in 1920.*" No trace of a Brooklyn exhibition has hitherto come to light. Of the 6 pictures listed in the 1920 *Indépendants,* no. 1909 is the only title which might be applied to the present work.

3. See above fn. 1.

fig. a.
Gleizes, sketch for *Equestrienne,* 1914,
pencil on paper, 10⅝ x 8¼ in., 27 x 21 cm.,
Collection A. Terrin.

fig. b.
Gleizes, sketch for *Equestrienne,* ink on
paper, 10¼ x 7⅞ in., 26 x 20 cm., Collection W. Firpo.

fig. c.
Gleizes, *Equestrienne,* 1914, etching, 9¼ x 7½
in., 23.5 x 19.1 cm., signed and dated l.c.:
"Alb Gleizes/14," The Solomon R. Guggenheim Museum, New York.

fig. d.
Gleizes, *Equestrienne,* 1919, oil on canvas,
37⅜ x 29½ in., 95 x 75 cm., Collection A. Terrin.

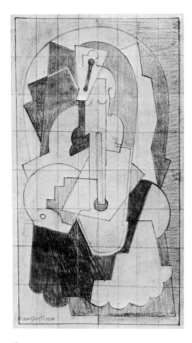

fig. e.
Gleizes, study for *Equestrienne*, 1920, pencil on light
ochre tinted paper, 11 x 5 ⅞
in., 28 x 15 cm., Collection
W. Firpo.

fig. f.
Gleizes, study for *Equestrienne*,
1921, pencil on paper,
10⅝ x 5 ⅞ in., 27 x 15 cm.,
The Solomon R. Guggenheim
Museum, New York.

fig. g.
Gleizes, *Equestrienne*, 1921, oil on canvas,
dimensions and present whereabouts
unknown.

56   Spanish Dancer. 1916.
(Danseuse espagnole; Peinture sur une danseuse rose[1]).

37.483

Oil with sand on board, 39⅞ x 30 (101.3 x 76.4)

Signed and dated l.r.: *Alb Gleizes / 16.*

PROVENANCE:

Purchased from the artist by Solomon R. Guggenheim, 1935; Gift of Solomon R. Guggenheim, 1937.

CONDITION:

In 1953 the board was mounted with PVA on Masonite supported by a wood frame. In 1954, apparently in response to further warping of the board, it was removed and flattened and remounted on an adjustable pine mount. At an unrecorded date (probably 1953 or 1954) some scattered losses along the right and left margins were inpainted, notably a 6 in. vertical line ½ in. from the right edge (a rabbet mark).

The edges and corners show considerable wear. The work is painted directly on the board with no ground, and the support shows through the thinly applied paint in many places, but there are only 2 actual paint losses. Apart from 4 scratches, the condition of the paint film is in general good. (Dec. 1973.)

Gleizes was in Barcelona from spring to December 1916 and produced a series of paintings of Spanish dancers. Several of them, including the present work, show marked affinities with the more abstract circus pictures of 1917 such as *Stunt Flying* (see below cat. no. 58) or *On a Circus Theme* (The Baltimore Museum of Art, Sadie A. May Collection, repr. D. Robbins, "From Cubism to Abstract Art," *The Baltimore Museum of Art News,* vol. xxv, Spring 1962, p. 19).

1. In a letter to Guggenheim's secretary dated July 24, 1935, Gleizes refers to the picture by this title.
2. This exhibition is cited by Robbins (1964). No catalogue has been located by the present author.

EXHIBITIONS:

New York, Bourgeois Galleries, *Exhibition of Modern Art,* Feb. 10-Mar. 10, 1917, no. 29; New York, Ardsley Studios, *Lithographs by Fantin-Latour and Recent Paintings by Albert Gleizes,* Mar. 1919, no. 3 (west room);[2] Charleston, S.C., SRGM 1-T, no. 113; Philadelphia, SRGM 3-T, no. 167; Charleston, S.C., SRGM 4-T, no. 239; Utica, N.Y., Munson Williams Proctor Institute, *Formal Organization in Modern Painting,* Nov. 1-29, 1953, no. 10; San Francisco, SRGM 164-T, *Albert Gleizes,* no. 104, repr. p. 84.

REFERENCE:

Robbins, 1964, p. 22, no. 104, repr. p. 84.

57 On Brooklyn Bridge. 1917.
(Sur Brooklyn Bridge).

37.489

Oil on canvas, 63¾ x 50⅞ (161.8 x 129.5)

Signed and dated l.l.: *Albert Gleizes / New York 1917*; inscribed by the artist l.c.: *sur Brooklin* [sic] *Bridge.*

PROVENANCE:
Purchased from the artist, 1937.

CONDITION:
In 1953 the work was cleaned with a mild solution of acetone and benzine and lined with wax resin. Some minor losses in the beige border areas were inpainted; the picture was placed on a new stretcher.

All edges are badly cracked and worn and there is extensive separation of the canvas from the lining. Several tears and punctures in the support were closed through the lining process, but are still visible. There is a horizontal line of abrasion across the top of the canvas 3 in. down, possibly caused by a stretcher impression. The condition in general is fair to good. (Dec. 1973.)

fig. a.
Gleizes, study for *On Brooklyn Bridge*,
1915, ink and gouache on paper, 9⅞ x 7½
in., 25 x 19 cm., signed and dated on
reverse: *"Albert Gleizes Brooklyn Bridge
1915,"* formerly Collection Juliette Roche
Gleizes, Paris.

Robbins suggested (in conversation with the author, November 1971) that the
1915 drawing formerly in Juliette Roche Gleizes' collection (fig. a) is a study
for the present painting. Gleizes' second visit to New York lasted from December 1916 to January 1919, interrupted by a brief journey to Bermuda early
in 1917. The present picture dates from the early part of this period and is
the last of Gleizes' *Brooklyn Bridge* works.

EXHIBITIONS:

Charleston, S.C., SRGM 4-T, no. 242; New York, SRGM 74, no. 50 (dated 1919); The
Brooklyn Museum, *The Brooklyn Bridge,* Apr. 28-July 27, 1958, repr.; New York, SRGM
129 (checklist); San Francisco, SRGM 164-T, *Albert Gleizes,* no. 86, repr. p. 73; London,
Tate Gallery, *Léger and Purist Paris,* Nov. 17, 1970-Jan. 24, 1971, no. 87.

REFERENCES:

C. Gray, "Gleizes," *Magazine of Art,* vol. 43, Oct. 1950, repr. p. 208; Robbins, 1964, no. 86,
repr. p. 73; Idem, 1975, chapter XI.

58   Stunt Flying. 1917.
      (Voltige aérienne).

37.230

Oil with sand on board, 39⅞ x 30
(101.3 x 76.4)

Signed and dated l.l.: *Alb Gleizes. / 1917;*
inscribed on reverse, probably by the artist
(transcribed but not photographed before
mounting): *Voltige aérienne, New York,
1917, Albert Gleizes.*

PROVENANCE:

Purchased from the artist by Solomon R.
Guggenheim, 1935; Gift of Solomon R.
Guggenheim, 1937.

CONDITION:

In 1953 the work was cleaned and mounted
on reinforced Masonite. Many losses along
the edges were inpainted and the picture
varnished (with unidentified varnish). In
1956 some further losses at the top right
were inpainted. There is a 2 in. dent in the
support (apparently built up by the artist)
near the lower right corner.

Apart from some wear along the edges and
in the corners, the condition of the paint
film is good. (Jan. 1974.)

As Robbins has pointed out (1962 and 1964), *Stunt Flying* is derived from the 1916 *Acrobats* formerly owned by Juliette Roche Gleizes (and dated by Robbins 1915 [in 1962] or 1914 [in 1964]). The 1916 *Acrobats* was painted after the couple had paid a visit to a circus in New York early that year (information provided by Juliette Roche Gleizes in conversation with the author, October 1971). Robbins convincingly describes *Stunt Flying* as the first fully successful expression of Gleizes' transition into abstraction.

The overlapping circles superimposed on a tilted background plane and the decorative patterning of the surface bring *Stunt Flying* into close relationship with *The Clowns,* also of 1917 (Musée d'Art Moderne de la Ville de Paris, Inv. AM 1061). But in the Paris picture, as in all of the previous circus scenes, the real subject of the work is clearly, if elliptically, defined and the two clowns stand palpably before us. In *Stunt Flying,* probably painted very shortly afterwards, the figures have disappeared, and only the sense of movement remains.

EXHIBITIONS:

New York, Ardsley Studios, *Lithographs by Fantin-Latour and Recent Paintings by Albert Gleizes,* Mar. 1919, no. 6 (west room);[1] Paris, *Salon des Indépendants,* Jan. 28-Feb. 29, 1920, no. 1910 *(Voltige);* Charleston, S.C., SRGM 1-T, no. 63, repr. p. 51; Philadelphia, SRGM 3-T, no. 68, repr. p. 86; Charleston, S.C., SRGM 4-T, no. 97, repr.; New York, SRGM 79 (checklist); Vancouver, SRGM 88-T, no. 12; New York, SRGM 129 (checklist); 163, *Albert Gleizes,* no. 112, repr. p. 86.

REFERENCES:

D. Robbins, "From Cubism to Abstract Art," *The Baltimore Museum of Art News,* vol. xxv, Spring 1962, pp. 15-16, repr.; Idem, 1964, p. 21, no. 112, repr. p. 86.

---

1. The exhibition is cited by Robbins (1964). No catalogue has been located by the present author.

59   Composition. 1929.
(*Religious Painting;*[1] *Peinture formelle*[2]).

37.235

Oil on canvas, 78¾ x 60¼ (200 x 153)

Signed and dated l.r.: *Alb. Gleizes. 29.*

PROVENANCE:
Purchased from the artist by Solomon R. Guggenheim by 1936; Gift of Solomon R. Guggenheim, 1937.

CONDITION:
Some minor inpaint along 6 in. of the lower edge is of unknown date.

The edges and corners are slightly worn with some minor losses of paint and ground. There is an 18 in. horizontal stain across the surface 17 in. up from the bottom; also a 16 in. curved scratch 4 in. down from the top, centered 16 in. from the left, apparently caused by pressure from the reverse. There is a pigment crackle scattered over the major portion of the surface with some cupping. The unevenly applied varnish is considerably discolored and there is heavy general soil, but the condition is otherwise good. (Mar. 1974.)

EXHIBITIONS:
Paris, *8ᵉ Salon des Tuileries,* 1930, no. 1224 *(Peinture formelle)*; Charleston, S.C., SRGM 1-T, no. 66, repr. *(Religious Painting)*; Philadelphia, SRGM 3-T, no. 72, repr.; Charleston, S.C., SRGM 4-T, no. 101, repr.

REFERENCE:
Art of Tomorrow, 1939, repr. p. 123, no. 235.

1. This title appears to have been invented by Hilla Rebay.
2. A label on the reverse reads: "*Salon des Tuileries 1930 / Gleizes (Albert) / Peinture.*"
   Gleizes' only entry in the catalogue is no. 1224: "*Peinture formelle.*"

60   Painting for Contemplation,
      Dominant Rose and Green. 1942.
      (Composition, Dominantes roses et vertes).

63.1668

Oil on burlap, 85 x 52 (216 x 132)

Signed and dated l.r.: *Alb Gleizes 42.*

PROVENANCE:

Juliette Roche Gleizes (Madame Albert
Gleizes), Paris, 1953-63; Gift of Madame
Albert Gleizes, Paris, 1963.

CONDITION:

All edges show fairly extensive inpainting of
an undetermined date.

All edges and corners show considerable
wear and loss. There is a circular area of
crackle at the upper center, but the condition is otherwise excellent. (Mar. 1974.)

André Dubois, in his 1970 catalogue *Albert Gleizes et le dessin* (Musée d'Art
et d'Industrie, Saint-Etienne), quotes passages from Gleizes' unpublished
L'Homme devenu peintre, 1948, which throw interesting light on the abstract
religious works of the artist's final phase. The clear superiority of these works
over figurative paintings lay, according to Gleizes, in their unique ability to
elicit the deepest possible spiritual response.

> *Que l'oeuvre strictement 'non figurative' soit au sommet de cette hiérarchie
> (allant de la figuration à la composition, puis à la nonfiguration par les lois
> de l'objet), cela n'est pas douteux ... Elle servira la tendance humaine à
> la rêverie, à la méditation, à la contemplation, à cette poésie desintéressée
> qui atteint ces régions de l'âme où l'esprit vit dans la conscience de sa propre
> inconscience* (Dubois, p. 19, no. 104).

Gleizes specifically denied that the forms were symbolic in nature and urged
the viewer rather to *"agir véritablement la substance de la peinture pour en
faire son object, par son corps aller vers la lumière"* (Ibid., p. 18, no. 101). The
abstract forms were literally intended "for contemplation" and hence for spiritual regeneration.

EXHIBITIONS:

Grenoble, Musée de Peinture et de Sculpture, *Albert Gleizes et tempête dans les salons 1910-
1914,* June 19-Aug. 31, 1963, no. 41; New York, SRGM 163, *Albert Gleizes,* no. 166, repr.
color p. 110.

REFERENCES:

Dom. A. Surchamp, "Présence d'Albert Gleizes," *Zodiaque,* no. 6-7, Jan. 1952, p. 42, pl. 16;
Robbins, 1964, no. 166, repr. color p. 110.

Natalia Goncharova

Born June 1881, Nechaevo, Russia.
Died October 1962, Paris.

61   Cats. 1913.

(Кошки [лучистое воспр. розовое,
черное и желтое], Koshki [luchistoe vospr.
rozovoe, chernoe i zheltoe], *Cats [rayonist
percep. in rose, black, and yellow]*; Кошки
[лучистое построение, комбинация
желтого, черного и розового], Koshki
[luchistoe postroenie, kombinatsiya
zheltogo, chernogo i rozovogo], *Cats
[rayonist construction, combination of
yellow, black, and rose]*; Кошки [черное,
желтое и розовое], Koshki [chernoe,
zheltoe i rozovoe], *Cats [black, yellow,
and rose]*).

57.1484

Oil on canvas, 33¼ x 33 (84.4 x 83.8)

Signed l.r.: *N Gontcharova.*; Inscribed by
the artist on reverse: *N. Gontcharova 43 rue
de Seine / Paris 6ᵉ / 1910* [sic]. *Rayonisme
1910. „LES CHATS;"* possibly by the artist:
Gontcharav[a] / *Katze*[n].

The signature on the face and the inscriptions on the reverse, all in western alphabet,
date either from 1914, when the painting
was exhibited in Paris, or from after 1915,
when the artist left Russia.

PROVENANCE:
Purchased from the artist, 1957.

CONDITION:
The painting was given a light surface cleaning in 1957 (it has not been varnished). In
1970 it was placed on a new stretcher.

Apart from 1 or 2 minor scratches and
abrasions, the condition is excellent.
(Jan. 1973.)

The dating of Goncharova's work is, as has been frequently noted, problematic. Chamot (author of the most recent monograph on the artist) has
commented (in correspondence with the author, August 1972) that the artist's
works were rarely signed and dated at the time of their execution, and that
the dates added in later years were often inaccurate. (For a discussion of the
related problems raised by the dating of Larionov's paintings and in particular
the dating of his earliest Rayonist works, see below cat. no. 160.)

The inscribed dates on the reverse of the present painting must, therefore,
be treated with some caution. The fact that one of the "*1910's*" was clearly
written over an already existing "*1912*" is a further indication that the artist
may have been unsure of the date of execution.

The earliest evidence for the dating of *Cats* is the catalogue of the exhibition
Target of March 1913 where the picture is dated 1913, as are the four other
explicitly Rayonist works (*Target*, nos. 45-48). Eganbyuri's book on Larionov
and Goncharova was published in the same year, and here the picture is also
listed among the works of 1913. In August 1913 the picture appeared in Goncharova's one-woman exhibition in Moscow, this time without date, but since
the catalogue of this exhibition is based directly upon Eganbyuri and follows
the same sequence, the implication is that his dates are acceptable.

In June 1914 an important exhibition of Goncharova's and Larionov's work
opened at the Galerie Paul Guillaume in Paris; for the first time *Cats* carried
the date 1910. Most subsequent publications have either tentatively or fully

accepted the 1910 date (see below EXHIBITIONS; also Seuphor, 1950 and 1955; Degand; SRGM *Handbook,* 1959). Alternative suggestions have been made. Gray dated the picture 1911 (in 1961) or 1911-12 (in 1962) and described it as perhaps Goncharova's earliest Rayonist work. Carrieri dated it 1912 and Cooper 1911-12.

Contemporary reviews of the two 1913 exhibitions neither cast doubt upon, nor effectively substantiate, the 1913 date then assigned to the painting. Parkin's review of *Target* mentions *Cats* and other Rayonist works as examples of the highest aspirations of contemporary Russian art and appears to imply that they are among the newest and most unusual works, but he does not specifically discuss their date. N. Lavrsky's review of *Target (Apollon,* no. 4, April 1913, pp. 57-59) refers briefly to *Rayonist Lilies* and discusses Larionov's Rayonism, but without reference to date. Rostislavov's review of Goncharova's one-woman exhibition (*Rech,* March 23, 1914) refers to the Rayonist works exhibited and implies that the style was her most recently developed one, but also offers no view on the date as such.

Goncharova herself, in the preface to the catalogue of her one-woman exhibition of 1913, attributes the theory of Rayonism to Larionov and states that among the objectives she is pursuing is "to put into practice M. F. Larionov's theory of Rayonism which I have elaborated" (trans. J. E. Bowlt). If one accepts the premise that Larionov's earliest Rayonist paintings date from 1912 (see below cat. no. 160), one is forced to place the *Cats* in late 1912 or early 1913, thus lending support to Eganbyuri's original 1913 date for the picture. Eganbyuri's dates have so far proved reasonably accurate, although some inconsistencies do occur. (Bowlt has recently drawn attention to Eganbyuri's own assertion that he completed the book in great haste and with little attention to accuracy, *Burlington Magazine,* vol. cxiv, October 1972, p. 719.) Chamot, in her 1972 monograph, finds Eganbyuri's dates in general acceptable (p. 54), and she places *Cats* in 1913 (p. 57). The cumulative evidence of the three 1913 catalogues argues strongly for a 1913 date, although one cannot rule out the possibility that the picture was completed at the end of 1912—the date originally inscribed on the reverse of the canvas. The stylistic maturity of the work suggests that it was painted at the height of Goncharova's Rayonist period, and not—as suggested by Gray—at its outset. Eganbyuri lists thirteen Rayonist constructions under 1912, and four specifically Rayonist pictures as well as nine Rayonist sketches under 1913. A date for *Cats* at the beginning of 1913 would thus seem entirely plausible.

EXHIBITIONS:

Moscow, Мишень (Mishen, *Target*), Mar. 24-Apr. 7, 1913, no. 49 (кошки [лучистое] черное, желтое и розовое, 1913, Koshki [luchistoe], chernoe, zheltoe i rozovoe, *Cats [rayonist] black, yellow and rose,* 1913");[1] Moscow, Художественный салон, Гончарова, 1900-1913 (Khudozhestvennyi salon, *Goncharova 1900-1913*), Aug. 1913, no. 645 (кошки [лучистое воспр. розовое, черное и желтое], Koshki [luchistoe vospr. rozovoe, chernoe i zheltoe], *"Cats [Rayonist percep. in rose, black and yellow]"*); Berlin, Der Sturm, *Erster Deutscher Herbstsalon,* Sept. 20-Nov. 1, 1913, no. 149 *(Katzen)*; Paris, Galerie Paul Guillaume, *Exposition Natalia Gontcharova et Michel Larionov,* June 17-30, 1914, no. 34 *("Les Chats [rayonnisme] 1910")*; Moscow, Выставка живописи 1915, год (Vystavka zhivopisi 1915 god, *Exhibition of Paintings of the Year 1915*), Mar.-May, 1915, no. 18? (кошки, koshki, *Cats*);[2] Dresden, *Internationale Kunstausstellung,* June-Sept. 1926, no. 284 *(Die Katzen)*; Palais des Beaux-Arts de Bruxelles, *La Peinture sous le signe d'Apollinaire,* Dec. 2-25, 1950, addenda to the catalogue, no. 82 (dated 1912); Paris, Galerie de l'Institut, *Nathalie Gontcharova: oeuvres anciennes et récentes,* May 4-23, 1956, p. 7, no. 7, repr. (dated 1910); Saint-Etienne, Musée d'Art et d'Industrie, *Art abstrait, les premières générations 1910-1939,* Apr. 10-June 1957, no. 64, fig. 12 (dated 1910); New York, SRGM 107, 118 (checklists, dated 1910?); Leeds, City Art Gallery, Arts Council of Great Britain, *Larionov and Goncharova,* Sept. 9-30, 1961, traveled to Bristol, City Art Gallery, Oct. 14-Nov. 4, 1961, London, Arts Council Gallery, Nov. 16-Dec. 16, 1961, no. 108, repr. (dated 1911); New York, SRGM 144, 151, 153, 196 (checklists, dated 1910); Los Angeles County Museum of Art, *The Cubist Epoch,* Dec. 15, 1970-Feb. 21, 1971, traveled to New York, The Metropolitan Museum of Art, Apr. 9-June 8, 1971, no. 105, color pl. 163, p. 160 (dated 1911-12?).

REFERENCES:

V. Parkin, Ослиный хвост и Мишень (Oslinyi khvost i Mishen, *Donkey's Tail and Target*), ed. Myunster, Moscow, 1913, p. 70; E. Eganbyuri (pseud. I. M. Zdanevich), Наталия Гончарова, Михаил Ларионов *(Natalia Goncharova, Mikhail Larionov),* ed. Myunster, Moscow, 1913, p. xii, repr. p. 11; M. Seuphor, *L'Art abstrait: ses origines, ses premiers maîtres,* Paris, 1950, repr. p. 154; L. Degand, "Le Rayonnisme, Larionov, Gontcharova," *Art d'aujourd'hui,* sér. 2, Nov. 1950, repr. p. 29; M. Seuphor, "Au temps de l'avant-garde," *L'Oeil,* no. 11, Nov. 1955, p. 29; SRGM *Handbook,* 1959, p. 67, repr.; C. Gray and M. Chamot, *Larionov and Goncharova,* exhibition catalogue, London, Arts Council, 1961, no. 108; C. Gray, *The Great Experiment: Russian Art 1863-1922,* New York, 1962, pl. 80; R. Carrieri, *Futurism,* Milan, 1963, p. 139, repr.; Cooper, *Cubist Epoch,* 1970, no. 105, pp. 160, 287, color pl. 163, p. 160 (dated 1911-12?); M. Chamot, *Gontcharova,* Paris, 1972, repr. color p. 57.

1. A picture entitled *Cats (study)* appeared in the exhibition *Donkey's Tail,* Mar. 1912, no. 40, but it cannot have been the present work. A review of that exhibition by Parkin published in *Donkey's Tail and Target,* ed. Myunster, Moscow, 1913, p. 56, cites the picture with a group of others as examples of Goncharova's "realistic" style. He compares the vibrant colors and realistic beauty of these paintings with those of van Gogh or Matisse.

2. It is not certain that the entry refers to the present picture. After the Paul Guillaume exhibition, the pictures were apparently sent back to Russia, but war broke out before they arrived (see Chamot, 1961, n.p.). The Germans seized the pictures, but Herwarth Walden of Der Sturm claimed ownership and was able to preserve them. After the war he returned them to the two artists. If the Guggenheim *Cats* did appear in the 1915 exhibition in Moscow, it must have been included in an early shipment of works that did reach Russia safely before the outbreak of hostilities. It is more likely, on the other hand, that one of Goncharova's other *Cats* (such as, for example, the picture mentioned in fn. 1 above) appeared in the 1915 show instead.

Adolph Gottlieb

Born March 1903, New York.
Died March 1974, New York.

62 The Sea Chest. 1942.

48.1172 x510

Oil on canvas, 26 x 34 (66 x 86.6)

Signed and dated l.r.: *Adolph Gottlieb* 42;
inscribed by the artist on reverse: *The Sea
Chest 1942 / Adolph Gottlieb.*

THE SEA CHEST 1942
ADOLPH GOTTLIEB

PROVENANCE:

Probably acquired directly from the artist by
Karl Nierendorf, New York, by 1948; acquired with the Estate of Karl Nierendorf,
1948.

CONDITION:

The work has received no treatment since
its acquisition.

The paint was thinly applied on a com-
mercially stretched canvas, and there are
slight stretcher impressions along the top
and left edges. All corners are somewhat
worn with loss of paint and ground, and the
edges are slightly worn with some abrasions.
There are ground cracks scattered over the
surface, but these have not penetrated the
paint layer. There is a 5 in. scratch in the
upper right corner, but the condition is
otherwise good. (Nov. 1973.)

178

W. Rubin first pointed to the stylistic continuity which characterizes Gottlieb's development from the Arizona still-lifes of 1938-39 to the more distinctive seaside still-lifes of 1939-40, and finally to his first pictographs of 1941 ("Adolph Gottlieb," *Art International,* vol. iii, no. 3/4, 1959, p. 36). The cacti in the desert pictures are usually arranged upon a table top, tipped up towards the picture plane, with glimpses of sea and sky behind. (See, for example, two unpublished works in the collection of Mrs. Esther Gottlieb, *Cactus Still-Life,* 1938, and *Cactus Arrangement,* 1938-39. Gottlieb's extensive pre-1941 oeuvre remains almost entirely unpublished.) The relationship of these sparsely arranged objects to the table upon which they rest is an essentially conventional one. In some of the seaside still-lifes of the following year, however, Gottlieb introduced a distinctly new element: the table is gone, and each individual object is placed in a box standing upon the beach. In *Souvenirs of the Sea,* 1939, for example (Collection Mrs. Esther Gottlieb, unpublished), three such boxes occupy about half of the picture surface; the sea, miniature sailboat, cliff, and sky act as a rather remote theatrical backdrop. In *Objects from the Sea,* 1939 (present whereabouts unknown), the boxes have been united into what Rubin has called "a large structure representing subdivided book-shelves." This structure occupies about two-thirds of the picture space, and the theatrical backdrop is even more remote. The pictographic grid structure of *The Eyes of Oedipus,* 1941, and subsequent works is, in some sense, as Rubin notes, a direct development out of this "compartmental system" which in the pictograph "cover[s] the entire surface" and is "deprived of its illusionistic depth."

The fact that Gottlieb in 1942 was still producing works such as *The Sea Chest* (so obviously reminiscent of *Objects from the Sea*) while already fully involved in his pictographic style suggests the extent to which he himself experienced the continuity which Rubin described. Thus, while Gottlieb's subject matter in the pictographs is so clearly different from that of the earlier still-lifes, the pictorial treatment of it develops directly out of this immediately preceding phase.

EXHIBITION:
New York, SRGM 195 (no cat.).

63   The Red Bird. 1944.

48.1172 X515

Oil on canvas, 40 x 30 (101.6 x 76.2)

Signed u.l.: *Adolph Gottlieb*. Not dated.

PROVENANCE:

Probably acquired directly from the artist by
Karl Nierendorf, New York, by 1948; acquired with the Estate of Karl Nierendorf,
1948.

CONDITION:

The work has received no treatment.

The edges and corners are in generally good
condition, apart from slight wear at the
upper corners and some rubs in the right
margin. There are several areas of crackle in
the paint layer, with some possible incipient
cleavage, but the condition in general is
good. (Nov. 1973.)

EXHIBITION:

New York, SRGM 200, *Adolph Gottlieb,* no. 4, repr. p. 29.

64   Augury. 1945.

48.1172 x516

Oil on canvas, 40 x 30 (101.6 x 76.1)

Signed l.l. of center: *Adolph Gottlieb*.
Not dated.

PROVENANCE:
Probably acquired directly from the artist by
Karl Nierendorf, New York, by 1948; acquired with the Estate of Karl Nierendorf,
1948.

CONDITION:
The work has received no treatment since
its acquisition.

The edges and corners are in generally good
condition, apart from slight wear along
the right edge. There is a faint 5 in. scratch
in the paint layer 11½ in. from the bottom
and 9½ in. from the left side. There are
several areas of crackle in the paint layer,
with some possible incipient cleavage, but
the condition in general is good. (Nov.
1973.)

Both *The Red Bird,* cat. no. 63, and *Augury* belong to Gottlieb's 1941-51 pictographic phrase. The artist's own explanations for his adoption of this style, a conscious decision, arrived at jointly with Rothko, to embark upon a series of works based upon classical mythology, have been extensively quoted and discussed in the literature on the artist. (See, in particular, *The New Decade,* ed. J. I. H. Bauer, Whitney Museum of American Art, New York, 1955, pp. 35-36; L. Alloway, "The New American Painting," *Art International,* vol. iii, no. 3/4, 1959, p. 23; W. Rubin, "Adolph Gottlieb," *Art International,* vol. iii, no. 3/4, 1959, p. 36; M. Friedman, *Adolph Gottlieb,* exhibition catalogue, Walker Art Center, Minneapolis, 1963, n.p.; D. Waldman, *Adolph Gottlieb,* exhibition catalogue, Whitney Museum of American Art and The Solomon R. Guggenheim Museum, New York, 1968, pp. 9 ff.; L. Alloway, "Melpomene and Graffiti," *Art International,* vol. xii, April 1968, pp. 21-24; J. Siegel, "Adolph Gottlieb: Two Views," *Arts Magazine,* vol. 42, February 1968, pp. 30-32.)

The pictorial continuity between this new style and the immediately preceding still-lifes has already been noted (see above cat. no. 62). The extent to which additional outside influences may have encouraged the development has been the subject of some dispute. Alloway (1959) convincingly suggested that Torres-García's works of the early 1930's must have played a formative role. Several of the Uruguayan artist's works, such as *Head,* 1930, or *Composition,* 1932, were indeed on exhibition at the Gallery of Living Art and elsewhere in New York, and it is difficult to imagine that Gottlieb was not aware of them. (For illustrations of some of Torres-García's most clearly similar works see, for example, catalogues of the Gallatin collection published in 1933 and 1940; also *The Latin American Collection of The Museum of Modern Art,* New York, 1943.) Torres-García's division of the canvas into an all-over grid of boxes in which fishes, fragments of anatomy, birds, and architectural or floral devices are displayed is so closely related to that of Gottlieb's works of the 1940's that it must have given impetus to the American artist's search for a new imagery. This seems especially true since Gottlieb's own recent work was, from a formal point of view, so clearly moving in the same direction already.

The insistence by some authors on the direct influence of North American Indian or Egyptian art on Gottlieb's pictographic language is, on the other hand, not so clearly demonstrable and has not been documented. Friedman's point (1963) that Gottlieb's pictographs are in a general sense a reflection of his wide-ranging explorations of many different art forms is probably an accurate one, although the specific relationship to traditions such as that of the Italian primitive predella panels (which Gottlieb often cited as an important precedent for his art) is difficult to sustain.

The actual use of the term "pictograph"—"A pictorial symbol or sign, a form of writing or record consisting of pictorial symbols" (*O.E.D.,* 1933)—was potentially misleading in that it carried with it the implication that the paintings were in some literary sense readable. Gottlieb took pains from the start to deny this, and Alloway (1968) has clearly stated the limits of meaning which these works contain: "Gottlieb . . . undoubtedly generates the atmosphere of meaning but, in fact, his sets of Pictographs are not transcribable. What he is doing is asserting the human by declaring his art, or Art, to be a symbolizing activity, but the basis of the combinations of signs is his own free associations or painterly improvisation." Alloway emphasizes, moreover, Gottlieb's insistence upon the anonymity, or lack of association, of his individual symbols: ". . . when [Gottlieb] happened to learn of pre-existing meanings attached to any of his pictographs, they became unusable. The signs needed to be evocative, but unassigned" (1968, p. 27. See also Rubin, p. 36: "The symbols of the Pictographs were selected by intuition, and constitute chains of 'associations'; they do not, however, form a rationalizable 'iconography'"). In this sense both *The Red Bird* and *Augury* are illustrative of Alloway's notion that the psychological atmosphere of myth and dream were central elements in Gottlieb's development of the pictograph as a mode of expression. The iconography of the individual motifs is impenetrable, but their combination and even the titles given to them result in the evocation of a "continuum of myth, partly archaic, partly the personal unconscious of the artist" (Alloway, unpublished notes, SRGM archives).

Balcomb Greene

Born May 1904, Niagara Falls, New York.
Lives in New York.

65   Composition. 1940.

40.848

Oil on canvas, 20 x 30 (50.5 x 76.0)

Not signed or dated.

PROVENANCE:
Purchased from the artist, 1940.

CONDITION:

At an unrecorded date the work was lined with wax resin and placed on a new stretcher. Some minor touches of inpainting may date from the same period.

Apart from some minor wear at the edges, the condition is excellent. (July 1974.)

EXHIBITIONS:

Portland, Or., SRGM 19-T, New York, SRGM 30 (no cats.); New York, Whitney Museum of American Art, *Balcomb Greene* (AFA traveling exhibition), May 23-July 23, 1961, no. 6, repr.; Albany, N.Y., SRGM 264-T (no cat.).

66   Criss Cross. 1940.

40.847

Oil on canvas, 19⅞ x 30 (50.5 x 76.1)

Not signed or dated.

PROVENANCE:
Purchased from the artist, 1940.

CONDITION:

The work has received no treatment since its acquisition.

Apart from some general soil and some scattered abrasions in the gray background, the condition is good. (Dec. 1972.)

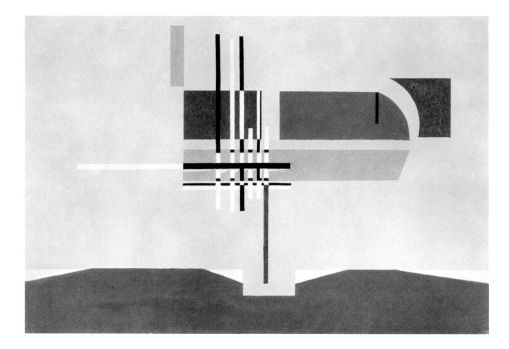

Juan Gris

(pseud. of Jose Victoriano Gonzales).

Born March 1887, Madrid.
Died May 1927, Paris.

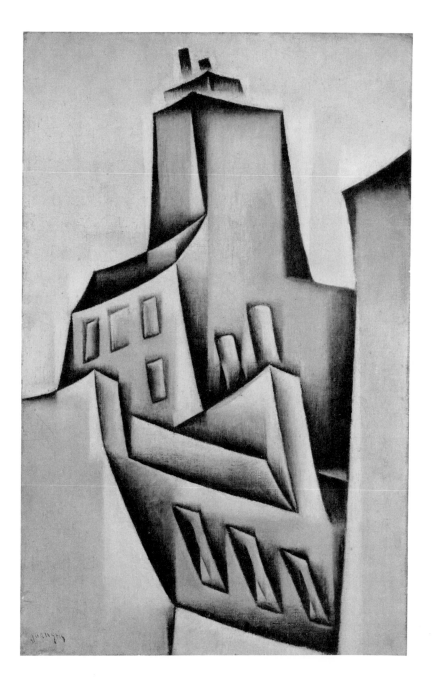

67 Houses in Paris. 1911.
*(Rooftops Barcelona; The Tower;
Rooftops; Les Toits).*

48.1172 x33

Oil on canvas, 20⅝ x 13½ (52.4 x 34.2)

Signed l.l.: *Juan Gris.* Not dated.

PROVENANCE:
Marcel Duchamp, Paris, possibly gift of the
artist (information supplied by Cooper,
correspondence with the author, July 1971);
Howard Putzel, San Francisco (Cooper, July
1971); Josef von Sternberg, Hollywood
(1948 correspondence in Museum files indicates that the picture was once in von
Sternberg's collection, information corroborated by Cooper, July 1971); Nierendorf
Gallery, New York; acquired with the
Estate of Karl Nierendorf, 1948.

CONDITION:
The painting was lined prior to its acquisition by the Museum. An old repair in the
upper right portion of the canvas apparently
necessitated extensive inpainting. The shaft
of sky between the 2 buildings and part of
the black shadow to the left of it (a section
4½ in. long, 3 in. wide at lowest point, 1¾
in. wide at its highest point) is entirely
repainted.

The application of paint overall is thin, especially in the black areas, and there has
been some abrasion, but the paint film is in
general well preserved. (Dec. 1971.)

The identification of the scene depicted has posed some problems. When the
picture was acquired it carried the title *The Tower.* It was exhibited several
times between 1953 and 1955 under the title *Rooftops Barcelona.* By 1957 this
title had been changed to *Rooftops*—the title by which it has since been known.
Since Gris lived in Paris from 1906 onwards and did not return to Spain, there
is no reason to suppose that the scene has any Spanish connections. Moreover,
the buildings represented are clearly recognizable as examples of architecture
to be found in the neighborhood of Gris' Paris studio at 13, rue Ravignan.

At least five other works depicting houses in this area, all correctly identified
as houses in Paris, throw light not only on the subject but on the date of the
Guggenheim painting. An oil, signed and dated 1911 and called *Houses in
Paris,* is in the Sprengel Collection, Hanover (D. H. Kahnweiler, *Juan Gris:
His Life and Work,* revised ed., London, 1969, repr. color, p. 13). A second oil,
Houses in Paris, dedicated to Picabia and dated by Kahnweiler 1912, is in a private collection (Kahnweiler, 2nd edition, London, 1947, pl. 3). A third oil was
destroyed in World War II (formerly Galerie Simon, 38⅝ x 25⅝ in., 98 x 65
cm., photo no. 5012; I am indebted to M. Potter for bringing this work to my
attention; according to Cooper, this picture appeared in the March 1912 *Salon
des Indépendants*). A pencil drawing formerly M. Knoedler & Co., Inc., now
The Museum of Modern Art, Joan and Lester Avnet Collection, entitled *Rue
Ravignan,* was exhibited in Dortmund in 1965 (*Juan Gris,* Museum am Ostwall, October 23-December 4, no. 103). A second pencil drawing entitled *Place
Ravignan* is dated 1912 by Kahnweiler (1969, p. 226, whereabouts unknown).
The architecture in all five works is strikingly similar and supports the identifi-
cation of the Guggenheim picture as *Houses in Paris.*

All six works share to some degree the characteristics of Gris' earliest
experiments with Cubism, which date from no later than 1911. The Guggenheim picture retains to a considerable extent the conventional shading and

modeling of three-dimensional form, but begins to show hints of Cubist definition, especially in the lower set of windows. The Sprengel painting, with its flattened street lamps and sequential triangular shadows, as well as its more arbitrary treatment of light sources, is a slightly later development. In the picture dedicated to Picabia, further development is visible in the much stronger emphasis on diagonal planes and in the breakdown of modeled forms into fragmented flat ones, especially at the lower left. In the drawings the breakdown of form is carried perhaps further. In the Avnet Collection drawing, although the house has a solid three-dimensional form and the fence recedes in space, the strong emphasis on repeated triangular shaded areas totally destroys the space between the house, tree, and fence, flattening the forms into one another. As in the other drawing, the tree trunk is broken down completely into a sequence of triangular planes and only at the top does the stylized foliage re-emerge. The modeled structure of the houses on the right is still intact, but the prominent triangular shadows again threaten to break down their relation to the space in which they stand.

These developments are eventually consistently and articulately applied in a work such as *Still Life* in The Museum of Modern Art, New York (Kahnweiler, 1969, p. 238), which is signed and dated 1911 and in which modeling has been abandoned in favor of a pattern of flattened, diagonally arranged shapes and lines arbitrarily lighted from several different directions. The destroyed rue Ravignan oil cited above, which is in some respects an elaboration of the version dedicated to Picabia, is sufficiently consistent in its application of these Cubist principles to have been painted either before or after The Museum of Modern Art *Still Life*. Its date is therefore difficult to establish, although according to Cooper's contention that it appeared in the 1912 *Salon*, it would have to have been completed by February of that year, and it probably does date from early in 1912.

The 1911 date of The Museum of Modern Art *Still Life* provides a firm *terminus post quem* for the other five rue Ravignan scenes and makes the Kahnweiler date of 1912 for two of them unacceptable. Since the Sprengel picture is also dated 1911, it is clear that all five must be dated in that year. Cooper has concurred that these three oils were painted in 1911, although he dates the destroyed work January-February 1912.

EXHIBITIONS:

New York, SRGM 74, 78 (checklists); 79 (checklist; withdrawn Oct. 28); 84, 87 (checklists); Boston, SRGM 90-T (no cat.); Montreal, SRGM 93-T, no. 14; London, SRGM 104-T, no. 25; New York, SRGM 118, p. 69, repr.; 129 (checklist); Philadelphia, SRGM 134-T, no. 39; New York, SRGM 144 (checklist); New York, Leonard Hutton Galleries, *Albert Gleizes and the Section d'Or,* Oct. 28-Nov. 21, 1964, no. 27, repr. p. 23; New York, SRGM 151, 153 (checklists); 173, no. 17, repr.; Dortmund, Museum am Ostwall, *Juan Gris,* Oct. 23-Dec. 4, 1965, traveled to Cologne, Wallraf-Richartz-Museum, Dec. 27, 1965-Feb. 13, 1966, no. 6, repr.; New York, SRGM 196 (checklist); 202, p. 102, repr. color; The Baltimore Museum of Art, *From El Greco to Pollock, Early and Late Works by European and American Artists,* Oct. 22-Dec. 8, 1968, no. 107, repr. p. 130; New York, SRGM 221 (no cat.); 232, pp. 144-145, repr. color; 240 (no cat.); 241, pp. 144-145, repr. color; 251, 266 (no cats.).

68   Newspaper and Fruit
Dish. March 1916.
*(Printer's Ink; Abstraction in Blue and
Yellow; Still Life).*

53.1341

Oil on canvas, 18⅛ x 14⅞ (46 x 37.8)

Signed and dated on reverse: *Juan Gris /
3-16 / 1.*

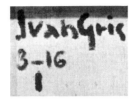

PROVENANCE:

Galerie l'Effort Moderne (Léonce Rosenberg), Paris (information supplied by D. H. Kahnweiler, correspondence with the author, March 1971, and D. Cooper, July 1971);[1]

purchased from Rosenberg by Katherine S. Dreier, West Redding, Connecticut (Cooper, July 1971), by 1921 (Worcester Museum exhibition catalogue);[2] Gift of the Estate of Katherine S. Dreier, 1953.

CONDITION:

Some time before 1953 a repair measuring ⅝ x ⅞ in. and located in the green triangle at the center of the canvas was made. The area was inpainted (clearly visible in photographs). The painting was cleaned in 1953, at which time some minor inpainting along the edges was necessary.

With the exception of some minor stress cracks in a few areas, the condition is excellent. (Dec. 1971.)

There are five other known oils of March 1916: (1) *Newspaper and Fruit Dish* (Yale University Art Gallery, New Haven, D. H. Kahnweiler, *Juan Gris: His Life and Work,* 2nd ed., London, 1947, repr. no. 27); (2) *The Lamp* (Philadelphia Museum of Art, Louise and Walter Arensberg Collection, J. T. Soby, *Juan Gris,* New York, 1958, repr. p. 54); (3) *Fruit Dish and Bottle* (Smith College Museum of Art, Northampton, Massachusetts, oval, *19th and 20th Century Paintings from the Collection of the Smith College Museum of Art,* Northampton, 1970, repr. no. 26); (4) *Newspaper and Bottle* (Detroit Institute of Arts, *Bulletin of the Detroit Institute of Arts,* vol. 44, no. 2, 1965, repr. p. 36); (5) *Fruit Dish on a Table* (Collection Gérard Bonnier, Stockholm, Cooper, *Cubist Epoch,* 1970, color pl. 273, p. 225). I am indebted to Cooper for bringing nos. 4 and 5 to my attention.

In all five still-lifes the same table, the same background door, and substantial areas of pointillist brush stroke appear. The newspaper appears in all but the Philadelphia and Smith College pictures; the compotier in all but the Detroit painting—where a bottle takes its place—and the Philadelphia one—where a lamp is substituted. All but the Guggenheim picture also contain a glass.

1. The picture does not appear among the Léonce Rosenberg photographic archives in Paris, but these are incomplete.

2. It has not been possible to establish with complete certainty whether the picture belonged to Dreier personally, or rather to the Société Anonyme. However, its presence in the 1952-53 exhibition (*Her Own Collection . . .*) would suggest that it was indeed her personal property. Further documentation on the entire question of Société Anonyme-Dreier ownership of works of art will probably emerge from the archives of Yale University presently being organized and catalogued under the direction of R. L. Herbert.

68

The Guggenheim work is undoubtedly the least complex of the six. The chronology of the group as a whole is difficult to establish since the elaborations and variations of the theme do not constitute an easily discernible stylistic development. The Guggenheim picture was, however, probably followed by the Yale one, to which it is compositionally closest. If the Yale picture is cropped approximately eight inches on the left and ten inches at the bottom it essentially represents, with some variations, the Guggenheim composition in reverse, and the colors in the two works are similar. It is probable that the

Guggenheim picture was a preparatory work for the more complex Yale composition. (Cooper concurred that the two pictures must be related in this way; correspondence with the author, July 1971.)

In this connection it is interesting to note that Dreier, who owned the Guggenheim picture by 1921, called it *Printer's Ink*. By 1926 she had acquired the Yale painting too, and the relationship between the two works obviously impressed itself upon her because she henceforth called them *Abstraction in Yellow and Blue 1 & 2* or, by 1932, *Study for Still Life in Yellow and Blue* (see below EXHIBITIONS) and *Still Life in Yellow and Blue*. The Yale picture, like the Guggenheim one, bears a signature and date on the reverse; beneath the date there is, instead of the "*1*" a "*2ᵉ*." Moreover, the Bonnier work is inscribed "*3-16-3ᵉ*" and the Philadelphia picture "*3-16-4ᵉ*." Since it was not Gris' practice to number his production from month to month, it seems likely that these numbers refer specifically to the chronological relationship between these four canvases. (I am indebted to M. Potter for drawing the inscriptions on the Bonnier and Philadelphia works to my attention.)

Herbert has pointed out that Gris' use of dabbed brush strokes, starting in 1914, constituted a "decorative homage to Neo-Impressionism" and did not reflect an interest in color theory (p. 232). The extent to which Seurat's technique occupied Gris' mind during the years 1915-16 is reflected in a letter he wrote to Kahnweiler on December 14, 1915: ". . . I can't find room in my pictures for that sensitive and sensuous side which I feel should always be there. . . . I find my pictures excessively cold. But Ingres too is cold, and yet he is good. Seurat also. Yes, Seurat also, although I dislike the meticulous element in his pictures almost as much as my own . . ." (*Letters of Juan Gris 1913-1927*, trans. Cooper, collected and edited by D. H. Kahnweiler, London, 1956). All six of the March 1916 still-lifes suggest Gris' consciousness of Seurat's legacy to which he refers in this letter.

EXHIBITIONS:

Mass., Worcester Art Museum, *Exhibition of Paintings by Members of the Société Anonyme*, Nov. 3-Dec. 5, 1921, no. 20 (*Printer's Ink*);[3] The Brooklyn Museum of Art, *An International Exhibition of Modern Art*, Nov. 19, 1926-Jan. 1, 1927, no. 206 (*Abstraction in Yellow and Blue, No. 1*); New York, The Anderson Galleries, *An International Exhibition of Modern Art*, Jan. 25-Feb. 5, 1927, no. 120 (*Abstraction in Yellow and Blue, No. 1*); New York, Marie Harriman Gallery, *Juan Gris*, opened Feb. 5, 1932, no. 20 (*Study for Still Life in Yellow and Blue*); New Haven, Yale University Art Gallery, *In Memory of Katherine S. Dreier 1877-1952: Her Own Collection of Modern Art*, Dec. 15, 1952-Feb. 1, 1953, no. 31 (*Abstraction in Blue and Yellow, No. 1*); New York, SRGM 79 (checklist, *Still Life*); Toronto, SRGM 85-T, no. 17; Vancouver, SRGM 88-T, no. 13, repr.; Boston, SRGM 90-T (no cat.); Montreal, SRGM

3. Although the painting is not illustrated in the catalogue, and the title used is otherwise unknown, a label from the back of the canvas carries information that corresponds precisely with that in the Worcester Art Museum's registration files. The records establish that the present painting was shipped to Worcester at the time of the exhibition, and that it was the only painting by Gris then present in the museum.

93-T, no. 15; New York, SRGM 95 (checklist); London, SRGM 104-T, no. 26; New York, SRGM 129, 196 (checklists); 199, *Neo-Impressionism,* no. 171, repr.; Columbus, Ohio, SRGM 207-T, p. 21, repr.; New York, SRGM 227 (no cat.); 232, p. 146, repr. p. 147; 240 (no cat.); 241, p. 146, repr. p. 147; 251, 266 (no cats.).

REFERENCES:

R. L. Herbert, *Neo-Impressionism,* exhibition catalogue, New York, 1968, no. 171; U. Apollonio, *Fauves e Cubisti,* Bergamo, 1959, repr. color, p. 66.

---

69   Bottle and Glass. February 1917.
(Bouteille et verre; Fruit Bowl; Black, White, Tan; Glass and Carafe).

38.237

Oil on wood panel, 21⅜ x 12⅝ (54.3 x 32.1)

Signed and dated l.l.: *Juan Gris / 2-1917.*

PROVENANCE:

Galerie l'Effort Moderne (Léonce Rosenberg), Paris (information supplied by D. Cooper, correspondence with the author, July 1971);[1] Pierre Faure, Paris, by 1933 (Kunsthaus Zürich exhibition catalogue); Rose Valland, Paris, by 1938; purchased from Valland by Solomon R. Guggenheim, October 1938; Gift of Solomon R. Guggenheim, 1938.

CONDITION:

The picture has not been cleaned since its acquisition, but a clear synthetic varnish has been applied. Under UV some retouchings within the various forms and along their edges flouresce considerably. It is difficult to say whether these are the work of the artist or later repaint.

The condition in general is good, although there is some horizontal cracking in the paint film throughout, and some minor abrasions and paint losses at the edges. (Dec. 1971.)

The picture is closely related to a work of January 1917, *Siphon and Glass,* now in the collection of Richard Weil, St. Louis (formerly Galerie Simon, Paris, photo no. 5107). Two other works of February 1917 are considerably more complex in compositional structure as well as in color: *Bottle and Fruit Dish* (The Minneapolis Institute of Arts, Cooper, *Cubist Epoch,* 1970, color pl. 274, p. 225) and *The Pot of Strawberry Jam* (Kunstmuseum Basel). However, in April 1917 Gris returned to many of the basic ideas of the Guggenheim painting in his composition of *Newspaper, Bottle, and Glass* (Private Collection, Bern, formerly Léonce Rosenberg, photo no. 014-N-945).

1. The painting does not appear among the Rosenberg photographic archives in Paris, but these are incomplete.

EXHIBITIONS:

Kunsthaus Zürich, *Juan Gris,* Apr. 2-26, 1933, no. 67 ("*Bouteille et verre,* coll. M. Faure, Paris;" this entry was identified with the Guggenheim picture by Cooper, correspondence 1971); New York, SRGM 74 (checklist, *Black, White, Tan*); 78 (checklist, *Fruit Bowl*; the title by which it has been known in all subsequent SRGM publications); 83 (no cat.); 87 (checklist); 89 (no cat.); 95, 97, 112 (checklists); Boston, 119-T, no. 14; New York, SRGM 129, 144, 151, 153 (checklists); 173, no. 42, repr.; 202, p. 36, repr.; 227 (no cat.); 232, p. 148, repr.; 240 (no cat.); 241, p. 148, repr.; 266 (no cat.).

70 Fruit Dish on a Check
Tablecloth. November 1917.
(Pink and Green; Compotier).

38.238

Oil on wood panel, 31¾ x 21¼ (80.6 x 53.9)

Signed and dated l.l.: *Juan Gris / Paris 11-17.*

PROVENANCE:

Galerie l'Effort Moderne (Léonce Rosenberg), Paris (information supplied by D. H. Kahnweiler, correspondence with the author, June 1971, and by Cooper, correspondence with the author, July 1971);[1] Pierre Faure, Paris (Cooper, July 1971); Rose Valland, Paris, by 1938; purchased from Valland by Solomon R. Guggenheim, October 1938; Gift of Solomon R. Guggenheim, 1938.

CONDITION:

In 1955 some slight warping of the wood panel was corrected with a press.

Cracking of the wood along the grain has resulted in vertical cracks in the paint film. There is considerable abrasion, with some paint loss. Certain glossy areas of the paint surface are soft and have not completely dried, making the surface extremely vulnerable. Dirt and fibers are imbedded in the paint film in these areas. This unusual phenomenon may be due to the artist's use of a plasticizer (castor oil?) mixed with the pigment. Heavy application of paint in these areas may have prevented the wood panel from completely absorbing the vehicle. Owing to its fragile condition, the painting has not been cleaned. (Dec. 1971.)

The painting was, upon its acquisition by Solomon Guggenheim, identified only as an abstract composition with the title *Pink and Green* (notice of acquisition in Foundation files dated 10/24/38; also *Art of Tomorrow*, 1939, no. 238). Kahnweiler correctly identified the work as *Fruit Dish on a Check Tablecloth*, and all subsequent publications have done likewise.

Other paintings of November 1917 which are closely related to the present work are *Bottle of Beaune and Fruit Dish* (formerly Collection Douglas Cooper, Kahnweiler, 1947, repr. facing p. 3); *Violin and Newspaper* (Private Collection, New York, J. T. Soby, *Juan Gris,* exhibition catalogue, N.Y., 1958, repr. p. 80); *Fruit Dish, Pipe, and Newspaper* (Kunstmuseum Basel, Kahnweiler, revised ed., New York, 1968, color pl. p. 139).

EXHIBITIONS:

New York, SRGM 74, 78, 79 (checklists); 81, 83 (no cats.); 87 (checklist); 89 (no cat.); 95, 97, 107 (checklists); New York, The Museum of Modern Art, *Juan Gris,* Apr. 9-June 1, 1958, p. 83, repr.; New York, SRGM 118, 129 (checklists); Philadelphia, SRGM 134-T, no. 40, repr.; New York, SRGM 144 (checklist); Mass., Worcester Art Museum, SRGM 148-T, no. 14, repr. p. 27; New York, SRGM 151, 153 (checklists); 173, no. 43, repr. p. 44; 196 (checklist); 202, p. 37, repr.; 227 (no cat.); 232, p. 149, repr.; 240 (no cat.); 241, p. 149, repr.; 251 (no cat.); Cleveland, SRGM 258-T, pl. 15; New York, SRGM 266 (no cat.).

REFERENCES:

D. H. Kahnweiler, *Juan Gris: His Life and Work,* 2nd ed., London, 1947, color pl. 2; SRGM *Handbook,* 1959, p. 70, repr. p. 71; SRGM *Handbook,* 1970, p. 149, repr.

1. The picture does not appear among the Rosenberg photographic archives in Paris, but these are incomplete.

Jean Hélion

Born April 1904, Couterne (Orne), France.
Lives in Paris.

71   Composition. April-May 1934.[1]

61.1586

Oil on canvas, 56¾ x 78¾ (144.3 x 199.8)

Inscribed by the artist on reverse (partially obscured by stretcher): *Hélion / Paris 34 / Top Haut.*

PROVENANCE:

Purchased from the artist by Paul Nelson, Paris, September 1935 (information from Hélion's working diary, confirmed by Paul Nelson, correspondence with the author, 1974); purchased from Paul Nelson by

Joseph Cantor, Carmel, Indiana, June 1961; purchased from Cantor, July 1961.

CONDITION:

The work has received no treatment.

Drying cracks are present in certain specific colored forms (the gray form at upper left, the blue-green strip upper center, the brown form lower center, the dark gray form to its right, blue-green and gray areas lower right). The overall condition is good. (May 1974.)

1. These precise dates were supplied by the artist, whose working diary contains detailed information on the sequence of his works, exhibitions in which the picture appeared, and collections to which they were sold. Hélion kindly provided the author with the entry on the Guggenheim picture, as well as information on several related works.

fig. a.
Hélion, final study for *Composition*, charcoal and water-
color on tracing paper, 12⅝ x 17¾ in., 32 x 45 cm.,
Collection of the artist.

Hélion's abstract compositions or *Equilibres* of 1932-33 were characterized by
sparsely arranged single configurations upon a unified ground. (See, for example, *Composition,* present whereabouts unknown, *Abstraction Création,*
no. 2, repr. p. 21; *Red Tensions,* Philadelphia Museum of Art, Louise and
Walter Arensberg Collection; *Equilibrium,* The Denver Art Museum.) These
compositions were all small in scale (approximately 24 x 30 in., 60 x 76 cm.).

In the spring of 1934 the artist for the first time combined several configurations into a densely organized all-over design of interconnected forms. The first
of these was extremely small in scale (*Composition:* ca. 8¼ x 10⅝ in., 21 x 27
cm., formerly Collection Pegeen Vail). This was followed in March by a large
painting now in the collection of Mr. and Mrs. Burton Tremaine (*Abstraction
Création,* no. 3, repr. p. 24, 51½ x 63¾ in., 130.8 x 161.9 cm.). The Guggenheim
painting which followed was somewhat larger and was seen by the artist as a
significant departure in terms of scale from all his previous work. His diary
entry for it reads in part: *"Mon 1ᵉʳ grand tableau. quelle envie me tourmenta de
le peindre! Je m'en suis tiré assez vite et bien. J'avais acheté à credit toile et
couleur. . . ."* A month later he completed a second large-scale work, closely
related to the Guggenheim picture though slightly smaller (Fine Arts Gallery
of San Diego, California, 51 x 76½ in., 129.5 x 194.3 cm.).

These four, and other large-scale works such as *Ile de France* of early 1935
(Tate Gallery, London), are composed of interlocking elements distributed in
an all-over design. They constitute Hélion's most fully developed expressions
of his notion of equilibrium. (For a detailed and illuminating discussion of
this 1932-35 phase in Hélion's oeuvre, see Schipper, pp. 107-125.) The compositions were almost always carefully worked out in a series of preparatory

studies, and four such studies for the Guggenheim painting are preserved in the artist's collection (fig. a is the final study for this work; for a discussion of how Hélion used the preparatory drawing stage towards his development of the final composition, see the artist's "Avowals and Comments," *The Painter's Object*, London, 1937, pp. 31-33). Hélion has described his development from the single isolated forms of 1932-33 to the more complex configurations of 1934-35 as one in which "elements, first dissociated, gather and combine to form 'figures.' Abstract figures, of course, deriving from nothing else than basic plastic elements. These figures became for me units, beings, that I kept on developing and associating in new ways. . . . All my evolution has been of that type: from single, to several; simple to complex; and back towards simple and single" (*Albright-Knox Gallery Notes*, 1970, p. 15).

By late in 1935 Hélion did indeed start to break down the elements again into individual figures. In works such as *The Three Figures* of November 1935 (Private Collection, Paris, *Hélion*, Grand Palais, exhibition catalogue, Paris, 1970, repr. p. 26, top, erroneously dated 1934), the forms are structured in such a way as to suggest something of what Hélion described as "abstract beings," a development which ultimately, by 1939, led him back to actual figuration.

EXHIBITIONS:

Paris, Galerie des "Cahiers d'Art," *Hans Arp-Ghika, Jean Hélion, S. H. Taueber-Arp*, July 3-Aug. 2, 1934 (no cat.);[2] Kunstmuseum Luzern, *Thèse, Antithèse, Synthèse*, Feb. 24-Mar. 31, 1935, no. 50 ("*Peinture, 1934*");[2] New York, SRGM 137 (no cat.); 144, 151, 153 (checklists); New York, Gallery of Modern Art, *Paintings by Jean Hélion, 1928-1964*, Nov. 3-Dec. 2, 1964, no. 6, repr.; New York, SRGM 173, no. 62, repr. color; 195 (no cat.); 196 (checklist); Columbus, Ohio, SRGM 207-T, p. 34, repr. color; New York, SRGM 227 (no cat.); 232, p. 158, repr. color p. 159; Paris, Grand Palais, *Hélion: cent tableaux 1928-1970*, Dec. 11, 1970-Feb. 1, 1971, repr. p. 25; New York, SRGM 241, p. 158, repr. color p. 159; 260 (no cat.).

REFERENCES:

G. Grigson, "Painting and Sculpture," *The Arts Today*, London, 1935, repr. opp. p. 92; S. J. W[oods], "Why Abstract?," *Decoration*, London, Mar. 1936, no. 11, repr. p. 44; T. M. Messer, *Elements of Modern Painting*, New York, 1961, n.p., repr. color; D. Robbins, *Painting between the Wars*, New York, 1966, p. 45, repr. color slide; New York, SRGM *Handbook*, 1970, p. 158, repr. color p. 159; "Letters from 31 Artists to the Albright-Knox Art Gallery," ed. E. Moore, *Albright-Knox Gallery Notes*, vol. xxxi, no. 2 and vol. xxxii, no. 2, Spring 1970, p. 15; M. S. Schipper, *Jean Hélion: The Abstract Years, 1929-1939*, unpublished Ph.D. dissertation, University of California at Los Angeles, 1974, pp. 115-117.

2. The picture's appearance in this exhibition is documented in the artist's working diary.

Alexej Jawlensky

Born March 1864, Torzok, Government of Tver, Russia.
Died March 1941, Wiesbaden.

72 Helene with Colored Turban. 1910.
*(Helene mit buntem Turban; Helen mit
rotem Turban; Helene with Red Turban).*

65.1773

Oil on board, 37⅛ x 31⅞ (94.2 x 81)

Signed and dated u.l.: *A. Jawlensky / 1910*;
inscribed on reverse, not in the artist's hand:
No. 19 1910 / Helene mit / buntem Turban.
(According to Andreas Jawlensky [corres-
pondence with the author, January 1974],
this is the handwriting of a Fr. Kümmel,
who helped Jawlensky to catalogue his
pictures.)

PROVENANCE:

Estate of the artist, 1941-61; purchased from
the estate by Galerie Wilhelm Grosshennig,
Dusseldorf, 1961; purchased from Grosshennig by Lock Galleries, New York, 1962;
Lock Galleries, New York, 1962-65;[1] with
Leonard Hutton Galleries, New York, 1965;
purchased from Hutton, 1965.

CONDITION:

At an unknown date, prior to acquisition
by the Museum, many small losses in the
background and some in the skirt were
inpainted.

3 abrasions are especially noticeable: a 2½
in. abrasion running from the top of the
canvas down between the "n" and the "s"
of the signature; a 2 in. one running horizontally from the center of the sitter's left
cheek into the ear; a ¾ in. one running vertically through the sitter's left eyebrow. 3
distracting vertical scratches through the
pigment to the board are visible: (1) from
the sitter's right hand down to the skirt;
(2) a 10 in. scratch running from above to
below the left forearm; (3) slightly to the
right of (2) a 5 in. scratch running upwards
from the upper edge of the forearm. In the
lower left corner there are cracks in the
veneer indicating a possible shrinkage of the
surface. The entire upper portion of the
figure's blouse reveals traction cracks. The
condition as a whole is fair. (July 1972.)

As Washton first pointed out, the picture was clearly influenced by Matisse's
portrait of Madame Matisse, *Red Madras Headdress* (Barnes Foundation,
Merion, Pennsylvania), and there are striking similarities between the two
works, although the use of color in each is, predictably, totally different. It
has so far proved impossible to establish with certainty when Jawlensky might
have seen the Matisse. He did visit the latter's studio in Paris late in 1907, and
since the work probably dates from that autumn or early winter, he probably
saw it on that occasion. (The painting was almost certainly included in
Matisse's one-man show at Paul Cassirer in Berlin in the winter of 1908-09,
but Jawlensky could not have seen it there since, according to information
provided by C. Weiler [in conversation with the author, May 1974], he did not
go to Berlin before 1913.)

Helene Nesnakomoff was born ca. 1880 of Ukranian peasant parents and
was brought up from infancy in the household of Marianne van Werefkin's
father, a high-ranking military commander. Jawlensky and Werefkin met and
became close friends in St. Petersburg ca. 1891 when she was a private pupil
of the painter Ilya Repin, teacher at the Imperial Art Academy, and Jawlensky,
an army officer, had enrolled in evening classes. Werefkin's father died in the

1. The picture was owned by Charles Lock during this entire period, although it appears in
   the 1964 Pasadena exhibition catalogue as jointly owned by him and Stephen Silagy. The
   latter had the work on consignment for a short time but never actually owned it (correspondence with Lock, 1972).

winter of 1895-96; that same year Jawlensky, Werefkin, and Helene left for Munich and established a household together that they maintained until 1922 when Jawlensky finally broke off with Werefkin and married Helene. Andreas, Jawlensky's only child, was born to Helene in January 1902 in Anspaki, Latvia, where the three had gone in 1901. At the outbreak of the war in 1914 all four fled to Switzerland and lived successively in St. Prex, Zurich, and Ascona. After their marriage in 1922 Helene and Alexej settled permanently in Wiesbaden where he died in 1941. In 1957 she moved with her son, Andreas, to Ascona and later to Locarno where she died in 1965.

72a   Portrait of a Young Girl. ca. 1909.
(reverse of cat. no. 72)

Oil on board, 37⅛ x 31⅞ (94.2 x 81). Since the edges of the background are only sketchily painted, the dimensions of the whole board are given.

Signed u.l.: *A. Jawlensky*; inscribed c.l., over red background, not in the artist's hand: *No. 19 1910 / Helene mit / buntem Turban.* This inscription refers to the portrait on the obverse.

CONDITION:

The work has received no treatment.

There is considerable paint loss from flaking in the red background to the left of the figure; this condition is stable. An area in the lower right corner, 3 in. from the right edge and 4½ in. from the bottom to 10 in. from the right edge and 4½ in. from bottom, shows considerable cracking in the pigment, possibly from shrinkage of the support. There are 3 horizontal scratches in the garment—each approximately 3 in. long —running from the figure's right shoulder to her face; the uppermost of the 3 has transfer material (wool or cotton?) attached to it. A large and distracting area of the figure's left forearm has extensive transfer material (white paint) adhering to the surface; the picture was apparently at some point placed against a wet painting. A scratch with transfer material runs from below the *"ban"* of *"Turban"* through the right hand of the figure. 4 in. below this is another scratch, approximately 3½ in. long. The rapid sketchiness of the technique has intentionally left large areas of the board unpainted. (There is no ground.) However, there are also many small paint losses throughout, especially in the garment. The condition in general is fair. (July 1972.)

According to Andreas Jawlensky (correspondence with the author, January 1974), the sketch dates from ca. 1906 and is a portrait of a neighbor, Resi, who frequently sat for the artist in the years 1906-09. (See, for example, two 1906 portraits in C. Weiler, *Alexej Jawlensky*, Cologne, 1959, nos. 22, 23, pp. 227-228.) The style of the sketch seems much more closely related, however, to several works of 1909. In particular, it may be compared to *Girl with Green Stole*, 1909 (Collection Galerie Wilhelm Grosshennig, Dusseldorf, E. von Rathke, *Alexej Jawlensky*, Hanau, 1968, pl. 11); *Girl with Gray Apron* (Private Collection, repr. Galerie Beyeler, Basel, *Alexej von Jawlensky, 1864-1941*, 1957, no. 40); and most compellingly with *Girl with Peonies*, 1909 (Städtisches Museum Wuppertal, Weiler, op. cit., repr. color p. 75), all of which also portray the

72a

neighbor Resi. The Guggenheim picture might even be a preliminary study for the latter, or else another portrait of the same Bavarian girl. Weiler (in conversation with the author, May 1974) concurred with the ca. 1909 dating of the Guggenheim *Portrait,* as well as with its relationship to *Girl with Peonies.*

EXHIBITIONS:

Munich, Haus der Kunst, *Der Blaue Reiter,* Sept.-Oct. 1949, no. 36;[2] Dusseldorf, Galerie Wilhelm Grosshennig, *Sonderausstellung Alexej von Jawlensky,* Oct. 3-31, 1961, repr. color cover; Dusseldorf, Galerie Wilhelm Grosshennig, *Auserlesene Meisterwerke des 19. und 20. Jahrhunderts,* June-Aug. 1962, repr.; Pasadena Art Museum, *Alexei Jawlensky: A Centennial Exhibition,* Apr. 14-May 19, 1964, no. 18; New York, Leonard Hutton Galleries, *A Centennial Exhibition of Paintings by Alexej Jawlensky, 1864-1941,* Apr. 17-Mar. 1965, no. 14, repr. color; The Baltimore Museum of Art, *A Centennial Exhibition of Paintings by Alexej Jawlensky, 1864-1941, A Selection from Each Year 1901-1917,* Apr. 20-May 23, 1965, no. 10; New York, SRGM 187 (checklist, commentary, repr. color); 196 (checklist); 221 (no cat.); 232, 241, p. 166, repr. color p. 167; Cleveland, SRGM 258-T, no. 3 repr.

REFERENCES:

C. Weiler, *Alexej Jawlensky,* Cologne, 1959, p. 230, no. 55, repr. color p. 79; [R-C. Washton], "Helene with Red Turban," *Gauguin and the Decorative Style,* New York, 1966, n.p.

2. The catalogue entry includes a reference to the *Neue Künstler Vereinigung,* Munich, 1911. It has so far not been possible to verify this from the *NKV* catalogues, and it seems to be a mistaken identification with *NKV, III. Ausstellung,* Dec. 1911, no. 33, *Im Turban,* which is not the present painting.

Wassily Kandinsky

Born December 1866, Moscow.
Died December 1944, Paris.

NOTE: Kandinsky kept his own handwritten "catalogue" or Handlist in six notebooks, now preserved in the collection of his widow, Nina Kandinsky. K. C. E. Lindsay first studied these notebooks and presented a great deal of the information contained in them in his unpublished Ph.D. dissertation, University of Wisconsin at Madison, 1951. I am much indebted to Nina Kandinsky and to Lindsay, who granted me permission to study his microfilms of these notebooks presently deposited with limited access in the library of The Museum of Modern Art. Of the six, one is in Russian, the others either in German or French. (For a description of the division of materials within the six books, see Grohmann, 1959, p. 329.) The Handlist includes various categories; only the following are relevant in the context of this catalogue: over seven hundred and thirty oil paintings of 1909-44 (a large proportion, but by no means all, of the artist's works in this medium; unrecorded works are especially frequent in the period up to 1920); seven hundred and thirty watercolors of 1910-44 (this too is an incomplete list, and the items up to ca. 1922 are not consistently numbered); one hundred and thirty-two small tempera paintings (*farbige Zeichnungen*) of 1901-08; one hundred and eight small oil studies (*kleine Oelstudien,* not dated, but datable from 1900-08); seventeen paintings on glass.

Also included are two important lists of pictures: first, a partial list of works, with their prices, that Kandinsky left with Herwarth Walden in Berlin when he returned to Russia at the outbreak of the 1914-18 war; second, a list of works sent by Walden to Stockholm in 1916 for the Der Sturm exhibition that was to be held at the Gummeson Gallery. (I am indebted to Nina Kandinsky for identifying and translating the latter two lists from the Russian. Neither is mentioned by Grohmann.)

The entries vary in the amount of information they provide. Besides the number and title, dimensions are often included, but these are not consistently accurate. Provenance information is often difficult to verify but has proved to be generally accurate. Exhibition data is in many cases full, in others non-existent. Some exhibitions are recorded for which no catalogue, reviews, or other substantiating evidence has ever come to light, and it is not clear whether they actually took place or were merely planned. The dates provided for the works are in general accurately recorded and correspond to the dates inscribed by Kandinsky on the works themselves. In a number of cases, however, especially among the early works, there are discrepancies between the dates on the works and the dates assigned to them in the Handlist. It is also clear that until about 1922 Kandinsky was not consistent in his recording habits; he failed to list many of the works of those years or the exhibition and other data on those he did record. In the case of these early years, the dates must therefore be treated with some caution.

References to Kandinsky's own "catalogue" in the present volume will be as follows: HL (Handlist), followed by the number of the work, its title in the original language, its date, month, and year (where given). In the case of the Russian entries, Kandinsky's original orthography is given. Additional information from the artist's entry will be cited where relevant.

Kandinsky's K enclosed by a full triangle, $\triangle$K, or an "open" triangle, <K, has occasionally been erroneously interpreted as a monogram for VK. Since Kandinsky always spelled his first name with a W (Wassily), there are no grounds for this interpretation.

The important catalogue *Wassily Kandinsky: Zeichnungen und Aquarelle im Lenbachhaus, München* by E. Hanfstaengl became available early in 1975 when the present manuscript was already complete. References to Hanfstaengl's discussion of many questions that relate directly to works in the SRGM collection are thus, unfortunately but unavoidably, missing from the entries that follow.

A catalogue raisonné of Kandinsky's paintings, drawings, and watercolors is in preparation. It is being written by H. K. Röthel with the collaboration of J. Benjamin.

73 Munich. ca. 1901-1902.

Not in HL.

50.1292

Oil on canvasboard, 9⅜ x 12⅝ (23.8 x 32.1)

Signed on reverse (photographed before mounting): *N 71 Kandinsky*; inscribed on reverse in Münter's hand: *München*. Not dated.

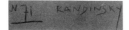

PROVENANCE:

Gabriele Münter, Murnau, 1914-49;[1] purchased from Münter by Otto Stangl, Munich, 1949 (information supplied by Stangl, correspondence with the author, March 1973); purchased from Stangl, 1950.

CONDITION:

In 1966 the canvasboard was mounted on a honeycomb panel.

The support is very slightly bent at the corners, and in these areas there is minor paint loss. The condition is otherwise excellent. (June 1972.)

Although the picture is inscribed on the reverse in Kandinsky's hand *"N 71,"* it does not correspond to his entry in the HL for that number (small oil studies, *"71. Binz auf Rügen [Dämmerung]"*). A picture which does correspond to this entry and which also bears the number 71 on the reverse is in a private collection in Paris (unpublished; I am indebted for this information to H. K. Röthel, but have not seen the painting in question or a photograph of it). Kandinsky apparently in this case inadvertently put the same number on two pictures and failed to record the Guggenheim work in the HL.

According to Röthel, who also tentatively dates the picture ca. 1901-02, the house depicted in the Guggenheim painting is typical of a small group of houses still standing in the vicinity of Kandinsky's first residence in Munich (Friedrichstrasse, Schwabing). Although difficult to establish with certainty, the date, based on a stylistic comparison with other oil studies which are recorded in the HL, is plausible.

1. When Kandinsky returned to Russia at the outbreak of the war, he left many of his pictures with Münter for safekeeping. After 1921, when he came back to Germany, he regained some of his pre-1914 works, the rest remaining in Münter's hands. In 1957 she gave her collection to the Städtische Galerie in Munich, with the exception of those few works that had since been sold—the present picture among them.

(For further details about the disposition of the Münter collection, see L. Eitner, "Kandinsky in Munich," *Burlington Magazine,* vol. xcix, June 1957, p. 193, who does, however, erroneously state that no works from the Münter collection were ever sold.)

EXHIBITIONS:

New York, SRGM 184, 208, 212, 226 (no cats.); 232, 241, p. 172, repr.; 252, repr.; 266 (no cat.).

REFERENCE:

Grohmann, 1959, p. 342 no. 55, repr. cc 539.

74 Amsterdam—View from the
Window. 1904.

HL small oil studies *52, Amsterdam,
aus d. Fenster.*

46.1055

Oil on board, 9⅜ x 13 (23.9 x 33.1)

Signed l.r.: *Kandinsky*; inscribed by the
artist on reverse (photographed before
mounting): *Kandinsky.—Amsterdam* (very
faint) *N° 52/1903.*

PROVENANCE:

Mrs. Hilda Bachrach, Forest Hills, New
York, by 1946;[1] purchased from Bachrach,
1946.

CONDITION:

In 1957 the board was mounted on a wood
support, and the picture was cleaned. A
small triangular area in the upper left corner
was inpainted at that time. In 1970 the picture was given a surface cleaning and coated
with clear synthetic varnish.

Apart from some minimal paint and support loss in the top right and bottom left
corners, the condition is excellent. (June
1972.)

Although the date inscribed by Kandinsky on the reverse is 1903, the artist's
visit to Holland with Münter is documented by J. Eichner as having taken place
from May 23 to June 21, 1904 ([1957], p. 205). The work is undated in the HL
and it is probable that the date was added substantially after the completion of
the painting, when the artist no longer exactly remembered the dates of his
Amsterdam visit. Grohmann gives no date for the picture. The scene depicted
is the view out of an upper window of the Americain Hotel on the Leidseplein
showing the bridge over the Singel gracht and the towers of the Lido and the
Park Hotel. On the right is the Vondelpark (fig. a). The Americain Hotel, Park

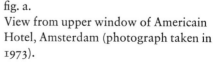
fig. a.
View from upper window of Americain
Hotel, Amsterdam (photograph taken in
1973).

1. The picture has previously been erroneously published as coming from the collection of
   B. C. Citroën, Amsterdam (SRGM 147, no. 3; SRGM *Handbook*, 1970, p. 170). Paul Citroën,
   Wassenaar (in correspondence with the author, April 1973), stated that B. C. Citroën never
   existed and that neither he, nor any of his relatives, ever owned the work.

Hotel, and Lido all existed in their present form in 1904. (I am indebted to Ems Magnus, Amsterdam, who supplied this information and the photograph, fig. a, April 1973.)

74

EXHIBITIONS:[2]

New York, SRGM 74 (checklist, dated 1903; so dated in all subsequent SRGM publications until SRGM 226, 1970); Brussels, SRGM 105-T, p. 1, repr.; Toronto, SRGM 117-T (no cat.); Philadelphia, SRGM 134-T, no. 45; New York, SRGM 147, *Kandinsky*, no. 3, repr. color p. 31; 173, no. 7, repr. color; 184 (no cat.); The Baltimore Museum of Art, *From El Greco to Pollock: Early and Late Works by European and American Artists,* Oct. 22-Dec. 18, 1968, no. 113, repr. p. 136; New York, SRGM 212, 226 (no cats.); 232, 241, pp. 170-171, repr.; 252, repr. color; New York, SRGM 266, 276 (no cats.).

REFERENCES:

Grohmann, 1959, p. 342 no. 52, repr. cc 538; SRGM 147, *Kandinsky,* exhibition catalogue, repr. color p. 31; SRGM *Handbook,* 1970, pp. 170-171, repr.

2. 2 labels preserved in the Museum's files remain unidentified with exhibitions; a printed label of the Sächsischer Kunstverein, Dresden, bearing the printed number "1475;" a printed label for a *"Kunstausstellung Der Sturm,"* with Kandinsky's name, address, and the title of the work handwritten in ink. It is possible that Herwarth Walden stored the picture at Der Sturm either during the war or at some other time and did not actually include it in the exhibition. Moreover, since he encouraged the artists associated with his gallery to put Der Sturm labels on the backs of all of their works, it is impossible to establish on the basis of labels alone whether or not the picture actually appeared in a Der Sturm exhibition.

75   Tunisian Sheep Festival. 1905.
     (Fête de moutons; Market Place in Tunis).

HL tempera paintings *88, Fete de moutons.*

46.1008

Tempera on board with colored paper
veneer, 16½ x 22½ (41.7 x 57.3)

Signed l.l.: *Kandinsky*; inscribed by the
artist on reverse: *No 88.* Not dated.

PROVENANCE:

Arthur Jerome Eddy (1859-1920), Chicago,
by 1913 *(Kandinsky 1901-1913,* 1913, pl. 26,

"*Fête de Muton* [sic] 1904, Samml.A.J.
Eddy"); Karl Nierendorf, New York, by
1946 (source and date of acquisition unknown); purchased from Nierendorf, 1946.

CONDITION:

The picture has received no treatment since
its acquisition.

There is a very faint stain (approximately
1 x 1½ in.) on the paper support upper
right. Apart from 3 minor damages to the
edges of the support (lower left corner; the
lower edge 3½ in. from the left side; left
edge 7 in. from the top), and rabbet marks
from a previous frame on all 4 edges, the
condition is excellent. (Sept. 1973.)

Kandinsky and Münter were in Tunis from December 25, 1904, until April 5,
1905 (Eichner [1957], p. 205), and the present picture certainly dates from this
journey. Kandinsky's own title for the work is somewhat misleading since
Tunis does not celebrate a sheep festival as such. However, Kandinsky was
present in Tunis during the Muslim pilgrimage month of *Dhū al-Ḥijja* (February 6-March 7, 1905), and, most importantly, for the major festival of the
Muslim year, the *al-ʿīd al-Kabir,* "the great feast," or *al-ʿ īd al-aḍḥa',* "the feast
of sacrifice," which takes place on the tenth day of *Dhū al-Ḥijja,* in this case
February 15, 1905. During this feast it is customary for the head of each household to slaughter a sheep, which is then roasted and consumed by the extended
family. Just before the feast Kandinsky undoubtedly saw the thousands of
sheep being brought into the city for the holiday, and indeed one of his unpublished Tunis sketchbooks contains an entire page of studies of sheep made
from life (GMS 324, p. 27). The scene depicted in the present painting is clearly
that of the market place (there are in fact no sheep visible in it) on or about the
day of this major feast which Kandinsky mistakenly identified as a "sheep festival." (I am indebted for information about the Muslim calendar dates and the
particular festival involved to Abraham L. Udovitch, Professor of Near Eastern
Studies, Princeton University.)

EXHIBITIONS:

Paris, *Salon d'Automne,* Oct. 18-Nov. 25, 1905, no. 825 ("*Fête de moutons a Tunis,* lith.");
Krefeld, Feb. 1906, Frankfurt am Main, Apr. 1906, Karlsruhe, *Neue Künstler Vereinigung,*
May 1906 (information from HL, but exhibitions not otherwise identified); The Art Institute
of Chicago, *Exhibition of Paintings from the Collection of A. J. Eddy,* Sept. 19-Oct. 22, 1922,
No. 41 ("*Fête de Meudon* [sic] 1904"); Pittsburgh, SRGM 53-T, *Kandinsky* (dated 1914);
New York, SRGM 74, no. 66 (dated 1903); Pasadena, SRGM 146-T, *Kandinsky,* no. 3, repr.
p. 33; New York, SRGM 184, 208 (no cats.); 252, repr.

REFERENCE:

Grohmann, 1959, p. 343 no. 88, repr. p. 259.

76   Pond in the Park. 1906(?).
      (Parkteich; Am Waldteich [?]).

Not in HL.

71.1936R 8

Oil on board, 13 x 16⅛ (33 x 40.8)

Signed and dated l.r.: Kandinsky. 190[...].

PROVENANCE:

Hilla Rebay, Greens Farms, Connecticut, 1967 (previous history and date of acquisition unknown); Estate of Hilla Rebay, 1967-71; acquired from the Estate of Hilla Rebay, 1971.

CONDITION:

Cardboard was apparently placed against the surface of the painting while it was still slightly wet, and it adhered to the pigment in a few places. In 1971 the board was mounted on a honeycomb panel; at this time, fumes from a solvent used in the treatment apparently penetrated the work, causing a break in the bond between pigment and ground. The result was some cleavage in the impasto areas; this was glued down immediately and the work is now stable. Some small areas of loss from the cleavage were filled with gesso and inpainted with watercolor. The surface, previously unvarnished, was coated with clear synthetic varnish.

Apart from considerable wear at the bottom 2 corners, the condition is good.
(June 1972.)

Grohmann publishes the picture as *"Pond in the Park, 1904."* However, he also reproduces an identical composition entitled *Pond in the Woods* (cc 2), which he associates with an entry for 1902 in the HL. The entry, no. 10 in a list of seventy-three oil paintings dating from 1900-09, reads as follows: "⊠ [sic] *Am Waldteich (Lack) Odessa, 1902, Moskau 1902, vernichtet."* The "*10*" is deleted. Grohmann states that the picture reproduced by him as cc 2 is the replacement of this no. 10, which was destroyed.

Although the dimensions given by Grohmann for cc 2 (13¼ x 21 in., 33.7 x 53.3 cm.) differ somewhat from those of the Guggenheim painting, a comparison of the photographs suggests that the two works are in fact one and the same. (Grohmann attributes cc 2 to a private collection in Paris, but widespread inquiries have failed to locate it.) The Guggenheim picture must thus be regarded as the replacement of the destroyed 1902 work.

The dating of the work presents some problems. The extremely heavy impasto, applied in part at least with a palette knife, is characteristic of 1906 works such as the *St. Cloud* series (Grohmann, 1959, cc 557-559) and the picture probably belongs to this group. However, works such as *The Sluice*, GMS 3 of ca. 1902, demonstrate a similar technique, and the dark palette is also characteristic of works painted in both periods. Most of the oil studies of 1901-07 are undated, and a satisfactory chronology for those which cannot be dated on the basis of specific journeys made by Kandinsky has yet to be developed. In the case of the present work, the style of which must be evaluated in the context of its possible relationship to a work of 1902, it is difficult to be certain of the 1906 date, but it is for the time being plausible.

EXHIBITIONS:
New York, SRGM 74, no. 68 ("*The Pool,* 1904"); 241 (addenda, "*The Pond,* 1904?"); Bridge-
port, Conn., Carlson Gallery, University of Bridgeport, *Homage to Hilla Rebay,* Apr. 18-
May 10, 1972, no. 21; New York, SRGM 252, repr.; 266, 276 (no cats.).

REFERENCE:
Grohmann, 1959, repr. cc 552.

77   Fishing Boats, Sestri. 1905-1906.
      (Fishing Boats, Rapallo).

Not in HL.

50.1293

Oil on canvasboard, 9⅜ x 12⅞ (23.7 x 32.8)

Signed on reverse (photographed before mounting): *Kandinsky.* Not dated.

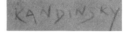

PROVENANCE:
Gabriele Münter, Murnau, 1914-49 (see above cat. no. 73, fn. 1); purchased from Münter by Otto Stangl, Munich, 1949 (information supplied by Stangl, correspondence with the author, March 1973); purchased from Stangl, 1950.

CONDITION:
In 1956 the board was mounted on a honeycomb panel.

The condition is excellent. (June 1972.)

Kandinsky and Münter were in Sestri some time between December 15 and 22, 1905, and in Rapallo from December 23, 1905, to April 30, 1906 (Eichner [1957], p. 206). Although the present work has hitherto been entitled *Fishing Boats, Rapallo,* H. K. Röthel and J. Benjamin have made the convincing suggestion that it was in fact painted at Sestri (conversation with the author, December 1974). The evidence to support their point is a pencil sketch which probably served as the preparatory study for this oil; it is inscribed *"Sestri-Dämmerung"* (fig. a). Although the work thus probably dates from December 1905, it is conceivable that Kandinsky actually painted it in Rapallo in 1906.

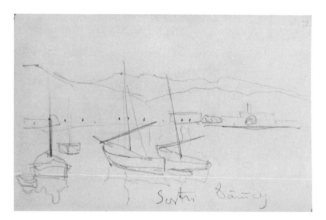

fig. a.
Kandinsky, pencil drawing, 4⅛ x 6¼ in., 10.3 x 15.8 cm., inscribed by the artist: *"Sestri—Dämmerung,"* Städtische Galerie im Lenbachhaus, Munich, GMS 327, p. 71.

77

EXHIBITIONS:

Brussels, SRGM 105-T, p. 3, repr.; Baltimore, SRGM 113-T (no cat.); Toronto, SRGM
117-T (no cat.); Pasadena, SRGM 146-T, *Kandinsky,* no. 4; New York, SRGM 184, 208, 212,
226 (no cats.); New York, SRGM 232, 241, p. 173, repr.; 252, repr.; 267 (no cat.).

REFERENCE:

Grohmann, 1959, p. 344, repr. cc 555.

78   Study for "Landscape with
      Tower." 1908.
      (Etude pour "Paysage avec une tour").

Not in HL.

38.501

Oil on board, 13 x 17½ (33 x 44.5)

Signed l.r.: *Kandinsky*. Not dated.

PROVENANCE:

Early history unknown; purchased from
Gutekunst und Klipstein, Bern, by Solomon
R. Guggenheim, February 1938;[1] Gift of
Solomon R. Guggenheim, 1938.

CONDITION:

In 1957 the board was mounted on a pine
panel; the surface was cleaned. Some paint
and support losses along the top and bottom
edges were filled with PVA and inpainted,
and the surface was coated with clear synthetic varnish.

The inpainting has discolored to some extent. The condition is otherwise good.
(June 1972.)

The picture does not appear in the HL. However, a much larger version, extremely close both compositionally and coloristically to the present work,
though more vibrant in the intensity of its tones, is recorded as *"72, Landschaft
mit Turm"* (29¾ x 39³⁄₁₆ in., 99.5 x 75.5 cm., Collection Nina Kandinsky, Paris,
Grohmann, 1959, repr. color p. 59). As Grohmann has pointed out (p. 58),
Kandinsky often during this period prepared for a painting by producing a detailed oil study which closely resembled the finished work, and it seems clear
that the Guggenheim picture is just such a study for the larger work recorded
in the HL. Grohmann himself seems, however, in the present instance to have
some doubts about the sequential relationship; he states that there were two

1. The picture presumably formed part of the group of works which were banned by the
   German government as degenerate art and acquired by Gutekunst und Klipstein during the
   course of 1937 and 1938. It has so far not been possible to discover the previous owner of
   this particular work.

fig. a.
Kandinsky, sketch of *Landscape with Tower,* oil on board, 12⅞ x 15¾ in., 32.7 x 40.2 cm., Städtische Galerie im Lenbachhaus, Munich, GMS 37.

versions of the *Landscape with Tower* (p. 58), but he dates the Guggenheim picture 1909 (cc 597), while dating Nina Kandinsky's alternately 1908-09 (p. 58) and 1909 (p. 330 no. 72), thus apparently suggesting that the Guggenheim version might even be the later of the two. Later (p. 60), he speaks of the Paris picture as the definitive one—a position that is certainly more convincing. It seems likely, however, that both works date from 1908 rather than 1909.

The Paris picture carries the date 1908 in the artist's hand both on its surface and on the reverse. Similarly the entry in the HL, though located among the paintings of 1909, is itself firmly dated 1908 (underlined), and it seems likely that Kandinsky inadvertently omitted it from the original list of 1908 works, thus being forced to include it with those of 1909. (The picture was first identified as a study for *Landscape with Tower* in the Paris, London, Oslo, and Rome catalogues of SRGM 105-T in 1957. The Paris catalogue gave no date, but in the latter three it was dated 1908. The Brussels catalogue of that show identified the picture simply as *Paysage avec une tour* and dated it 1911.)

A small landscape in the Städtische Galerie, Munich (fig. a), depicts the same church in the same setting, although the vantage point is different, and the handling of the color and light, as well as the nature of the composition are much more characteristic of Kandinsky's open-air sketches of this period. The conception was significantly altered by Kandinsky in the two other works where the carefully organized composition, the arbitrary use of light, and the intense colors bring the landscape somewhat closer to Kandinsky's *Improvisations.* The Munich nature study, though probably also of 1908, cannot be described as a study for the Guggenheim or the Paris painting.

EXHIBITIONS:

New York, SRGM 43, *Kandinsky,* no. 3 (dated 1909); Milwaukee, SRGM 49-T (no cat.); New York, SRGM 74, no. 63; Brussels, SRGM 105-T, p. 8, repr.; Toronto, SRGM 117-T (no cat.); Pasadena Art Museum, *German Expressionism,* Apr. 23-June 4, 1961, no. 36; Worcester, Mass., SRGM 148-T, no. 18, repr.; New York, SRGM 173, no. 11, repr.; 184 (no cat.); 202, p. 42, repr.; 212 (no cat.); 226 (no cat.); 252, repr.; 276 (no cat.).

REFERENCES:

Brisch, 1955, pp. 184-186, 190-193; Grohmann, 1959, pp. 58, 60, repr. cc 597.

79   Blue Mountain. 1908-1909.
     (Der Blaue Berg).

HL *1908-1909, 84,* Синяя гора (Siniaia gora, Blue Mountain).

41.505

Oil on canvas, 41¾ x 38 (106 x 96.6)

Signed and dated l.r.: *Kandinsky / 1908;*[1] signed on stretcher (photographed before replacement of stretcher): *Kandinsky;* on stretcher, not in the artist's hand: *Nr. 84.*

PROVENANCE:

Left with Herwarth Walden in Berlin when Kandinsky departed for Russia in 1914;[2] purchased by unknown private collector after 1919;[3] purchased from an unknown source by Staatliche Gemäldegalerie, Dresden, through their Patronatsverein, 1931;[4] banned by the German government as degenerate art, 1937;[5] purchased from Gutekunst und Klipstein, Bern, by Solomon R. Guggenheim, February 1939; Gift of Solomon R. Guggenheim, 1941.

CONDITION:

In 1954 some small areas of scattered cleaving paint were reattached with wax resin; in 1967 the canvas was lined with wax resin and placed on a new stretcher. After cleaning, the surface was coated with clear synthetic varnish. At some date prior to 1967 (probably 1957), a few scattered losses were inpainted; these are concentrated mostly in the whitish impasto above the mountain, ca. 3 to 8 in. from the top; a larger area of inpainting (ca. 2½ in.) is in the black and red area to the right of the mountain.

The general fragility of the paint film appears to be due to poor bonding between the layers, and the danger of further flaking is still present. (June 1972.)

The conflict between the 1908 date on the canvas and the 1908-09 date of the HL is difficult to resolve on stylistic grounds and is further complicated by the fact that the date on the work may possibly have been changed.[1] A date of 1908-09 is for the moment the most plausible.

1. The signature is in blue paint. The date is in black, painted over blue. Under strong magnification there is some suggestion, although not conclusive, that the original date, inscribed in blue, was 1909 not 1908.

2. A list of some of the works Kandinsky left with Walden, together with their prices, appears in the HL. See above, p. 204, NOTE. The present picture is not included.

3. The picture was still in Walden's hands at the time of the 1919 Der Sturm exhibition.

4. Information supplied by the Staatliche Gemäldegalerie, Dresden, which has no record of the previous owner. An unpublished postcard from Kandinsky to Grohmann dated Feb. 26, 1931, indicates that the artist had also lost track of the picture's whereabouts between 1914 and 1931: *"Aus einem Zeitungsausschnitt (Sächsische Staatsztg, Dresden, 12.11) muss ich entnehmen, dass ein älteres Bild von mir 'Blauer Berg' aus dritter Hand vom Patronatsverein für Ihre Gemäldegal. angekauft wurde. Da ich sonst nichts davon hörte, habe ich die Richtigkeit der Notiz in Verdacht . . ."* (Grohmann Archiv, Stuttgart, copy in the library of The Museum of Modern Art, New York).

5. Information supplied by the Staatliche Gemäldegalerie, Dresden, Apr. 1972. The work is also published by F. Roh, *Entartete Kunst,* Hanover, 1962, p. 151, as among the works seized by the Nazis from Dresden's collection. Gutekunst und Klipstein acquired a large group of these banned works during the course of 1937 and 1938.

It is well known that in Kandinsky's work up to 1913 the theme of the horse and rider occurs a great many times in a variety of contexts and is clearly of central importance to the artist. Starting in 1909 his preoccupation with this motif becomes especially intense; in that year, apart from *Blue Mountain* he produced *Blue Rider* (HL 69, later painted over), *Picture with Archer* (HL 75), *Improvisation 2* (HL 77), *Improvisation 3* (HL 78), *Sketch (Rider)* (HL 82), *Improvisation 9* (HL 100), and *Mountain* (not in HL, GMS 54), as well as the woodcut for the membership card of the *Neue Künstler Vereinigung* (Röthel, *Gr. W.,* 1970, no. 78) and several watercolors and drawings.

At the beginning of 1910 and increasingly throughout 1911, the motif acquires religious and spiritual connotations which, if present at all, are not clearly evident in the works of 1909. While the connections between Kandinsky's earlier and later uses of the horse and rider imagery are not entirely clear, it is nonetheless important to view these various works in relationship to each other, recognizing the extent to which the art of 1909 and before contained the motifs that were given far more explicit significance by 1911.

Early in 1910 Kandinsky painted *Composition I* (HL 92) in which three riders are shown riding from left to right before a mountain. Brisch describes them as riders of the Apocalypse and bases his identification on their giant size and on the fact that the surrounding landscape is filled with signs of violence and catastrophe (1955, pp. 213, 231-233; for a discussion of why Kandinsky omitted the fourth rider—death—from all of his representations of the apocalyptic horsemen, thus emphasizing their positive, regenerative aspects, see H. Nishida, "Genèse du Cavalier bleu," *XXᵉ Siècle,* no. xxvii, December 1966, pp. 23-24, and Washton, 1968, pp. 179-180; both accept Brisch's reading of the horsemen in *Composition I* as apocalyptic).

Although it is difficult to accept this interpretation of *Composition I* without some clearer evidence, the horsemen of the Apocalypse do appear elsewhere in Kandinsky's paintings of the coming years, with their identifying attributes (*Horsemen of the Apocalypse I & II,* glass paintings, GMS 121 and 106). The three horsemen in *Blue Mountain,* small in scale and riding through a peaceful landscape, bear no such connotations, but they must be seen in the context of Kandinsky's developing preoccupation in the years 1909-11 with the motif of three horsemen and a mountain. (The specific visual inspiration for the configuration used by Kandinsky in this work may possibly—as Washton has suggested—have been Gerhard Munthe's tapestry, *König Sigurds Reise nach Jerusalem* [*Dekorative Kunst,* vii, 1901, repr. p. 37], where three horsemen similarly grouped ride from left to right; the mountain is, however, missing from the Munthe work.)

During this period Kandinsky also concentrated heavily on representations of a single horse and rider—a motif that culminated in the series of studies preparatory to the 1911 cover designs for the first *Blaue Reiter* exhibition catalogue, the *Blaue Reiter* announcement, and the covers of *Über das Geistige in der Kunst* and the *Blaue Reiter Almanach.* For discussions of the sources and significance of the single rider motifs, see the following: Brisch (1955, pp. 209

ff.), who misleadingly implies that the horse and rider theme in Kandinsky's work always carries an apocalyptic connotation; K. C. E. Lindsay ("The Genesis and Meaning of the Cover Design for the first *Blaue Reiter* Exhibition Catalogue," *Art Bulletin,* vol. xxxv, March 1953, pp. 47-50), who sees the horseman leaping off the mountain as a symbol of Kandinsky's own artistic development—the emancipation of his "poetic inspiration" and his breakthrough to abstraction; Roters (pp. 201-226), who emphasizes on the one hand the folk art sources for the rider motif and on the other the romanticized medieval ones and sees the *Blaue Reiter* of the almanac cover as a combination of St. George and St. Martin—the newly created patron saint of an art which will shape the future; Nishida (loc. cit., pp. 18-24), who sees the rider of the almanac cover as St. George, and many of the other riders as deriving from the Apocalypse—symbols of Kandinsky's faith in the idea of regeneration and a new era; Washton (1968, pp. 166-174), who suggests that Theosophical ideas influenced Kandinsky's rider imagery in the designs for the *Blaue Reiter* publications and the cover of *Über das Geistige,* and who cites a variety of sources for this imagery: Kandinsky's own earlier religious pictures, folk art, the Apocalypse itself, and Steiner's writings; she also refers in passing to the more personal identification of the rider and his mount in Kandinsky's "Rückblicke" as the artist and his talent *(Kandinsky 1901-1913,* 1913, p. xvi), but describes the image as having much wider significance—representing in various ways the religious regeneration which the *Blaue Reiter* movement was to bring; Weiss (1973, pp. 451-464), who traces the stylistic and symbolic development of the horse and rider motif from its earliest manifestation in Kandinsky's oeuvre at the turn of the century through its transformation in the later geometric work.

Only Roters suggests a connection between the motif of three riders and that of one. He proposes that Kandinsky's development of the *Blaue Reiter* motif goes back ultimately to *Mountain* of 1909, and beyond that to *Blue Mountain,* in both of which the rider (or riders) are for the first time juxtaposed with a mountain (pp. 218-219). He sees the motif as gradually evolving out of these 1909 pictures and reaching its final expression in works such as the design for the *Blaue Reiter* exhibition catalogue. In that context he suggests that Kandinsky has constructed a world in which he himself is the *Blaue Reiter* and the landscape a symbol and outward sign of his spiritual world.

The imagery of 1908-09 works such as *Blue Mountain* is certainly not inspired by Christian sources, and the significance of the *Blaue Reiter* motif clearly different from that of the apocalyptic horsemen. However, it is important to consider Kandinsky's preoccupation in these early years with the horseman and mountain motif as part of his evolution in the immediately following period towards a body of work in which biblical motifs are used.

EXHIBITIONS:
Munich, Atelier, 1909 (information from HL, but exhibition not otherwise identified);
Odessa, Салон 2 Международная худ- нная выставка устройтель В.А. Издебский
(Salon 2, Mezhdunarodnaia khud-nnaia vystavka ustroitel' V. A. Izdebskii, *Salon 2,*

International Exhibition organized by V. A. Izdebsky), Dec. (?) 1910, no. 200 ("Всадник у синей горы 1908," Vsadnik u sinei gory, *Rider by the Blue Mountain,* 1908); Berlin, Der Sturm, *Wassily Kandinsky: 1902-1912,* Oct. 2-30, 1912, no. 48 (Munich ed.), no. 44 (Berlin ed.);[6] Munich, Galerie Thannhauser, *Kandinsky,* Jan. 1914;[7] Berlin, Der Sturm, 37. *Ausstellung,* Apr. 1919, no. 32; New York, SRGM 43, *Kandinsky,* no. 1 (dated 1908; so dated in all subsequent SRGM publications); Chicago, SRGM 47-T, *Kandinsky,* no. 1; Pittsburgh, SRGM 53-T, *Kandinsky,* no. 1; New York, SRGM 74, no. 69; Brussels, SRGM 105-T, no. 5; Baltimore, SRGM 113-T (no cat.); Toronto, SRGM 117-T (no cat.); New York, SRGM 118 (checklist); Philadelphia, SRGM 134-T, no. 46; New York, SRGM 144 (checklist); New York, SRGM 147, *Kandinsky,* no. 9, repr. color, p. 37; New York, SRGM 162 (checklist); 173, no. 10, repr. color; 184 (no cat.; withdrawn before closing); 187, *Gauguin and the Decorative Style* (checklist; commentary, repr. color); Montreal, Expo 67, *Man and his World,* Apr. 28-Oct. 27, 1967, no. 92, repr.; New York, SRGM 202, p. 66, repr. color p. 67; Columbus, Ohio, SRGM 207-T, repr. color p. 11; New York, SRGM 221, 226 (no cats.); 232, 241, p. 174, repr. color p. 175; 252, repr. color; 266, 276 (no cats.).

REFERENCES:

Kandinsky 1901-1913, 1913, repr. p. 37 (dated 1908); Grohmann, 1930, p. xxiv (dated 1908); Grohmann, 1959, p. 331 no. 84, repr. p. 263 (dated 1909); D. Robbins, "Vasily Kandinsky: Abstraction and Image," *College Art Journal,* vol. xxii, Spring 1963, repr. color cover (dated 1908); E. Roters, "Wassily Kandinsky und die Gestalt des Blauen Reiters," *Jahrbuch der Berliner Museen,* N.S. Band 5, Heft 2, 1963, pp. 219-220 (dated 1909); R. C. Washton, *Man and his World,* exhibition catalogue, Montreal, 1967, no. 92 (dated 1908); Washton, 1968, p. 59, fn. 2 (dated 1908); SRGM *Handbook,* 1970, pp. 174-175, repr. color (dated 1908).

6. The exhibition was also to have been shown in modified form at the Galerie Hans Goltz in Munich, and this latter exhibition is widely referred to in the literature as Kandinsky's first major 1-man show. According to an unpublished letter from Kandinsky to Goltz, dated Sept. 12, 1912, the exhibition was originally scheduled to open in Munich, Oct. 15. (I am much indebted to H. K. Röthel for bringing this and other letters to my attention. It is from the Kandinsky-Goltz-Walden correspondence that the following facts about the 2 exhibitions are derived.)

Published catalogues of both the Munich and the Berlin exhibitions exist; the Munich catalogue, which was published by Verlag "Neue Kunst" Hans Goltz in Sept. 1912, contains 73 items. The Berlin catalogue, which was apparently not published until the end of 1913 (i.e., long after the Oct. 1912 Der Sturm exhibition), contains 64 items. Only 36 of the items appear in both catalogues. Various facts combine to establish that the Munich exhibition at Hans Goltz did not in fact take place. First, the letters exchanged by Kandinsky and Walden (preserved in the Der Sturm Archiv, Berlin) strongly imply, though they never explicitly state, that the exhibition plans collapsed owing to personal difficulties between the various parties concerned. The letters also dwell at some length on the possibility of J. K. Thannhauser doing an exhibition of Kandinsky's work in Munich at the beginning of 1914, and in a letter of Nov. 12, 1913, Kandinsky writes to Walden that he feels he absolutely must have an exhibition in Munich some time *("Ich muss mal in München ausstellen.")*—suggesting that he had not yet had one. Finally, no reviews of the Goltz exhibition have ever come to light, and its actual opening is referred to neither in the Kandinsky correspondence, nor, for example, in that of Macke and Marc. Evidence for the Berlin exhibition is, on the other hand, plentiful. It is advertised throughout its run in the 3 Oct. issues of *Der Sturm* (nos. 130, 131, 132); and 2 review articles on it appear in that journal (1 in no. 132, p. 182, dealing mainly with the criticism that the show has already inspired in other newspapers; the second, in no. 134-135, Nov. 1912, p. 204, dealing more directly with the works of Kandinsky himself). Thus it is clear that whereas the Munich Hans Goltz catalogue was undoubtedly printed and sold, the exhibition itself never took place at Goltz's gallery. The Goltz catalogue was used instead by Walden for his Oct. 1912 exhibition in Berlin. From Nov. 1912 until Nov. 1913, Kandinsky's *Kollektiv-Ausstellung* traveled under Walden's auspices to Rotterdam, Leyden, Utrecht, Hamburg, Groningen, Amsterdam, Brussels, Antwerp (?), Karlsruhe (?), Frankfurt, Aachen. On this journey the Goltz catalogue was also probably used (a second printing, still with the Goltz cover, and probably dating from Jan. 1913, contained Kandinsky's *"Ergänzung"*).

On Nov. 18, 1913, Kandinsky wrote to Walden that the first edition of the catalogue was out of print. Walden then had a second edition printed, this time with his own imprint— *"Verlag Der Sturm"*—instead of Goltz's on the cover. In Jan. 1914 a Kandinsky exhibition opened at Galerie Thannhauser in Munich, and although the 1913 correspondence refers repeatedly to concrete plans for a new edition of the catalogue which would be printed with Thannhauser's name on the cover, no such catalogue has hitherto come to light. Thannhauser may thus have used Walden's second edition of the Der Sturm catalogue; and although it has not hitherto been possible to prove that the Thannhauser exhibition contained precisely those works which were included in the Der Sturm *Kollektiv-Ausstellung* version, this does seem likely.

7. In an unpublished letter from Kandinsky dated Jan. 2, 1914 (Der Sturm Archiv, Berlin), the artist states that the exhibition has just opened, and that *Blue Mountain* had already been reserved, together with *Improvisation 24*, for the Reiffmuseum in Aachen. Whereas this museum did indeed purchase the latter work, they apparently later decided against *Blue Mountain*.

80   Landscape near Murnau with
      Locomotive. 1909.
      (Murnaulandschaft).

Not in HL.

50.1295

Oil on board, 19⅞ x 25⅝ (50.4 x 65)

Signed and dated l.l.: *Kandinsky 1909.*

PROVENANCE:

Possibly purchased directly from the artist
by Rudolf Ibach, Barmen, Wuppertal;[1] purchased from Ibach by Otto Stangl, Munich,
before 1950; purchased from Stangl, 1950.

CONDITION:

In 1953 the board was mounted on Masonite and the Masonite on pine. Some losses in
paint and support along the edges were
filled and inpainted at this time. Surface dirt
was removed and the picture coated with
clear synthetic varnish.

A few areas of abrasion and loss along the
edges still exist. The condition is otherwise
good. (June 1972.)

The picture is closely related in color and technique to *Railroad near Murnau*
in the collection of the Städtische Galerie, Munich, also of 1909 (GMS 49).

EXHIBITIONS:

New York, SRGM 132 (checklist); Pasadena, SRGM 146-T, *Kandinsky,* no. 10, repr. p. 39;
New York, SRGM 184 (no cat.); 196 (checklist); 208, 212, 226 (no cats.); 252, repr.; 276
(no cat.).

REFERENCES:

Grohmann, 1959, p. 345, repr. cc 599 *(Landscape near Murnau with Locomotive)*; Weiss,
1973, p. 448.

1. Ibach purchased several works directly from Kandinsky and this may have been one of
   them. In a letter of July 1972 to the author, Stangl states that he acquired the work from
   Ibach, but he was unable to provide the date of the transaction, nor could he say how long
   Ibach had owned the work.

81   Group in Crinolines. 1909.
(Reifrockgesellschaft).

HL *1909, 89,* Общество [в] кринолинам (Obshchestvo [v] krinolinam, A Gathering [in] Crinolines).

45.966

Oil on canvas, 37½ x 59⅛ (95.2 x 150.1)

Signed and dated l.l.: *Kandinsky 1909*; inscribed by the artist on stretcher (transcribed but not photographed before replacement of stretcher): *Kandin*[sky R]*eifrock-*[damen] *(1909).*

PROVENANCE:

Purchased from the artist by W. Beffie, Amsterdam and Brussels, August 1913 (information from HL and *Kandinsky 1901-1913,* 1913, p. 46); remained in Beffie collection until at least 1938 (lender to New Burlington Galleries); Karl Nierendorf, New York, by 1942 (exhibition catalogue); purchased from Nierendorf, 1945.

CONDITION:

In 1963 the canvas was cleaned, surfaced with clear synthetic varnish, lined with wax resin, and placed on a new stretcher.

Apart from some wear along the top, right, and bottom margins, the condition is excellent. (Aug. 1972.)

Grohmann drew attention to the fact that Kandinsky's interest in mid-19th century costume is discernible as early as 1902 when he painted *Bright Air* (Collection Nina Kandinsky, HL 1902, 13). In fact this interest goes back even earlier and is part of a general Biedermeier revival at the turn of the century, when many early artists introduced costumes of the 1840's into their work. (For a brief discussion of this Biedermeier revival in the Jugendstil crafts, see Weiss, p. 206, fn. 35.) The Russian artists of this period (Bakst, Benois, Somow, and especially Borisoff Mussatoff) experienced what Louis Réau described as a *"rétrospectivisme—c'est-à-dire le goût des époques abolies"* (*L'Art russe,* Bd. 2, Paris, 1922, p. 224), and ladies in crinolines abound in the ca. 1900-01 works of Borissoff Mussatoff reproduced in *Mir Iskusstva* and elsewhere. Brisch makes the point that this romantic Russian interest in the "fairy-tale" or historically removed (and hence unreal) setting played an important role in Kandinsky's development towards abstraction (1955, pp. 157 ff.).

Kandinsky's preoccupation with the Biedermeier style is traceable in the early part of the century in his sketchbooks (see, for example, GMS 330, pp. 33-34; GMS 333, p. 44), in drawings (GMS 97, 184, 391, 987/1, 989), and in several paintings. In 1909 he produced a second painting entitled *Group in Crinolines* (State Tretiakov Gallery, Moscow, HL 1909, 64, Grohmann, 1959, repr. p. 350). It shows a large group of ladies, formally attired with fans and high coiffures, posed in a garden against an almost theatrical background of pseudo-classical architecture. The ladies appear again, in a veiled and almost illegible form in *Pastorale* of 1911 (see below cat. no. 86), and then not again until 1916 where they are to be found in a series of fourteen Biedermeier watercolors. In 1917-18 they appear for the last time in a highly decorative series of glass paintings. (Some of these are illustrated in H. K. Röthel, *Kandinsky: Painting on Glass,* exhibition catalogue, New York, 1966, nos. 36, 43, 45.)

Weiss has convincingly suggested that the composition of the Guggenheim *Group in Crinolines* may have been inspired by an Adolf Münzer mural shown at the 1900 Glaspalast exhibition and reproduced in the September 1, 1900, *Kunst für Alle.* She notes, moreover, that Kandinsky referred to Münzer in his October 3, 1909, "letter from Munich," published in the Russian periodical *Apollon.*

Weiss' further suggestion that a painting such as *Group in Crinolines* may owe something to August Endell's 1896 essay *"Um die Schönheit"* (which Kandinsky must have known) is both plausible and illuminating.

EXHIBITIONS:

Berlin, Der Sturm, *Wassily Kandinsky: 1902-12,* Oct. 2-30, 1912, no. 6 (Munich and Berlin
eds.), "*Reifrockdamen, 1909*";[1] Munich, Galerie Thannhauser, *Kandinsky,* Jan. 1914;[2] Berlin,
Kreis für Kunst Köln im Deutschen Theater, *Kandinsky Ausstellung,* Jan. 30-Feb. 15, 1914,
no. 2 ("*Reifrockdamen 1909*");[3] Berlin, Der Sturm, *Kandinsky Münter,* 1916, no. 1 ("*Reifrockdamen 1909*");[3] London, New Burlington Galleries, *Twentieth Century German Art,* July
1938, no. 75 ("*Crinoline, 1910,* Collection Beffie, Brussels"); New York, Nierendorf Gallery,
Kandinsky Retrospective, Dec. 1942-Feb. 1943 (checklist); New York, SRGM 43, *Kandinsky,*
no. 4; Chicago, SRGM 47-T, *Kandinsky,* no. 2; Toronto, SRGM 85-T, no. 18; New York,
SRGM 87 (checklist); Boston, SRGM 90-T (no cat.); Montreal, SRGM 93-T, no. 16, repr.;
Brussels, SRGM 105-T, p. 4, repr.; Toronto, SRGM 117-T (no cat.); New York, SRGM 118
(checklist); Philadelphia, SRGM 134-T, no. 47, repr.; New York, SRGM 147, *Kandinsky,*
no. 12, repr. p. 42; 184 (no cat.); 202, p. 88, repr.; 208, 212, 214, 221, 226 (no cats.); 232, 241,
p. 176, repr. p. 177; 252, repr. color; 276 (no cat.).

REFERENCES:

Kandinsky 1901-1913, 1913, repr. p. 46; *V. V. Kandinsky,* 1918, repr. p. 12; Grohmann, 1959,
p. 50, repr. cc 30; Weiss, 1973, pp. 497-501.

1. It is not clear whether this entry refers to the Guggenheim picture or to the version now in
the State Tretiakov Gallery, Moscow (HL 64), also of 1909 (see above). For information on
the cancellation of the Munich showing of this exhibition, see above, *Blue Mountain,*
cat. no. 79, fn. 6.

2. See above cat. no. 79, fn. 6.

3. It is not clear whether this entry refers to the Guggenheim or to the Tretiakov picture.

82   Study for "Composition II." 1909-1910.
      (*Skizze für Komposition 2; Composition 2;*
      Composition No. 35).

HL *1909, 89a,* Эскиз композиции 2 (Eskiz
kompozitsii 2).

45.961

Oil on canvas, 38⅜ x 51⅝ (97.5 x 131.2)

Signed and dated l.r.: *Kandinsky / 1910.*

PROVENANCE:

Purchased from the artist by W. Beffie, Amsterdam and Brussels, August 1913 (information from HL); remained in Beffie
collection until at least 1938;[1] Karl Nierendorf, New York, by 1942 (exhibition catalogue); purchased from Nierendorf, 1945.

CONDITION:

In 1964 the picture was given a superficial
cleaning and surfaced with PBM; it had not
been varnished previously.

Apart from considerable wear along the
margins, the condition is excellent. Visible
at certain points throughout the canvas are
the remains of a grid obviously drawn with
soft black crayon on the canvas beneath the
paint layer. In addition there are some
scattered color notations (fig. a). Infra-red
photographs made with transmitted light
do not reveal any additional lines or color
notations. Although Kandinsky habitually
penciled color notes on preparatory studies
for paintings, examples of such notations on
canvas have not hitherto come to light. The
use of a grid appears to have been extremely
rare in Kandinsky's work. One appears in a
watercolor sketch for *Composition IV*
(Collection Nina Kandinsky, Paris, Grohmann, 1959, repr. p. 73), and one on an unpublished sketchbook page of anatomical
studies (GMS 342, p. 17); but no other
canvases with a grid infra-structure are
known to the author. (June 1972.)

fig. a.
Kandinsky, *Study for "Composition II,"*
with the grid underdrawing and penciled
color notations indicated.

The present picture is the final study for a much larger work (78¾ x 108¼ in.,
200 x 275 cm.) formerly in the collection of Baron von Gamp, Berlin (destroyed during the Second World War, *Über das Geistige in der Kunst,* 2nd ed.,
Munich, 1912, repr. p. 123, *Kandinsky 1901-1913,* 1913, repr. p. 48). The two
versions are extremely close, and only two obvious differences serve to distinguish them: in the final painting the four figures huddled in the lower left

1. No lenders are listed in the 1937 Bern exhibition catalogue, but the picture was not for sale,
   and it presumably still belonged to Beffie at that time. It was for sale at the 1938 Burlington
   exhibition, and it is possible that Nierendorf purchased it on this occasion.

82

corner have become one amorphous shape, and the central white vertical form extends to the top edge of the canvas instead of stopping short of it.

The study has frequently been identified as the final version (see below EX-HIBITIONS and REFERENCES). Grohmann suggested (1959, p. 120) that Kandinsky himself in 1930 intentionally submitted a photograph of the study to serve as the illustration for *Composition II* in his monograph then being prepared for publication by *Cahiers d'Art* (Grohmann, 1930, p. 3). Grohmann wonders whether Kandinsky at that time saw the study as more "significant," or possibly "more in line with his subsequent intentions," and therefore specifically designated it as the final work. Lindsay, in his 1959 review of Grohmann's monograph, dismisses this theory as unacceptable and blames Grohmann for the confusion between the two works. Lindsay's interpretation is especially compelling in view of the fact that Grohmann clearly confused the two works in 1924 when he published the study with the title, dimensions, and "collection von Gamp" of the larger work.

The final work appears in the HL 1910, 98, but it is described there as having been painted during the winter of 1909-10, a fact accepted by Brisch (p. 231) and Grohmann (1959, p. 118). Washton without comment dates both the final study and the destroyed final work 1910 (1968, p. 180 and figs. 162 and 165). Three of the preliminary studies and the Guggenheim work are signed and dated 1910, although the latter appears in the HL under 1909. It is possible that the ideas for the work originated in 1909, although it is more likely that the Guggenheim picture and several of the studies were completed in 1910.

A woodcut of the composition was made for *Klänge*. H. K. Röthel convincingly dates the woodcut, with most of the other *Klänge* woodcuts, 1911 (*Gr. W.*, 1970, no. 97 and p. 445); he states there that it was probably based on the Guggenheim study rather than on the final work, but has since revised this view (in conversation with the author, December 1974). Grohmann (1959, p. 121) dates the woodcut 1913, the year of *Klänge*'s publication, and convincingly relates it to the final version.

The themes, imagery, and spiritual significance of Kandinsky's seven pre-1914 *Compositions* have been the subject of considerable discussion, and Kandinsky himself made it clear that these were his most ambitious and important works (*Kandinsky 1901-1913*, 1913, p. xiii). Whereas he did not himself offer explanations of their imagery, he did in a limited way comment on the spiritual and aesthetic intentions of some of them and on their sources of inspiration. In *Über das Geistige in der Kunst* he wrote that, unlike the *Impressions* (which are based on direct observation of nature) and *Improvisations* (which are largely spontaneous expressions of inner character or non-material nature), the *Compositions* are the result of a long and painstaking process of formulating an expression of inner feeling (2nd ed., 1912, p. 124). In this respect he said that the work of art must be the outward expression of the inner emotion in the soul of the artist.

In the 1913 "Rückblicke," he reemphasized the fact that the *Compositions* must evolve as independent beings from within the artist (*Kandinsky 1901-1913*, 1913, p. xxv, NOTE), and the 1918 Russian edition contains—as Brisch has pointed out (p. 163)—some important additional sentences on the ways in which these paintings came into being:

> *It became the great ambition of my life to paint a Composition. They appeared before me in my dreams—indistinct and fragmentary visions, sometimes frightening in their clarity. Sometimes I saw whole paintings, but when I awoke only the vaguest details, a faint trace, remained. Once when I lay sick with typhoid fever I visualized an entire painting with great clarity. But when the fever had left me, it somehow crumbled in my memory* (V. V. Kandinsky, 1918, p. 25, trans. N. Berberova).

It is interesting to note that he then cites *Composition II* as one of the three works which most closely approximates his memory of the feverish visions that originally inspired them.

Elsewhere Kandinsky takes pains to explain that the titles or subtitles that sometimes accompany the *Compositions* are in no sense intended to be descriptive in a literal sense. Thus, in his essay on *Composition VI (Deluge)* he states: "nothing would be more erroneous than to think of this painting as the depiction of an event" (*Kandinsky 1901-1913*, 1913, p. xxxviii). He describes the agonizing process involved in extricating himself from the very specific details of the catastrophe of the Flood (depicted in a 1912 glass painting of the subject), until he felt able at last to express the inner sound *(Klang)* of the word "Flood" instead of the event to which the word is normally attached. Thus, his stated aim in *Composition VI (Deluge)* is to submerge the theme of the Deluge totally and to be left with an independent statement of inner feeling. (For a further discussion of the creation of *Composition VI* and of the significance of the "inner feeling" and "inner sound," see S. Ringbom, *The Sounding Cosmos,* Abo, 1970, pp. 116 ff., 150 ff.; Weiss has pointed out that Kandinsky's use of terms such as *Klang, innere Notwendigkeit,* and *geistig* was consistent with the aesthetic vocabulary of German criticism at the turn of the century [1973, pp. 64, 388, 479, 483 et passim].)

While Kandinsky's essay on *Composition VI* identifies the original stimulus for that painting as the Deluge, it is interesting to note that in connection with *Composition II* he specifically denies having used any theme at all: "Composition 2 was painted without a theme, and perhaps I would have been afraid at that time to take a theme as my starting point" (Eichner [1957], p. 114).

This statement raises obvious problems for those attempting to decipher the contents of the picture, as well as questions about the artist's intentions, especially since the subject matter of the work is in parts clearly legible and—on the basis of comparison with works that bear explanatory titles—susceptible of interpretation. This is further complicated by the fact that Kandinsky implies a few paragraphs earlier in the same lecture that whereas he may not have started with a specific theme in mind, he did know what tone or spiritual message he wished the *Composition* to convey: he describes the initial drawing and composition as "tragic," and his use of color in the work as calculated to lessen the tragedy (Ibid., p. 113). His meaning here is not entirely clear, but the interpretations of the painting offered by Brisch and Washton provide some illumination.

Brisch first made the suggestion that *Composition II* is in part a representation of the Deluge, in part of The Garden of Love. On the left side he notes a drowning figure with arm raised, a group of four figures huddled against the approaching waves, and a prostrate figure already drowned. In the center he points out two figures on horseback fleeing one after the other up the central white form which he sees as a rock or a mountain. This rock form is balanced on the left by another which leans towards the left edge, and between the two he sees a mountain with trees, toppling towers, a figure with arms spread out in a gesture either of blessing or exorcism, and a sky full of jagged clouds. On the right-hand side Brisch describes a contrasting scene of lyrical peace. In the lower right two figures are reclining—a motif that appears here for the first time, but recurs several times in the years to come, notably in *Improvisation 27 (Garden of Love),* 1912, HL 149, where the figures are clearly intended to be seen as lovers. (The motif occurs at least twice in works of 1911: in the woodcut vignette for chapter III, "Geistige Wendung," in the 1912 editions of *Über das Geistige in der Kunst* [Röthel, *Gr. W.,* no. 86]; and on the far right of *Com-*

position IV, 1911, HL 125, as well as of its studies.) Behind the couple Brisch sees five kneeling figures apparently making offerings to the reclining pair, and to the left of them a mother and child; higher up is a weeping willow-like tree and another rock form. (The weeping willow occurs for the first time in the woodcut *Sterne* dated 1907 by Röthel [*Gr. W.,* no. 75].) The effect of the *Composition* is, according to Brisch's analysis, that of a dream; the dramatic contrast between the idyllic arcadian quality of the right side and the destruction and chaos of the left creates a tension of expressive power. Brisch further suggests that one of Kandinsky's own statements about *Composition VI (Deluge)* is equally applicable to its forerunner *Composition II:* "one can divide the picture into two independent halves each of which stands on its own although they have grown into one" *(Kandinsky 1901-1913,* 1913, p. xxxix).

Washton for the most part repeats Brisch's reading of the individual motifs, although she sees the central white form as a tree rather than a rock, and agrees with Grohmann (1959, pp. 120-121) that some of the five figures on the right are children playing ball. She departs from Brisch's reading of the picture's motifs in only one important respect: she sees the two central horsemen as confronting and battling one another as do those on the left side of *Composition IV,* rather than as escaping from the rising flood. In this respect they play an important role in her interpretation of the picture's meaning, which differs in significant ways from that of Brisch. She sees the work as a reflection of Kandinsky's sense (expressed both in *Über das Geistige in der Kunst* and in his 1914 lecture) of the confusion and disharmony of his age. Thus the horsemen represent the conflict of individual elements with one another and the sense of tragedy inherent in that conflict. The "nightmare" of the age is, however, brightened by a "glimmer of light," represented here by the lyrical quality of the composition's right-hand side. (For a fuller discussion of the role in Kandinsky's work of the Garden of Love image as a symbol of the coming rebirth of society, see Brisch, pp. 219 ff. and Washton, 1968, pp. 76-82, 181-185.)

The interpretations of both Brisch and Washton remain to some extent problematic. Washton's reading of the two horsemen is difficult to sustain: whereas the horsemen in *Composition IV* seem clearly to be engaged in conflict, their forelegs intertwined and their bodies seen in strict profile, the juxtaposition of the horsemen in *Composition II* is much more ambiguous. The perspective from which they are shown, both apparently retreating into the picture plane, lends support, however, to Brisch's theory that they are galloping rapidly upwards, rather than battling one another. An early drawing for the picture (fig. b), although extremely diagrammatic and elliptical, further supports this reading. The two horses are sketched in, the lower one with a directional arrow pointing towards the upper left, the upper one curved to the right and decorated with six spots, and they are in this drawing clearly conceived of as separate entities mounting the field, rather than as engaged in battle. Although the black clouds, windswept trees, and darkened sky of the upper left portion of the painting lends credence to the notion that a storm is taking place, whether the entire left side of the painting depicts a Deluge remains un-

fig. b.
Kandinsky, drawing for *Composition II,*
ink on paper, 11 7/8 x 9 7/8 in., 30 x 23.8 cm.,
Private Collection, Paris.

clear. Similarly ambiguous is the role of the foreground figures in the lower left corner and the prostrate figure in the foreground. Are they drowning or drowned? Or are they much less drastic pictorial beings, standing and reclining? A lack of clearly identified precedents makes it difficult to be sure.

Within the context of either Brisch's or Washton's analysis, Kandinsky's own 1914 statement that the composition was "tragic" and his use of color intended to lessen the tragedy is comprehensible; his use of bright colors throughout the painting does indeed effectively work to obscure the tragic implications which a Deluge might otherwise suggest. In fact Grohmann was misled, apparently by the use of color alone, into describing the entire picture as a "festive scene" (1959, p. 120).

The sense in which Kandinsky claims to have taken no specific theme as the starting point for this work, while he emerges with a partially legible subject matter, remains to some extent problematic. While the imagery may ultimately remain ambiguous, further study of it and of related works may throw more light on the problem.

Three studies which are conceivably early ideas for the center section for *Composition II,* but which have hitherto not been associated with it, throw some possible light on the gradual formation of Kandinsky's compositional ideas for the picture. A page from one of the artist's unpublished notebooks

fig. c.
Kandinsky, study for *Composition II* (?), sketchbook page, 5⅜ x 3⅜ in., 13.5 x 8.5 cm., Städtische Galerie im Lenbachhaus, Munich, GMS 345/66.

fig. d.
Kandinsky, study for *Composition II* (?), watercolor on paper, 13 x 12⅞ in., 33 x 32.8 cm., Städtische Galerie im Lenbachhaus, Munich, GMS 353.

fig. e.
Kandinsky, *Composition I,* oil on canvas, 47⅛ x 55⅛ in., 119.8 x 140 cm., signed and dated l.r.: *"Kandinsky 1910,"* destroyed.

(fig. c) and a watercolor (fig. d), both in the Städtische Galerie, Munich, seem at first glance to be closely related to *Composition I* (fig. e): the pose of the left-hand rider with arms spread wide as his horse leaps across the central mountain, and the leaning towers poised on the summit in the background seem to be directly related to the earlier picture. Upon closer inspection, however, the relationships to *Composition II* are even more compelling: there are two horse-men, rather than three, and they are juxtaposed exactly in the fashion of the latter picture; more important, at their feet in the foreground lies a prostrate

fig. f.
Kandinsky, study for *Composition II*,
oil on board, 23 x 19¼ in., 58.5 x 49
cm., Private Collection, Germany.

figure identical to the one in *Composition II*. The cruciform gesture of the
horseman in the drawings and the watercolor is transferred in *Composition II*
to the small figure standing in a boat at the left. (A nude figure with arms spread
out becomes a recurring central motif in 1912 depictions of the Deluge: see for
example, a glass painting, now lost, Röthel, *Kandinsky: Painting on Glass*,
exhibition catalogue, New York, 1966, repr. p. 13; and HL 151a; 159a.) The
colors carefully inscribed in the pencil sketch do not correspond exactly to
those of the Guggenheim picture, but to a remarkable degree they approximate
them. In certain instances the colors in the final picture have been reversed: the
"drowned" figure (if such she is) is designated red in the drawing and the adjacent ground dark green; in the final version the reverse is the case. Similarly,
the sky in the upper right corner is in the drawing designated red surrounding
white; in the painting white surrounds red, and so on. The relationships which
emerge here between *Composition I* and *II* suggest that Kandinsky's early ideas
for *Composition II* were much more dependent upon *Composition I* than has
hitherto been recognized.

The detailed oil study for the right side of the picture (fig. f) is close to the
Guggenheim version, although some changes, especially in the distribution
of colors, are introduced. Whereas in the final version the two white figures
recline upon orange ground, in the earlier study one of them is orange and
they recline on a blue/white ground; the two green kneeling figures in the
foreground are in the earlier version differentiated, one being olive green and
the other pale blue. The clear rectangle of blue-violet shaded with redder
violet that lies just behind the figures in the Paris oil is omitted entirely from
the Guggenheim picture, where a quite new distribution of somewhat ambiguous landscape forms has been introduced.

EXHIBITIONS:

Kunsthalle Bern, *Wassily Kandinsky,* Feb. 21-Mar. 29, 1937, no. 5; London, New Burlington Galleries, *Twentieth Century German Art,* July 1938, no. 76 ("Composition No. 2, 1912, for sale");[2] New York, Nierendorf Gallery, *Kandinsky,* Dec. 1942-Jan. 1943 *(Composition 2);* New York, Art of this Century, *15 Early, 15 Late,* Mar. 13-Apr. 10, 1943, no. 215; New York, SRGM 43, *Kandinsky,* no. 7 ("Composition No. 2, 1910");[3] Chicago, SRGM 47-T, *Kandinsky,* no. 3; Pittsburgh, SRGM 53-T, *Kandinsky,* no. 5; New York, SRGM 74, 79 (checklists); Toronto, SRGM 85-T, no. 19 ("Composition No. 35, 1910"); Vancouver, SRGM 88-T, no. 18; Cambridge, Mass., Harvard University, Busch-Reisinger Museum, *Artists of the Blaue Reiter,* Jan. 21-Feb. 24, 1955, no. 17, repr.; SRGM 105-T, no. 6 (withdrawn after London showing); Palais des Beaux-Arts de Bruxelles, *50 Ans d'art moderne,* Apr. 17-July 21, 1958, no. 142, repr.; New York, SRGM 118 (checklist); Philadelphia, SRGM 134-T, no. 48; New York, SRGM 147, *Kandinsky,* no. 13, repr. color, p. 41; 162, *Van Gogh and Expressionism* (checklist); University of California at Los Angeles Art Galleries, *Years of Ferment: The Birth of Twentieth Century Art,* Jan. 24-Mar. 7, 1965, no. 89, repr., traveled to San Francisco, Museum of Art, Mar. 28-May 16, 1965, Cleveland Museum of Art, July 13-Aug. 22, 1965; New York, SRGM 184, 198-T (no cats.); 202, p. 86, repr. color p. 87; 208, 212, 214, 221, 226 (no cats.); 232, 241, p. 178, repr. color p. 179; 252 (withdrawn after New York showing), repr. color; Cleveland, SRGM 258-T, no. 6, repr.; New York, SRGM 276 (no cat.).

REFERENCES:

G. J. W[olf], *Kunst für Alle,* Nov. 1, 1910, pp. 68-70 (review of *Neue Künstler Vereinigung* in which *Composition II* appeared; the painting is the target of particular abuse); W. Kandinsky, lecture dated Jan. 30, 1914, not delivered, first published in Eichner [1957], pp. 111, 113, 114; Grohmann, 1924, p. 6, repr. n.p. ("Composition II, Coll. von Gamp, Berlin"); Grohmann, 1930, repr. p. 3 ("Composition 2, 1910, Coll. de Gamp, Berlin"); Grohmann, 1933, repr. p. 81 ("Composition Nº 2 1910, Coll. v. Gamp, Berlin"); M. Bill, *Wassily Kandinsky,* Paris, 1951, repr. p. 125 *(Composition 2);* Brisch, 1955, pp. 189, 233-238; Grohmann, 1956, p. 7, color pl. 1; Grohmann, 1959, pp. 118, 120-121, repr. color p. 109; K. Lindsay, review of Grohmann, *The Art Bulletin,* vol. 41, Dec. 1959, p. 350; D. Robbins, "Vasily Kandinsky: Abstraction and Image," *College Art Journal,* vol. xxii, Spring 1963, pp. 145-147; R. C. Washton, "Kandinsky's Paintings on Glass," *Artforum,* vol. v, Feb. 1967, p. 25; G. H. Hamilton, *Painting and Sculpture in Europe 1880-1940,* Baltimore, 1967, p. 370; Washton, 1968, pp. 180-185, 220-221, fig. 165 (dated 1910).

2. The catalogue entry erroneously refers to W. H. Wright's *Modern Painting,* New York, 1915, for a reproduction; Wright reproduces the final version, not the study. Although the Burlington exhibition entry carries the title of the final work, its dimensions are those of the Guggenheim study. Moreover, the final work was at the time in the Collection of Baron von Gamp in Berlin, where it remained until its destruction during the war.

3. Until 1963 the Guggenheim consistently used the title *Composition 2* instead of *Study for "Composition II."* In 1954-55, for no apparent reason, the picture appeared in 4 separate exhibitions as *Composition No. 35* (SRGM 79, 85-T, 88-T, and Busch-Reisinger, 1955).

83   Landscape with Factory
Chimney. 1910.
(Landschaft mit Fabrikschornstein; Land-
schaft mit Schornstein).

HL *1910, 105,* Пейзаж с фабр[ичной]
трубой (Peizazh s fabr[ichnoi] truboi,
Landscape with Factory Chimney).

41.504

Oil on canvas, 26 x 32¼ (66.2 x 82)

Signed and dated l.r.: *Kandinsky / 1910.*

PROVENANCE:

Purchased from Herwarth Walden by Paul
Citroën, Berlin and Amsterdam, ca. 1919;[1]
purchased from Citroën by Kunstsammlungen zu Weimar 1923 (information
supplied by Citroën, correspondence with
the author, April 1973); banned by the German government as degenerate art, 1937;
purchased from Gutekunst und Klipstein,
Bern, by Solomon R. Guggenheim, February 1939; Gift of Solomon R. Guggenheim, 1941.

CONDITION:

In 1953 the picture was cleaned and surfaced with PBM. In 1962 it was lined with
wax resin.

Scattered over the surface in approximately
12 impasto areas, there are small paint
losses with accompanying cracks, a condition apparently due to weakened bonding of
the paint film. The edges and corners are
worn in places, but the condition is otherwise good. (June 1972.)

1. Citroën (in a letter to the author, Apr. 1973) stated that he purchased the picture during the
First World War. However, since Walden still owned the work at the time of the 1919
exhibition, it is likely Citroën purchased it at that time.

The HL records a sketch (hitherto unlocated) for the picture which was at that time in the collection of the artist Erma Barrera Bossi (b.1885). The painting published by Kandinsky in 1913 as *Landschaft mit Schornstein, 1910*, has the dimensions 90 x 72 cm. (35½ x 28⅜ in.; *Kandinsky 1901-1913*, p. 49). However, the dimensions given by Kandinsky are often inaccurate, and the picture in question is almost certainly the present one rather than another version. Neither the HL nor Grohmann, who publishes the Guggenheim picture as 1910, no. 105 (1959, p. 331), suggest that there was another version of the composition.

EXHIBITIONS:

Munich, *Neue Künstler Vereinigung: II Ausstellung*, Sept. 1-14, 1910, no. 60 *(Landschaft);*[2] Berlin, Der Sturm, *Wassily Kandinsky: 1902-12*, Oct. 2-30, 1912, no. 9 or 10? (Munich ed.), no. 8 (Berlin ed.), "*Landschaft, 1910;*"[3] Barmen, May 1912 (information from HL, but exhibition not otherwise identified); Amsterdam, Stedelijk Museum, *Moderne Kunstkring*, Nov. 7-Dec. 8, 1913, no. 92 ("*Paysage avec cheminée 1910*," information from HL); Berlin, Der Sturm, *73 Ausstellung*, Apr. 1919, no. 37 *(Landschaft mit Schornstein)*; Milwaukee, SRGM 49-T (no cat.); Pittsburgh, SRGM 53-T, *Kandinsky*, no. 14; New York, SRGM 79 (checklist); 83 (no cat.); 84 (checklist); Vancouver, B.C., SRGM 88-T, no. 17; Cambridge, Mass., Harvard University, Busch-Reisinger Museum, *Artists of the Blaue Reiter*, Jan. 21-Feb. 24, 1955, no. 16; New York, SRGM 95 (checklist); Brussels, SRGM 105-T, no. 5, repr.; Toronto, SRGM 117-T (no cat.); Boston, SRGM 119-T, no. 15; Paris, Musée National d'Art Moderne, *Les Sources du XXe siècle: les arts en Europe de 1884 à 1914*, no. 84; Pasadena, SRGM 146-T, *Kandinsky*, no. 13, repr. p. 48; New York, SRGM 184 (no cat.); 196 (checklist); 208, 212 (added Sept. 6), 226 (no cats.); 252, repr.

REFERENCES:

Kandinsky 1901-1913, 1913, repr. p. 49; Grohmann, 1959, p. 331 no. 105, repr. cc 40.

2. The HL states that this picture appeared in the 1910 *NKV*, and no. 60 is the only landscape listed in the catalogue. I am indebted to D. Gordon for establishing the correct dates of this exhibition.

3. A copy of the catalogue annotated by Münter contains the handwritten note "*mit Schornstein*" next to no. 8. I am indebted to H. K. Röthel and J. Benjamin for bringing this to my attention. For information on the cancellation of the Munich showing of this exhibition, see cat. no. 79, fn. 6.

84 Landscape with Rolling
Hills. 1910-1911.
*(Landschaft mit welligen Hugeln;
Mountain Landscape; Gebirgslandschaft;
Berglandschaft).*

HL *1910, 104a,* Пейзаж с волн[истыми] горами (Peizazh s voln[istymi] gorami, Landscape with rolling hills).

41.503

Oil on board, 13 x 17⅝ (33 x 44.7)

Signed l.l.: *Kandinsky*; inscribed by the artist on reverse (photographed before mounting): *Kandinsky Studie (Ettaler Mandel) 1911.* (The Ettaler Mandel is a flat-topped mountain peak near Murnau.)

PROVENANCE:
Purchased from Herwarth Walden by an unknown private collector, possibly "Passman," September 27, 1916;[1] acquired from "Stiftung Passman" by Städtische Landesmuseum, Hanover, June 17, 1930; banned by the German government as degenerate art, 1937;[2] purchased from Gutekunst und Klipstein, Bern, by Solomon R. Guggenheim, February 1939; Gift of Solomon R. Guggenheim, 1941.

CONDITION:
In 1955 the edges were filled with PVA emulsion; the board was mounted on a wooden cradled sub-support with moveable horizontal members. A small area in the bottom right corner was inpainted; the canvas was surfaced with PBM front and back.

The corners are worn and there have been some losses along the top and right edges. The condition is otherwise excellent. (June 1972.)

Grohmann dates the work 1910, presumably on the basis of its location in the HL. He asserts in addition that the work appeared in the *Neue Künstler Vereinigung* in Munich, 1910-11. However, only one landscape is recorded in the catalogue of that exhibition (no. 60), and Grohmann also claims that *Landscape with Factory Chimney,* HL 1910, 105, appeared there. Since the HL entry for the latter does include a reference to the *Neue Künstler Vereinigung,* 1910-11, while that of 104a does not, it would seem unlikely that the present picture appeared in the show.

Since its acquisition, the painting has been consistently dated 1911 by the Guggenheim Museum on the basis of Kandinsky's inscribed date on the reverse of the work itself. The conflicting evidence presented by the HL (1910) and the artist's inscription (1911) is difficult to resolve for reasons cited in relation to *Winter Study with Church,* 1910-11, cat. no. 85. The picture was probably painted in the latter half of 1910, or the very beginning of 1911.

1. The HL states that the work was *"verkauft von Walden 27. ix.16, 500."* Ludwig Schreiner, Director of the Städtische Landesmuseum in Hanover, deduced from the Museum records that Alexander Dorner, then Director of the Museum, acquired the picture in exchange for a Nolde from the *"Stiftung Passman"* (correspondence with the author, Mar. 29, 1972). No further information about Passman has hitherto come to light.

2. Information supplied by Dr. Schreiner. The work is also published by F. Roh, *Entartete Kunst,* Hanover, 1962, p. 194 *(Gebirgige Landschaft),* as among the works seized by the Nazis from Hanover's collection.

84

EXHIBITIONS:

Berlin, Der Sturm, *Wassily Kandinsky: 1902-1912*, Oct. 2-30, no. 44 ? (Munich ed.), no. 9 (Berlin ed.), *Landschaft*;[3] New York, SRGM 43, *Kandinsky*, no. 11 ("*Landscape, 1911*;" so dated in all subsequent SRGM publications); Pittsburgh, SRGM 53-T, *Kandinsky*, no. 12; New York, SRGM 74, no. 64; 111 (checklist); Baltimore, SRGM 113-T (no cat.); Boston, SRGM 119-T, no. 16; Pasadena, SRGM 146-T, *Kandinsky*, no. 16, repr. p. 44; New York, SRGM 184, 208, 212, 226 (no cats.); 252 repr.; New York, SRGM 266, 276 (no cats.).

REFERENCE:

Grohmann, 1959, p. 331 no. 104a, repr. cc 39.

3. The HL gives no indication of exhibitions in which the picture might have appeared; however, a copy of the Berlin catalogue annotated by Münter contains the handwritten note "104a" next to no. 9. I am indebted to H. K. Röthel and J. Benjamin for bringing this to my attention. For information on the cancellation of the Munich showing of this exhibition, see cat. no. 79, fn. 6.

85 Winter Study with Church. 1910-1911.
*(Winterstudie mit Kirche; Murnau in
Winter with Church).*

Not in HL.

37.502

Oil on board, 13 x 17½ (33 x 44.5)

Signed l.r.: *Kandinsky*; inscribed by the
artist on reverse (photographed before
mounting): *Kandinsky-Winterstudie mit
Kirche (1911)*.

PROVENANCE:

Early history unknown; purchased from

Rudolf Bauer, Berlin, by Solomon R. Guggenheim, 1936; Gift of Solomon R. Guggenheim, 1937.

CONDITION:

In 1957 the board was mounted on a pine
sub-support, the edges filled with PVA, and
the surface sprayed with PBM. In 1972
cleavage of the board at the lower center
margin was arrested.

Apart from some losses in paint film and
support along the edges (some of which
were inpainted in 1957), the condition is
excellent. (July 1972.)

The five closely related landscapes with church are difficult to date precisely.[1]
Only two—the Guggenheim and Eindhoven pictures—are dated by Kandinsky

1. There are at least 4 other approximately contemporary landscapes which include a similar
church (Grohmann, 1959, p. 400, cc 612, formerly Collection Ziersch, subsequently sold by
Wilhelm Grosshennig to an unknown private collection; cc 613, Stedelijk van Abbemuseum, Eindhoven; cc 614, GMS 59; cc 616, GMS 46, dated in Eichner's hand "1910").
None of these appear in the HL, and only 1 (cc 613) is dated by Kandinsky 1910, although
Grohmann places all of them, including the Guggenheim picture, in 1910. It has thus far
proved impossible to establish which of the 5 appeared in the Der Sturm exhibition.

himself, the former 1911, the latter 1910. Grohmann, apparently unaware of Kandinsky's 1911 date on the reverse of the Guggenheim picture, places all five paintings in 1910, the Guggenheim version first in the sequence and the Eindhoven one third (1959). In an article published in 1966 he pushes the Guggenheim painting even further back—into the winter of 1909. Although Grohmann's distinction between works of 1909 (such as *Study for "Landscape with Tower,"* above, cat. no. 78) and the present group is entirely convincing, it is difficult to claim that Kandinsky's stylistic development in the years 1909-11 is sufficiently clear to allow in every case for the tracing of an evolution from one canvas to the next. As Grohmann himself acknowledged, several tendencies existed side by side "influencing each other and contrasting with each other in the most various ways" (1959). Kandinsky's occasional lapses of memory in the dating of his early work have already been noted (see above, NOTE, p. 204), and it is certainly possible that the 1911 date on the Guggenheim canvas represents such a lapse, the picture actually dating from 1910. However, there is no compelling stylistic evidence to support such a theory, and the group of five landscapes may well have been painted between mid 1910 and early 1911, the Guggenheim picture coming towards the end of the sequence rather than necessarily at its outset.

Although several of these works have been described as Murnau landscapes, it is not certain that they are in fact based on specific landscape motifs. The church tower in some of them resembles that of the Parish Church in Murnau, but H. K. Röthel and J. Benjamin, who have made a detailed study of the area surrounding Kandinsky's Murnau residence, suggest that the topography of the landscape, especially in the Eindhoven and Guggenheim paintings, does not correspond to that of the Church's actual setting (conversation with the author, December 1974). Both the Eindhoven and the Guggenheim paintings are in any event more suggestive of composed *Improvisations* than of landscape studies, and the question of whether they were inspired by a specific location must thus be treated with some caution.

For a discussion of the relationship between this picture and Kandinsky's 1913 development into abstraction, see below cat. no. 93.

EXHIBITIONS:

Berlin, Der Sturm, *Wassily Kandinsky: 1902-1912,* Oct. 2-30, 1912, no. 64? (Munich ed.), no. 58? (Berlin ed.), "*Landschaft [Kirche],* 1911;"[1] Berlin, Der Sturm, *Kandinsky,* Sept. 1916, no. 3 (*Landschaft mit Kirche*);[1] Philadelphia, SRGM 3-T, no. 173; Charleston, S.C., SRGM 4-T, no. 247; New York, SRGM 43, *Kandinsky,* no. 10; Milwaukee, SRGM 49-T (no cat.); Pittsburgh, SRGM 53-T, no. 4; Brussels, SRGM 105-T, p. 10, repr.; Toronto, SRGM 117-T (no cat.); New York, SRGM 118 (not in checklist; added Mar. 3); Pasadena, SRGM 146-T, *Kandinsky,* no. 15, repr. p. 44; New York, SRGM 184 (no cat.); 202, p. 25, repr.; 208, 212, 226 (no cats.); 252, repr.; 276 (no cat.).

REFERENCES:

Grohmann, 1959, pp. 60-61, repr. cc 611 (dated 1910); Idem, "La grande unité d'une grande oeuvre," *XXe Siècle,* xxvii, Dec. 1966, repr. p. 12 (dated 1909).

86   Pastorale. February 1911.

HL *ii/1911, 132*, Пастораль (Pastoral).

45.965

Oil on canvas, 41⅝ x 61⅝ (105.8 x 156.7)

Signed and dated l.r.: *Kandinsky 1911.*

PROVENANCE:

Purchased from Herwarth Walden by Fritz Schön,[1] Berlin, before 1930 (Grohmann, 1930, repr. p. 8); purchased from Schön, Quebec, by Dominion Gallery, Montreal, 1943 (information on this and subsequent provenance supplied by Max Stern, Dominion Gallery, correspondence, 1967, 1971-72); purchased from Dominion Gallery by Karl Nierendorf, New York, November 1943; purchased from Nierendorf 1945.

CONDITION:

By 1954 the canvas had been stretched so that ¼-½ in. of bare canvas and several tack holes were visible on the left, top, and right margins. The tack holes were filled with gesso and the margins inpainted; a small puncture right of center (above the flower) was also filled and inpainted. The surface was cleaned and sprayed with PBM.

Apart from some slight wear along the bottom edge, the condition is excellent. (Aug. 1972.)

1. The HL states (in Russian): "Sold by Walden / 1800 / Coll. Schön 2500 / Coll. Schön, Berlin." The implication is that Walden did not perhaps sell the work directly to Schön: a label of the Galerie Arnold, Dresden, on the reverse possibly indicates that the picture may have passed through their hands on consignment from Walden. The 2 prices in the HL would thus be explained. Apart from the fact that it is known that Kandinsky paintings were being handled by the Galerie Arnold from an early date, and that Schoen purchased many works from this gallery, there is no further evidence to substantiate the hypothesis.

As was noted above (cat. no. 81), this painting belongs to a group of works in which ladies in Biedermeier costume are placed in "fairy-tale," theatrical, or otherwise unreal settings. Here the three Biedermeier ladies on the right (who Weiss suggests are reminiscent of Guillaume Roget's *Phantasie* of ca. 1898) share a pastoral landscape with two sheep, a shepherdess with one leg raised and a pipe at her lips reclining on the ground, a cow, and a horse. The outlines of the figures are unclear, their forms veiled, and, as Weiss points out, the composition offers a perfect illustration of Kandinsky's own discussion of the fairy-tale element in painting published in *Über das Geistige in der Kunst* in December 1911, the year in which *Pastorale* was painted. He warns that this fairy-tale element runs the risk of being purely anecdotal and thus interfering both with the viewer's response to color and with his ability to experience a real "vibration of the soul." Thus the painting becomes worthless. The artist must find a way of using form, movement, and color which will suppress the anecdotal and allow the work to convey its pure, deep, profound effect (2nd ed., Munich, 1912, pp. 105-106). Kandinsky added an anguished and revealing footnote to this description of representation and abstraction: *"Dieser Kampf mit der Märchenluft ist dem Kampfe mit der Natur Gleich. . . . Es ist leichter, die Natur zu malen, als mit ihr zu kämpfen!"* ("This battle with the fairy-tale atmosphere is similar to the battle against Nature. . . . How much easier it is to paint nature than to fight against it!") The veiled forms of *Pastorale*, barely legible through their brilliant colors, may be said to represent Kandinsky's almost exactly contemporary solution to the dilemma posed in both the text and in the footnote.

EXHIBITIONS:

Berlin, Der Sturm, *Der Blaue Reiter*, Mar. 1912 (hors catalogue?);[2] Barmen, May 1912 (information from HL, but exhibition not otherwise identified); Berlin, Der Sturm, *Ausstellung von zurückgestellten Bilder des Sonderbundes Köln*, June-July, 1912 (no cat.);[3] Berlin, Der Sturm, *Kandinsky*, Sept. 1916, no. 15; New York, Buchholz Gallery, *The Blue Four*, Oct. 31-Nov. 25, 1944, no. 29; New York, SRGM 43, *Kandinsky*, no. 12; New York, SRGM 87 (checklist); Brussels, SRGM 105-T, p. 9, repr.; Toronto, SRGM 117-T (no cat.); New York, SRGM 118 (checklist); Lexington, Ky., SRGM 122-T, no. 9; New York, SRGM 144 (checklist); 147, *Kandinsky*, no. 24, repr. color p. 51; 173, no. 18, repr. color; 184 (no cat.); 202, p. 86, repr. p. 87; 208, 221, 226 (no cats.); 232, 241, p. 180, repr. p. 181; 252, repr. color; 266, 276 (no cats.).

REFERENCES:

Grohmann, 1930, repr. p. 8, pl. 10; Idem, "L'Art non figurative en Allemagne," *L'Amour de l'art*, 15, Sept. 1934, p. 433; Idem, 1959, pp. 112-114, 332 no. 132, repr. color p. 127; Weiss, 1973, pp. 502-503.

---

2. Information from the HL entry reads: *"D.B.R. Sturm."* The picture does not appear in the catalogue, but it might have been included hors catalogue.

3. The HL entry includes *"Sturm vi. 12."* D. Gordon, in conversation with the author, verified the fact that no catalogue was published for this exhibition.

87   Sancta Francisca. 1911.

Not in HL.

53.1361

Oil and tempera (?)[1] on glass, 6⅛ x 4⅝
(15.6 x 11.8)

Not signed or dated; inscribed on board
backing, not in the artist's hand (transcribed
but not photographed before discarding of
backing): *Fanny*.[2]

PROVENANCE:

Franzisca Dengler, Munich, ca. 1911-ca.
1940 (information supplied by Francke,
correspondence with the author, 1972);
purchased from Dengler by Günther
Francke, Munich, ca. 1940; purchased from
Francke, 1953.

CONDITION:

The work has received no treatment.

Apart from a few pinpoint losses, the condition is excellent. (Oct. 1973.)

1. Although both oil and tempera seem to be present in the medium, this fact has not been
   finally established, and further study of the medium used by Kandinsky in this and other
   glass paintings is required.
2. According to Röthel, the handwriting was that of Franzisca Dengler, for whom the picture
   was painted.

Sancta Francisca of Rome (1384-1440, canonized in 1608) was the Patron Saint of Christian housewives. Röthel has convincingly identified the painting, not as a portrait of the Saint herself, but as a humorous homage to Kandinsky's servant Franzisca Dengler (known as "Fanny") who was—as it were—the saint of the household. Röthel quotes from the reminiscences of Elisabeth Erdmann-Macke, who described Fanny as *"der gute Geist des Hauses."* The fact that Fanny herself owned the work lends support to Röthel's hypothesis.

Washton, in her article on the glass paintings, refers to the influence of Bavarian *hinterglasmalerei* on Kandinsky's 1910-11 glass paintings and cogently illustrates her point by reproducing a Bavarian *Virgin and Child* of ca. 1800 which shows striking similarities to the *Sancta Francisca*.

The work is difficult to date precisely, but its stylistic relationship to *St. Vladimir* (GMS 127, dated June 1911) makes the 1911 date proposed by Röthel (and accepted by Washton, as well as by Grohmann) convincing. Brisch's 1913 date for the work is not substantiated by any discussion and seems less plausible.

EXHIBITIONS:

New York, SRGM 84 (checklist); 184 (no cat.); 191, *Kandinsky: Painting on Glass*, no. 4, repr. color; 212 (no cat.; added Sept. 6); 252, repr. (withdrawn after New York showing).

REFERENCES:

Brisch, 1955, p. 230; Grohmann, 1959, p. 346, repr. cc 662; H. K. Röthel, *Kandinsky: Painting on Glass,* exhibition catalogue, New York, 1966, p. 10; R. C. Washton, "Kandinsky's Paintings on Glass," *Artforum,* vol. v, Feb. 1967, p. 23.

---

88   No. 160b (Improvisation 28 [?]). 1912.
        (Improvisation 28; No. 160b).

HL *1912, 160b* (no title).

37.239

Oil on canvas, 43 7/8 x 63 7/8 (111.4 x 162.1)

Signed and dated l.l.: *Kandinsky / 1912;* inscribed twice on stretcher, possibly by the artist (transcribed but not photographed before replacement of stretcher): *Improvisation No. 28;* signed on stretcher: *Kandinsky.*

PROVENANCE:

Museum Folkwang, Essen, before 1922-36;[1] Galerie Ferdinand Möller, Berlin, 1936?;[2] purchased from Möller(?) by Solomon R. Guggenheim, 1936; Gift of Solomon R. Guggenheim, 1937.

CONDITION:

In 1954 the picture was cleaned. In 1958 it was lined with wax resin; prior to lining, 5 patches and some residual glue on the reverse were removed. 1 of the patches had covered a right-angled tear through the canvas (1 1/2 x 3 in., located 13 3/4 in. from the bottom, 13 3/4 in. from the left) which had been repaired in 1952. The area around the tear was inpainted, the canvas placed on a new stretcher and surfaced with clear synthetic varnish. 7 in. of the upper margin, starting at the left corner, was repainted at an unspecified date.

Apart from a 4 in. horizontal abrasion along the lower left margin, 3 small losses in the canvas, and some wear along all 4 margins, the condition is good. (June 1972.)

88

Although there is no title for the work in the HL, various pieces of evidence suggest that Kandinsky intended to give it the title *Improvisation 28*. The inscription on the stretcher has been lost (see above), and there is no way of knowing whether it was in the artist's hand. However, a letter from Kandinsky to Hilla Rebay about the painting, dated November 27, 1936, suggests that this inscription was his: "Could you be so kind as to let me know the number of this Improvisation? You can find it on the reverse of the stretcher"

1. In 1922 the Museum Folkwang was taken over by the Kunstmuseum in Essen. All works that had formed part of the Folkwang collection are so identified in the 1929 catalogue of the new museum. For the entry on this picture see A. Waldstein, *Museum Folkwang Essen, Moderne Kunst,* Essen, 1929, p. 19, no. 180, "Improvisation." The entry for this picture in the HL reads: *"Coll. S.R. Guggenheim, N.Y., acheté du Folkwang Museum Essen en 1936."*

2. Paul Vogt, Director of the Museum Folkwang, in correspondence with the author, June 1972, stated that the records of the Museum had all been destroyed during the war and that no date either of acquisition or sale was recorded. The source from which Guggenheim acquired the picture is also not recorded; however, a deleted entry in the HL suggests that Möller might have been an intermediary. It reads: *"88.Improvisation. gemalt in Murnau / Folkwang Museum? / und vom Museum an Möller / Coll. S.R. Guggenheim, N.Y. verkauft /."* Since the entire entry, apart from the title and *"gemalt in Murnau,"* was deleted by Kandinsky himself, he had apparently attached the information to the wrong painting. Since *160b* was the only Kandinsky from Essen acquired by Guggenheim, it is possible that the deleted entry describes the Essen-Möller-Guggenheim transaction for this work. A Galerie Möller label formerly on the reverse carries the information *"W. Kandinsky / Improvisation 1912."*

(The Hilla von Rebay Foundation Archive). A Der Sturm label on the reverse (see fn. 3) also carries the title *Improvisation 28*. The entry in the HL for no. 150 reads: *Improvisation 28 (War)*. This picture has never been located and may have been destroyed, but the sketch accompanying its entry in the HL is quite different from that accompanying the entry for *160b*, and it is clear that another work is involved. It seems plausible to tentatively suggest, therefore, that Kandinsky mistakenly assigned the title *Improvisation 28* to two numbers in the HL, *No. 150* and *No. 160b*.

A watercolor study for the picture is in the collection of The Hilla von Rebay Foundation (fig. a). As is usually the case at this point in Kandinsky's development, the imagery in the watercolor is in general much more clearly legible than that in the final work. Washton has proposed that the painting should, like *Composition II*, be seen as divided into halves. On the left she points out, as Grohmann did before her, the boat with parallel oars and the waves beneath it. In the upper left corner she draws attention to a cannon (which is far more clearly depicted in the watercolor) and the mountain behind it. Further to the right she sees a group of giant-size candles with flames, a sun in the upper right-hand corner, a standing couple with arms entwined at the center of the right margin (also more clearly decipherable in the sketch than in the final work), and in the lower right corner a whale or serpent. The long tubular forms which stretch up from the bottom edge are not identified by Washton, although she ascribes to them a dividing function similar to that of the tree form (or rock form) in *Composition II* (see above cat. no. 82). As in the case of the latter, she sees the motifs on the left side as symbolic of destruction, those on the right as symbolic of hope.

fig. a.
Kandinsky, study for *No. 160b*, watercolor on paper,
15½ x 22¼ in., 39.4 x 56.5 cm., Collection The Hilla von
Rebay Foundation, Greens Farms, Connecticut.

Even if, as seems likely, the present picture is in some sense related to the entry in the HL for *Improvisation 28 (War)*, the subtitle may not necessarily apply to the Guggenheim work, and if it does, it should be treated with caution. In a long and frequently discussed letter to A. J. Eddy (published in *Cubists and Post-Impressionists*, New York, 1914, pp. 125-126), Kandinsky discussed the painting *Improvisation 30 (Cannon)* which is in several important respects iconographically related to *160b*. He insisted that the subtitle should not be taken as a description of the content; thus, whereas cannons might be discernible, they should not suggest that the picture is to be taken either as a comment on war, or as a picture about war; "they might be explained by the constant war talk that had been going on throughout the year. But I did not intend to give a representation of war; to do so would have required different pictorial means; besides, such tasks do not interest me." The recognizable motifs are, he insists, entirely peripheral to the essential inner meaning and impact of the work.

Nonetheless, although the imagery may not reflect a preoccupation with the subject of war, it is conceivable that it results from Kandinsky's overall preoccupation with the anxieties of his age, the spiritual unrest which he describes in *Über das Geistige in der Kunst*, published less than a year before this picture was painted. Thus, as Washton points out (pp. 88-89), the war-like motifs of these paintings do not constitute "conscious or 'unconscious' representations of historical events," but rather may perhaps be seen as symbolically related to Kandinsky's contemporary spiritual and religious preoccupations.

EXHIBITIONS:[3]

Philadelphia, SRGM 3-T, no. 74, repr. p. 76 *(Improvisation)*; Charleston, S.C., SRGM 4-T, no. 103, repr. p. 106; New York, SRGM 43, *Kandinsky*, no. 18, repr.; Milwaukee, SRGM 49-T (no cat.); New York, SRGM 64 (no cat.); Montreal, SRGM 93-T, no. 18; Brussels, SRGM 105-T, p. 11, repr.; Toronto, SRGM 117-T (no cat.); Boston, SRGM 119-T, no. 17; Cleveland Museum of Art, *Paths of Abstract Art*, Oct. 4-Nov. 13, 1960, no. 30, repr.; Philadelphia, SRGM 134-T, no. 49; New York, SRGM 144 (checklist); 147, *Kandinsky*, no. 29, repr. p. 55; 162 (checklist; commentary, repr. color); New York, Stephen Hahn Gallery, *Kandinsky Paintings from 1903-1942*, Oct. 6-24, 1964 (no cat.); New York, SRGM 173, no. 24, repr. color; 184, 208, 212, 226 (no cats.); New York, Sidney Janis Gallery, *20th Century European Art*, Feb. 4-Mar. 7, 1970, no. 47, repr.; New York, SRGM 252, repr.

REFERENCES:

A. Waldstein, *Museum Folkwang Essen, Moderne Kunst*, Essen, 1929, no. 180; Grohmann, 1959, pp. 126-127, 332 no. 160b, repr. color p. 131; J. Lassaigne, *Kandinsky*, Geneva, 1964, repr. color p. 67; H. Nishida, "Genèse du Cavalier bleu," *XXᵉ Siècle*, no. xxvii, Dec. 1966, p. 23, repr.; Washton, 1968, pp. 211-214.

3. 2 labels preserved in the Museum files remain unidentified with exhibitions; a printed label from the Galerie Flechtheim, Berlin, bearing the number "3835;" a printed label for a *"Kunstausstellung Der Sturm / Herwarth Walden"* with the handwritten information *"Kandinsky / Improvisation 28."* (See above cat. no. 74, fn. 2, for a note on the interpretation of Der Sturm labels.) The canvas was also formerly stamped with the imprint of Rudolf Bauer's Berlin gallery Das Geistreich, suggesting either that it was exhibited there, or else that Bauer had it on consignment at some point.

89 Painting with White Form. 1913.
(Bild mit weisser Form).

HL *1913, 166,* Картина с бел[ой] формой
(Kartina s bel[oi] formoi, Painting with
White Form).

37.240

Oil on canvas, 47⅜ x 55 (120.3 x 139.6)

Signed and dated l.l.: *Kandinsky i9i3*;
inscribed by the artist on stretcher: *Kandinsky Bild mit weisser Form.i9i3*; barely
visible: *Bild No. 166; No. 166.*

PROVENANCE:

Purchased from the artist by Herwarth
Walden, Berlin, 1913 (information from HL
and from *Kandinsky 1901-1913,* 1913, p. 7);
reacquired by the artist, 1924;[1] purchased
from the artist by Otto Rolfs, Braunschweig,
by 1929 (information from HL and from
Grohmann, 1929, p. 325); Rudolf Bauer,
Berlin, by 1937; purchased from Rudolf
Bauer by Solomon R. Guggenheim, 1937;
Gift of Solomon R. Guggenheim, 1937.

CONDITION:

Although the work has apparently received
no treatment since its acquisition by the
Museum, several small areas of repaint are
visible under UV; the largest of these is a
vertical line ca. 6¾ in. long below and to
the right of center. Smaller areas of repaint
are in the white, ca. 9½ in. from the bottom,
28 in. from the right side; in the red and
orange ca. 23 in. from the bottom, 22 in.
from the right side; in the yellow-beige ca.
19½ in. from the bottom, 22 in. from the
right; left of center ca. 1½ in. from the
bottom, 18½ in. from the left. There is a
puncture with accompanying fine cracks
and some cleavage in the beige area 9 in.
from the bottom, 11 in. from the right. The
unpainted ground now visible along the top,
right, and bottom margins is considerably
worn and there are some losses in the support in those areas. The overall condition of
the paint film is good. (June 1972.)

a.

b.

fig. a.
Kandinsky, study for
*Painting with White
Form,* watercolor on
paper, 14⅞ x 10¾ in.,
37.7 x 27.4 cm., Städt-
ische Galerie im Len-
bachhaus, Munich,
GMS 151.

fig. b.
Kandinsky, study for
*Painting with White
Form,* HL 1913, 165, oil
on canvas, 39¼ x 34¾
in., 100.6 x 87.9 cm.,
Courtesy of The Detroit
Institute of Arts. Gift of
Mrs. Ferdinand
Moeller.

1. When Kandinsky returned to Germany from Russia in 1921, *Painting with White Form*
was among the few works by him still left in Walden's possession. The HL entry includes
the information *"von Walden zurück—Vergleich 1924,"* referring to the 1924 out of court
settlement reached between them regarding Kandinsky's claims against his former dealer.

Grohmann (1959, p. 134) knew of only two studies for the composition (figs. b and d). Since the publication of his book two others have come to light: a watercolor in the Städtische Galerie in Munich (fig. a), long recognized by E. Hanfstaengl as a study for the painting and identified as such by Washton (p. 223); and a pen and ink drawing in a private collection (fig. c). It is conceivable that the Munich watercolor and the oil version in Detroit that clearly

89

followed it (figs. a and b) may represent the early conception for the whole work rather than direct studies for the left side of it. The only argument in favor of such an interpretation is the fact that the Detroit oil appeared in two exhibitions in 1921 as *Bild mit weisser Form, I Fassung* (Hanover, Galerie von Garvens and Berlin, *Grosser Berliner Kunstausstellung)*, thus suggesting that it represented Kandinsky's first solution, rather than a study for the large work. The two other studies (figs. c and d) are clearly directly preparatory to the Guggenheim painting.

With the help of these studies, the origins of certain motifs in the painting can be clarified, although it emerges as one of the most impenetrable works of early 1913.

Washton's reading of the motifs presents several problems. She sees the two forms in the upper right corner as horses engaged in battle, reminiscent of those in *Composition IV*. However, the treatment of this area in the watercolor (fig. d) and even more so in the drawing (fig. c) suggests that these two forms were probably conceived rather as domed towers similar to those used again and again by Kandinsky in 1912-13. In the upper center Washton sees the red roof and yellow chimney (so clearly legible in the studies, though much less so in the final work) as having their origins in the "familiar tumbling towers," which she sees most clearly depicted in the upper right corner of the Munich watercolor. Although difficult to read, the drawing and the New York watercolor seem rather to show a relatively stable country house with chimney, partly hidden by shrubbery and foliage. In the final painting this jagged foliage is transformed into the forceful ultramarine almost amoebic form which becomes one of the central elements in the composition.

Washton's reading of the white semi-circle halfway up the right edge as a boat tipped onto its side with the black mast projecting deep into the center of the composition is suggestive, especially if one compares the motif with a perhaps more legible boat at the left in *Improvisation 31 (Sea Battle)*. Much more problematic, however, is her reading of the central subject of the picture. She sees the white form on the left side of the composition as an anthropomorphic shape with a head, raised right arm, and in the New York watercolor a left arm too. As such she suggests that the figure was probably derived from the "materialization of spirits" (reproduced in A. Aksakov's *Animismus and Spiritismus*, Leningrad, 1890) and hence may represent in some sense not only Kandinsky's attempt to dematerialize his motifs in order "to reveal their spiritual essence," but also to embody Rudolf Steiner's astral man.

Grohmann (1959) and Hamilton see the picture as essentially lacking in recognizable imagery, although Grohmann points out the appearance here for the first time of the round form with one jagged edge that is to become a common motif in later years. Ringbom relates this embryonic "tentacled" form to A. Besant and C. W. Leadbeater's diagram for "Selfish Greed" or "Greed for Drink" (his figs. 122-125). As such he sees Kandinsky's use of the motif as an instance of the way in which the artist used Theosophical imagery as a starting point for the development of his own highly personal vocabulary.

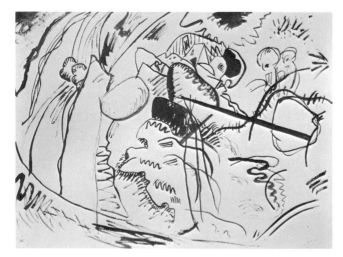

fig. c.
Kandinsky, study for *Painting with White Form,* pen
and ink on paper, 10½ x 14¾ in., 26.6 x 37.4 cm.,
Private Collection, Paris.

fig. d.
Kandinsky, study for *Painting with White Form,* water-
color on paper, 10⅞ x 15 in., 27.6 x 38.1 cm., The
Museum of Modern Art, New York. Katherine S.
Dreier Bequest.

EXHIBITIONS:

Berlin, *Erster Deutscher Herbstsalon,* Sept.-Nov. 1913, no. 185; Berlin, Der Sturm,
Expressionisten, Futuristen, Kubisten, July 1916, no. 25; Berlin, Der Sturm, *Sammlung
Walden,* Oct. 1919, no. 172; Berlin, *Kunstausstellung Berlin, Abteilung der Novembergruppe,*
1920, no. 1262 (for sale); Charleston, S.C., SRGM 4-T, no. 104, repr. color p. 91 ("*Light Form,*
1912"); Baltimore, SRGM 5-T, no. 104, repr. color; New York, SRGM 43, *Kandinsky,* no. 19
("*Light Form,* 1912"); 64 (no cat.); Boston, Institute of Contemporary Art, *Kandinsky,* Mar.
25-Apr. 18, 1952, traveled to New York, M. Knoedler & Co., Inc., May 10-June 6, 1952, San
Francisco Museum of Art, July 20-Aug. 26, 1952, Minneapolis, Walker Art Center, Sept. 14-
Oct. 26, 1952, Cleveland Museum of Art, Nov. 6-Dec. 7, 1952, no. 29; New York, SRGM 79
(checklist); Andover, Mass., Addison Gallery of American Art, *Variations,* Jan. 8-Feb. 15,
1954, no. 23; Brussels, SRGM 105-T, p. 14, repr.; Toronto, SRGM 117-T (no cat.); Boston,
SRGM 119-T, no. 18; Cleveland Museum of Art, *Paths of Abstract Art,* Oct. 4-Nov. 13, 1960,
no. 31, repr.; Philadelphia, SRGM 134-T, no. 51; Paris, Galerie Maeght, *Der Blaue Reiter,*
Oct. 26-Nov. 1962, cat. published in *Derrière le miroir,* no. 133-134, p. 16, repr.; New York,
SRGM 147, *Kandinsky,* no. 31, repr. p. 57; 162 (checklist); New York, Sidney Janis Gallery, *3
Generations,* Nov. 24-Dec. 26, 1964, no. 11, repr.; Museum of Fine Arts of St. Petersburg,
Florida, Inc., *Inaugural Exhibition,* Feb. 7-Mar. 7, 1965, no. 82, repr.; New York, SRGM 184
(no cat.); Buenos Aires, Museo Nacional de Bellas Artes, *De Cézanne à Miró,* May 15-June 5,
1968, traveled to Santiago, Museo de Arte Contemporaneo de la Universidad de Chile, June
26-July 17, 1968, Caracas, Venezuela, Museo de Bellas Artes, Aug. 4-25, 1968, p. 46, repr.;
New York, SRGM 208, 212, 221, 226 (no cats.); 232, pp. 186-187, repr.; 236 (no cat.); 241,
pp. 186-187, repr.; 252, repr.; 266 (no cat.).

REFERENCES:

Kandinsky 1901-1913, 1913, repr. p. 7; *V. V. Kandinsky,* 1918, repr. p. 31; H. Bahr, *Expressionismus,* Munich, 1920, repr. opp. p. 120 ("*Samml. Walden, Berlin*"); F. Burger, *Cézanne
und Hodler,* Munich, 1923, repr. no. 178; W. Grohmann "Wassily Kandinsky," *Cahiers d'art,*
4 année, no. 7, 1929, repr. p. 325 (upside down, "*Coll. Otto Rolfs, Braunschweig*"); Brisch,
1955, pp. 228, 246; Grohmann, 1959, pp. 134, 332 no. 166 (*Painting with White Forms*), repr.
color p. 135; Washton, 1968, pp. 86-87, 223-225; S. Ringbom, *The Sounding Cosmos,* Abo,
1970, pp. 204-205, pl. 121; G. H. Hamilton, *19th and 20th Century Art,* New York, 1970,
p. 229, color pl. 37.

90   **Landscape with Rain.** January 1913.
   (Landschaft mit Regen; Rain).

HL *i/1913, 167,* Пейзаж с дождем (Peizazh
s dozhdem, Landscape with Rain).

45.962

Oil on canvas, 27⅝ x 30¾ (70.2 x 78.1)

Signed l.l.: *Kandinsky*. Not dated.

PROVENANCE:
Heinz Braune, Munich, 1913- at least 1920;[1]
Fritz Schön, Berlin, by 1928 (Nationalgalerie
exhibition catalogue)-1943; purchased from
Schön, Quebec, by Dominion Gallery,
Montreal, 1943 (information on this and
subsequent provenance supplied by Max

Stern, Dominion Gallery, correspondence,
1967, 1971-72); sold by Dominion Gallery to
Karl Nierendorf, New York, November
1943; purchased from Nierendorf, 1945.

CONDITION:
In 1953 the picture was cleaned; in 1962 the
canvas was lined with wax resin, the
stretcher was replaced, and the margins
waxed. The left margin was inpainted along
its entire length (approximately ½ in. in
width) and the picture surfaced with PBM.

Apart from some small paint losses along
the edges, the condition is excellent. (July
1972.)

An earlier smaller version of the same scene from the identical vantage point
is in the Clayeux Collection, Paris (oil on board, 28 x 31⅛ in., 33 x 44.5 cm.,
Grohmann, 1959, cc 38; *Cahiers d'Art*, 1956-57, repr. p. 187). Grohmann
(p. 62) identifies the Clayeux oil, which appears in the HL under 1910, as the
study for the 1913 Guggenheim picture, implying thereby that the Clayeux
oil was preparatory in nature rather than a completed painting in its own
right. Although it is clear that the Guggenheim painting has been developed
from the earlier version, the relationship between the two would seem to be
that of two different conceptions of the same scene rather than that of a "study"
to a completed painting.

The 1913 date for the Guggenheim picture has not been questioned in the
literature, and it is not clear why the picture carried the date 1911 for the
fifteen years between 1953 and 1968 (see below EXHIBITIONS).

1. The HL states that the picture was painted for an auction to be held at the Russian Ball in
   Munich, where it was purchased for 150 CH by Dr. Braune; it later belonged to *"Schön,
   Berlin."* The picture is reproduced in *Kandinsky 1901-1913*, pl. 10, as *"Privatbesitz,
   München"* (the Braune collection), and it still belonged to him when the Russian edition of
   Kandinsky 1901-1913 was published in 1918, and when H. Zehder's monograph *Wassily
   Kandinsky* was published in Dresden, 1920 (pl. 2). It has not been possible to establish the
   date of its sale to Fritz Schön.

EXHIBITIONS:

Berlin, Nationalgalerie, *Neuerer Deutscher Kunst aus Berliner Privatbesitz*, Apr. 1928, no. 47 ("*Stadt in Regen*, Samml. Fritz Schön, Grunewald"); New York, Nierendorf Gallery, *Gestation-Formation*, Mar. 1944, no. 9; New York, SRGM 43, *Kandinsky*, no. 22; Chicago, SRGM 47-T, *Kandinsky*, no. 4; Pittsburgh, SRGM 53-T, *Kandinsky*, no. 10; New York, SRGM 79 (checklist, dated 1911?; so dated in all subsequent SRGM publications until SRGM 212, 1968; withdrawn Oct. 20); Toronto, SRGM 85-T, no. 20, repr.; New York, SRGM 87 (checklist); 89 (no cat.); Montreal, SRGM 93-T, no. 17; New York, SRGM 95, 97 (checklists); London, SRGM 104-T, no. 29; New York, SRGM 112, 118 (checklists); Lexington, Ky., SRGM 122-T, no. 10; Pasadena, SRGM 146-T, *Kandinsky*, no. 17, repr. p. 45; New York, SRGM 184 (no cat.); New York, Spencer Samuels Gallery, *Expressionismus*, Apr. 22-Sept. 6, 1968, no. 47 (dated 1911); New York, Sidney Janis Gallery, *European XXth Century Artists*, Jan. 8-Feb. 1, 1969, no. 22 (dated 1911); New York, SRGM 212, 226 (no cats.); 252, repr.; New York, SRGM 266, 276 (no cats.).

REFERENCES:

Kandinsky 1901-1913, 1913, repr. p. 10; *V. V. Kandinsky*, 1918, p. 29; H. Zehder, *Wassily Kandinsky*, Dresden, 1920, no. 2; Grohmann, 1959, pp. 62, 332 no. 167, repr. cc 85.

91 ## Painting with White Border. May 1913.
(Das Bild mit weissem Rand; The White Edge; No. 173).

HL *v/1913, 173,* Картина с бел[ой] каймой (Kartina c bel[oi] kaimoi, Painting with White Border).

37.245

Oil on canvas, 55¼ x 78⅞ (140.3 x 200.3)

Signed and dated l.l.: *Kandinsky 1913.*; inscribed by the artist on stretcher (barely visible): *Kandinsky Bild mit weissem Rand (1913)* (clearly visible): *No 173.*

PROVENANCE:
Purchased from the artist through Herwarth Walden, Berlin, by F. Kluxen, Münster, November 1, 1913;[1] returned to Walden, 1918 or 1919;[2] purchased from an unknown source by Solomon R. Guggenheim before 1937; Gift of Solomon R. Guggenheim, 1937.

CONDITION:
In 1953 the canvas was cleaned; 3 small holes (1 at the bottom edge, 1 at the left edge, and 1 in the left corner) were filled with gesso and inpainted with PVA. The canvas was surfaced with PBM. In 1955 2 damages to the support were repaired (1 1¼ in. long in the green and blue area left of center; the second ½ in. long in the white bar at the center); the inpainting in these areas is now discolored and cracked. In 1970 a 1 in. puncture in the lower right white arc was repaired and inpainted.

There is considerable wear in the margin areas, especially at the corners. The support is fragile, but the paint film in general well preserved. (Sept. 1972.)

Kandinsky's own essay on this picture was written shortly after the completion of the work itself and throws some light on the process of composition, on the artist's sense of the final effect, and on his theories of the symbolism of color.

Regarding the thematic content he offers an explanation only of the troika motif which dominates the upper left of the composition, a form derived, he says, from the curving backs of the horses in a Russian *Dreigespann* (or three-horse carriage). The picture was composed under the spell of his recent visit to Moscow, and Grohmann describes the work as a kind of "apotheosis of Moscow."

Washton convincingly argues that the central motif of the man on horseback holding a strikingly long white lance is a figure of St. George, and the three white claw-like projections in the lower left corner a serpent or dragon. (Kandinsky does not identify this element of the composition, but he does describe

1. Unpublished letters from Herwarth Walden to Kandinsky in the Gabriele Münter und Johannes Eichner Stiftung, Munich, dated Oct. 31, 1913, and Nov. 1, 1913. (I am indebted to H. K. Röthel for bringing these letters to my attention and for making copies of them available to me.) In the first letter Walden reports that Kluxen is ready to buy the picture and in the second that he has bought it.

2. HL: "sold to Kluxen" (in Russian); *"getauscht 1918 gegen No. 188. Samml. S. R. Guggenheim."* In 1918 or 1919 Kluxen apparently returned some pictures to Walden in exchange for others. He acquired *Black Lines* (see below cat. no. 94) in exchange for *Improvisation 10* at the same time.

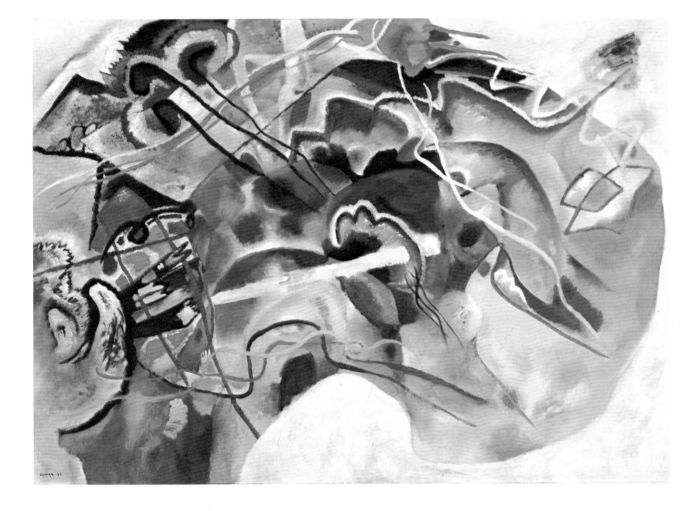

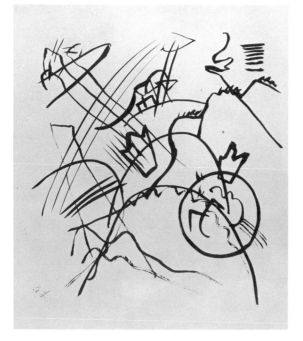

fig. a.
Kandinsky, study for *Painting with White Border*, 1912, ink on paper, 10 x 9¾ in., 25.5 x 24.6 cm., Musée National d'Art Moderne, Paris.

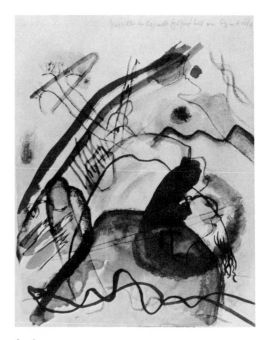

fig. b.
Kandinsky, study for *Painting with White Border,* watercolor on paper, 12 x 9½ in., 30.5 x 24.1 cm., Städtische Galerie im Lenbachhaus, Munich, GMS 354.

fig. c.
Kandinsky, study for *Painting with White Border*, watercolor on paper, 15 x 13⅜ in., 38 x 34 cm., formerly Collection van Assendelft.

fig. d.
Kandinsky, study for *Painting with White Border,* watercolor on paper, 12½ x 9⅜ in., 31.6 x 23.9 cm., inscribed: *"Zu Bild no. 173,"* Städtische Galerie im Lenbachhaus, Munich, GMS 160.

fig. e.
Kandinsky, study for *Painting with White Border,* oil on canvas, 39¼ x 31 in.,
99.7 x 78.7 cm., The Phillips Collection, Washington, D.C.

the lower left as a *"Kampf in Weiss und Schwartz"* ["a battle in white and
black"].) Washton sees the clear outline of the head, neck, and crossed forelegs
of the horse, as well as its tail and the rider in only one watercolor (fig. b), but
it is in fact also present in the 1912 ink drawing (fig. a) and in the enlarged version of the watercolor (fig. c). In subsequent versions this horse and rider has
been simplified to the double-humped curved form which it takes in the final
painting.

Washton further convincingly associates the trumpet form at the upper right
of figs. b and d—in both these cases clearly held and blown by an angel figure
—with the apocalyptic trumpet found in the paintings of the Resurrection, Last
Judgment, and All Saints' Day. In the later studies and in the final painting, the
angel is gone and the trumpet has been reduced to a barely outlined transparent
area, recognizable only in the light of these earlier representations.

The earliest conception for the picture seems to have been vertical in format.
A group of studies (figs. a-d) culminating in the Phillips oil sketch (fig. e) record
this phase. The horizontal format represented by the watercolor (fig. g), the
second oil study (fig. h), and all the remaining studies was probably developed
during a second stage. The sequence proposed here is, however, extremely tentative, and Kandinsky's gradual evolution of the composition requires more

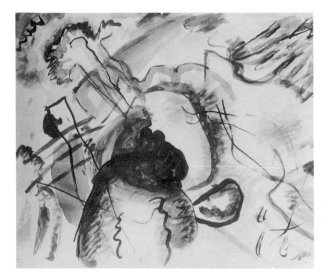

fig. f.
Kandinsky, study for *Painting with White Border,* water-
color on paper, 10¾ x 14⅞ in., 27.4 x 37.8 cm., inscribed:
"Zu Bild no. 173," Städtische Galerie im Lenbachhaus,
Munich, GMS 131.

fig. g.
Kandinsky, study for *Painting with White Border,* watercolor on paper, 5 x 13¼ in.,
12.7 x 33 cm., Collection The Hilla von Rebay Foundation, Greens Farms, Connecticut.

fig. h.
Kandinsky, study for *Painting with White Border,* oil on
canvas, 27⅝ x 41 in., 70.2 x 104.1 cm., State Tretiakov
Gallery, Moscow.

fig. i.
Kandinsky, study for *Painting with White Border*, ink on paper, 8 x 21 in., 20.3 x 53.3 cm., inscribed: *"Zu Bild mit Weissem Rand,"* Städtische Galerie im Lenbachhaus, Munich, GMS 379.

fig. j.
Kandinsky, study for *Painting with White Border*, pencil on paper, 10⅞ x 14⅞ in., 27.5 x 37.8 cm., Städtische Galerie im Lenbachhaus, Munich, GMS 396.

detailed study. Nonetheless, the painstaking resolution of the compositional problems described in his essay are traceable within the present sequence. Throughout all the studies except the final one (fig. p), the area in the lower right corner remains vague, undefined, and open. Indeed the first inkling of the white edge appears in this very last extremely rapid skeleton study where the solution apparently suddenly presented itself.

The apocalyptic trumpet persists throughout most of the sketches; toppling towers, part of Kandinsky's traditionally apocalyptic imagery, are the subject of one small horizontal sketch (fig. i); in two late studies they are moved over to the far left (figs. k and l; Washton sees these forms as the outline of a horse and rider, but they seem on the contrary much more clearly associable with the earlier toppling towers of fig. i). These towers are reduced almost to nothing in figs. m and n. By the final painting they are no longer legible as such.

The "serpent"—target of St. George's labors—is most clearly defined in the hitherto unpublished and unidentified watercolor (fig. g), where great curved monstrous jaws appear to fasten upon the lance. These jaws are subsequently simplified to either two or three more rigidly projecting arms (or heads?) which lunge out at the oncoming rider.

The arched thick forms of the lower right (which gave Kandinsky so much trouble) appear in their final form only in the painting itself and in the probably penultimate schematic drawing (fig. o; this drawing, identified by Washton as a study for *Composition II,* is clearly an outline schema for the present work; it contains all of the essential elements of the composition apart from the crucial final white edge).

fig. k.
Kandinsky, study for *Painting with White Border,* pencil
on paper, 5 ⅞ x 9 ⅞ in., 15 x 25 cm., Städtische Galerie
im Lenbachhaus, Munich, GMS 429.

fig. l.
Kandinsky, study for *Painting with White Border,* pencil
on paper, 5 ⅞ x 9 ⅞ in., 15 x 25 cm., Städtische Galerie
im Lenbachhaus, Munich, GMS 429.

fig. m.
Kandinsky, study for *Painting with White Border,* ink on
paper, 10 ⅞ x 15 ¼ in., 27.5 x 38.8 cm., inscribed: *"Zu
Bild no. 173,"* Städtische Galerie im Lenbachhaus,
Munich, GMS 397.

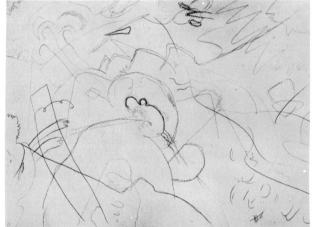

fig. n.
Kandinsky, study for *Painting with White Border,* pencil
on paper, 10 ⅞ x 14 ⅞ in., 27.5 x 37.8 cm., inscribed: *"Zu
Bild no. 173,"* Städtische Galerie im Lenbachhaus,
Munich, GMS 395.

Washton sees the composition as a whole as an expression of Kandinsky's
apocalyptic vision and his "belief in the spiritual upheaval to come."

The horse within a circle depicted in fig. a has been seen by Lindsay (1951,
pp. 152 ff.), then by Brisch (p. 228) and Weiss (1973, p. 460) as an early prophetic suggestion of Kandinsky's later use of the circle in place of the horse,
and his endowment of that form with much of the symbolic content previously
carried by the horse. (For further discussion of this aspect of Kandinsky's iconographic development, see below cat. nos. 105 and 111.) The remarkable appearance of the circle at this early date, as well as its clear association with the
horse, raise important issues of chronology which require further study.

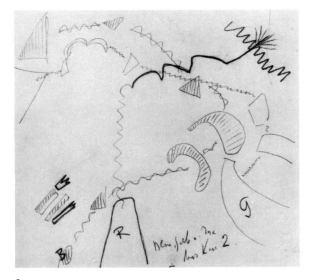

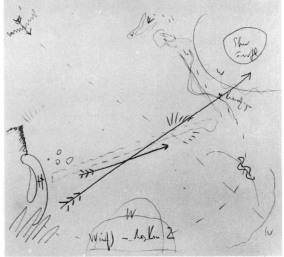

fig. o.
Kandinsky, study for *Painting with White Border,* pencil
on paper, 8¼ x 9⅞ in., 20.9 x 24.9 cm., Städtische
Galerie im Lenbachhaus, Munich, GMS 452.

fig. p.
Kandinsky, study for *Painting with White Border,* pencil
on paper, 8¼ x 9⅝ in., 21.1 x 24.6 cm., Städtische
Galerie im Lenbachhaus, Munich, GMS 451.

EXHIBITIONS:

Berlin, Der Sturm, *Erster Deutscher Herbstsalon,* Sept.-Nov. 1913, no. 182; Dresden, Galerie
Arnold, *Die Neue Malerei,* Jan. 1914, no. 67, repr.; Berlin, Der Sturm, *Kandinsky,* Sept. 1916,
no. 20; Berlin, Graphisches Kabinett Neumann, *Kunstausstellung,* 1919-20 (?);[3] Charleston,
S.C., SRGM 1-T, no. 67, repr. p. 53 (*The White Edge;* the title by which the picture was
known in all subsequent SRGM publications until SRGM 88-T, 1954); Philadelphia, SRGM
3-T, no. 76, repr. p. 75; Charleston, S.C., SRGM 4-T, no. 106, repr. p. 105; New York, SRGM
43, *Kandinsky,* no. 24, repr.; Pittsburgh, SRGM 53-T, *Kandinsky,* no. 3, repr.; New York,
SRGM 78 (checklist; added Apr. 24); 79 (checklist); Toronto, SRGM 85-T, no. 21; Vancouver,
SRGM 88-T, no. 19, repr. (*Picture with White Edge,* the title by which the picture has been
known in all subsequent SRGM publications); San Francisco Museum of Art, *Art in the
Twentieth Century,* June 17-July 10, 1955, p. 14; New York, SRGM 95 (checklist); The
Denver Art Museum, *Turn of the Century, 1880-1920,* Oct. 1-Nov. 18, 1956, no. 16; London,
SRGM 104-T, no. 31; New York, SRGM 118 (checklist); World's Fair, *Masterpieces of
Modern Art,* Apr. 21-Sept. 4, 1962, no. 59, repr.; Philadelphia, SRGM 134-T, no. 52; New
York, SRGM 147, *Kandinsky,* no. 32, repr. p. 58; New York, SRGM 184, 208, 212, 221, 226
(no cats.); 232, p. 185, repr. p. 184; 236 (no cat.); 241, p. 185, repr. 184; 252, repr. n.p. (with-
drawn after New York showing); 266 (no cat.).

REFERENCES:

W. Kandinsky, "Das Bild mit weissem Rand," *Kandinsky 1901-1913,* 1913, pp. xxxix-xxxxi,
repr. p. 13; *V. V. Kandinsky,* 1918, repr. p. 33 ("Coll. Kluxen"); Brisch, 1955, pp. 228-229,
296, 318; Grohmann, 1959, pp. 132, 134, 332 no. 173, repr. cc 90; Washton, 1968, pp. 217-223;
P. Overy, *The Language of the Eye,* New York, 1969, pp. 68, 118-119, pl. 25; Weiss, 1973,
pp. 460 ff., 507 ff.

3. A printed label on the stretcher carries this information, but no catalogue of the exhibition
   has so far come to light.

92   Small Pleasures. June 1913.
        (Kleine Freuden; No. 174).

HL *vi/1913, 174,* Маленькие радости
(Malenkie radosti, Small Pleasures).

43.921

Oil on canvas, 43¼ x 47⅛ (109.8 x 119.7)

Signed and dated l.l.: *Kandinsky 1913;* inscribed by the artist on stretcher (barely
visible): *Kandinsky Kleine Freuden (1913) /
(No 174).*

PROVENANCE:

Purchased from the artist by W. Beffie, Amsterdam and Brussels, 1913 (information
from HL and from *Kandinsky 1901-1913,*
1913, p. 6); remained in Beffie collection
until at least 1938 (lender to New Burlington Galleries); Karl Nierendorf, New York,
by 1942 (exhibition catalogue); purchased
from Nierendorf, 1943.

CONDITION:

In 1954 the surface was cleaned; an 8 in. tear
below and to the right of center had at some
unspecified earlier date been patched and retouched. The surface was coated with PBM.

Apart from the edges where there is some
wear (especially in the 4 corners where the
support is worn through to the stretcher),
the condition is excellent. (Aug. 1972.)

The origin of the composition is to be found in a glass painting entitled *With
Sun* (fig. b), dated 1910 by Grohmann on the basis of a photograph apparently
so dated in Kandinsky's hand (1959, p. 111; the present whereabouts of the
photograph are unknown). Röthel, who originally dated the glass painting ca.
1912 (1966), now more convincingly also inclines to date it 1910 (conversation
with the author, December 1974). The glass painting and the preparatory study
for it (fig. a) present the imagery of *Small Pleasures* in its most clearly legible

fig. a.
Kandinsky, study for glass painting *With Sun,* pencil on
paper, 11½ x 15⅜ in., 29.3 x 38.9 cm., Städtische Galerie
im Lenbachhaus, Munich, GMS 443.

fig. b.
Kandinsky, *With Sun,* 1910, oil and tempera (?) on glass,
12 x 15⅞ in., 30.6 x 40.3 cm., Städtische Galerie im
Lenbachhaus, Munich, GMS 120.

92

form. In the center are two hills, each surmounted by a citadel. On the left a silvery couple is walking at an angle (or possibly reclining?) and three brightly colored horsemen are galloping up the hillside; on the right a purple row boat with three black oars is tossed in a blue sea. In the upper left corner is a brilliant blue, white, and yellow sun, in the upper right a black cloud with white center.

fig. c.
Kandinsky, *Improvisation 21a,* oil on canvas,
37¾ x 41⅜ in., 96 x 105 cm., Städtische Galerie
im Lenbachhaus, Munich, GMS 82.

fig. d.
Kandinsky, study for *Small Pleasures,* ink on
paper, 9½ x 9¾ in., 24 x 24.7 cm., inscribed:
"zu 'kleine Freuden'," Städtische Galerie im
Lenbachhaus, Munich, GMS 393.

This composition clearly provided the model for *Improvisation 21a* (fig. c),
where the underlying structure is identical to that of the glass painting, but the
forms are to some extent veiled and less legible. The 1911 date for *Improvisation 21a,* recorded both in the HL and on the work itself, has presented no
problems, and Grohmann's 1910 date for the glass painting is thus entirely
plausible. The colors of the oil are, as Washton has noted, subdued blues,
pinks, and grayish-whites, and the contrasts of the more vibrant glass painting
have been suppressed (1972). The sun in the upper left corner has become a
pinkish-red cloud, and the threatening nature of the cloud in the upper right is
somewhat reduced by the use of brown-beige, blue, and some pink/white,
rather than pure black.

Small Pleasures, preceded by at least three further studies (figs. d-f), was
painted approximately two years later than *Improvisation 21a,* and the colors
have changed considerably. However, the compositional relationship, as well
as the extent to which the images are veiled, is remarkably close in the two
works.

Grohmann discusses *Small Pleasures* in isolation from the earlier versions
and therefore fails to identify some of the images; he sees the painting as divided into a "ponderous" right side and a "playful" left side, the whole suggesting a relationship with the All Saints' pictures of the immediately preceding
period.

Washton takes Grohmann's analysis still further and sees the title as "ironic."
Far from depicting actual "pleasures" such as rowing, loving, riding (as Röthel

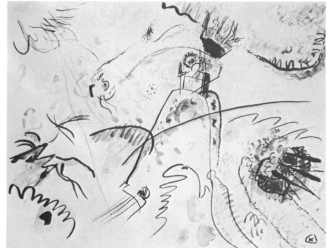

fig. e.
Kandinsky, study for *Small Pleasures*, 1913, watercolor on paper, 9⅜ x 11¾ in., 23.8 x 29.9 cm.,
formerly Collection Jan W. E. Buijs, The Hague.

fig. f.
Kandinsky, study for *Small Pleasures,* 1913, watercolor
on paper, 9¼ x 12⅜ in., 23.5 x 31.5 cm., Private
Collection, Paris.

suggested), the picture is to be seen, she argues, as a logical extension of Kandinsky's preoccupation in works such as *Resurrection II, All Saints' Day,* and
Deluge with the notion of "regenerative" Apocalypse, with a striving for en-
lightenment, and with a tension between dissonance and hope (1968 and 1972).
The three horsemen are in her view the apocalyptic riders, and the boat is
tossed in a stormy sea, surrounded by threatening waves, black clouds, and at
the lower center a whale.

Ringbom too places the work in the context of Kandinsky's notion of the
Apocalypse announcing a new spiritual era. Although he does not discuss the
imagery of the painting as a whole, he sees the ubiquitous hill with the "onion
dome towers"—also used on the cover of *Über das Geistige*—as a direct reflection of that passage in the book where "a large city, solidly built according to
the rules of architecture and mathematics [is] suddenly shaken by an immense
force," the towers crumble and fall, the sun grows dark, and one searches in
vain for the power with which to battle the darkness (*Über das Geistige,* 1912,
p. 22). This central image of the collapsing or threatened city is, Ringbom argues, a metaphor for a shattered material world on the eve of spiritual
regeneration.

The most difficult problem raised by Washton's (and to a lesser extent Ringbom's) reading and interpretation of the picture, a problem which remains unresolved, is its introduction into Kandinsky's language of an otherwise unknown note of deep irony. Although many of the paintings of the years 1911-13
contain apocalyptic imagery, and although this imagery is often veiled beneath

a tapestry of vibrant color and blurred forms, the notion of irony is absent. Kandinsky repeatedly warns against interpretations of his paintings which are based on their titles or subtitles, since these do not, he emphasizes, provide the clue to their deepest meaning (see above *Study for "Composition II"* and *160b*, cat. nos. 82, 88); but no other case has hitherto emerged in which he may be said to have used a title to deliberately obscure what lies within the work. Moreover, while it is true that the three horsemen, the boat, the citadel perched upon a hilltop, the couple, and the dark cloud are significant images in much of Kandinsky's pre-war oeuvre, it is also true that they do appear in contexts which do not carry explicitly apocalyptic meaning. (See, for example, *Picture with Archer*, 1909, 75; *Blue Mountain*, 1909, 84; *Romantic Landscape*, 1911, 115; *Garden of Love*, 1912, 149; *Improvisation 26 (Rowing)*, 1912, 148.) Washton's designation of the sea in *Small Pleasures* as stormy, and the right side of the painting as dominated by dark colors, is at least debatable. The overall coloring of the canvas, with the exception of the cloud in the upper right corner, is in fact vibrant, and the waves, which are blue, do not give an especially ominous impression. The identification of the foreground form as a whale is not certain. Ringbom's identification of the citadel as toppling is also in this instance difficult to sustain.

The possibility must be borne in mind, therefore, that the extraordinarily lyrical and decorative nature of the preparatory watercolor (fig. f) and of the final painting does not in fact mask a deeper underlying warning of impending Apocalypse, but rather recalls the memory of "small pleasures."

A recently discovered, unpublished essay on this painting written by Kandinsky in June 1913, tends to support the notion that the title is an accurate reflection of the painting's content rather than an ironic comment upon it. At the same time this text also gives some hint of a more profound content. (I am indebted to Röthel for a transcribed copy of this essay, the original of which is in the Gabriele Münter und Johannes Eichner Stiftung, Munich, and for his permission to quote from it.)

In the essay Kandinsky establishes first that it was the delicacy of color in the glass painting *With Sun*, combined with its gold, silver, and transparent glazes, which inspired him to attempt the composition on a larger scale. He made a preparatory drawing (presumably fig. d) in which he suggested this delicacy through a use of fine and very fine lines. (*"Ich habe erst eine Zeichnung gemacht [das Weiche habe ich da durch feine und sehr feine Linien unterstrichen] um das Verschobene in der grossen Komposition zu entfernen und diese Komposition kühl und von grossem Gleichgewicht der Teile für das Bild zu machen."*) He describes the background of the painting as *"geistig,"* and although he chose it unconsciously, he then realized that it provided the ideal "playground" (*"Spielplatz"*) for the small pleasures. His aim was to let himself go and to scatter a heap of small pleasures upon the canvas. (*"Mein Ziel war ja—sich gehen zu lassen und eine Menge kleine Freuden auf die Leinwand zu schütten."*)

His description of the actual process of execution evokes similarly pleasurable memories. It went easily, joyfully, happily. Within this framework, however, Kandinsky does provide a clue to the significance of the black cloud in the upper right. He acknowledges that within the generally joyful setting of this playful scene the black cloud introduces a slightly somber note in the form of *"das feine innere Kochen"* ("the subtle interior simmering") and *"die Über-fliessungen"* ("overflowings"), both of which terms he apparently borrowed from his description of the "melancholy" passages in *The Painting with White Border* (*Kandinsky 1901-1913, 1913,* p. xxxx). In the context of *Small Pleasures,* he takes pains to emphasize that these "simmerings" remain mere suggestions which never assume a really painful tone, but they are nonetheless present. *("Aber überall blieb das alles im Bereich der Kleinen Freuden und bekam keinen schmerzlichen Beiklang.")* The generally playful nature of the picture's tone is compared to clear, individual drops of water falling into a pool; the dark cloud is thus analogous to one drop which suddenly sounds a melancholy bass note, but which arouses no fear. Similarly, a young yellow pug might be sitting in a pensive and serious mood; the distant memory of a dangerous bulldog is there, but who could possibly fear the little yellow pug! *("Das ganze Bild erinnert mich an in's Wasser fallende Tropfen, die hell und verschieden klingen und wenn plötzlich ein Tropfen schwermütig im Basston aufplumpst [die obere rechte düstere Ecke!] so wird es einem nicht bange. So sitzt manchmal nachdenklich und ernst ein junger gelber Mops. Es ist schon eine entfernte Erinnerung an einen gefährlichen Bulldog da - wer wird aber Angst vor dem kleinen Mops haben!")*

The overall atmosphere of the painting as described by Kandinsky is thus clearly one of pleasure. A flickering reminder of more serious things hovers in the background, but this does not destroy the essentially carefree tone.

Although it has repeatedly been demonstrated that Kandinsky's own descriptions of his paintings must be treated with considerable caution (see, for example, *Study for "Composition II,"* cat. no. 82), it is clear that the essay provides a coherent framework for both the imagery and the title of the painting, a framework which implies neither an ironic nor an apocalyptic stance. Some of the motifs which appear here in a light-hearted context may possibly evoke the memory of apocalyptic contexts within which they are used elsewhere. But the shadowy reminder of "an inner simmering melancholy" in *Small Pleasures* should be seen not as the dominant theme, but rather as a note, barely sensed, of the turbulent movement and restless energy of *Painting with White Border, Composition VII,* and other much more explicitly apocalyptic paintings of this same year. It lingers only in the background, allowing the vibrant gaiety of the painting as a whole to dominate.

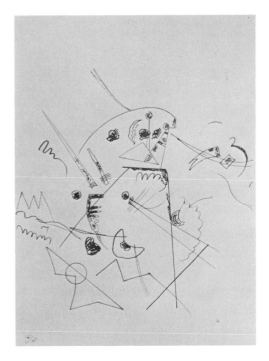

fig. g.
Kandinsky, study for *Reminiscences,*
ca. 1924(?), tusche on paper, 14 x 12 in.,
35.5 x 30.5 cm., Private Collection, Paris.

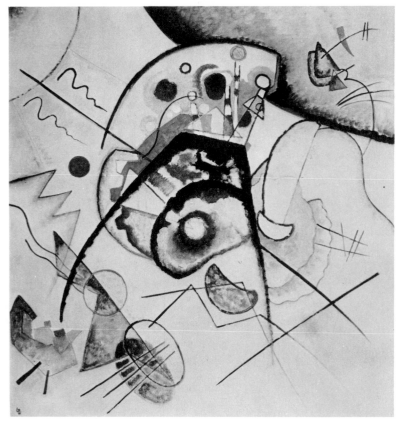

fig. h.
Kandinsky, *Reminiscences,* 1924, oil on canvas, 38⅝ x 37⅜ in., 98 x 95
cm., Private Collection, Paris.

NOTE: Lindsay's attribution to 1913 of the drawing which formed the basis of Kandinsky's 1924 painting *Reminiscences* raises problems which must be discussed in the present context. The drawing (fig. g), which is signed and dated 1913, is described by Lindsay as a study for the 1913 *Small Pleasures,* and Brisch, Grohmann, and Weiss, among others, have accepted his argument (1953, pp. 50-52). The drawing is, as Lindsay states, stylistically and iconographically closely related to the 1924 picture (fig. h), while its relationship to that of 1913 is both stylistically and formally remote. Precisely because of its extraordinarily advanced style, however, Lindsay argues that it accurately represents the nature of Kandinsky's 1913 preoccupation with the notion of a purely abstract art and his rapidly growing confidence in the potentialities for such an art. (For a brief comment on this issue, see below cat. no. 93; for a detailed analysis, see Lindsay, 1953.) Since other paintings and drawings of the period do not similarly reflect this development, the drawing in question would constitute a uniquely prophetic statement of later developments, paralleled by nothing else in Kandinsky's career.

Although it cannot be ruled out that Lindsay's analysis reflects what actually happened in Kandinsky's art rather early in 1913, the visual evidence argues strongly against it. For even though, as Lindsay so cogently argues, Kandinsky's theoretical writings in 1913-14 demonstrate a new attitude to geometric and precise form, the actual works of art produced, in all media, do not. And, although it is true, as Weiss has pointed out, that geometric figures such as circles and triangles occurred already in Kandinsky's early Jugendstil designs and graphics (pp. 430-432, 455-458), the stylistic context in which they were then used is quite different. Thus it is only the presence of the 1913 date on the drawing which argues for its attribution to this early phase. However, another plausible explanation for this inscribed date does exist. In 1924 as Kandinsky looked back to the *Small Pleasures* watercolor (fig. f) which he still owned—the painting having long been sold—and decided to recreate it in his by then fully developed abstract style, he would naturally have begun with a preparatory drawing. In order to pinpoint the era to which the title *Reminiscences* referred, it would seem plausible that he might sign the drawing with the triangle-enclosed K and the date of the earlier model, thus, as it were, establishing the provenance of the theme represented and indicating the extent to which he wished this to be a link with the past. A date of 1924 for the *Reminiscences* drawing seems thus more plausible than one of 1913.

EXHIBITIONS:

Amsterdam, Stedelijk Museum, *Moderne Kunstkring,* Nov. 7-Dec. 8, 1913, no. 96; London, New Burlington Galleries, *Twentieth Century German Art,* July 1938 (not in cat.);[1] New York, Nierendorf Gallery, *Kandinsky Retrospective,* Dec. 1942-Feb. 1943 (checklist); New York, SRGM 43, *Kandinsky,* no. 21, repr. p. 10; Pittsburgh, SRGM 53-T, *Kandinsky,* no. 17; Munich, Haus der Kunst, *Der Blaue Reiter,* Sept.-Oct. 1949, no. 67, repr.; New York, SRGM 74, no. 71; 87 (checklist); Brussels, SRGM 105-T, p. 12, repr.; Baltimore, SRGM 113-T (no cat.); Toronto, SRGM 117-T (no cat.); Boston, SRGM 119-T, no. 19; New York, SRGM 147, *Kandinsky,* no. 33, repr. p. 59; 184 (no cat.); 202, p. 80, repr. p. 81; 208, 212, 221, 226 (no cats.); 232, 241, p. 189, repr.; 252, repr.; 266, 276 (no cats.).

REFERENCES:

Kandinsky 1901-1913, 1913, repr. p. 6; *V. V. Kandinsky,* 1918, repr. p. 37; Idem, *On the Spiritual in Art,* trans. M. Sadler, London, 1914, repr. foll. p. 106; Grohmann, 1930, p. xxiv, repr. p. 10; Lindsay, 1951, pp. 152-155; Idem, "The Genesis and Meaning of the Cover Design for the first *Blaue Reiter* Exhibition Catalogue," *Art Bulletin,* vol. xxxv, March 1953, pp. 49-52; Brisch, 1955, pp. 226-230; Grohmann, 1959, pp. 110-111, 130, 194, 332 no. 174, repr. p. 137; H. K. Röthel, *Kandinsky: Painting on Glass,* exhibition catalogue, New York, 1966, no. 19; R. C. Washton, "Kandinsky's Paintings on Glass," *Artforum,* vol. v, Feb. 1967, p. 25; Washton, 1968, pp. 207-211; S. Ringbom, *The Sounding Cosmos,* Abo, 1970, pp. 167-168; R. C. Washton-Long, "Kandinsky and Abstraction: The Role of the Hidden Image," *Artforum,* vol. x, June 1972, pp. 47-49, repr. color p. 44; Weiss, 1973, pp. 461-462.

1. A label for the exhibition appears on the reverse: "Exhibition 'Modern German Art' / New Burlington Galleries / London / Kleine Freuden / Kandinsky / Owner: W. Beffie / Not for sale." Beffie also lent *Group in Crinolines* to this exhibition (see above cat. no. 81). After the catalogue had gone to press he apparently agreed to lend *Small Pleasures* in addition.

93 Light Picture. December 1913.
(Helles Bild; Bright Picture).

HL *xii / 1913, 188*, Светлая картина
(Svetlaia kartina, Light Picture).

37.244

Oil on canvas, 30⅝ x 39½ (77.8 x 100.2)

Signed and dated l.l.: *Kandinsky 1913;* inscribed by the artist on stretcher (barely visible): *Kandinsky—Helles Bild* (fully visible): *Nᵒ 188.*

PROVENANCE:

Left by Kandinsky with Gabriele Münter, Murnau, 1914;[1] purchased from Münter by Herwarth Walden, Berlin, 1916 or 1917;[2] acquired from Walden by F. Kluxen, Münster, in exchange for *Painting with White Border*, 1918 or 1919;[3] remained in Kluxen collection until at least 1924 (Grohmann, 1924, repr. n.p.); purchased from an unknown source by Solomon R. Guggenheim, before September 1930;[4] Gift of Solomon R. Guggenheim, 1937.

CONDITION:

In 1957 the painting was lined with wax resin.

The 4 corners show considerable wear, as do the margins. There is some cracking in the pigment, with a few tiny scattered losses, notably in the blacks, yellows, and reds. (Aug. 1972.)

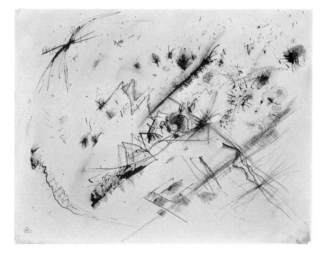

fig. a.
Kandinsky, study for *Light Picture,* 1913, watercolor and ink on paper, 10 x 13⅝ in., 25.4 x 34.5 cm., Germanisches Nationalmuseum, Nuremberg.

1. When Kandinsky returned to Russia at the outbreak of the war, he left many of his pictures with Münter for safekeeping.
2. HL: *"Münter verkauft an Walden. 1500. 1917."* Since the picture appeared in a 1916 exhibition at Der Sturm it is possible that Münter sold it at that time, but that Kandinsky did not hear about it until later.
3. HL: *"Bes. Kluxen getauscht 1918 (od. 19) gegen für (No. 173)."* See above cat. no. 91, fn. 2.
4. The Guggenheim records do not reveal the source or date of purchase, but an unpublished letter from Kandinsky to Grohmann dated 7/9/30 refers to the picture as "Coll. Guggenheim" (Grohmann Archiv, Stuttgart, copy in the library of The Museum of Modern Art, New York).

93

A very detailed watercolor and ink study for the picture is in the collection of the Germanisches Nationalmuseum, Nurenberg (fig. a). It has not been possible to verify whether the colors in the final painting closely follow those of the study.

Kandinsky's works of 1913 were, until the early 1950's, traditionally regarded as totally abstract. But as Brisch, Grohmann, H. K. Röthel, Washton, Ringbom, and others have amply demonstrated, these works are in fact filled with the religious imagery so characteristic of the immediately preceding years. Though veiled and in many instances virtually undecipherable without the aid of the preparatory studies and/or the earlier glass paintings, these images still constitute in many cases a more or less explicit eschatological content for the 1913 paintings. (See above, for example, *Painting with White Border*, cat. no. 91.) It is only towards the end of 1913 and during the course of 1914 and later that Kandinsky actually appears to have abandoned recognizable imagery in ~or of a more clearly abstract mode of expression, although the old motifs continue to appear throughout the later years. Exactly which paintings represent this break with the *gegenständlich* is still the subject of dispute. Moreover, definitions of the actual terms involved vary considerably—whether they are the German *abstrakt, gegenstandlos, absolut,* and *ungegenständlich* or the English "abstract," "purely abstract," "non-objective," or more recently "objectless." Kandinsky's own use of these various terms in relation to his work remains far from clear. (For a discussion of many of the problems involved, see Washton, 1968, chapter 1; also Weiss, 1973, pp. 130-131, 150-151, et passim.)

Washton suggests that *"Light Picture* [appears] to have dispensed with apocalyptic imagery and to have substituted what Kandinsky would later call a sensation of the cosmos or infinity." Ringbom, on the other hand, sees the composition as directly dependent upon a series of 1910-13 landscapes of which the first is *Murnau with Church.* He traces the gradual "disintegration" of this landscape through the 1913 *Landscapes with a Church I* and *II* and suggests that *Light Picture* represents the final phase in the progression, not only in the disintegration of the legible forms through the emancipation of color, but also in the "spiritualization" of these forms—a process which Ringbom relates directly to the influence of Steiner's Theosophical texts. However, Kandinsky himself, in hitherto partially unpublished 1936-37 correspondence with Hilla Rebay, stated in the strongest possible terms that both *Light Picture* and *Black Lines* belonged to that group of pictures which had "nothing whatsoever to do with an object." Since it was largely in response to Rebay's definitions that his notion of an explicitly "non-objective" art was formulated, it is important to examine the context in which his statements occurred.

In a letter of December 16, 1936, he addressed himself for the first time to her definitions of "abstract" and "non-objective" art, as she had expressed them in the introduction to the 1936 Charleston, South Carolina, catalogue, *Solomon R. Guggenheim Collection of Non-Objective Paintings* (SRGM 1-T). He wrote: *Sie machen, wie Sie mir selbst sagten, einen wesentlichen Unterschied zwischen "abstract" und "non-objectiv"* [sic]. *Der Unterschied ist, wie ich Sie verstehe, der, dass "abstract" eine Abstraktion bedeutet, die aus dem Gegenstand herausgezogen wird, wogegen "non-objectivity" eine Kunst bedeutet, die in ihrer Entstehung keinen Gegenstand braucht und ihm also in keiner Form verwendet. Es befindet sich in Moskau mein erstes "abstraktes" Bild, das Sie ruhig "non-objectiv" nennen durften, da es auch in der Entstehung nichts mit irgend einem Gegenstand zu tun hatte. Da ich nicht sofort und ununterbrochen auf diesem Wege weiter gehen konnte (ich war damals ganz allein und kannte keine Vorbilder), so kam ich im Laufe der weiteren paar Jahre zum Gegenstand zurück um die Form zu bilden. D.h. in einigen Teilen der Bilder war auch hier und da eine Spur vom Gegenstand sichtbar. Aber schon 1913 kamen solchen Fälle fast nie vor. Die Bilder z.B., die zur Sammlung Guggenheim gehören, sind restlos "non-objectiv"—"Helles Bild," 1913, "Schwarze Striche," 1913 ... So ist auch die grosse "Komposition 7" (300 x 200), 1913, die sich auch in Moskau befindet. "Bild mit drei Flecken," 1914 ... usw* (Letter preserved in The Hilla von Rebay Foundation Archive).

("As you tell me yourself, you make a firm distinction between 'abstract' and 'non-objective.' The difference, if I understand you correctly, is that 'abstract' means an abstraction from the object, while 'non-objectivity' describes an art which requires no object and therefore uses none. My first 'abstract' painting is in Moscow, and you could certainly call that 'non-objective' since its origin had nothing whatever to do with an object. Since I was unable to continue along that road immediately and without interruption [I was all alone at that time and had no precedents to follow], I returned to the object during the course of the following years. That is, in some of those paintings, traces of an object are visible here and there. However, by 1913 such incidents were rare. The [1913] paintings in the Guggenheim collection, such as 'Light Picture' and 'Black Lines' are totally 'non-objective.' So is the large 'Composition 7' [300 x 200], 1913, which is also in Moscow. Also 'Picture with Three Spots,' 1914, and so on.")

On January 16, 1937, he returned to the subject once more, apparently in response to a request from Rebay, who had mislaid his earlier letter. A translation of the January letter, which differs in only a few important details from the earlier version, was published by Rebay in the 1945 catalogue, *In Memory of Wassily Kandinsky*:

Nach Ihrer Terminologie operiert die "abstrakte" Kunst mit Elementen, die aus irgend welchen Gegenständen "abstrahiert" wurden. Die "non-objective" dagegen ihre Elemente selbst schafft, ohne sich irgendwie der Gegenstände zu bedienen. Wenn es so ist, verstehe ich nicht, warum Sie meine Malerei als "abstrakte" bezeichnen, da schon in der Sammlung Guggenheim mehrere Bilder von mir vorhanden sind (schon aus der Vorkriegszeit), die in keiner Weise mit dem Gegenstand zu tun haben. Wie soll ich mir das erklären? . . . Im verlorenen Brief erwähnte ich auch, dass ich nicht sofort zur "reinen Abstraktion" gelangen konnte, weil ich damals ganz allein in der Welt stand. Trotzdem habe ich bereits 1911 mein erstes "non-objectiv" Bild gemacht ("Volksmuseum" in Moskau). Aus 1913 befinden sich in der Sammlung Guggenheim "non-objectiv" Bilder von mir - "Helles Bild," und "Schwarze Striche." Und dann aus den Jahren 1918, 1922, 1923, 1924, 1925, usw (Letter preserved in The Hilla von Rebay Foundation Archive).

("According to your terminology 'abstract' art operates with elements which have been 'abstracted' from some object. 'Non-objective' art creates its own elements, without making use of any objects whatsoever. If that is the case, I do not understand why you term my painting 'abstract' since the Guggenheim collection already has several of my paintings [even from the pre-war era] which have nothing to do with an object. How am I to understand that? . . . In the letter which was lost I also mentioned that I could not immediately come to 'pure abstraction' because at that time I was *totally alone* in the world. In spite of that I painted *my first non-objective painting in 1911* [People's Museum, Moscow]. The Guggenheim collection has some 1913 'non-objective' paintings of mine—'Light Picture' and 'Black Lines.' Then also some from the years 1918, 1922, 1923, 1924, 1925, etc.")

Two points about these letters must be noted. First, the 1911 "non-objective" work mentioned in both letters has never been identified, and it is therefore impossible to evaluate Kandinsky's designation of it as such. Second, if the term "non-objective" is to be understood in Rebay's terms—as having no representational function, depicting no recognizable object, and having no recognizable source as its original inspiration—Kandinsky's careful use of it in this context would seem to present a clear case for the acceptance of *Light Picture* and *Black Lines* as genuinely "non-objective" works.

The issue is complicated, however, by Kandinsky's inclusion in the December 1936 letter of *Composition VII* on the list of those works totally lacking any trace of an object. For although Grohmann, among others, felt that *Composition VII* was not susceptible of interpretation (1959, p. 138), subsequent studies have shown that this is far from the truth. Röthel in 1961 first convincingly suggested that *Composition VII* grew out of a whole series of paintings with eschatological motifs: angels of the Apocalypse, All Saints' Day, and the Last Judgment (*Kandinsky: the Road to Abstraction,* exhibition catalogue, Marlborough Fine Art, London, 1961). In 1966 he specified further that the motifs in *Composition VII* might be considered "abstract," though certainly not "non-objective" (*Kandinsky: Painting on Glass,* exhibition catalogue, SRGM 1966, p. 12). Washton pointed to many of the same images—clearly legible in the studies though almost totally obscured in the final version—which are also to be found in earlier apocalyptic paintings (boats, oars, men, a horse and rider, a couple, trumpets), and she suggested that the original conception for the work was probably rooted specifically in the theme of the Last Judgment (1968, pp. 197-203). Similarly Ringbom described *Composition VII* as the culmination of all the earlier apocalyptic paintings (chapter V). Whether or not the final painting clearly reflects any such coherent theme, the presence in its preparatory studies of innumerable recognizable objects places it outside the confines of Kandinsky's explicitly defined notion of the "non-objective" cited in the two letters. The fact that he omitted any mention of *Composition VII* from his second letter might suggest that he recognized this problem and wished to separate *Light Picture* and *Black Lines* from the earlier work, thereby more clearly associating their "non-objective" quality with the works of "1918, 1922, 1923, 1924, 1925, etc."

The careful analysis of Kandinsky's 1910-14 writings undertaken by Lindsay in 1951 reveals the probing and fluctuating nature of the artist's thoughts on the subject of the *ungegenständlich,* the *abstrakt,* or the *absolut* in the period immediately preceding his departure for Russia in 1914. For example, in the earliest editions of *Über das Geistige in der Kunst* (published 1911-12), Kandinsky had written that an exclusively abstract art—one totally lacking in objective origins—was not yet possible: *"Mit ausschliesslich rein abstrakten Formen kann der Künstler heute nicht auskommen"* (2nd ed., 1912, p. 56). Early in 1914, he made some notes for corrections to be made in the next edition (the so-called *"kleine Änderungen"*). These were published for the first time in the 1947 Wittenborn translation, and the important phrase had been changed to read: *"Heute können nur wenige Künstler mit rein abstrakten Form auskommen."* ("Purely abstract forms are within the reach of only a few artists at present.") Between 1912 and 1914, namely, in June 1913, he wrote the autobiographical essay "Rückblicke," in which he celebrated his discovery that an explicitly "abstract" *(abstrakten)* as opposed to representational *(gegenständlichen)* art was possible *(Kandinsky 1901-1913,* 1913, p. vi). Thus it is clear that *Light Picture* and *Black Lines,* painted at the end of 1913 and just after *Composition VII* was completed, were conceived at a time when Kandinsky's convictions about the potentialities of a totally abstract (or in Rebay's terms "non-objective") art were barely established. It is within the context of these writings that the definition of *Composition VII* as an "abstract" work, and of *Light Picture* and *Black Lines as* "non-objective" works, becomes clear.

EXHIBITIONS:

Munich, Galerie Thannhauser, *Kandinsky,* Jan. 1914 (no cat.; information from HL);[5] Berlin, Der Sturm, *Kandinsky,* Sept. 1916, no. 23; New York, The Museum of Modern Art, *Summer Exhibition,* 1933 (checklist); Charleston, S.C., SRGM 1-T, no. 68, repr. p. 31; New York, The Museum of Modern Art, *Fantastic Art, Dada, Surrealism,* Dec. 7, 1936-Jan. 17, 1937, no. 226, repr.; Philadelphia SRGM 3-T, no. 77, repr. p. 77; Charleston, S.C., SRGM 4-T, no. 107, repr. p. 107; New York, SRGM 43, *Kandinsky,* no. 28, repr.; Chicago, SRGM 47-T, *Kandinsky,* no. 7; New York, SRGM 64 (no cat.); 78 (checklist); 79 (checklist; withdrawn Oct. 20); Vancouver, SRGM 88-T, no. 20; Boston, SRGM 90-T (no cat.); Brussels, SRGM 105-T, p. 13, repr.; Bloomington, University of Indiana, *German Art in Our Time,* Oct. 1-22, 1958, no. 12; Toronto, SRGM 117-T (no cat.); New York, SRGM 118 (checklist); Lexington, Ky., SRGM 122-T, no. 11, repr.; Paris, Musée National d'Art Moderne, *Les Sources du XXe siècle: Les arts en Europe de 1884 à 1914,* Nov. 9, 1960-Jan. 23, 1961, no. 294; Pasadena, SRGM 146-T, *Kandinsky,* no. 23, repr. color p. 51; New York, SRGM 173, no. 29, repr.; 184 (no cat.); 202, p. 16, repr.; 208, 212, 221, 226 (no cats.); 232, 241, p. 192, repr. p. 193; Cal., Fine Arts Gallery of San Diego, *Color and Form 1909-1914,* Nov. 20, 1971-Jan. 2, 1972, no. 32, traveled to The Oakland Museum, Jan. 26-Mar. 5, 1972, Seattle Art Museum, Mar. 24-May 7, 1972; New York, SRGM 252, repr. n.p. (withdrawn after New York showing); Cleveland, SRGM 258-T, no. 12, repr.; New York, SRGM 276 (no cat.).

REFERENCES:

V. V. Kandinsky, 1918, repr. p. 44; W. Grohmann, 1924, repr. n.p. (*"Samml. Kluxen"*); Brisch, 1955, pp. 256, 259; S. Ringbom, *The Sounding Cosmos,* Abo, 1970, pp. 142-149, fig. 52; R. C. Washton-Long, "Kandinsky and Abstraction: The Role of the Hidden Image," *Artforum,* vol. x, June 1972, p. 49, repr. p. 48.

5. See above cat. no. 79, fn. 6. Thannhauser may have used the 2nd edition of the Berlin catalogue for his exhibition, but the present picture, which was not completed until December 1913, is naturally not included there.

94 Black Lines. December 1913.
(Schwarze Linien; Schwarze Striche; Bild mit schwarzen Linien; Bild mit schwarzen Strichen).

HL *xii / 1913, 189,* Черные штрихи (Chernye shtrikhi, Black Lines).

37.241

Oil on canvas, 51 x 51¼ (129.4 x 131.1)

Signed and dated l.l.: *Kandinsky i9i3*; inscribed by the artist on stretcher (partially obscured by tape adhesive): *Kandinsky— Schwarze Linien (Dez 1913). (No. 189).*

PROVENANCE:

F. Kluxen, Münster, 1914-18;[1] acquired in exchange for *Improvisation 10* (HL 1910, 101) by Herwarth Walden, Berlin, ca. 1918;[2] Georg Muche, Berlin, by 1928 (National-galerie exhibition catalogue); Solomon R. Guggenheim by 1930;[3] Gift of Solomon R. Guggenheim, 1937.

CONDITION:

In 1953 the canvas was given a surface cleaning (natural varnish was not removed) and some losses in the black and dark green areas upper left were inpainted; the canvas was coated with PBM and restretched on the original stretcher.

There are large areas of cracking pigment throughout, sometimes combined with small losses due to flaking. The condition is fragile. (Sept. 1972.)

fig. a.
Kandinsky, study for *Black Lines,* 1913, black chalk on paper, 8¼ x 8 in., 21.1 x 20.4 cm., inscribed on gray mount: *"zu schwarze Linien,"* inscribed on the drawing: *"W"* [Weiss]; *"pr"* [preussisch]; *"ultra"* [ultra-marin]; *"Zinn"* [Zinnober]; *"K . . . hell"* [? unclear], Städtische Galerie im Lenbach-haus, Munich, GMS 428.

fig. b.
Kandinsky, study for *Black Lines,* 1913, ink on paper, 15¾ x 14 in., 40 x 35.8 cm., inscribed on reverse: *"Kandinsky, Zeich-nung zu Bild Schwarze Linien (1913),"* Städtische Galerie im Lenbachhaus, Munich, GMS 394.

1. The HL entry includes the information: *"Kreis für Kunst 2.14, Kluxen ausgestellt. Bes. Kluxen getauscht 1918 (od 19) gegen (für) No. 101."* Kluxen is not listed as the lender in the 1916 Der Sturm catalogues, and it is possible that he had already given the work to Walden by then.

94

2. Kluxen's purchases from Walden started in 1913; since Walden handled Kandinsky's work during the latter's absence in Russia 1914-21, the exchange must have been made through him. V. V. *Kandinsky,* p. 39, lists no owner for the picture, suggesting that Kandinsky himself was unaware of these transactions until later.

3. The Guggenheim records do not reveal the source or date of purchase, but an unpublished letter from Kandinsky to Grohmann dated 7/9/30 refers to the picture as "Coll. Guggenheim" (Grohmann Archiv, Stuttgart, copy in the library of The Museum of Modern Art). Grohmann calls the picture *Schwarze Striche.*

Two studies for the picture exist. The first (fig. a) is in black chalk and includes some color notes; it is clearly an early overall conception for the work. Many of the elements, especially on the periphery of the composition, are carried through into the final work, and the indications for color, although sparse, roughly approximate those used in the corresponding sections of the painting itself.

In the second study (fig. b), the compositional ideas have been further developed and the focal point of the organization of the black areas considerably refined. The linear elements are to a large extent worked out in this detailed drawing, although important further changes are made in the next stage. The divisions between the color areas, which in the final painting lack specific outlines, are in the study to a large extent undefined.

Kandinsky's description of this work as one of his first abstract (or in Rebay's terms "non-objective") paintings is discussed above; see cat. no. 93.

EXHIBITIONS:

Berlin, Kreis für Kunst Köln im Deutschen Theater, *Kandinsky Ausstellung,* Jan. 30-Feb. 15, 1914, no. 3;[1] Berlin, Der Sturm, *Expressionisten, Futuristen, Kubisten,* July 1916, no. 24 *(Bild mit schwarzen Linien)*; Berlin, Der Sturm, *Kandinsky,* Sept. 1916, no. 22 *(Bild mit schwarzen Strichen)*;[4] Berlin, Nationalgalerie, *Neuerer Deutscher Kunst aus Berliner Privatbesitz,* Apr. 1928, no. 48; Charleston, S.C., SRGM 1-T, no. 69, repr. color p. 47; Philadelphia, SRGM 3-T, no. 79, repr. color p. 71; Charleston, S.C., SRGM 4-T, no. 109, repr. color p. 93; Baltimore, SRGM 5-T, no. 109, repr. color; New York, SRGM 43, *Kandinsky,* no. 27, repr. color; Paris, Musée National d'Art Moderne, *L'Oeuvre du XXe siècle,* May-June 1952, no. 42, repr., traveled to London, Tate Gallery, July 15-Aug. 17, 1952, no. 37, repr.; New York, SRGM 78 (checklist); 81, 83 (no cats.); 87 (checklist); 89 (no cat.); 95, 97 (checklists); London, SRGM 104-T, no. 30, pl. 5; New York, SRGM 118 (checklist); Philadelphia, SRGM 134-T, no. 53; New York, SRGM 147, *Kandinsky,* no. 35, repr. p. 65; New York, Marlborough-Gerson Gallery, *Artists and Maecenas; A Tribute to Curt Valentin,* Nov. 12-Dec. 27, 1963 (not in cat.); New York, SRGM 162 (checklist); 184 (no cat.; withdrawn before closing); 187, 196 (checklists); 198-T (no cat.); 202, p. 15, repr. p. 14; 208, 212, 214, 221, 226 (no cats.); 232, 241, p. 190, repr. p. 191; 252, repr. color (withdrawn after New York showing); 266 (no cat.).

REFERENCES:

V. V. *Kandinsky,* 1918, repr. p. 39; Grohmann, 1933, repr. p. 84; K. Kuh, *Break-Up: The Core of Modern Art,* Greenwich, Conn., 1965, pp. 96-97, pl. 66; G. Heard Hamilton, *Painting and Sculpture in Europe 1880-1940,* Baltimore, 1967, p. 133, pl. 72B.

4. A watercolor in Munich (GMS 161) is inscribed on the back—in Münter's hand—*"Mit schwarzen Strichen 1913."* The picture bears no relation to the Guggenheim work or to its studies, nor does it appear to relate in any way to the 1920 picture *Schwarze Striche* (HL 226). It may well have been mistitled. Pre-1920 exhibition references to *Bild mit schwarzen Strichen* almost certainly refer to the Guggenheim picture.

95   Painting No. 199.[1] 1914.
(Autumn; Intense; Souvenir; Tableau;
Composition).

HL *1914, 199,* Панно по заказу Кемпбелла
(Panno po zakazu Kempbella, Panel ordered
by Campbell).

41.869

Oil on canvas, 63⅞ x 48⅛ (162.4 x 122.3)

Signed and dated l.l.: *K / 1914.*

PROVENANCE:

Edwin R. Campbell (1874-1929), New York,
1916-29; intervening history unknown; acquired by Murray Hoffman, Palm Beach,
Florida, 1940;[2] given by Hoffman on consignment to James St. L. O'Toole, New
York, 1940; purchased from O'Toole, 1941.

CONDITION:

In 1954 the canvas was cleaned, and 2 small
areas of loss were inpainted (1 at the left
margin, 3½ in. from the top; 1 9 in. from
the left side, 21¼ from the bottom). The
picture was surfaced with PBM and had apparently not been previously varnished.

There is slight wear along parts of the edges
and considerable wear in the corners and
some slight surface soil, but the condition is
otherwise excellent. (July 1972.)

Painting No. 199 and *Painting No. 201* (see below cat. no. 96) were, together
with *Painting No. 200* and *Painting No. 198* (figs. e and h), now in the collection of The Museum of Modern Art, New York, commissioned by Edwin R.
Campbell to decorate the circular vestibule of his apartment at 635 Park
Avenue, New York. (The background and history of these paintings was first
established by Lindsay.) As Lindsay reports, Campbell was apparently introduced to Kandinsky's work by his friend Arthur J. Eddy, who had himself
discovered the artist in the 1913 Armory Show. The complete circumstances
of the original commission are unknown since Eddy's first letter on the subject
has apparently not survived. However, a letter to Münter dated June 15, 1914,
written when the commission had clearly already been accepted by Kandinsky,
reveals that the artist was provided with a detailed description of the architectural setting for which his panels were destined:

1. The 4 panels were numbered by Kandinsky in the HL 198-201, but the entries contained no
   other information, and he inscribed no corresponding numbers on the works themselves.
   The numbers assigned to them here derive from a set of photographs in the Gabriele
   Münter und Johannes Eichner Stiftung, Munich, inscribed by the artist with the numbers
   1-4, thus possibly corresponding with the sequence 198-201 in the HL. I am indebted to J.
   Benjamin for drawing my attention to these photographs.
2. William McKim of Palm Beach, Florida, in conversation with Hoffman, learned the following details of the acquisition and reported them to A. H. Barr, Jr., in a letter dated Jan. 1,
   1956. (I am indebted to The Museum of Modern Art for making a copy of this letter available to me.) In 1940 Hoffman was called by a woman who had been asked to decorate an
   old house on South Ocean Boulevard; the two panels had been discovered by the new
   owners in the attic of the old house, and they had instructed her to dispose of them as she
   saw fit. Knowing that Hoffman was a painter, and that canvas was at that time scarce, she
   offered them to him for re-use. He accepted them and stored them in his studio without
   knowing what they were. During the summer on a visit to The Museum of Modern Art in
   New York, he happened to see the two matching panels and realized that his two were also
   by Kandinsky. He then mentioned the pictures to the dealer O'Toole and asked whether
   he might be able to sell them for him. He later received payment from O'Toole.

95

. . . I enclose a rough pencil sketch of the reception hall.

You will see that the hall is almost a circle with three large openings leading to other parts of the house.

The woodwork of this circular hall is pure white and the ceiling is white. Each picture will hang in its own particular space, and when all are in place they will look exactly as if originally intended as part of the hall. The idea is to put a three inch gold frame about each picture, and when this is done and the pictures are in place, just outside the frame there will be a small white moulding, which is already on the wall, so that the pictures will be framed first in three inches of gold, and then outside of that will be the small raised moulding, which is now a part of the decoration.

The floor is dark hardwood, polished, with oriental rugs.

So you see the pictures will have every advantage. They will be seen not only from the hall itself, but through the three entrances. People will see them from a distance and close to, and I have the feeling that the pictures will prove very beautiful decorations, and will make what might be called a "stunning" hall. The word "stunning" in this connection means very striking and handsome.

I was glad to get this commission for Herr Kandinsky because it gives him an entrance in New York, and while the price is not large, yet it is quite a venture for my friend to hang four such extremely modern pictures in a place where everybody must see them. I think my friend has a good deal of courage, but I am very sure he will be very much pleased with the result.

I am sure Kandinsky will choose a beautiful color scheme.

Of course, my letter made it clear that the pictures are upright, that is each one is taller than it is wide; they stand upright.

With kindest regards to Herr Kandinsky, I am

Yours very sincerely,
A. J. Eddy

Encls.

P.S. My friend will frame the pictures after they arrive in New York. I think the canvases better be mounted on stretchers and shipped already [sic] for framing. They will be so freshly painted that I do not think it is wise to roll them.

They should be shipped to

E. R. Campbell
635 Park Ave.,
New York City."

(Letter preserved in the Gabriele Münter und Johannes Eichner Stiftung, Munich. I am indebted to H. K. Röthel for permission to quote from this and other letters in the Eddy correspondence.)

Although the dimensions of the walls were not included in this letter, they must have been supplied in an earlier one. The four canvases fit, with seven inches to spare on each side, into the panels surrounded by mouldings in the vestibule (Lindsay, p. 58). Kandinsky thus apparently chose a slightly smaller canvas size in each case than Campbell had in mind: even with the three-inch gold frame, there would have been four inches of white wall between the edge of the frame and the surrounding moulding. Whether Campbell or Eddy made any additional suggestions to Kandinsky is for the time being unknown; but according to the HL, Campbell agreed to pay five hundred marks for each panel.

The frames themselves have not survived, and no photograph of the vestibule with the paintings installed has hitherto come to light.

Shortly after the completion of the commission, the war broke out, and Kandinsky fled to Russia, leaving the works behind. Lindsay suggests that the panels were stored by Walden until October 1915, when he sent a group of pictures to Stockholm for exhibition at the Gummeson Gallery. Additional letters from Eddy to Münter and to Kandinsky himself reveal that the pictures were not stored by Walden, but rather were sent to W. Beffie in Amsterdam, who was to ship them to New York. ("I regret to say that I have heard nothing regarding the panels painted for Dr. Campbell since the receipt of Mr. Beffie's letter saying they were in Amsterdam. I wrote him urging him to get them out and ship to this country as soon as possible, but have never received any reply to my letter . . ." (September 7, 1915, Gabriele Münter und Johannes Eichner Stiftung, Munich). On December 31, Eddy wrote to Kandinsky in Moscow telling him that he had acquired papers from the British Consul General in Chicago which would help to get the four pictures out of Amsterdam. How the pictures were shipped to Stockholm, and at whose request, is not clear. Although they do not appear in the catalogue of the Gummeson exhibition (see below EXHIBITIONS), they were, according to Lindsay, sent together with the other works and shown there before being shipped on to New York in the summer of 1916.

The subsequent history and dispersal of the panels remains somewhat unclear. Campbell was divorced in 1921, left his apartment, and moved to Pasadena. His widow, later Mrs. Fitzhugh Green, New Canaan, Connecticut, assumed that he had taken the paintings with him, but he apparently did not do so, since two of them later turned up in her storage and were purchased by Mrs. Virginia Freeman at the March 1953 sale of the Green Estate. These two subsequently came into the collection of The Museum of Modern Art, New York (information from The Museum of Modern Art files). The history of the two Guggenheim panels is obscure until their emergence in Palm Beach, Florida, in 1940.

The pictures have been known by various titles, although Kandinsky gave them none. Lindsay first tentatively suggested that the works might have been inspired by the four seasons, drawing attention to Kandinsky's *Winter* (1911, 122) and *Autumn* (1912, 156) as precedents for Kandinsky's interest in repre-

fig. a.
Kandinsky, study for *Painting No.
200*, pencil on paper, 6¾ x 3⅜ in.,
17 x 9.4 cm., Städtische Galerie im
Lenbachhaus, Munich, GMS 408.

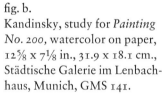

fig. b.
Kandinsky, study for *Painting
No. 200*, watercolor on paper,
12⅝ x 7⅛ in., 31.9 x 18.1 cm.,
Städtische Galerie im Lenbach-
haus, Munich, GMS 141.

senting the contrasts between seasons through the use of color and form.
Grohmann (like most subsequent authors) was inclined to accept Lindsay's
descriptive titles, although he suggested that Kandinsky would probably have
called the works *Improvisations*. However, since Kandinsky himself gave the
pictures only numbers, since Eddy's June letter speaks only of a "beautiful
color scheme," and since the paintings bear no striking resemblance either in
color or forms to works that he did designate with seasonal titles, the association must remain at best speculative.

Several preparatory studies for the series are in the collection of the
Städtische Galerie in Munich. Four of these are for *Painting No. 200* (figs. a-d).
Several of the elements that are carried through to the final painting are already
present in the early sketch (fig. a), although its prominent central mountain
and subsidiary hillock are discarded in the subsequent stages.

fig. c.
Kandinsky, small study for *Painting No. 200*, oil on board, 25⅜ x 19½ in., 64.5 x 49.5 cm., Städtische Galerie im Lenbachhaus, Munich, GMS 65.

fig. e.
Kandinsky, *Painting No. 200*, 1914, oil on canvas, 64 x 36¼ in., 162.5 x 92.1 cm., The Museum of Modern Art, New York. Mrs. Simon Guggenheim Fund.

fig. d.
Kandinsky, large study for *Painting No. 200*, oil on board, 39 x 23⅜ in., 99 x 59.5 cm., Städtische Galerie im Lenbachhaus, Munich, GMS 75.

fig. f.
Kandinsky, study for *Painting No. 198*, ink on paper, 6¾ x 3¼ in., 17 x 8.4 cm., Städtische Galerie im Lenbachhaus, Munich, GMS 383.

fig. g.
Kandinsky, study for *Painting No. 198*, watercolor on paper, 12⅝ x 6¼ in., 32.1 x 15.9 cm., Städtische Galerie im Lenbachhaus, Munich, GMS 140.

The sequence of the three later studies is difficult to establish with certainty. The watercolor (fig. b) and the large oil study (fig. d) are detailed and very brightly colored; white dominates and there is a prominent use of bright blue, red, some yellow, and green, all of which also appear in The Museum of Modern Art painting. The format and proportions of these two studies are also close to the final work. The smaller oil study (fig. c), while compositionally much closer to the final work, is of a squarer format and its colors are much more subdued than either those of *Painting No. 200,* or of the other two studies (figs. b and d). Even though this is due in part to the clearly visible darkening of the board, the overall tone of the latter is without doubt much closer to that of the Guggenheim *Painting No. 199* than to The Museum of Modern Art's picture. This might suggest that Kandinsky was to some extent working on the four panels simultaneously rather than completing them one at a time.

A black ink study (fig. f), inscribed on the reverse in J. Eichner's hand *"Idee zu einem Wandbild für Campbell,"* is clearly the first study for *Painting No. 198,* and already all the essentials of the composition are included. It was followed by a detailed watercolor (fig. g) in which the colors in general correspond to those of the final painting.

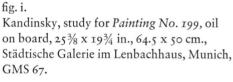

fig. i.
Kandinsky, study for *Painting No. 199,* oil
on board, 25⅜ x 19¾ in., 64.5 x 50 cm.,
Städtische Galerie im Lenbachhaus, Munich,
GMS 67.

fig. h.
Kandinsky, *Painting No. 198,* 1914,
oil on canvas, 64 x 31½ in., 162.5 x
80 cm., The Museum of Modern Art,
New York. Mrs. Simon Guggenheim
Fund.

Only one definite study for *Painting No. 199*—a detailed oil—has so far
come to light (fig. i). Its colors are in general very close to the final work,
although the overall effect both of color and of brushwork is considerably
more dynamic in the Guggenheim painting. In particular, the lower right
corner in the study lacks both the striking ultramarine and the vitality of brush
stroke used in the painting; more important still, the study does not have the
dynamic white form which is the central focus of *No. 199.* Although the
subdued tone of the study is—as in the case of fig. c—possibly due in part to
the darkening of the board, it is clear that the differentiation and vitality of
brushwork in the final work is matched by an intensification of the color. It is
possible that *Large Study* of 1914 (oil on canvas, Museum Boymans-van Beuningen, Rotterdam, not in HL, Grohmann, 1959, cc 630) was also a study for
Painting No. 199, as both Grohmann (who on p. 142 confused the Guggenheim
No. 199 with The Museum of Modern Art's *No. 200)* and Sihari suggested.
The central white "amoeba" form is present in both the Rotterdam and Guggenheim pictures, as is the mountain form above it. Sihari sees the "amoeba"

fig. j.
Kandinsky, drawing, possibly an early
idea for *Painting No. 199* or *No. 201* (?),
pencil on paper, 6⅜ x 4⅞ in., 16.3 x 12.5
cm., Städtische Galerie im Lenbachhaus,
Munich, GMS 380.

fig. k.
Kandinsky, study from sketchbook, pos-
sibly an early idea for *Painting No. 199* or
No. 201 (?), pencil on paper, 8⅛ x 6⅜ in.,
20.7 x 16.3 cm., Städtische Galerie im
Lenbachhaus, Munich, GMS 323/5.

form as symbolic of the notion of evolution from inorganic to organic matter.
(See below cat. no. 141 for further elaboration of this point.)

No study for *Painting No. 201* has yet come to light, although it is most
likely that studies for this picture, as well as additional ones for *No. 199*, were
made. A small oil in the Städtische Galerie (GMS 70) which has frequently
been identified as a study for *No. 201* (see, for example, Grohmann, 1959,
cc 635, and Röthel, *Städtische Galerie München: Der Blaue Reiter,* 3rd ed.,
Munich, 1970, p. 21, and earlier eds.) may in fact be an independent work.
The lower right corner is treated somewhat similarly in the two works, but
the remainder of the composition bears no relation to the Guggenheim picture.

A pencil drawing in the Städtische Galerie (fig. j), which is identified on the
reverse in J. Eichner's hand as a sketch for a Campbell *"Wandbild,"* is also
difficult to accept as a study for this series, although it may have been a very
early idea for one of the two Guggenheim paintings. A watercolor based upon
it is in the Städtische Galerie (GMS 144). Another such early idea may possibly
be represented by a pencil study in one of the unpublished Munich sketchbooks (fig. k), but this too can be associated with the series in only the most
tentative fashion.

EXHIBITIONS:

Stockholm, Carl Gummesons Konsthandel, *Kandinsky,* Feb. 1916 (not in cat.);[3] New York, SRGM 30 (no cat.); 43, *Kandinsky,* no. 31, repr. *(Souvenir)*; Chicago, SRGM 47-T, *Kandinsky,* no. 8; New York, SRGM 64 (no cat.); 84 (checklist); Vancouver, SRGM 88-T, no. 21 *(Composition)*; New York, The Museum of Modern Art, *Kandinsky Murals Re-United after 25 Years,* May 23-Aug. 3, 1956 (no cat.); Brussels, SRGM 105-T, p. 15, repr.; Baltimore, SRGM 113-T (no cat.); Toronto, SRGM 117-T (no cat.); New York, SRGM 118 (checklist; *Painting [Autumn]*); Philadelphia, SRGM 134-T, no. 54; New York, SRGM 147, *Kandinsky,* no. 41, repr. color p. 62; 173, no. 36, repr. color; 184 (no cat.); 202, p. 77, repr.; 208, 212, 214, 221, 226 (no cats.); 232, 241, p. 196, repr. p. 197; 252, repr. color (withdrawn after New York showing); 276 (no cat.).

REFERENCES:

K. Lindsay, "Kandinsky in 1914 New York: Solving a Riddle," *Art News,* vol. 55, May 1956, pp. 32-33, 58-60; Grohmann, 1959, pp. 142, 144, 333 no. 198, p. 281, fig. a; L. P. Sihari, *Oriental Influences on W. Kandinsky and P. Mondrian, 1909-1917,* unpublished Ph.D. dissertation, Institute of Fine Arts, New York University, 1967, pp. 160-161.

3. The entry in the HL includes the information *"bis zur Absendung in Stockholm II.16 Gummeson."* According to Lindsay, 1956, the panels were included in the exhibition and then sent on to New York. Confirmation of the fact was contained in a 1958 letter to A. H. Barr, Jr., from Jan Runnqvist, Stockholm.

---

96   Painting No. 201. 1914.
      (Winter; Carneval; Composition).

HL *1914, 201,* Панно по заказу Кемпбелла (Panno po zakazu Kempbella; Panel ordered by Campbell).

41.868

Oil on canvas, 63⅞ x 48⅛ (162.3 x 122.8)

Signed and dated l.l.: *K / 1914.*

PROVENANCE:

See above cat. no. 95 *Painting No. 199.*

CONDITION:

The work has received no treatment.

Apart from some slight wear along the edges, considerable wear with paint loss in the corners, and some surface soil, the condition is excellent. (July 1972.)

EXHIBITIONS:

Stockholm, Carl Gummesons Konsthandel, *Kandinsky,* Feb. 1916 (not in cat.);[1] New York, SRGM 30 (no cat.); 43, *Kandinsky,* no. 30, repr. *(Carneval)*; 64 (no cat.); Toronto, SRGM 85-T, no. 22 *(Composition)*; New York, The Museum of Modern Art, *Kandinsky Murals Re-United after 25 Years,* May 23-Aug. 3, 1956 (no cat.); Brussels, SRGM 105-T, p. 16; Toronto, SRGM 117-T (no cat.); New York, SRGM 118 (checklist; *Painting [Winter]*); Philadelphia, SRGM 134-T, no. 55; New York, SRGM 147, *Kandinsky,* no. 42, repr. color p. 63; 162 (checklist); 173, no. 37, repr. color; 184 (no cat.); 202, p. 76, repr.; 208, 212, 214,

1. See above cat. no. 95, fn. 3.

96

221, 226 (no cats.); 232, 241, p. 199, repr. p. 198; 252, repr. color (withdrawn after New York showing); 276 (no cat.).

REFERENCES:

K. Lindsay, "Kandinsky in 1914 New York: Solving a Riddle," *Art News,* vol. 55, May 1956, pp. 32-33, 58-60; Grohmann, 1959, pp. 142, 144, 333 no. 198, repr. p. 281b; H. Read, *Kandinsky*, London, 1959, p. 12, repr. color.

97   Fugue. March 1914.
      (No. 193; Great Fugue).

HL *iii / 1914, 193,* фуга. (Fuga, Fugue).

37.243

Oil on canvas, 51 x 51 (129.5 x 129.5)

Not signed or dated. (Grohmann records
that the picture is signed and dated l.l.:
"*Kandinsky 1914.*")

PROVENANCE:

Collection Herwarth Walden, Berlin (information from HL); Rudolf Bauer, Berlin (?);[1]
purchased from an unknown source by
Solomon R. Guggenheim by 1937;[2] Gift of
Solomon R. Guggenheim, 1937.

CONDITION:

No treatment has been recorded, but inpainting of uncertain date is visible along
15 in. of the top edge, approx. ⅛ in. in
width.

A puncture from the reverse caused cracking
and flaking in a ⅜ in. area in the region of
the crossed white lines (16 in. from the top,
21¾ in. from the right side). The edges are
worn in places, and there are a few virtually
invisible traction cracks, but the condition
is otherwise excellent. (July 1972.)

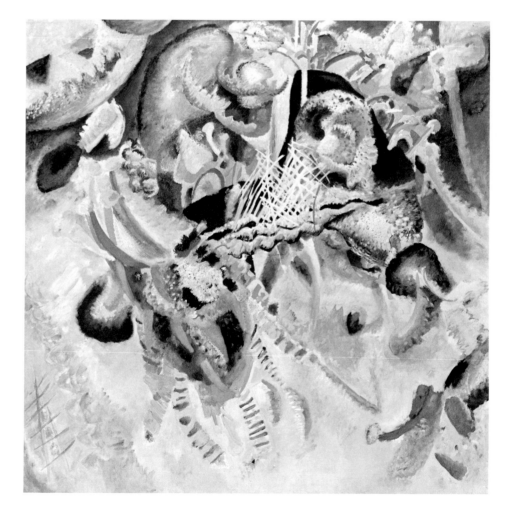

1. The stamp of Bauer's Berlin gallery Das Geistreich is on the reverse, indicating either that
   he once exhibited the picture, or that he owned it himself, or that he purchased it on
   Guggenheim's behalf. No further evidence on this point has hitherto been found.
2. The HL entry includes a reference to "*Galerie F. Möller, Berlin,*" which has been deleted,
   presumably by Kandinsky himself. It is possible that Guggenheim purchased the picture
   from Möller, but no additional evidence on this point has yet come to light.

fig. a.
Kandinsky, study for *Engraving V*
(Röthel, *Gr. W.*, 1970, no. 151), 1914,
pencil on paper, 8⅝ x 11⅛ in.,
21.9 x 28.2 cm., Städtische Galerie im
Lenbachhaus, Munich, GMS 471.

An undated drypoint engraving and a preparatory pencil drawing for it (fig. a)
were first associated with this composition by H. K. Röthel (*Gr.W*, 1970, no.
151), and he convincingly dates the engraving 1913-14. The greater elaboration of detail in the drawing and print, as well as the legibility of motifs would
support his notion that they pre-date the Guggenheim painting. Motifs such
as the hill surmounted by toppling towers at the top and right of center of
the drawing are almost totally obscured by color in the painting; the three
overlapping rounded forms at the top left of center in the drawing (reminiscent
of the horseman and rider in the many drawings for *Painting with White
Border,* see above cat. no. 91) have become in the painting one immense and
somewhat amorphous shape. The broadness of treatment and freedom of
handling in the painting obscure almost all of the individual forms that are
so carefully delineated in the earlier conception.

According to Grohmann, Kandinsky called this work a "controlled Improvisation;" and indeed, Münter's copy of the HL lists the picture as *"beherrschte
Improvisation—Fuga."* The title, *Fugue,* which Kandinsky used in the HL, as
well as, for example, in his 1937 correspondence with Rebay, was the only
title carried by the picture until its acquisition by the Museum, when it
inexplicably became *Great Fugue.*

EXHIBITIONS:

Berlin, Der Sturm, *Kandinsky,* Sept. 1916, no. 27 *(Fuge)*; Philadelphia, SRGM 3-T, no. 75,
repr. p. 32 (*Great Fugue;* the title by which the picture has been known since its acquisition);
Charleston, S.C., SRGM 4-T, no. 105, repr. p. 38; Toledo, Ohio, *Contemporary Movements
in European Painting,* Nov. 6-Dec. 11, 1938, no. 47; New York, SRGM 43, *Kandinsky,* no. 25;
Chicago, SRGM 47-T, *Kandinsky,* no. 6; Pittsburgh, SRGM 53-T, *Kandinsky,* no. 13; New
York, SRGM 64 (no cat.); 147, *Kandinsky,* no. 38, repr.; 184 (no cat.), 212 (no cat.; added
Sept. 6); Staatliche Kunsthalle Baden-Baden, *Vasily Kandinsky,* July 10-Sept. 27, 1970, no.
43, repr.; Cal., Fine Arts Gallery of San Diego, *Color and Form 1909-1914,* Nov. 20, 1971-
Jan. 2, 1972, traveled to The Oakland Museum, Jan. 26-Mar. 5, 1972, Seattle Art Museum
(Pavillion), Mar. 24-May 7, 1972, no. 34, repr. color; New York, SRGM 252, repr.

REFERENCE:

Grohmann, 1959, pp. 140, 333 no. 193, repr. color p. 147.

98   Red Oval. 1920.
      (Rotes Oval).

HL 1920, 227, Красный овал (Krasnyi oval,
Red Oval).

51.1311

Oil on canvas, 28⅛ x 28⅛ (71.5 x 71.2)

Signed and dated l.l.: *K 20*; inscribed by the
artist on reverse: *K / N° 227 / 1920.*

PROVENANCE:

Collection Ernst Heyer, Bielefeld, 1923-?;[1]
Collection Hella Nebelung, Dusseldorf,
before 1950 (information supplied by Otto
Stangl, correspondence with the author,

July 1972); purchased from Nebelung by
Otto Stangl before 1950; purchased from
Stangl, Munich, 1951.

CONDITION:

In 1953 the painting was restretched on the
original stretcher; the alteration in the
margins necessitated inpainting along the
entire top edge (approximately ⅛ in. in
width), 10¼ in. of right edge from the top
(approximately ½ in. in width), 13 in. of
the left edge from the bottom (approximately ½ in. in width). A small puncture
in the green background near the top
margin right of center was repaired and
inpainted; 2 small losses near the bottom
margin were also inpainted. The canvas was
surfaced with PBM.

Some minor cracking in the paint film is
present in the upper right corner and at
intervals along the right margin. Apart from
surface soil which is especially apparent in
the light areas, the condition is good. (Aug.
1972.)

As Grohmann has observed (p. 164), Kandinsky painted no pictures between
November 9, 1917 (when the Bolsheviks came to power), and July 1919. In
the remaining months of 1919 he produced six oils and in 1920 ten, among
which is the present work. He remained in Russia until December 1921.
Whether he was substantially influenced during these years by the contemporary work of Malevich and Lissitsky is unclear. Overy claims that such
influence was absent; Elderfield describes the present picture as a traditional
work, but does not specify Russian influence as such. The presence for the
first time of the receding rectangle suspended in a unified square field—an
element which is taken up again in later works such as *In the Black Square*
(see below cat. no. 104)—does suggest a reference to the work of Malevich
which is difficult to ignore. (See, for example, Malevich's *Suprematist Painting*,
1917-18, Stedelijk Museum, Amsterdam, A7670.) However, the question of
interrelationship between the work of Kandinsky and that of his Russian
avant-garde colleagues during the period 1916-21 requires further study and
documentation.

1. The entry in the HL includes the information *"Hannover ii. 23 (Kestner). verkauft von
   Kestner. / Sammlung Ernst Heyer Bielefeld."* It has not been possible to confirm whether
   Heyer purchased the picture directly from the Hanover exhibition or to establish how long
   he owned it.

EXHIBITIONS:

Berlin, Galerie Goldschmidt Wallerstein, *Wassily Kandinsky,* May 1922 (information from HL entry);[2] Munich, Galerie Thannhauser, *W. Kandinsky,* July 1-14, 1922, no. 2; Stockholm, Carl Gummesons Konsthandel, Oct. 1922 (information from HL, but exhibition not other-wise identified); Hanover, Kestner Gesellschaft, *Kandinsky,* Feb. 1923 (no cat.); New York, SRGM 74, no. 89; Brussels, SRGM 105-T, no. 19; Toronto, SRGM 117-T (no cat.); Pasadena, SRGM 146-T, *Kandinsky,* no. 26, repr. color p. 16; New York, SRGM 173, no. 49, repr. color; New York, SRGM 208, 212, 226, 228 (no cats.); Ithaca, N.Y., Andrew Dickson White Museum of Art, *Russian Art of the Revolution,* Feb. 24-Mar. 25, 1971, traveled to The Brooklyn Museum, June 14-July 25, 1971, no. 32, repr.; New York, SRGM 252, repr. color; 266 (no cat.).

REFERENCES:

Grohmann, 1959, pp. 168, 333 no. 227, repr. cc 120; P. Overy, *Kandinsky: The Language of the Eye,* New York, 1969, p. 16, repr. p. 75; J. Elderfield, "On Constructivism," *Artforum,* vol. ix, May 1971, pp. 60-61, repr.

2. The exhibition was reviewed by L. Hilbersheimer, "Berliner Ausstellungen," *Sozialistische Monatshefte,* 1922, vol. 1, p. 699; no catalogue has come to light.

99   Blue Segment. 1921.
     (Blaues Segment).

HL *1921, 235,* Синий сегмент (Sinii segment, Blue Segment).

49.1181

Oil on canvas, 47½ x 55⅛ (120.6 x 140.1)

Signed and dated l.l.: *K 21*; inscribed on
reverse, possibly by the artist: КАНДИ-
НСКІЙ / *K/№ 235./1921.*

PROVENANCE:

Collection Lafitte, Anvers;[1] Nina Kandinsky, Paris ?-1948; purchased from Nina
Kandinsky by Galerie René Drouin, Paris,
1948; purchased from Drouin, 1949.

CONDITION:

In 1953 the picture was cleaned and some
minor losses retouched. Cleavage in several
areas was noted at that time. In 1957 the
areas of cleavage were infused with wax
resin; it was noted that several old repaints
(dating from before acquisition by the
Museum) had discolored, and that there
was some scattered flaking in the paint surface.

There is some cracking in the thick white
impasto areas in the lower left and along
the right-hand side of the upper margin.
(Aug. 1972.)

EXHIBITIONS:

Berlin, Galerie Goldschmidt Wallerstein, *Wassily Kandinsky,* May 1922 (information from
HL);[2] Munich, Galerie Thannhauser, *W. Kandinsky,* July 1-14, 1922, no. 4; Stockholm, Carl
Gummesons Konsthandel, Oct. 1922 (information from HL, but exhibition not otherwise
identified); New York, Société Anonyme, *Kandinsky: First One-Man Exhibition,* Mar. 23-
May 4, 1923 (no cat.); Cal., The Oakland Art Gallery, *The Blue Four,* May 2-31, 1926, no. 11;
The Arts Club of Chicago, *The Blue Four,* Apr. 1-15, 1932, no. 91; Kunsthalle Bern, *Wassily
Kandinsky,* Feb. 21-Mar. 29, 1937, no. 11 (for sale); [erroneously listed by Grohmann as hav-
ing appeared in Jeu de Paume exhibition of 1937]; Amsterdam, Stedelijk Museum, *Kandinsky,*
Feb. 13-Mar. 14, 1948, no. 27, repr.; New York, SRGM 64 (no cat.); 74, no. 85; 79 (checklist);
Vancouver, SRGM 88-T, no. 22; Brussels, SRGM 105-T, p. 20; Toronto, SRGM 117-T (no
cat.); New York, SRGM 118 (checklist); Philadelphia, SRGM 134-T, no. 58; New York,
SRGM 147, *Kandinsky,* no. 48, repr. p. 74; Buffalo, N.Y., Albright-Knox Art Gallery, *Plus by
Minus: Today's Half-Century,* Mar. 3-Apr. 14, 1968, no. 62; New York, SRGM 208, 212, 214,
226 (no cats.); 252, repr. (withdrawn after New York showing).

REFERENCES:

C. Estienne, *Kandinsky,* Paris, 1950, p. 12, pl. xv (recorded as "Collection Lafitte"); Grohmann, 1959, pp. 168-169, 334 no. 235, repr. cc 128.

1. According to the HL entry, the picture was at some stage in the Lafitte Collection, but it
has not been possible to confirm this. Since the picture was acquired by Drouin directly
from Nina Kandinsky (correspondence between Drouin and Rebay, Sept. 1948, The Hilla
von Rebay Foundation Archive), the picture apparently came back into her collection,
probably sometime after Kandinsky's death.

2. See above cat. no. 98, fn. 2.

100 Earth Center.[1] 1921.
(White Center; Weisses Zentrum).

HL *1921, 236,* Земной центр (Zemnoi tsentr, Earth Center).

71.1936R 98

Oil on canvas, 46¾ x 53¾ (118.7 x 136.5)

Signed and dated l.l.: *K 2i*; inscribed by the artist on reverse: *K / Nº 236. / 192i.*

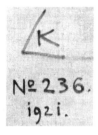

PROVENANCE:

Hans Goltz, Munich, ca. 1925;[2] Maurice J. Speiser, Philadelphia, by 1939 (lender to The Museum of Modern Art exhibition); Karl Nierendorf, New York, by 1944 (see below EXHIBITIONS); purchased from Nierendorf by Hilla Rebay, 1944 (invoice in The Hilla von Rebay Foundation Archive); Estate of Hilla Rebay, 1967-71; acquired from the Estate of Hilla Rebay, 1971.

CONDITION:

There are 9 small areas of inpainting in the light-colored diagonal bands at lower left; these appear to be of considerable age.

There is some slight wear along the edges, a small dent in the canvas above and slightly to the left of center, and general soil. The condition is otherwise excellent. (July 1972.)

EXHIBITIONS:

Moscow, Мир искусства (Mir Iskusstva, *World of Art*), Oct.-Nov. 1921, no. 44 *(Kartina No. 236)*; Berlin, Galerie Goldschmidt Wallerstein, *Wassily Kandinsky,* May 1922 (information from HL);[3] Munich, Galerie Hans Goltz, *Kandinsky Jubiläums-Ausstellung,* Jan. 1923 (information from HL, but exhibition not otherwise identified); New York, The Museum of Modern Art, *Art in our Time; 10th Anniversary Exhibition,* May-Nov. 1939, no. 180 (dated 1916, lent Maurice J. Speiser); New York, Nierendorf Gallery, *Gestation-Formation,* Mar. 1944, no. 10; New York, SRGM 43, *Kandinsky,* no. 43, repr.; Chicago, SRGM 47-T, *Kandinsky,* no. 34; Pittsburgh, SRGM 53-T, *Kandinsky,* no. 23; Paris, Musée National d'Art Moderne, *L'Oeuvre du XXᵉ siècle,* May-June 1952, no. 43, traveled to London, Tate Gallery, July 15-Aug. 17, 1952, no. 38; New York, SRGM 241 (addenda); Bridgeport, Conn., Carlson Gallery, University of Bridgeport, *Homage to Hilla Rebay,* Apr. 18-May 10, 1972, no. 30; New York, SRGM 252, repr. color, n.p. (withdrawn after New York showing); 260, 276 (no cats.).

REFERENCE:

Grohmann, 1959, pp. 168, 334 no. 236, repr. cc 129.

1. I am indebted to Nina Berberova, Princeton, N.J., for a correct reading and translation of the Russian title, which has been erroneously given as *White Center* in all previous records and publications.

2. An unpublished letter from Kandinsky to Grohmann dated Apr. 13, 1930, contains the following information: *"No. 236 wurde noch vomjetzt verstorbenen Hans Goltz nach New York verkauft (vor 4-5 Jahren)."* It has not been possible to establish whether the buyer was Maurice J. Speiser or whether there was an intermediate owner.

3. See above cat. no. 98, fn. 2.

101 Circles on Black. 1921.
(Kreise auf Schwarz; Kreise im Schwarz;
Russian Carnival; Black Composition).

HL *1921, 241,* Круги на черном (Krugi na chernom, Circles on Black).

46.1050

Oil on canvas, 53¾ x 47⅛ (136.5 x 120)

Signed and dated l.l.: *K/21;* inscribed by the artist on reverse: *K / № 241. / 1921.*

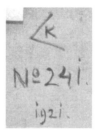

PROVENANCE:

Purchased from the artist by Katherine S. Dreier, West Redding, Connecticut, March 1926 (information from HL); purchased from Dreier, 1946 (she retaining lifetime ownership); transferred to Museum, 1952.

CONDITION:

Some inpainting along the edges—upper center, center to upper right, center to bottom left—dates from before acquisition. There is a certain slackness in the support due to weakness of the stretcher, although the stretcher keys were replaced in 1954 and the stretcher keyed out.

Cracking of the paint film is present in certain limited areas, and there are a few tiny paint losses. The painting has not been cleaned, but is generally in good condition. (Aug. 1972.)

The picture is identified by Grohmann as the last work painted by Kandinsky before he left Russia in December 1921 (p. 169). As early as 1922, Hilbersheimer commented on its transitional nature: "the titles of [these] paintings betray [Kandinsky's] intentions . . . a striving towards geometrization, towards the constructive." This picture, together with *Variegated Circle,* 1921, HL 238, represents the beginning of the artist's intense preoccupation with the circle. (See below *Composition 8,* cat. no. 105, for a discussion of this element.)

Grohmann convincingly suggests (p. 185) that the woodcut *Kleine Welten No. VI* of 1922 (Röthel, *Gr. W.,* 1970, no. 169) is a variation of this composition and that it represents one of the only instances in this series of prints in which Kandinsky was inspired by his own earlier work. The degree of geometrization has increased in the print as has the economy, but many of the basic compositional ideas are clearly drawn from the 1921 painting.

EXHIBITIONS:

Moscow, Мир искусства (Mir Iskusstva, *World of Art*), Oct.-Nov. 1921, no. 45 *(Kartina No. 241)*; Berlin, Galerie Goldschmidt Wallerstein, *Wassily Kandinsky,* May 1922 (cited in review by Hilbersheimer); Munich, Galerie Thannhauser, *W. Kandinsky,* July 1-14, 1922, no. 8; Stockholm, Carl Gummesons Konsthandel, Oct. 1922 (information from HL, but exhibition not otherwise identified); New York, Société Anonyme, *Kandinsky: First One-Man Exhibition,* Mar. 23-May 4, 1923 (information from HL, no cat.); Springfield, Mass., Museum of Fine Arts, *Modern German Art,* Jan. 10-30, 1939, no. 28 *(Russian Carnival)*; New York, SRGM 43, *Kandinsky,* no. 44; Chicago, SRGM 47-T, *Kandinsky,* no. 41; Pittsburgh, SRGM 53-T, *Kandinsky,* no. 15 *(Black Composition)*; New York, SRGM 64 (no cat.); 78 (checklist, *No. 241*); Toronto, SRGM 85-T, no. 23; Brussels, SRGM 105-T, no. 21 repr.; Toronto, SRGM 117-T (no cat.); New York, SRGM 118 (checklist); Philadelphia, SRGM 134-T, no. 59; Pasa-

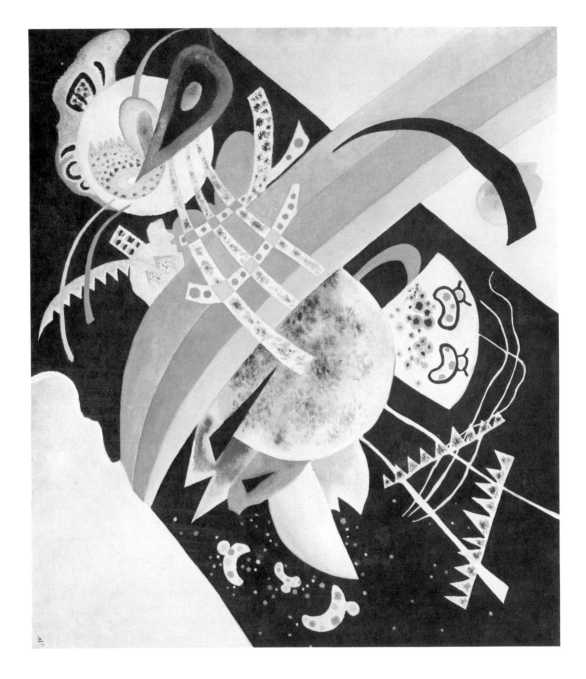

dena, SRGM 146-T, *Kandinsky*, no. 27, repr. p. 54; New York, SRGM 195 (no cat.); New York, SRGM 196 (checklist); 202, p. 94, repr. p. 95; 208, 212, 214, 226, 228 (no cats.); 252, repr.

REFERENCES:
L. Hilbersheimer, "Berliner Ausstellungen," *Sozialistische Monatshefte,* vol. 1, July 1922, p. 699; Grohmann, 1959, pp. 169, 185, 334 no. 241, repr. p. 286.

102   Blue Circle. 1922.
(Blauer Kreis; Cercle bleu).

HL *1922, 242,* Синий круг (Sinii krug, Blue Circle).

46.1051

Oil on canvas, 43 x 39 (109.2 x 99.2)

Signed and dated l.l.: *K/22;* inscribed by the artist on reverse: *K/i922/Nº 242.*

PROVENANCE:

Purchased from the artist by Katherine S. Dreier, West Redding, Connecticut (information from HL) by 1924 (Grohmann, 1924); purchased from Dreier, 1946.

CONDITION:

In 1953 the painting was cleaned; numerous old repaints in the background areas, especially along the edges, in the lower left corner, the lower right corner, and across the top, were not removed. In 1956 an area above the lower edge, right of center, was retouched, as were 4 other minor losses. The canvas was infused with wax resin from the reverse and lightly surfaced with PBM. In 1967 2 dents and an abrasion in the off-white area upper left of center were repaired and inpainted.

The paint is in general extremely thinly applied, but its condition is stable. (July 1972.)

As early as 1924 Grohmann was able to describe 1922, the year Kandinsky joined the Bauhaus, as a crucial transitional year in the artist's development. Works such as *Blue Circle* were, he wrote, the "upbeat" before the artist's unequivocal commitment to works in a "constructive" mode from the beginning of 1923. Writing in 1958 he placed less emphasis upon 1922. (See below cat. no. 105 for a discussion of the significance of the circle during these years.)

EXHIBITIONS:

Dusseldorf, *Internationale Kunstausstellung,* June 1922 (information from HL but exhibition not otherwise identified); Weimar, *Bauhaus Ausstellung,* Aug.-Sept. 1923 (no cat.; information from HL); Berlin, *Grosser Berliner Kunstausstellung,* 1926, pl. 12, bottom; New York, The Museum of Modern Art, *Modern Works of Art: Fifth Anniversary Exhibition,* Nov. 19, 1934-Jan. 20, 1935, no. 34, repr.; New York, SRGM 43, *Kandinsky,* no. 47, repr.; Chicago, SRGM 47-T, *Kandinsky,* no. 42; Pittsburgh, SRGM 53-T, *Kandinsky,* no. 19; New York, SRGM 78 (checklist); Vancouver, SRGM 88-T, no. 15; The Newark Museum, *Abstract Art 1910 to Today,* Apr. 27-June 10, 1956, no. 32; Brussels, SRGM 105-T, p. 23 repr.; Baltimore, SRGM 113-T (no cat.); Toronto, SRGM 117-T (no cat.); New York, SRGM 118 (checklist); 147, *Kandinsky,* no. 49, repr. p. 74; New York, M. Knoedler & Co., Inc., *Space and Dream,* Dec. 5-29, 1967, p. 52, repr.; New York, SRGM 226, 227, 228 (no cats.); 232, 241, p. 203, repr. p. 202; 252, repr. (withdrawn after New York showing); New York, SRGM 266, 276 (no cats.).

REFERENCES:

Staatliches Bauhaus Weimar, 1919-1923, Weimar-Munich [1923], repr. p. 186; Grohmann, 1924, repr. [n.p.]; K. S. Dreier, *Modern Art,* New York, 1926, frontispiece; Grohmann, 1930, repr. p. 20 (dated 1921 on list of pls.); Grohmann, 1959, pp. 184, 334 no. 242, repr. cc 133; J. Lassaigne, *Kandinsky,* Geneva, 1964, pp. 94, 96, repr. color p. 87.

103   On Gray. 1923.
       (Auf Grau).

HL *1923, 252, Auf Grau.*

49.1214

Oil on canvas, 47½ x 55¼ (120.2 x 140.5)

Signed and dated l.l.: *K/23*; inscribed by the artist on reverse: *K / 1923 / Nº 252.*

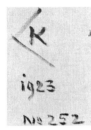

PROVENANCE:

Herwarth Walden, Berlin, 1924;[1] Nell Urech-Walden, Schniznach-Bad, Switzer-land, 1924-49; purchased from Nell Walden, 1949.

CONDITION:

In 1954 the surface was cleaned and coated with clear synthetic varnish; the stretcher was keyed out. Apparently, prior to acquisition, 4 small losses were inpainted: 3 of these are close to the lower edge approximately 20 to 22 in. from the left margin, the fourth (a repair approximately 1 in. in diameter) is 12½ in. from the left margin and 5½ in. from the top.

A blister in the lower right corner has caused some cracking in the adjacent paint film, and minimal cracking is present at the left margin above center and in the black areas right of center. The condition is otherwise excellent. (Aug. 1972.)

The general compositional emphasis, as well as several of the individual motifs, are reminiscent of the color lithograph *Kleine Welten No. 1* of 1912 (H. K. Röthel, *Gr. W.,* 1970, no. 164).

EXHIBITIONS:

Darmstadt, May-June, 1923 (information from HL, but exhibition not otherwise identified); Kunstmuseum Bern, *Der Sturm: Sammlung Nell Walden aus den Jahren 1912-1920,* Oct. 1944-Mar. 1945, no. 305; Kunsthalle Basel, *Francis Picabia: Sammlung Nell Walden,* Jan. 12-Feb. 3, 1946, no. 233; New York, SRGM 64 (no cat.); Pasadena, SRGM 146-T, *Kandinsky,* no. 29, repr. p. 56; New York, SRGM 228 (no cat.); 252, repr.

REFERENCE:

Grohmann, 1959, p. 334 no. 252, repr. cc 143.

1. The HL entry includes the information *"Sammlung Walden,"* but gives no indication of the date of acquisition. The picture was presumably among the works Nell Walden took with her when she left Walden in 1924.

104   In the Black Square. 1923.
       (Im schwarzem Viereck).

HL *1923, 259, Im Schwarzem Viereck.*

37.254

Oil on canvas, 38⅜ x 36⅝ (97.5 x 93)

Signed and dated l.l.: *K/23*; inscribed by the artist on reverse: *K / N⁰ 259. / i923.*

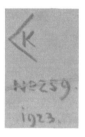

PROVENANCE:

Victor Rubin, Berlin, September 1923-April 1936 (information from HL); purchased

from Rubin through J. B. Neumann, New York, by Solomon R. Guggenheim, April 1936; Gift of Solomon R. Guggenheim, 1937.

CONDITION:

In 1953 the surface was cleaned, but the scattered applications of natural varnish were not removed; the canvas was surfaced with clear synthetic varnish. In 1958 the stretcher was replaced and the margins waxed. In 1974 the work was cleaned. PBM, which had crosslinked, was successfully removed with T-323. The work was lined on fiberglass with BEVA and coated with AYAF.

Apart from some wear at the edges and a minimal amount of cracking in the paint film just above the center, the condition is excellent. (Sept. 1974.)

A preparatory watercolor is in the collection of Karl Flinker, Paris (fig. a). With some minor exceptions, the colors and forms in the two works are the same. The most notable differences between the watercolor and the painting are in the areas of dabbed or spray-like color; whereas in the watercolor these are amorphous and free in character, in the final version they are carefully confined within specific or implied outlines. The black area within which the white trapezoid is placed is considerably larger proportionately in the watercolor than in the final picture.

The dabbed technique used in parts of this composition reappears in graphic form in *Lithograph No. III* of 1925 (Röthel, *Gr. W.,* 1970, no. 187).

fig. a.
Kandinsky, study for *In the Black Square,* watercolor on paper, 14⅛ x 14⅛ in., 36 x 36 cm., Collection Karl Flinker, Paris.

104

EXHIBITIONS:

Weimar, *Bauhaus Ausstellung,* Aug.-Sept. 1923 (no cat.; information from HL); Berlin, *Grosser Berliner Kunstausstellung,* 1926, pl. 12, top; Berlin, Galerie Alfred Flechtheim, *Kandinsky,* Feb. 1931, no. 29; Philadelphia, SRGM 3-T, no. 84, repr. p. 33; Charleston, S.C., SRGM 4-T, no. 114, repr. p. 39; Washington, D.C., SRGM 38-T (no cat.); Milwaukee, SRGM 49-T (no cat.); Munich, Haus der Kunst, *Die Maler am Bauhaus,* Apr. 27, 1950-Jan. 15, 1951, no. 75; New York, SRGM 87 (checklist); Brussels, SRGM 105-T, p. 25, repr.; Baltimore, SRGM 113-T (no cat.); Toronto, SRGM 117-T (no cat.); New York, SRGM 118 (checklist); Philadelphia, SRGM 134-T, no. 61; New York, SRGM 147, *Kandinsky,* no. 52, repr. p. 75; New York, Sidney Janis Gallery, *Two Generations of 20th Century Art,* Jan. 2-31, 1967, no. 20; New York, SRGM 195 (no cat.); 196 (checklist); 202, p. 17, repr.; 208, 212, 214, 226, 227, 228 (no cats.); 232, 241, p. 204, repr. p. 205; 252, repr. color (withdrawn after New York showing); New York, SRGM 266 (no cat.).

REFERENCES:

Grohmann, 1924, n.p. ("*Samml. Rubin, Berlin*"); Grohmann, 1930, p. 21, repr.; J. B. Neumann, ed., *Artlover,* vol. 3, no. 4, 1936, p. 60, repr.; *Art of Tomorrow,* 1939, no. 254, repr.; Grohmann, 1959, pp. 186, 334 no. 259, repr. cc 147; H. Read, *Kandinsky,* London, 1959, pp. 6, 14, repr. color.

105   Composition 8. 1923.

HL *1923, 260, Komposition 8.*

37.262

Oil on canvas, 55⅛ x 79⅛ (104 x 201)

Signed and dated l.l.: *K / 23*; inscribed by
the artist on reverse: *K / N⁰ 260. / 1923.*;
on stretcher: *„Komposition 8."*

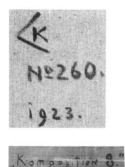

PROVENANCE:
Purchased from the artist by Solomon R.
Guggenheim, 1929; Gift of Solomon R.
Guggenheim, 1937.

CONDITION:
Some small areas of inpainting along the
top, right, and bottom edges are of uncertain date. In 1954 the surface was cleaned
but the natural varnish, which was selec-
tively applied mainly in the black areas, was
not removed.

The edges are worn in several places; there
are a small number of minor abrasions in
the paint film. The pin-sized hole made by
a compass point is visible at the center of
most of the circular forms. (July 1972.)

A watercolor study for the right side of the composition is owned by the
Galleria Galatea, Turin (fig. a). The colors of the study closely approximate
those of the final work, although sèveral small changes in the composition
have been made.

As early as 1933 Grohmann described this painting as the masterpiece of
the Bauhaus period, and in 1958 he more specifically stated that Kandinsky
himself regarded it as "the highpoint of his postwar achievement" (1959,
p. 188).

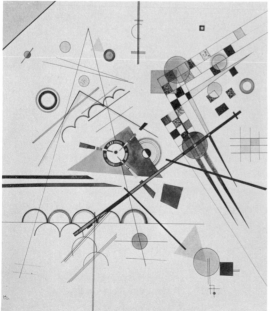

fig. a.
Kandinsky, study for *Composition 8,*
1923, watercolor on paper, 18½ x 16¾
in., 47 x 42.5 cm., Galleria Galatea,
Turin.

105

Kandinsky had started to use circles in 1921, and although it was not until
1923 that they began to play a dominant compositional role, Weiss points out
that the circle was an important motif for the artist from his earliest Jugendstil
period (1973, pp. 430-432, 455-458). Between 1923 and 1929 the circle was
used by Kandinsky as the sole motif in approximately ten works (see below
Several Circles, 1926, cat. no. 111). In 1925, 1929, and 1930 Kandinsky offered

several different explanations of the significance of this development. In a letter to Grohmann of November 21, 1925, he wrote: "I want people to perceive what lies behind my painting since this is finally what interests me; the formal problems only play a minor role. It is not enough merely to recognize that I use triangles or circles . . ." On October 12, 1930, he wrote:

> You mention the circle, and I agree with your definition. It is a link with the cosmic. But I use it above all formally. Have I sent you the few lines I wrote for you way back in April? I have just come upon them again.—Why does the circle fascinate me? It is (1) the most modest form, but asserts itself unconditionally, (2) a precise but inexhaustible variable, (3) simultaneously stable and unstable, (4) simultaneously loud and soft, (5) a single tension that carries countless tensions within it. The circle is the synthesis of the greatest oppositions. It combines the concentric and the excentric in a single form, and in equilibrium. Of the three primary forms [triangle, square, circle], it points most clearly to the fourth dimension (quoted by Grohmann, 1959, pp. 187-188; the originals are in the Grohmann Archiv, Stuttgart).

The previous year, in response to a psychologist's questionnaire, he had again stressed the symbolic significance of the circle over its formal qualities:

> If I make such frequent, vehement use of the circle in recent years, the reason (or cause) for this is not the geometric form of the circle, or its geometric properties, but my strong feeling for the inner force of the circle and its countless variations; I love the circle today as I formerly loved the horse, for instance—perhaps even more, since I find more inner potentialities in the circle, which is why it has taken the horse's place . . . In my pictures, I have said a great many "new" things about the circle, but theoretically, although I have often tried, I cannot say very much (P. Plaut, *Die Psychologie der Productiven Persönlichkeit*, Stuttgart, 1929, pp. 306-308, quoted by Brisch, 1955, p. 229 and by Grohmann, 1959, p. 188).

Lindsay, in his analysis of the circle's significance (pp. 48 ff.), dwells upon this latter aspect; he sees the circle as a source of symbolic energy, a kind of "power-giving sun," and cites *Composition 8* as a compelling example of the use of this central symbol of the Bauhaus years. For a further discussion of the process whereby the symbolism inherent in Kandinsky's image of the horse was gradually transferred to that of the circle, see Weiss, 1973, pp. 452-464.

Composition 8 contains yet another motif which Kandinsky was later to cite as an example of the powerful qualities of abstract configuration. In the upper right the acute angle of a yellow triangle rests on the black outline of a blue circle. In 1931 Kandinsky wrote: "The contact of the acute angle of a triangle with a circle is no less powerful in its effect than that of the finger of God with the finger of Adam in Michelangelo's painting" (*Cahiers d'Art*, vol. 6, 1931, p. 352, cited by Lindsay, p. 46). Whether Kandinsky intends this statement to be taken as an evaluation of the comparable "intrinsic meaning" in the two works (as Lindsay argues) or whether he is referring, as seems more plausible, to the extraordinary formal tension created in both by the moment of contact is impossible to say. It is clear, however, that he saw the motif as an especially powerful one and that he used it extremely rarely. Its earliest appearance—and in a peripheral role—is in *Composition 8*. The following year it becomes the central subject of the painting *Contact* (HL 1924, 284, Lindsay, 1966, repr. p. 51). Kandinsky used it in this form in only one other painting—*Tension in Red* of 1926 (see below cat. no. 112), where it appears at the top of the field in an important but not central role.

In three other cases he used the motif in a modified form: *Theme Point* of 1927 (HL 381, Grohmann, 1959, repr. cc 249) contains a series of triangles poised upon the edges of semi-circles; the ceramic decoration of the music room in the *Internationale Kunstausstellung* in Berlin, 1931 (HL 554C, Grohmann, 1959, repr. cc 398) also reduces the full circle of the original conception to a semi-circle, although the motif here plays as central a role as it does in *Contact*. In *Sharp Quiet* of 1927 (HL 384, Grohmann, 1959, repr. cc 251) a further modification occurs in that the angle of the triangle rests upon the interior edge of the circle rather than its exterior, and the formal tension of the contact between the two elements is thus removed.

EXHIBITIONS:

Weimar, *Bauhaus Ausstellung,* Aug.-Sept. 1923 (no cat.; information from HL); Dresden, *Fides,* Oct. 1924, Wiesbaden, Jan.-Feb. 1925, Barmen, Mar. 1925, Bochom, Apr. 1925, Dusseldorf, Nov. 1925, Braunschweig, *Jubiläums Ausstellung,* Oct. 1926 (information from HL, but exhibitions not otherwise identified); Städtische Kunsthalle Mannheim, *Wege u. Richtungen der Abstrakten Malerei in Europa,* Jan. 30-May 27, 1927, no. 81; Charleston, S.C., SRGM 1-T, no. 76, repr. p. 32; Philadelphia, SRGM 3-T, no. 87, repr. p. 78; Charleston, S.C., SRGM 4-T, no. 117, repr. p. 108; New York, SRGM 43, *Kandinsky,* no. 57, repr.; Pittsburgh, SRGM 53-T, *Kandinsky,* no. 21, repr.; Paris, Musée National d'Art Moderne, *L'Oeuvre du XXe siècle,* May-June, 1952, no. 44, traveled to London, Tate Gallery, July 15-Aug. 17, 1952, no. 39 (dated 1925); New York, SRGM 84 (checklist); San Francisco Museum of Art, *Art in the Twentieth Century,* June 17-July 10, 1955, p. 14; New York, The Museum of Modern Art, *German Art of the Twentieth Century,* Oct. 1-Dec. 8, 1957, traveled to City Art Museum of Saint Louis, Jan. 8-Feb. 24, 1958, no. 67, repr. color; Kansas City, Mo., Nelson Gallery and Atkins Museum, *The Logic of Modern Art,* Jan. 19-Feb. 26, 1961, no. 27; New York, SRGM 147, *Kandinsky,* no. 53, repr. p. 77; Cleveland Museum of Art, *50 Years of Modern Art: 1916-1966,* June 15-July 31, 1966, no. 26, repr.; Stuttgart, Württembergischer Kunstverein, *50 Jahre Bauhaus,* May 5-July 28, 1968, no. 111, repr., traveled to London, Royal Academy, Sept. 21-Oct. 27, 1968, Amsterdam, Stedelijk Museum, Nov. 30, 1968-Jan. 8, 1969, Paris, Musée d'Art Moderne, Apr. 1-June 22, 1969, Chicago, Illinois Institute of Technology, Aug. 25-Sept. 26, 1969, Toronto, The Art Gallery of Ontario, Dec. 5, 1969-Feb. 8, 1970, Pasadena Art Museum, Mar. 16-May 10, 1970, Buenos Aires, Museo Nacional de Bellas Artes, Sept. 1-Oct. 10, 1970; New York, SRGM 252, repr. (withdrawn after New York showing); 266, 276 (no cats.).

REFERENCES:

Grohmann, 1930, repr. p. 24; Idem, 1933, p. 5; Idem, 1959, pp. 188, 190, 219, 334 no. 260, repr. color p. 189; J. Lassaigne, *Kandinsky,* Geneva, 1964, pp. 97-98; K. Lindsay, "Les Thèmes de l'inconscient," *XXe Siècle,* vol. xxvii, Dec. 1966, pp. 48-49, repr. p. 46; P. Overy, *Kandinsky: The Language of the Eye,* New York, 1969, pp. 67-68, 83, 107-108, 121-122, color pl. 29.

106   Yellow Accompaniment. 1924.
       (Gelbe Begleitung).

HL *1924, 269, Gelbe Begleitung.*

39.264

Oil on canvas, 39⅛ x 38⅜ (99.2 x 97.4)

Signed and dated l.l.: *K/24*; inscribed by the artist on reverse: *K „Gelbe Begleitung." / N⁰ 269. / 1924.*

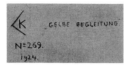

PROVENANCE:

Purchased from Gutbier, Dresden, by Dr. [Curt] Glaser, Dresden, 1926;[1] Rudolf

Bauer, Berlin, by 1939; purchased from Rudolf Bauer by Solomon R. Guggenheim, 1939; Gift of Solomon R. Guggenheim, 1939.

CONDITION:

Some time prior to 1953 (when the conservator's record on the picture begins) some apparent losses along the 4 edges were inpainted.

The paint over the entire surface was applied extremely thinly, and since there was no varnish, a certain amount of soil has penetrated the paint layer, which is, however, otherwise well preserved. (Aug. 1972.)

EXHIBITIONS:

Vienna, *Internationale Ausstellung,* Sept. 1924, Wiesbaden, Jan.-Feb. 1925, Barmen, Mar. 1925, Bochom, Apr. 1925, Dusseldorf, Nov. 1925, Braunschweig, *Jubiläums Ausstellung,* May 1926 (information from HL, but exhibitions not otherwise identified); Dresden, Galerie Arnold, *Jubiläums-Ausstellung: Kandinsky,* Oct. 16-Nov. 10, 1926, no. 22; Cazenovia, N.Y., SRGM 33-T (no cat.); New York, SRGM 43, *Kandinsky,* no. 63; 64 (no cat.); 78, 79 (checklists); Brussels, SRGM 105-T, p. 27, repr.; Baltimore, SRGM 113-T (no cat.); Toronto, SRGM 117-T (no cat.); Pasadena, SRGM 146-T, *Kandinsky,* no. 33, repr. p. 62; New York, SRGM 228 (no cat.); 252, repr.

REFERENCE:

Grohmann, 1959, pp. 186, 334 no. 269, repr. cc 158.

1. The HL entry states: *"Samml. Dr. Glaser, Dresden (verkauft in Ausst. B. Gutbier Okt. 26)."* Gutbier was the owner of the Galerie Arnold, Dresden, where the picture was exhibited in 1926. H. K. Röthel suggested (in conversation with the author) that the reference might be to the art historian Curt Glaser.

107 Deep Brown. 1924.
(*Tiefes Braun*).

HL *1924, 271, Tiefes Braun.*

48.1172 x81

Oil on canvas, 32¾ x 28⅝ (83.1 x 72.7)

Signed and dated l.l.: *K / 24*; inscribed by
the artist on reverse (photographed before
lining): *K / „Tiefes Braun." / N° 27i. /
i924.*

PROVENANCE:

Given by the artist on consignment (?) to
Karl Nierendorf, New York, before 1937;[1]
with Nierendorf until 1948; acquired with
the Estate of Karl Nierendorf, 1948.

CONDITION:

In 1953 the painting was cleaned, and a few
tiny losses were retouched; the picture was
surfaced with PBM and restretched on a
new stretcher. In 1966 the canvas was lined
with wax resin.

The margins show some wear, and there are
2 abrasions in the light brown area lower
left, but the condition is otherwise good.
(Aug. 1972.)

EXHIBITIONS:

Dresden, *Sezession,* July-Sept. 1924, Wiesbaden, Jan.-Feb. 1925, Barmen, Mar. 1925, Bochom,
Apr. 1925, Dusseldorf, Nov. 1925 (information from HL, but exhibitions otherwise not
identified); New York, College Art Association, *Kandinsky: A Retrospective View,* 1937, no.
4;[2] New York, Nierendorf Gallery, *Group Exhibition,* Apr. 17-May 6, 1939 (no cat.); New
York, Nierendorf Gallery, *Kandinsky,* Mar. 1941, no. 6; New York, Nierendorf Gallery,
Works by Kandinsky, Dec. 1942-Feb. 1943 (checklist); New York, SRGM 43, *Kandinsky,*
no. 78; New York, SRGM 147, *Kandinsky,* no. 54, repr. color p. 78; Cambridge, Mass.,
Busch-Reisinger Museum, *Masters of the Bauhaus,* Nov. 1-Dec. 10, 1966, p. 19; New York,
SRGM 226, 228 (no cats.); Staatliche Kunsthalle Baden-Baden, *Kandinsky Gemälde, 1900-
1944,* no. 56, repr. color; New York, SRGM 252, repr.; 276 (no cat.).

REFERENCE:

Grohmann, 1959, p. 334 no. 271, repr. cc 159.

1. The HL entry includes Nierendorf's name, but without price, suggesting that the work was
   sent to him on consignment, as some paintings apparently were (information supplied by
   Nina Kandinsky in conversation with the author, Oct. 1972). The picture was in Nierendorf's hands by the time of the 1937 exhibition, but was still unsold at the time of his death.
2. This exhibition and the picture's appearance in it is recorded in the Museum's files, but no
   catalogue or other record of the exhibition has hitherto been located by the Museum or by
   the College Art Association.

108   One Center. 1924.
       (*Ein Zentrum*).

HL *1924, 285, Ein Zentrum.*

37.263

Oil on canvas, 55⅜ x 39⅛ (140.6 x 99.5)

Signed and dated l.l.: *K / 24*; inscribed by
the artist on reverse: *K „Ein Zentrum" /
N⁰ 285. / 1924.*

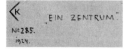

PROVENANCE:

C. H. Kirchhoff, Wiesbaden, 1925-37?;[1]
purchased, possibly through Rudolf Bauer,
by Solomon R. Guggenheim by 1937;[2] Gift
of Solomon R. Guggenheim, 1937.

CONDITION:

The work has received no treatment.

The condition is excellent. (Aug. 1972.)

EXHIBITIONS:

Wiesbaden, Jan.-Feb. 1925 (information from HL, but exhibition not otherwise identified);
Philadelphia, SRGM 3-T, no. 90, repr. p. 81; Charleston, S.C., SRGM 4-T, no. 121, repr. color,
p. 95; Baltimore, SRGM 5-T, no. 121, repr. color; Cazenovia, N.Y., SRGM 33-T; Washington,
D.C., SRGM 38-T (no cats.); New York, SRGM 43, *Kandinsky,* no. 62; Pittsburgh, SRGM
53-T, no. 27; Munich, Haus der Kunst, *Die Maler am Bauhaus,* May-June 1950, no. 77;
Boston, Institute of Contemporary Art, *Kandinsky,* Mar. 25-Apr. 18, 1952, traveled to New
York, M. Knoedler & Co., Inc., May 10-June 6, 1952, San Francisco Museum of Art, July 20-
Aug. 26, 1952, Minneapolis, Walker Art Center, Sept. 14-Oct. 26, 1952, Cleveland Museum of
Art, Nov. 6-Dec. 7, 1952, no. 33; New York, SRGM 147, *Kandinsky,* no. 55, repr. p. 79; 252,
repr.

REFERENCES:

W. Grohmann, "W. Kandinsky," *Cahiers d'Art,* année 7, 4, 1929, repr. p. 326; Idem, 1930,
p. 25, repr. no. 31 ("*Collection Kirchhoff, Wiesbaden*"); Idem, 1959, p. 335 no. 285, repr.
p. 288.

1. Kirchhoff is listed in the HL as the first owner. An unpublished letter from Kandinsky to
   Grohmann dated Aug. 31, 1926, refers to the fact that Kirchhoff is especially fond of the
   work; it seems likely that he purchased it at the time of the Jan. 1925 Wiesbaden exhibition.
   There is no record of how long he owned the work, but Guggenheim is listed in the HL as
   the second owner.
2. Guggenheim's financial records do not indicate from whom he purchased the picture. The
   stamp of Bauer's gallery Das Geistreich is on the reverse of the canvas, indicating either
   that the picture passed through his hands, or that it was at some point exhibited in his
   gallery. It has not been possible to clarify this point.

109   Pointed and Round. 1925.
        (Spitz und Rund; Pointu et rond).

HL *1925, 293, Spitz und Rund.*

37·333

Oil on board, 27½ x 19⅝ (69.8 x 50)

Signed and dated l.l.: *K / 25*; inscribed by
the artist on reverse: *K / N⁰ 293. / 1925. /
«Spitz u. Rund.» 50 x 70.*

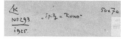

PROVENANCE:

Given by the artist to N. Ehmsen, Munich
(information from HL);[1] reverted to the
artist; purchased from the artist through
Valentine Gallery, Paris, by Solomon R.
Guggenheim, February 1933; Gift of Solomon R. Guggenheim, 1937.

CONDITION:

The brown circular form at the upper left
was originally painted reddish-brown and
later extensively retouched with orange-
brown. Kandinsky probably did this retouching when he reacquired the picture
from Ehmsen, sometime before 1933. It is
impossible to judge whether the 2 pigments
were originally more closely matched than
they now appear. A few scattered small
areas of inpainting which are also under
the natural varnish may have been made by
Kandinsky at the same time. In 1953 the
board was mounted on Masonite with PVA
emulsion and the Masonite was mounted on
a pine grid. The surface was cleaned but
the varnish not removed. The edges were
filled and the losses in this area inpainted.

The overall condition is good. (Aug. 1972.)

EXHIBITIONS:

Charleston, S.C., SRGM 1-T, no. 81, repr. color p. 45; Philadelphia, SRGM 3-T, no. 93, repr.
color p. 73; Charleston, S.C., SRGM 4-T, no. 123, repr. color p. 97; Baltimore, SRGM 5-T,
no. 123, repr. color; New York, SRGM 43, *Kandinsky* (dated 1935), no. 20; Pittsburgh, SRGM
53-T, *Kandinsky,* no. 49; Brussels, SRGM 105-T, p. 28, repr.; Toronto, SRGM 117-T, New
York, SRGM 228 (no cats.); 252, repr.; 276 (no cat.).

REFERENCES:

H. Rebay, *Innovation: une nouvelle ère artistique,* Paris, 1937, repr. color p. 53; Grohmann,
1959, pp. 195, 335 no. 293, repr. cc 180.

1. Ehmsen was, according to Nina Kandinsky (in conversation with the author, Nov. 1972), a
   painter and a friend of Kandinsky. It has not been possible to establish when Kandinsky
   gave him the picture, or when it reverted to the artist, although this must have been prior
   to 1933.

110   Bright Unity. 1925.
       (Helle Einheit).

HL *1925, 308, Helle Einheit.*

37.273

Oil on board, 27½ x 19⅝ (69.8 x 49.8)

Signed and dated l.l.: *K / 25*; inscribed by
the artist on reverse: *K __ Helle Einheit ‾ /
N⁰ 308. / 1925 / 50 x 70.*

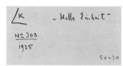

PROVENANCE:

Rudolf Bauer, Berlin; purchased from Bauer
by Solomon R. Guggenheim, June 1930
(information from HL, confirmed by Nina

Kandinsky in conversation with the author,
October 1972); Gift of Solomon R. Guggenheim, 1937.

CONDITION:

In 1953 some soil was removed from the surface, the board was mounted on reinforced
Masonite, and the surface was sprayed with
PBM. Considerable inpainting along the 4
edges and tiny touches scattered throughout
the background pre-date 1953, but cannot
be accurately dated.

There is some fine cracking in the paint film
of the tan background, the blue square upper left, and the light green quadrilateral below the black triangle. There is slight wear
along the edges of the support, and a few
scattered abrasions and losses. The condition is otherwise good. (Aug. 1972.)

EXHIBITIONS:

Charleston, S.C., SRGM 1-T, no. 80, repr. p. 33; Philadelphia, SRGM 3-T, no. 92, repr. p. 35;
Charleston S.C., SRGM 4-T, no. 124, repr. p. 41; Portland, Or., SRGM 19-T (no cat.); New
York, SRGM 43, *Kandinsky,* no. 87, repr. p. 30; Milwaukee, SRGM 49-T (no cat.); Pitts-
burgh, SRGM 53-T, *Kandinsky,* no. 53; Munich, Haus der Kunst, *Die Bauhausmeister,* May 6-
June 6, 1950, no. 79; New York, SRGM 111, 132 (checklists); Pasadena, SRGM 146-T, *Kan-
dinsky,* no. 36, repr. p. 63; N.Y., Albany Institute of History and Art, *Art in Science,* Sept. 24-
Oct. 31, 1965, no. 33, repr.; Stuttgart, Württembergischer Kunstverein, *50 Jahre Bauhaus,*
May 5-July 28, 1968, no. 115, traveled to London, Royal Academy of Arts, Sept. 21-Oct. 27,
1968, Amsterdam, Stedelijk Museum, Nov. 30, 1968-Jan. 8, 1969, Paris, Musée d'Art Moderne,
Apr. 1-June 22, 1969, Chicago, Illinois Institute of Technology, Aug. 25-Sept. 26, 1969,
Toronto, Art Gallery of Ontario, Dec. 5, 1969-Feb. 8, 1970, Pasadena Art Museum, Mar. 16-
May 10, 1970; New York, SRGM 252, repr.; New York, SRGM 276 (no cat.).

REFERENCE:

Grohmann, 1959, pp. 195, 335 no. 308, repr. cc 194.

111   Several Circles. 1926.
       (Einige Kreise; Some Circles).

HL *1926, No. 323, Einige Kreise.*

41.283

Oil on canvas, 55¼ x 55⅜ (140.3 x 140.7)

Signed and dated l.l.: *K / 26*; inscribed by
the artist on reverse: *K / N° 323. / 1926 /
„Einige Kreise."*

PROVENANCE:
Purchased from the artist by Staatliche
Gemäldegalerie, Dresden, through their
Patronatsverein, 1926 (information supplied
by Staatliche Gemäldegalerie in correspondence with the author, April 1972); banned
by the German government as degenerate
art, 1937;[1] purchased from Gutekunst und
Klipstein, Bern, by Solomon R. Guggenheim, February 1939; Gift of Solomon R.
Guggenheim, 1941.

CONDITION:
The work has received no treatment.

Apart from some minor wear along the
edges and at the corners, and a few minor
abrasions, the condition is excellent. (May
1974.)

A sketch for this work is listed in the HL as the first painting of 1926 (1926,
322). Grohmann describes it as oil on canvas (Collection Anne Lewenstein,
27⅜ x 27⅜ in., 70.2 x 70.2 cm.) but does not reproduce it. Nina Kandinsky
(in conversation with the author, November 1972) said that the picture was
sold in April 1944, shortly before Kandinsky's death, to Madame Lecouture,
who included it in an exhibition. No trace of it has since been found and no
photograph located. The identification of the buyer as Madame Lewenstein

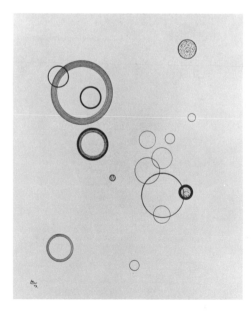

fig. a.
Kandinsky, ink on paper, signed and dated
l.l.: "K 23," 12¾ x 9⅜ in., 32.5 x 23.7 cm.,
Private Collection, Paris.

1. The work is published by F. Roh, *Entartete Kunst,* Hanover, 1962, p. 150, as among the
   works seized by the Nazis from Dresden's collection.

derives from the HL, but neither she nor Madame Lecouture have hitherto been identified.

As has already been noted above, the circle became a dominant motif for Kandinsky during the Bauhaus years and clearly acquired a significance comparable only to that of the horse in the pre-1914 period. (For a discussion of this development, see above *Composition 8*, cat. no. 105.) Between 1923 and 1929 Kandinsky produced a series of works in which the circle was not only the dominant but the sole motif. The earliest examples are probably two ink drawings in a private collection in Paris; one of these (fig. a) is described by Grohmann (1959) as the first drawing of 1923.

III

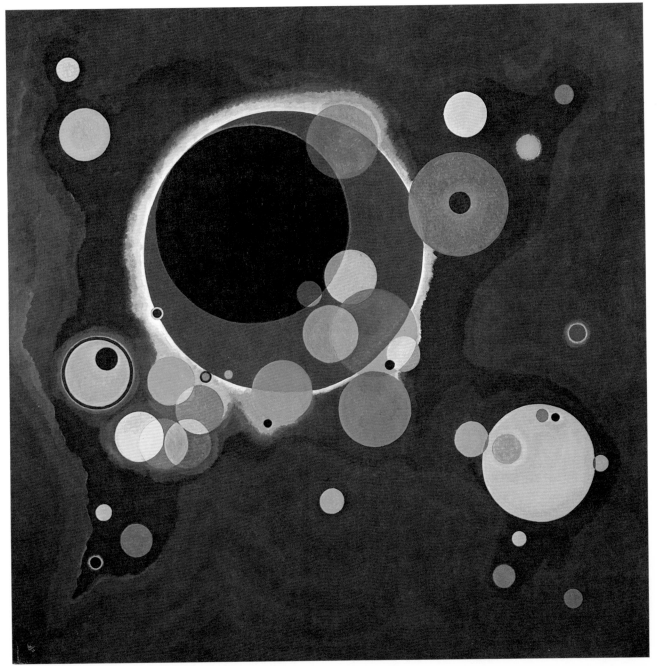

The circle pictures that followed are of three types. In the first type the circles are suspended, as if in mid-air, against a unified color field (*Several Circles; Blue,* 1927, 393; *Heavy Circles* 1927, 398; *Circles in Brown* 1929, 477). The 1923 ink drawing (fig. a) clearly belongs to this group. In the second type, the circles are placed against a background of amorphous shapes which are themselves suspended in a color field (*In Itself,* 1926, 330; *Black Increasing,* 1927, 373; *Deepened Impulse,* 1928, 424). In the third type, the circles are combined in some limited way with other geometric shapes, but clearly remain the unique focus of the composition (*Circles within the Circle,* 1923, 261; *Accent in Pink,* 1926, 325). In addition, there were, of course, dozens of works produced during these years in which the role of the circle was less central.

Grohmann (1959, pp. 204-206) has convincingly pointed out that the cosmic reference implicit in Kandinsky's use of the circle cannot be ignored, and that the circle pictures of the 1920's must be seen within the context of the artist's November 21, 1925, letter. Kandinsky states in that letter that he wants the viewer to perceive the inner meaning that lies *behind* the formal structures of his paintings, and that "of the three primary forms . . . the circle points most clearly to the fourth dimension." In a letter of October 1930 he goes further and concurs with Grohmann's suggestion that the circle provides a definite link with the cosmic. For further discussion and fuller quotations from both letters, see above cat. no. 105.

As S. Ringbom points out (*The Sounding Cosmos,* Abo, 1970, pp. 199-200), the "inner meaning" which Kandinsky wished the viewer to grasp is not readily susceptible of verbal explanation. Rather it appeals to the inner eye and the "finer emotions" which Kandinsky saw as coming to maturity in the new Spiritual Epoch—emotions that were beyond the scope of simple verbal analysis. Ringbom also draws attention to a 1937 article in which Kandinsky refers again, as he had in the pre-World War I period, to the notion of "hearing" the sound (*Klang)* of form: "This is the solution of the question of 'abstract art.' Art is mute only to those who cannot 'hear' the form" (W. Kandinsky, *Kunst und Künstler,* ed.M.Bill, 2nd ed., Bern, 1963, p. 208. For a discussion of the pre-1914 notion of *Klang,* see above cat. no. 82 and Ringbom, op. cit., pp. 116 ff.). Ringbom suggests that the cosmic interpretation of geometric forms which is expanded in Kandinsky's *Punkt und Linie zu Fläche (Point and Line to Plane),* first published in 1926, is traceable to Theosophical sources, and in particular that his description of the birth of the circle (4th ed., Bern, 1959, pp. 61 ff.) closely approximates that of the Theosophical notion of the development from spirit to matter. (For a discussion of this point, see Ringbom, op. cit., pp. 200 ff.)

P. Weiss's detailed discussion of Kandinsky's Munich environment provides additional sources which must be taken into account in any consideration of Kandinsky's theory of geometric form and his breakthrough into abstraction. (See also Weiss, "Kandinsky and the 'Jugendstil' Arts and Crafts Movement," *Burlington Magazine,* vol. cxvii, May 1975, pp. 270-279.) One such source is Karl Scheffler, whose work Kandinsky is known to have admired (see Weiss,

1973, pp. 381 ff.). In Kandinsky's October 1930 letter to Grohmann cited above, he had stated: "The circle is the synthesis of the greatest oppositions. It combines the concentric and the excentric in a single form, and in equilibrium." Scheffler, in his 1901 article on ornament in which—as Weiss states—he had identified abstraction as the essential area of the decorative artist, Scheffler wrote: "The circle is the eternally beautiful and complete ornament, because within it the most obvious possible equilibrium of two forces—the centrifugal and the centripetal—occurs" ("Meditationen über das Ornament," *Dekorative Kunst,* vol. viii, July 1901, p. 400, trans. P. Weiss, 1973, pp. 453-454, fn. 19). In this and in innumerable other instances Kandinsky's thinking is related to and grows naturally out of the intellectual environment in which he found himself in Munich from 1896 onwards. Weiss's analysis of Jugendstil theory and practice and of the contributions made by the crafts movement, by Endell, Obrist, Hölzel, and by the Symbolist insistence on "inner significance" to developing ideas of a new visual language must clearly be taken into account as immensely important ingredients in the formation of Kandinsky's art and theory. Together with the Theosophical sources explored by Ringbom, R. C. Washton, and others, they provide a rich and complex network of overlapping strands which cannot usefully be studied in isolation from one another.

EXHIBITIONS:

Dresden, *Internationale Kunstausstellung,* June-Sept. 1926, no. 519, repr.; New York, SRGM 43, *Kandinsky,* no. 97; Pittsburgh, SRGM 53-T, *Kandinsky,* no. 45, repr.; New York, SRGM 64 (no cat.); 147, *Kandinsky,* no. 57, repr. color p. 81; New York, Marlborough-Gerson Gallery, *Artists and Maecenas: A Tribute to Curt Valentin,* Nov. 12-Dec. 27, 1963 (not in cat.); New York, SRGM 173, no. 56, repr. color; Cambridge, Mass., Busch-Reisinger Museum, *Masters of the Bauhaus,* Nov. 1-Dec. 10, 1966, p. 19, repr.; New York, SRGM 195 (no cat.); 196 (checklist); Buffalo, N.Y., Albright-Knox Art Gallery, *Plus by Minus: Today's Half Century,* Mar. 2-Apr. 14, 1968, no. 65; New York, SRGM 198-T, 226, 227, 228 (no cats.); 232, 241, p. 206, repr. color p. 207; 252, repr. color (withdrawn after New York showing); Cleveland, SRGM 258-T, no. 21, repr.; New York, SRGM 276 (no cat.).

REFERENCES:

Offset, Heft 7, 1926, repr. p. 409; Grohmann, 1930, p. xxix, repr. p. 34; M. Bill, *Kandinsky,* Paris, 1951, repr. p. 53; Grohmann, 1959, pp. 206, 335 no. 323, repr. color p. 205; M. Brion, *Kandinsky,* London, 1961, pp. 72-73; Grohmann, "La Grande unité d'une grande oeuvre," *XXᵉ Siècle,* vol. xxvii, Dec. 1966, pp. 13-16, repr. color foll. p. 56.

112   Tension in Red. 1926.
(Spannung in Rot; Tension en rouge).

HL *1926, 326, Spannung in Rot.*

38.286

Oil on board, 26 x 21⅛ (66 x 53.7)

Signed and dated l.l.: *K / 26*; inscribed by the artist on reverse (transcribed but not photographed before mounting): *K / N⁰ 326 / 1926. «Spannung in Rot.»*

PROVENANCE:

Given by the artist on consignment to Galerie Gradiva (André Breton), Paris, September 1937?;[1] purchased from the artist by Galerie Jeanne Bucher, Paris, 1938 (information supplied by Galerie Jeanne Bucher, correspondence with the author, October 1971); purchased from Bucher by Solomon R. Guggenheim, July 1938;[2] Gift of Solomon R. Guggenheim, 1938.

CONDITION:

In 1953 the board was mounted on Masonite reinforced with a wooden frame. Some inpainting of abraded areas has taken place along all 4 edges and in an area approximately ⅞ in. long near the upper left-hand corner of the red pentagon. The date of this retouching is not recorded.

Some additional abrasions and tiny losses along the edges have occurred since. The condition is otherwise good. (July 1972.)

EXHIBITIONS:

Dresden, *Internationale Kunstausstellung*, June-Sept. 1926, no. 520; Städtische Kunsthalle Mannheim, *Wege u. Richtungen der Abstrakten Malerei*, Jan. 30-Mar. 27, 1927, no. 84; The Arts Club of Chicago, *The Blue Four*, Apr. 1-15, 1932, no. 86; Kunsthalle Bern, *Wassily Kandinsky, Französische Meister der Gegenwart*, Feb. 21-Mar. 29, 1937, no. 28; Washington, D.C., SRGM 38-T (no cat.); New York, SRGM 43, *Kandinsky*, no. 102 (erroneously listed as watercolor); 74, no. 91; 147, *Kandinsky*, no. 59, repr. p. 84; Richmond, Va., SRGM 188-T, New York, SRGM 228 (no cats.); 252, repr.; New York, SRGM 266, 276 (no cats.).

REFERENCE:

Grohmann, 1959, pp. 210, 335 no. 329, repr. cc 208.

1. The HL includes a reference to *"Gradiva"* and the date *"16.9.37."* André Breton opened his Surrealist gallery on the rue de Seine in 1937, and it was closed when he left for Mexico in 1938. In 1938 he also wrote a short piece on Kandinsky (reprinted in *Le Surréalisme et la peinture, 1925-1965*, Paris, 1965, pp. 286-287). It seems possible that the present picture was sent to the gallery on consignment and returned to Kandinsky in 1938.

2. The HL erroneously lists Hilla Rebay as the owner although the work was paid for by Guggenheim. Rebay probably negotiated the purchase.

113   Extended. 1926.
(Ausgedehnt).

HL *1926, 333, Ausgedehnt.*

39.279

Oil on panel, 37½ x 17⅜ (95.3 x 44.2)

Signed and dated l.l.: *K / 26;* inscribed by
the artist on reverse: *K / No 333 / 1926. /
«Ausgedehnt."*

PROVENANCE:

Purchased from the artist by C. H. Kirchhoff, Wiesbaden, February 1927 (information from HL);[1] Rudolf Bauer, Berlin, by
1939; purchased from Rudolf Bauer by
Solomon R. Guggenheim, 1939; Gift of
Solomon R. Guggenheim, 1939.

CONDITION:

In 1953 the surface was cleaned and the soft
resin varnish was largely removed. Scattered
losses along the edges were retouched with
colors in PVA. The picture was surfaced
with Ozenfant's wax.

The condition is excellent. (July 1972.)

EXHIBITIONS:

New York, SRGM 43, *Kandinsky,* no. 90; 64 (no cat.); 78 (checklist); Toronto, SRGM 85-T,
no. 25; Vancouver, SRGM 88-T, no. 23; Brussels, SRGM 105-T, p. 30, repr.; Baltimore,
SRGM 113-T (no cat.); Toronto, SRGM 117-T (no cat.); New York, SRGM 118 (checklist);
252, repr.

REFERENCES:

Grohmann, 1959, p. 335 no. 333, repr. cc 213; H. Read, *Kandinsky,* London, 1959, repr.
color opp. p. 16.

1. The HL entry also includes the note *"(K-Ges),"* which has been interpreted by Grohmann
as a reference to the Kestner Gesellschaft. Nina Kandinsky, however, has explained (in
conversation with the author, Oct. 1972) that the reference is to the Kandinsky Gesellschaft of which Kirchhoff was a member. The subscribers to the Gesellschaft supported
Kandinsky with a small annual income in exchange for which they each received one or
more works by the artist per year. The present picture was thus acquired by Kirchhoff in
his capacity as a member of the group.

114   Three Sounds. 1926.
        (Drei Klänge).

HL *1926, 343, Drei Klänge.*

41.282

Oil on canvas, 23⅝ x 23½ (59.9 x 59.6)

Signed and dated l.l.: *K / 26*; inscribed by
the artist on reverse: *K „Drei Klänge." / N⁰
343. 1926. / 59 x 59.*

PROVENANCE:

Purchased from the artist by Anhältische
Gemäldegalerie, Dessau, November 1928
(information from HL); banned by the German government as degenerate art, 1937;[1]
purchased from Gutekunst und Klipstein,
Bern, by Solomon R. Guggenheim, February
1939; Gift of Solomon R. Guggenheim, 1941.

CONDITION:

Some extremely minor touches of inpaint
predate acquisition.

The edges, although unevenly painted, are
in good condition. There is a slight stretcher
impression along the lower margin, and
some scattered areas of fine ground cracks
(some penetrating the paint layer) in the
pale blue area. There are a few extremely
minor paint losses, but the condition in general is excellent. (Nov. 1973.)

EXHIBITIONS:

Hanover, spring 1928 (information from HL, but exhibition not otherwise identified); New
York, SRGM 43, *Kandinsky*, no. 96; 79 (checklist); Toronto, SRGM 85-T, no. 26; Brussels,
SRGM 105-T, p. 29, repr.; Toronto, SRGM 117-T (no cat.); New York, SRGM 118 (check-
list); Cleveland Museum of Art, *Paths of Abstract Art*, Oct. 4-Nov. 13, 1960, no. 32; New
York, SRGM 147, *Kandinsky*, no. 60, repr. p. 85; Stuttgart, Württembergischer Kunstverein,
50 Jahre Bauhaus, May 5-July 28, 1968, no. 116, repr., traveled to London, Royal Academy of
Arts, Sept. 21-Oct. 27, 1968, Amsterdam, Stedelijk Museum, Nov. 30, 1968-Jan. 8, 1969, Paris,
Musée d'Art Moderne, Apr. 1-June 22, 1969, Chicago, Illinois Institute of Technology, Aug.
25-Sept. 26, 1969, Toronto, The Art Gallery of Ontario, Dec. 5, 1969-Feb. 8, 1970, Pasadena
Art Museum, Mar. 16-May 10, 1970; Kunsthalle Nürnberg, *Was die Schönheit sei, das weiss
ich nicht*, Apr. 30-Aug. 1, 1971, no. 165; New York, SRGM 252, repr.; New York, SRGM
266, 276 (no cats.).

REFERENCES:

Grohmann, "W. Kandinsky," *Cahiers d'Art*, année 7, 4, 1929, repr. p. 328; Idem, 1930, repr.
p. 35; Idem, 1959, p. 336 no. 343, repr. cc 223.

1. Although it has not been possible to verify this directly from Dessau, it can be deduced
   from the fact that the large number of works from German collections that were acquired
   by Gutekunst und Klipstein in 1937-38 were available only because of the government's
   policy on degenerate art. For other examples now in the Guggenheim collection see cat.
   nos. 32, 78, 79, 83, and 84.

115   Calm. 1926.
(Stilles; Ruhe; Quiet).

HL 1926, 357, Stilles.

41.284

Oil on wood panel, 19 x 18¼ (48.3 x 46.3)

Signed and dated l.l.: K / 26; inscribed by
the artist on reverse: K / No 357. / i926 /
«Stilles" / 47 x 50. / Erfurt.; not in the
artist's hand: Wunder der Tiefsee.

PROVENANCE:

Purchased from the artist by Angermuseum,
Erfurt, ca. 1926;[1] banned by the German
government as degenerate art, 1937;[2] purchased from Gutekunst und Klipstein, Bern,
by Solomon R. Guggenheim, February 1939;
Gift of Solomon R. Guggenheim, 1941.

CONDITION:

2 very small areas of inpainting of uncertain
date exist; 1 is in the lower left corner, 1 in
the lower right corner.

Cracks in the paint film have developed
around the circumferences of 4 nail-heads
which were present in the panel before the
painting was begun. Several abrasions with
some paint loss are visible along the left
edge and 1 on the lower right edge. The
condition is otherwise good. (July 1972.)

EXHIBITIONS:

New York, SRGM 43, Kandinsky, no. 98, repr. p. 31; Pasadena, SRGM 146-T, Kandinsky,
no. 37, repr. p. 64; Stuttgart, Württembergischer Kunstverein, 50 Jahre Bauhaus, May 5-July
28, 1968, no. 119, traveled to London, Royal Academy, Sept. 21-Oct. 27, 1968, Amsterdam,
Stedelijk Museum, Nov. 30, 1968-Jan. 8, 1969, Paris, Musée d'Art Moderne, Apr. 1-June 22,
1969, Chicago, Illinois Institute of Technology, Aug. 25-Sept. 26, 1969, Toronto, Art Gallery
of Ontario, Dec. 5, 1969-Feb. 8, 1970, Pasadena Art Museum, Mar. 16-May 10, 1970; New
York, SRGM 252, repr.; 276 (no cat.).

REFERENCES:

Grohmann, 1930, p. xxviii, repr. p. 33, no. 42; Idem, 1959, pp. 207-208, 336 no. 357, repr.
color, p. 209 (Quiet).

1. Grohmann (1959, p. 208) states that the picture was purchased by Erfurt soon after it was
painted. An unpublished letter from Kandinsky to Grohmann dated 13/4/30 suggests that
Grohmann could obtain a photograph of the work from Dr. Kunze, then Director of the
Angermuseum (Grohmann Archiv, Stuttgart, copy in the library of The Museum of
Modern Art, New York).

2. This has not been verified directly by Erfurt; see above cat. no. 114, fn. 1.

116   Colored Sticks. 1928.
       (Bunte Stäbchen, Mottled Bars).

HL *1928, 434, Bunte Stäbchen.*

38.306

Varnished tempera on board, 16⅞ x 12⅞
(42.7 x 32.7)

Inscribed by the artist on reverse: *K / Nº
434 / 1928 «Bunte Stäbchen" / 42 x 57.*

PROVENANCE:

Purchased from the artist by Galerie Jeanne
Bucher, Paris, 1938 (information supplied by
Galerie Jeanne Bucher, correspondence with
the author, October 1971); purchased from
Bucher by Solomon R. Guggenheim, July
1938;[1] Gift of Solomon R. Guggenheim,
1938.

CONDITION:

The work has received no treatment.

The varnish was originally unevenly applied
and has discolored slightly, but the condition is excellent. (Sept. 1973.)

EXHIBITIONS:

Kunsthalle Basel, *Bauhaus Dessau,* Apr. 20-May 9, 1929, no. 86 (for sale); New York, SRGM
43, *Kandinsky,* no. 131 (erroneously listed as watercolor); Stuttgart, Württembergischer
Kunstverein, *50 Jahre Bauhaus,* May 5-July 28, 1968, no. 124, traveled to London, Royal
Academy, Sept. 21-Oct. 27, 1968, Amsterdam, Stedelijk Museum, Nov. 30, 1968-Jan. 8, 1969,
Paris, Musée d'Art Moderne, Apr. 1-June 22, 1969, Chicago, Illinois Institute of Technology,
Aug. 25-Sept. 26, 1969, Toronto, Art Gallery of Ontario, Dec. 5, 1969-Feb. 8, 1970, Pasadena
Art Museum, Mar. 16-May 10, 1970; New York, SRGM 252, repr.

REFERENCE:

Grohmann, 1959, p. 337 no. 434 (*Mottled Bars,* incorrect dimensions listed), repr. cc 292.

1. The HL erroneously lists Hilla Rebay as the owner although the work was paid for by
   Guggenheim. Rebay probably negotiated the purchase.

117   Two Sides Red. 1928.
(Zwei Seiten Rot).

HL *1928, 437, 2 Seiten Rot.*

45.981

Oil on canvas, 22⅞ x 17¼ (58.3 x 43.9)

Signed and dated l.l.: *K / 28;* inscribed by
the artist on reverse: *K / Nº 437 / 1928. /
«Zwei Seiten Rot" / 43 x 57.*

PROVENANCE:

Given by the artist on consignment to Karl
Nierendorf, New York, ca. 1937 (information from HL); purchased from Nierendorf,
1945.

CONDITION:

In 1954 the margins were extensively inpainted. In 1957 the canvas was infused with
wax resin, rabbet marks were inpainted,
and the surface sprayed with PBM.

There are scattered areas of fine crackle in
the black areas (barely visible to the naked
eye). The artist's unevenly applied natural
varnish is somewhat discolored; penetration
of the wax resin is visible on the surface at
some points, creating a mottled appearance.
The condition in general is fair to good.
(Nov. 1973.)

EXHIBITIONS:

New York, Nierendorf Gallery, *Kandinsky,* Mar. 1941, no. 55; New York, SRGM 43, *Kan-
dinsky,* no. 138; Chicago, SRGM 47-T, *Kandinsky,* no. 29; Boston, Institute of Contemporary
Art, *Kandinsky,* Mar. 27-Apr. 27, 1952, traveled to New York, M. Knoedler & Co., Inc.,
May 10-June 6, 1952, San Francisco Museum of Art, July 20-Aug. 26, 1952, Minneapolis,
Walker Art Center, Sept. 14-Oct. 26, 1952, no. 40; New York, SRGM 81 (no cat.), 83 (checklist); Vancouver, SRGM 88-T, no. 25; New York, SRGM 89 (no cat.), 95 (checklist); Brussels,
SRGM 105-T, p. 32, repr.; Baltimore, SRGM 113-T (no cat.); Toronto, SRGM 117-T (no
cat.); New York, SRGM 118 (checklist); Pasadena, SRGM 146-T, *Kandinsky,* no. 41, repr.
p. 47; New York, SRGM 195 (no cat.); 196 (checklist); 226, 227, 228 (no cats.); 232, 241,
p. 208, repr.; 252, repr. color; 266, 276 (no cats.).

REFERENCE:

Grohmann, 1959, pp. 210, 337 no. 437, repr. cc 294.

118 Some Red. 1929.
(Etwas Rot).

HL *1929, 441, Etwas Rot.*

45.980

Oil on board, 16 x 12½ (40.5 x 31.8)

Signed and dated l.l.: *K / 29*; inscribed by the artist on reverse: *K / No 44i / 1929 «Etwas Rot." / 32 x 4i.*

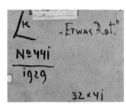

PROVENANCE:

Dr. Otto Baier, Cologne (information from HL);[1] Karl Nierendorf, New York, by 1941 (exhibition catalogue); purchased from Nierendorf, 1945.

CONDITION:

Considerable inpainting of the 4 edges occurred at an unspecified date. This seems to have been in areas of rabbeting from an earlier frame.

A number of abrasions in the black areas (appearing as gray lines) exist; also a few scattered tiny paint losses revealing the light-colored support beneath. The condition is otherwise good. (Aug. 1972.)

EXHIBITIONS:

New York, College Art Association, *Kandinsky: A Retrospective View,* 1937, no. 10;[2] New York, Nierendorf Gallery, *Kandinsky,* Mar. 1941, no. 57 *(Slightly Red)*; New York, Nierendorf Gallery, *Works by Kandinsky,* Dec. 1942-Feb. 1943 (checklist); New York, SRGM 43, *Kandinsky,* no. 158; Chicago, SRGM 47-T, *Kandinsky,* no. 17; Anniston, Ala., SRGM 51-T (no cat.); Brussels, SRGM 105-T, p. 34, repr.; Toronto, SRGM 117-T (no cat.); New York, SRGM 147, *Kandinsky,* no. 63, repr. p. 87; 228 (no cat.); 252, repr.

REFERENCE:

Grohmann, 1959, p. 337 no. 441, repr. cc 297.

1. The HL specifies that the picture was acquired by Baier in his capacity as a member of the Kandinsky Gesellschaft (see above cat. no. 113, fn. 1). He thus probably acquired the work in 1929 or 1930.

2. This exhibition and the picture's appearance in it is recorded in the Museum's files, but no catalogue or other record of the exhibition has hitherto been located by the Museum or by the College Art Association.

119   Levels. 1929.
        (Etagen).

HL *1929, 452, Etagen.*

46.1049

Oil on board, 22¼ x 16 (56.6 x 40.6)

Signed and dated l.l.: *K / 29;* inscribed by
the artist on reverse (photographed before
mounting): *K / Nº 452 / 1929 / «Etagen» /
41 x 56.*

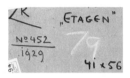

PROVENANCE:

Purchased from the artist by E. Tériade,
Paris, ca. 1930 (information from HL, confirmed by Tériade in correspondence with
the author, April 1974);[1] Ilse Shryer, New
York, by 1946; purchased from Shryer, 1946.

CONDITION:

In 1957 the board was mounted on a rigid
pine support with PVA and light pressure.
The edges of the board were filled with PVA
emulsion.

Apart from a few scattered abrasions the
condition is excellent. (Aug. 1972.)

EXHIBITIONS:

New York, SRGM 64 (no cat.); Munich, Haus der Kunst, *Die Maler am Bauhaus,* May-June
1950, no. 88; Boston, Institute of Contemporary Art, *Kandinsky,* Mar. 25-Apr. 18, 1952,
traveled to New York, M. Knoedler & Co., Inc., May 10-June 6, 1952, San Francisco Museum
of Art, July 20-Aug. 26, 1952, Minneapolis, Walker Art Center, Sept. 14-Oct. 26, 1952, no. 42;
Brussels, SRGM 105-T, p. 35, repr.; Toronto, SRGM 117-T (no cat.); Boston, SRGM 119-T,
no. 21; London, Institute of Contemporary Art, *The Mysterious Sign,* Oct. 26-Dec. 3, 1960;
New York, SRGM 147, *Kandinsky,* no. 64, repr. p. 87; 195 (no cat.); 196 (checklist); 212, 226,
227, 228 (no cats.); 232, 241, p. 209, repr.; 252, repr.; 266, 276 (no cats.).

REFERENCES:

E. Tériade, "Documentaire sur la jeune peinture," *Cahiers d'Art,* 5ᵉ année, 1930, p. 79, repr.;
Grohmann, 1959, pp. 216, 337 no. 452, repr. cc 307; J. Lassaigne, *Kandinsky,* Geneva, 1964,
repr. color p. 95.

1. Tériade, who purchased the picture directly from Kandinsky about 1930, published it in
   1930 with the caption *"Galerie de France."* Although no exhibition of Kandinsky's work
   apparently took place at this gallery, his pictures were probably there on consignment, since
   in a letter of June 8, 1931, he urges Solomon R. Guggenheim to go there to look at some of
   his recent work (The Hilla von Rebay Foundation Archive).

   Tériade is uncertain to whom he sold the picture or when, although he suggested it might
   have been to Anthony Zwemmer in London. Zwemmer does not recall buying it, but is not
   absolutely certain (correspondence with the author, June 1974).

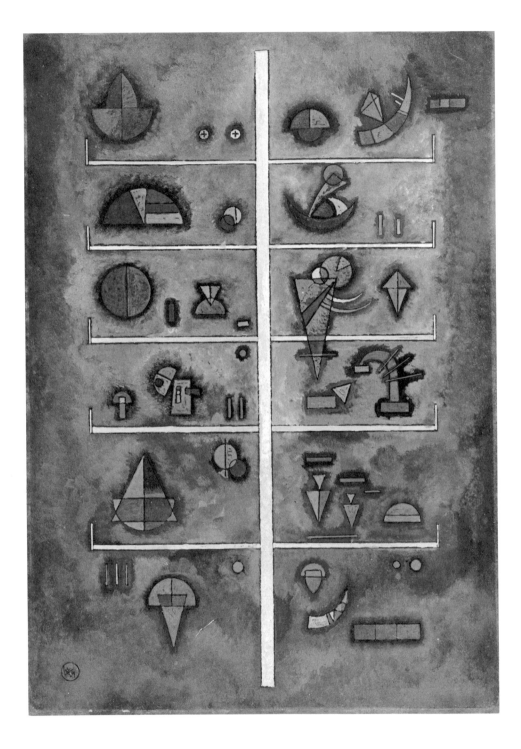

120 Pink-Sweet. 1929.
(Rosa-Süss).

HL *1929, 481, Rosa-Süss.*

71.1936R 69

Oil on board, 27¼ x 18⅞ (69.2 x 47.8)

Signed and dated l.l.: *K / 29*; inscribed by
the artist on reverse: *K / Nº 48i / 1929. /
«Rosa Süss." / 49 x 70.*

PROVENANCE:

J. B. Neumann, New York (information
from HL reads *"bei Neumann,"* indicating
that it was on consignment); Karl Nierendorf, New York?;[1] purchased from Nierendorf or Neumann by Hilla Rebay, 1944;
Estate of Hilla Rebay, 1967-71; acquired
from the Estate of Hilla Rebay, 1971.

CONDITION:

A diagonal abrasion in the lower right
corner (visible in photograph) has been inpainted. Some abraded areas along the left,
top, and right margins have also been
inpainted.

The condition is otherwise excellent.
(Aug. 1972.)

EXHIBITIONS:

Berlin, Galerie Flechtheim, *Kandinsky,* Feb. 1931, no. 42; London, The Mayor Gallery, *Ex-
hibition of Drawings by Paul Nash, Zadkine, Kandinsky, Hillier,* Dec. 1933, no. 13 *(Quiet
Pink)*;[2] New York, SRGM 43, *Kandinsky,* no. 156; Chicago, SRGM 47-T, *Kandinsky,* no. 38;
Pittsburgh, SRGM 53-T, *Kandinsky,* no. 41; New York, SRGM 74, no. 94; 241 (addenda);
Bridgeport, Conn., Carlson Gallery, University of Bridgeport, *Homage to Hilla Rebay,* Apr.
18-May 10, 1972, no. 49; New York, SRGM 252, repr. color; 276 (no cat.).

REFERENCE:

Grohmann, 1959, pp. 211, 338 no. 481, repr. cc 333.

1. A Nierendorf label on the reverse does not necessarily prove that the picture passed through
   his hands, since it might well date from an exhibition (hitherto untraced) at the Nierendorf
   Gallery. It has so far not been possible to ascertain whether Hilla Rebay purchased the
   work from Neumann or Nierendorf, although a label on the reverse in her hand states that
   she bought the picture in 1944.
2. A Mayor Gallery label on the reverse confirms that it is the present work, rather than a
   watercolor *Rose doux* formerly in the Kirchhoff collection, that was exhibited in London.
   The Kirchhoff picture, not recorded in the HL and present whereabouts unknown, appeared in the 1929 exhibition at the Galerie Zak in Paris as no. 42.

121   Far Away. 1930.
       (Fern).

HL *1930, 533, Fern.*

48.1172 x521

Oil on board, 13⅝ x 9⅝ (34.6 x 24.4)

Signed and dated l.l.: *K / 30*; inscribed by
the artist on reverse: *K / Nº 533 / i930 /
«Fern" / 24 x 34.*

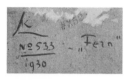

PROVENANCE:

Given by the artist on consignment to Karl
Nierendorf, New York, before 1937;[1] acquired with the Estate of Karl Nierendorf,
1948.

CONDITION:

At some point prior to acquisition, portions
of the red circle were inpainted and these
have since discolored. In 1970 some cleavage between the board and lamination was
repaired; a loss at the top left corner was
built up and inpainted, and the work was
cleaned, but the fragility of the paint film
and thinness of application made it impossible to remove 2 stains—1 below and 1 to
the left of the red globe, as well as the
earlier inpainting. Some further loss on the
right side of the circle was inpainted and the
surface was coated with Lucite 44.

Partly due to the thinness of the paint application, and partly to some abrasion with
paint loss, the board shows through in certain areas. (Sept. 1973.)

EXHIBITIONS:

Berlin, Galerie Flechtheim, *W. Kandinsky,* Feb. 1931, no. 66; New York, College Art Association, *Kandinsky: A Retrospective View,* 1937, no. 21;[2] New York, Nierendorf Gallery, *Kandinsky,* Mar. 1941, no. 22 *(Distant)*; New York, SRGM 43, *Kandinsky,* no. 167; Boston,
Institute of Contemporary Art, *Kandinsky,* Mar. 25-Apr. 18, 1952, traveled to New York, M.
Knoedler & Co., Inc., May 10-June 6, 1952, San Francisco Museum of Art, July 20-Aug. 26,
1952, Minneapolis, Walker Art Center, Sept. 14-Oct. 26, 1952, no. 46; New York, SRGM 228
(no cat.); 252, repr.

REFERENCE:

Grohmann, 1959, p. 339 no. 533.

1. Information from HL. The picture was in Nierendorf's hands by the time of the 1937 exhibition, but was still unsold at the time of his death.

2. The exhibition and the picture's appearance in it is recorded in the SRGM files, but no
   catalogue or other record of the exhibition has hitherto been located either by the Museum
   or by the College Art Association.

122   Bias. 1931.
(Neigung; Inclination).

HL *1931, 568, Neigung.*

49.1176

Oil and tempera on board, 27½ x 27½
(70 x 70)

Signed and dated l.l.: *K/ 31*; inscribed by
the artist on reverse (transcribed but not
photographed before mounting): *K / No
568 / 193i / «Neigung" / 70 x 70.*

PROVENANCE:

Given by the artist on consignment to Galka
Scheyer (d. 1945);[1] Hildegarde Prytek (secretary to Karl Nierendorf), New York, 1945-
48; purchased from Prytek, 1949.

CONDITION:

In 1953 the work was mounted on Masonite
with PVA, and the edges were filled; the surface was cleaned and coated with PBM. In
1958 it was reglued and dried under
pressure.

There is some lifting and tearing with losses
of the board at all edges, and the corners
are slightly crushed. A few small areas of
inpainting are visible at the edges, and 3
small touches in the red circle upper left.

There are some paint losses in the white
areas, although the method of paint application, intended to leave the board visible
in many places, makes it difficult to establish with the naked eye where these
losses are .The overall condition is good.
(Oct. 1973.)

EXHIBITIONS:

Los Angeles, Stendhal Gallery, *Kandinsky,* Feb. 1936 (checklist); New York, SRGM 64 (no
cat.); Pasadena, SRGM 146-T, no. 46, repr. p. 73; New York, SRGM 226, 228 (no cats.); 252,
repr.; 276 (no cat.).

REFERENCE:

Grohmann, 1959, p. 339 no. 568, repr. cc 410 *(Inclination).*

1. The picture was in Scheyer's hands at the time of the 1936 Los Angeles exhibition (information supplied by Stendhal Gallery, in correspondence with the author, Oct. 1973). Nina
   Kandinsky (in conversation with the author, Oct. 1972) explained that many of the pictures
   of the late 1920's and early 1930's were taken by Scheyer to California, where she hoped to
   sell them. After her death some of the unsold works passed into the hands of Nierendorf.
   Upon his death in 1948, or possibly before, a few works from the Estate were apparently
   acquired by Hildegarde Prytek, who in turn sold them.

123   Pronounced Rose. March 1932.
       (Entscheidendes Rosa; Rose prononcé).

HL *iii / 1931/2, 573, Entscheidendes Rosa.*

49.1178

Oil on canvas, 31⅞ x 39⅜ (80.9 x 100)

Signed and dated l.l.: *K / 32*; inscribed by
the artist on reverse: *K / Nº 573 / i932.*

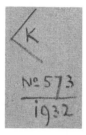

PROVENANCE:

Given by the artist on consignment to Galka
Scheyer (d. 1945);[1] on consignment to Karl
Nierendorf, New York, 1945-48; Hildegarde
Prytek (secretary to Nierendorf), New York,
1948-49; purchased from Prytek, 1949.

CONDITION:

At an undetermined date an area ½ x ¼ in.
in the lower center was retouched.

There are small losses in paint and support
in each of the 4 corners, and some cracking
and small losses along the margins. The condition is otherwise excellent. (Aug. 1972.)

EXHIBITIONS:

New York, SRGM 64 (no cat.); Boston, Institute of Contemporary Art, *Kandinsky,* Mar. 25-
Apr. 18, 1952, traveled to New York, M. Knoedler & Co., Inc., May 10-June 6, 1952, San
Francisco Museum of Art, July 20-Aug. 26, 1952, Minneapolis, Walker Art Center, Sept. 14-
Oct. 26, 1952, no. 47; New York, SRGM 87 (checklist); Brussels, SRGM 105-T, no. 36, repr.;
Baltimore, SRGM 113-T (no cat.); Toronto, SRGM 117-T (no cat.); New York, SRGM 147,
Kandinsky, no. 67, repr. p. 92; 226, 228 (no cats.); 252, repr. (withdrawn after Los Angeles
showing); Rochester, N.Y., SRGM 263-T (no cat.); New York, SRGM 276 (no cat.).

REFERENCES:

Grohmann, 1959, pp. 217, 339 no. 573, repr. cc 413; J. Lassaigne, *Kandinsky,* Geneva, 1964,
repr. color p. 97.

1. The HL contains the information *"b. Emmy."* For an explanation of how the works on
   consignment to Galka Scheyer came into the hands of Nierendorf and then Hildegarde
   Prytek, see above cat. no. 122, fn. 1.

124   Development Upwards. 1934.
(Montée gracieuse; Graceful Ascent;
Développement en haut; No. 596).

HL *1934, 596, Montée gracieuse.*

45.970

Oil on canvas, 31⅝ x 31¾ (80.4 x 80.7)

Signed and dated l.l.: *K / 34;* inscribed by
the artist on reverse: *K / Nº 596 / 1934 /*
partially obscured by stretcher:
"[De]*veloppement en*[haut]."

PROVENANCE:

Purchased from the artist by Karl Nierendorf, New York, September 1938 (information from HL);[1] purchased from Nierendorf,
1945.

CONDITION:

In 1956 a rubbed area at the right margin
just above center was inpainted. In addition
there are 5 other areas of minor retouching
(⅛-½ in.) and 1 large area (ca. 3 in. long)
to the right and below the yellow rectangle
at the right margin. These retouchings are
of uncertain date. There are 3 visible lines
of abrasion of 3 in. each with apparent
transfer material in the upper right section
of the canvas.

Throughout the composition black lines are
beginning to show through the paint layer;
these do not correspond to the present composition and suggest that Kandinsky was
using a canvas upon which he had previously sketched out another painting. The
condition is very good. (Oct. 1973.)

EXHIBITIONS:

Paris, Galerie Cahiers d'Art, *Kandinsky,* May 1934 (information from HL and from review
by C. Zervos); San Francisco Museum of Art, *Seven Additional Kandinsky Oils,* July 20-
Aug. 9, 1939 (no cat.); New York, Nierendorf Gallery, *Kandinsky,* Mar. 1941, no. 63; New
York, SRGM 43, *Kandinsky,* no. 201, repr. p. 40 *(Development in Height);* Milwaukee, SRGM
49-T (no cat.); Pittsburgh, SRGM 53-T, *Kandinsky,* no. 50; Boston, Institute of Contemporary
Art, *Kandinsky,* Mar. 25-Apr. 18, 1952, traveled to New York, M. Knoedler & Co., Inc., May
10-June 6, 1952, San Francisco Museum of Art, July 20-Aug. 26, 1952, Minneapolis, Walker
Art Center, Sept. 14-Oct. 26, 1952, no. 48; New York, SRGM 79 (checklist); Toronto, SRGM
85-T, no. 27; Vancouver, SRGM 88-T, no. 26; Brussels, SRGM 105-T, no. 37; Baltimore,
SRGM 113-T, Toronto, SRGM 117-T (no cats.); New York, SRGM 147, *Kandinsky,* no. 69,
repr. p. 92; New York, SRGM 208, 212, 226 (no cats.); 252, repr.; 276 (no cat.).

REFERENCES:

C. Zervos, "Notes sur Kandinsky," *Cahiers d'Art,* vol. 9, no. 5-8, 1934, p. 156; Grohmann,
1959, pp. 228, 340 no. 596, repr. cc 433; H. Read, *Kandinsky,* London, 1959, repr. color opp.
p.20.

1. The HL also includes the information *"b.Emmy,"* suggesting that the picture was at some
point (like cat. nos. 122 and 123) sent on consignment to Galka Scheyer. Whether this was
before or after 1938 is not clear.

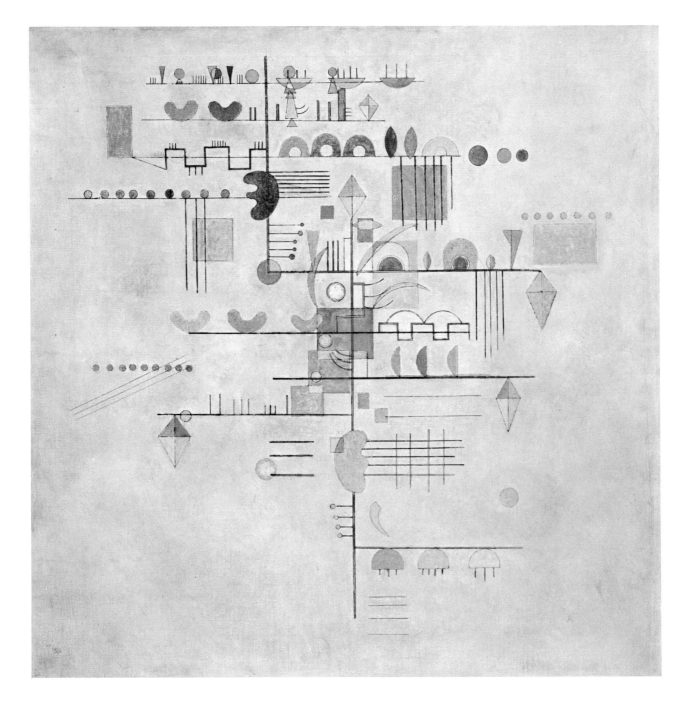

125   Blue World. 1934.
       (Monde bleu; Blue Theme, Blue Realm).

HL *1934, 602, Monde bleu.*

45.969

Oil with sand on canvas, 43½ x 47⅝
(110.6 x 120.2)

Signed and dated l.l.: *K / 34;* inscribed by
the artist on reverse: *K/ Nº 602 / i934;*
on stretcher: *"Monde Bleu."*

PROVENANCE:

Gift of the artist to his wife, Nina Kandin-
sky, 1934 (information supplied by Nina
Kandinsky in conversation with the author,
November 1972); given on consignment to
Karl Nierendorf, New York, 1939-45;[1] pur-
chased from Nierendorf by Solomon R.
Guggenheim, 1945; Gift of Solomon R.
Guggenheim, 1945.

CONDITION:

In 1954 and 1958 the border areas were
cleaned, the rest of the surface being left
untouched.

The corners show considerable wear; there
are losses of sand and pigment in several
places, concentrated especially in the vertical line corresponding to the center
stretcher member, and at the lower right in
the blue/green and pink areas. The surface
has never been varnished and there is considerable surface soil, but the condition is
otherwise good. (Oct. 1973.)

EXHIBITIONS:

Paris, Galerie Cahiers d'Art, *Kandinsky,* May 1934 (information from HL and review by
Zervos); Kunstmuseum Lucerne, *Thèse, antithèse, synthèse,* Feb. 24-Mar. 31, 1935, no. 56;
Kunsthalle Bern, *Wassily Kandinsky,* Feb. 21-Mar. 29, 1937, no. 56, repr.; Pittsburgh,
Carnegie Institute, *International Exhibition of Paintings,* Oct. 19-Dec. 10, 1939, no. 323, repr.;
New York, Nierendorf Gallery, *Kandinsky,* Mar. 1941, no. 13 *(Blue Theme);* New York,
Nierendorf Gallery, *Works by Kandinsky,* Dec. 1942-Feb. 1943 (checklist); New York, SRGM
43, *Kandinsky,* no. 226 (dated 1938); Pittsburgh, SRGM 53-T, *Kandinsky,* no. 34; New York,
SRGM 64 (no cat.); 74, no. 93; Toronto, SRGM 85-T, no. 28 *(Blue Realm);* Vancouver,
SRGM 88-T, no. 16; Brussels, SRGM 105-T, no. 38; Pittsburgh, Carnegie Institute, *Retro-
spective Exhibition of Carnegie Internationals,* Dec. 5, 1958-Feb. 8, 1959, no. 82, repr.; New
York, SRGM 118, 151, 153 (checklists); 208, 212, 214, 226 (no cats.); 252, repr. (withdrawn
after New York showing); 276 (no cat.).

REFERENCES:

C. Zervos, "Notes sur Kandinsky," *Cahiers d'Art,* vol. 9, no. 5-8, 1934, p. 156, repr.; H. Rebay,
"Pioneer in Non-Objective Painting," *Carnegie Magazine,* vol. xx, May 1946, repr. p. 9;
Grohmann, 1959, pp. 228, 340 no. 602, repr. cc 437.

1. The picture was sent to America for the exhibition in Pittsburgh in 1939, and, probably
   owing to the war, was never returned. According to the HL it was then *"chez Nierendorf,"*
   presumably on consignment, although Nina Kandinsky herself had expected and awaited
   its return (in conversation with the author, Nov. 1972).

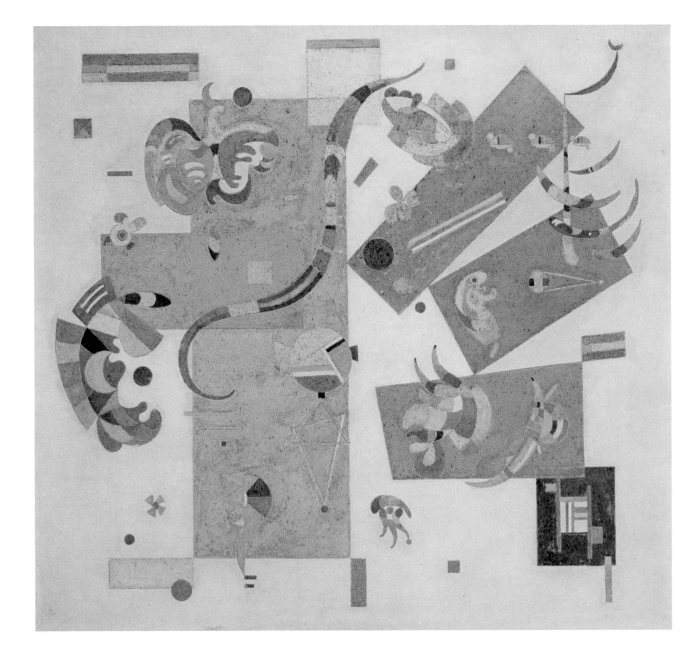

126   Striped. 1934.
       (Rayé; No. 609).

HL *1934, 609, Rayé.*

46.1022

Oil with sand on canvas, 31⅞ x 39⅜
(81 x 100)

Signed and dated l.l.: *K / 34*; inscribed by
the artist on reverse: *K / N⁰ 609 / i934.*

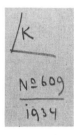

PROVENANCE:

With Peggy Guggenheim, London, 1938;
purchased by Karl Nierendorf, New York,
ca. 1941;[1] purchased from Nierendorf, 1946.

CONDITION:

In 1956 some losses in the black areas were
retouched, but since their locations were not
recorded and they are not visible with the
naked eye or under UV, it is impossible to
know how widespread they were.

All margins are rubbed with some loss,
especially the upper left margin where there
is a loss 5 in. from the top, and the top
margin where there is a ¾ in. loss 7 in. from
the left. There are a few small brown stains,
clearly visible to the naked eye, in the white
areas; there are also some minor pinpoint
losses in the black areas. Apart from some
general soil the condition is good. (Oct.
1973.)

EXHIBITIONS:

Paris, Galerie Cahiers d'Art, *Kandinsky,* June-July 1935 (no cat.; information from HL);
London, Guggenheim Jeune, *Kandinsky,* Mar. 1938, no. 6; New York, SRGM 84 (checklist);
Vancouver, SRGM 88-T, no. 27; London, SRGM 104-T, no. 33; New York, SRGM 118
(checklist); Pasadena, SRGM 146-T, *Kandinsky,* no. 51, repr. color p. 76; New York, SRGM
173, no. 63 repr. color; 208, 212, 226 (no cats.); 252, repr. (withdrawn after New York showing); 276 (no cat.).

REFERENCES:

Grohmann, 1959, pp. 232, 340 no. 609, repr. p. 305; J. Elderfield, "Geometric Abstract Painting and Paris in the Thirties," *Artforum,* vol. viii, June 1970, p. 72.

1. The picture was not sold at the end of the London exhibition. Peggy Guggenheim brought
   the picture to New York in 1941 and sold it to Nierendorf on Kandinsky's behalf
   (information supplied by Peggy Guggenheim, correspondence with the author, Oct. 1973).

127   Accompanied Contrast. 1935.
        (Contraste accompagné; No. 613).

HL *1935, 613, Contraste accompagné.*

37.338

Oil with sand on canvas, 38¼ x 63⅞
(97.1 x 162.1)

Signed and dated l.l.: *K / 35*; inscribed by
the artist on reverse: *K / № 613 / 1935.*

PROVENANCE:

Purchased from the artist by Solomon R.
Guggenheim, August 1935; Gift of Solomon
R. Guggenheim, 1937.

CONDITION:

In 1955 a tear at the left margin, 3½ in. from
the bottom, was repaired with linen and
wax resin; the loss was filled and inpainted
with PBM, and small flakes near the lower
edge were also filled and inpainted. 5 other
scattered areas of inpainting (¼-¾ in.)
probably date from 1957.

All edges, especially the top, are somewhat
abraded, as are all 4 corners. There are
some minor losses in the sanded areas, and
some minor scratches and abrasions, but the
condition in general is good. (Dec. 1973.)

Kandinsky first painted this composition in a 1931 watercolor (fig. a), and the
earlier version is identical in both composition and color to the later one. The
entry for the watercolor in the HL (432) carries the notation *"Esquisse,"* suggesting that Kandinsky's intention from the start was to paint a larger version.
The fact that he did not do so until four years later is difficult to explain and
does not correspond to his usual practice.

EXHIBITIONS:

Paris, Galerie Cahiers d'Art, *Kandinsky,* June-July 1935 (no cat.; information from HL);
Charleston, S.C., SRGM 1-T, no. 92, repr. p. 35; Philadelphia, SRGM 3-T, no. 111, repr.
p. 39; Charleston, S.C., SRGM 4-T, no. 144, repr. p. 46; Cazenovia, N.Y., SRGM 33-T (no
cat.); New York, SRGM 43, *Kandinsky,* no. 210; Chicago, SRGM 47-T, *Kandinsky,* no. 24;
Pittsburgh, SRGM 53-T, *Kandinsky,* no. 54; New York, SRGM 64 (no cat.); 84 (checklist);
Tex., Fort Worth Art Center Museum; *Inaugural Exhibition,* Oct. 8-31, 1954, no. 43; New

fig. a.
Kandinsky, study for *Accompanied Contrast,* 1931, HL
432, *"Fleckig,"* watercolor on paper, 10⅝ x 18⅞ in.,
27 x 48 cm., Collection Berggruen, Paris.

127

York, SRGM 95 (checklist); Brussels, SRGM 105-T (withdrawn after London showing), no. 40, repr.; Brussels, *50 Ans d'art moderne,* Apr. 17-July 21, 1958, no. 145, repr.; Toronto, SRGM 117-T (no cat.); New York, SRGM 118 (checklist); New York, SRGM 147, *Kandinsky,* no. 71, repr. p. 94; 195 (no cat.); 196 (checklist); 208, 212, 214, 226, 227 (no cats.); 232, 241, p. 210, repr. p. 211; 252, repr. color (withdrawn after New York showing); New York, SRGM 266, 276 (no cats.).

REFERENCES:

Grohmann, 1959, p. 340 no. 613, repr. cc 443; J. Lassaigne, *Kandinsky,* Geneva, 1964, repr. color, p. 105.

128   Two Circles. 1935.
        (Deux Cercles; No. 614).

HL *1935, 614, Deux Cercles.*

41.339

Oil and tempera on canvas, 25⅝ x 36⅜
(72.8 x 92.3)

Signed and dated l.l.: *K / 35*; inscribed by
the artist on reverse (transcribed but not
photographed before lining): *K / No 614 /
1935 «Deux Cercles.»*

PROVENANCE:

Purchased from the artist by Hilla Rebay,
Greens Farms, Connecticut, July 1936 (information from HL); transferred to the Collection of Solomon R. Guggenheim, 1938;
Gift of Solomon R. Guggenheim, 1941.

CONDITION:

At an unrecorded date, the canvas was lined
with wax resin adhesive. In 1953 the work
was cleaned, and in 1957 losses to the left
of center were inpainted. A 3½ x 2½ in.
wedge-shaped area of heavy inpaint is visible 17 in. from the left and 6 in. from the
bottom. 3 other minor areas of inpaint are
visible under UV.

There is a heavy irregular crackle pattern
over a 4½ in. area along the top, right, and
bottom sides of the canvas, as well as some
scattered crackle in the center of the composition. This widespread condition does
not at this point show evidence of incipient
cleavage. There is a certain amount of wear
at the edges and in the corners. The overall
condition is fair. (Oct. 1973.)

EXHIBITIONS:

Paris, Galerie Cahiers d'Art, *Kandinsky,* June-July 1935 (no cat.; information from HL);
Philadelphia, SRGM 3-T, no. 115, repr. p. 41; Charleston, S.C., SRGM 4-T, no. 148, repr. p.
47; New York, SRGM 43, *Kandinsky,* no. 211; Milwaukee, SRGM 49-T (no cat.); New York,
SRGM 78, 87 (checklists); Montreal, SRGM 93-T, no. 20; New York, SRGM 107 (checklist);
Pasadena, SRGM 146-T, *Kandinsky,* no. 53, repr. p. 78; New York, SRGM 208, 212, 226 (no
cats.); 252, repr. (withdrawn after New York showing).

REFERENCE:

Grohmann, 1959, p. 340 no. 614, repr. cc 452.

129   Violet-Orange. 1935.
       (No. 622).

HL *1935, 622, Violet-Orange.*

37·334

Oil on canvas, 35 x 45¾ (88.9 x 116.2)

Signed and dated l.l.: *K/ 35*; inscribed by
the artist on reverse (transcribed but not
photographed before lining): *K / No 622 /
1935 – «Violet-orange.»*

PROVENANCE:

Purchased from the artist by Solomon R.
Guggenheim, July 1936; Gift of Solomon R.
Guggenheim, 1937.

CONDITION:

In 1955 the work was lined with wax resin
on natural linen and restretched on the
original stretcher. Surface wax was removed
with petroleum benzine, and extremely
minor losses at the edges were retouched
with watercolor. The work was surfaced
with PBM.

There are 3 small areas of ground and pigment cracks with some loss and possible incipient cleavage: 22 in. from top and 6 in.
from the right; 17 in. from the top and 10
in. from the right; 22 in. from the top and
24 in. from the right. Apart from some
minor soil and wear at the edges, the condition is otherwise excellent. (Apr. 1974.)

EXHIBITIONS:

Philadelphia, SRGM 3-T, no. 114, repr. p. 40; Charleston, S.C., SRGM 4-T, no. 146, repr.
p. 47; New York, SRGM 43, *Kandinsky,* no. 206; Chicago, SRGM 47-T, *Kandinsky,* no. 21;
Brussels, SRGM 105-T, p. 39; Toronto, SRGM 117-T (no cat.); Boston, SRGM 119-T, no. 22;
Pasadena, SRGM 146-T, *Kandinsky,* no. 55, repr. color p. 81; New York, SRGM 173, no. 64
repr. color; 195 (no cat.); 196 (checklist); 202, p. 19, repr. p. 18; 226 (no cat.); 252, repr.;
New York, SRGM 266, 276 (no cats.).

REFERENCE:

Grohmann, 1959, p. 340 no. 622, repr. cc 449.

130   Green Accent. 1935.
       (No. 623).

HL *1935, 623, Accent vert.*

37.340

Tempera and oil on canvas, 32 x 39⅜
(81.1 x 100.2)

Signed and dated l.l.: *K / 35*; inscribed by
the artist on reverse: *K / N⁰ 623 / 1935 /
«Accent Vert.»*

PROVENANCE:

Purchased from the artist by Solomon R.
Guggenheim, July 1936; Gift of Solomon R.
Guggenheim, 1937.

CONDITION:

The work has received no treatment.

All edges show moderate wear in places
and some loss due to cracking at the turn of
the canvas; the lower left and upper right
corners are badly worn with loss of paint
and ground. There are 6 isolated areas of
minor crackle varying in size from ½ to
1 in. The condition is excellent. (Nov. 1973.)

EXHIBITIONS:

London, Feb.-June, 1936 (no cat. located; information from HL and from *Axis,* 1936);
Philadelphia, SRGM 3-T, no. 116, repr. p. 41; Charleston, S.C., SRGM 4-T, no. 149, repr.
p. 47; New York, SRGM 43, *Kandinsky,* no. 212, repr. p. 41; Chicago, SRGM 47-T, *Kandinsky,* no. 23; Pittsburgh, SRGM 53-T, *Kandinsky,* no. 25; New York, SRGM 79 (checklist);
Toronto, SRGM 85-T, no. 29; Vancouver, SRGM 88-T, no. 28; Boston, SRGM 90-T (no cat.);
New York, SRGM 95 (checklist; withdrawn Sept. 12); 97 (checklist); London, SRGM 104-T,
no. 34; New York, SRGM 112, 118 (checklists); 147, *Kandinsky,* no. 72, repr. p. 95; 195 (no
cat.); 196 (checklist); 202, p. 19, repr. p. 18; 208, 212 (no cats.); New York, M. Knoedler &
Co., Inc., *Kandinsky: Parisian Period 1934-1944,* Oct. 21-Nov. 22, 1969, no. 8, repr.; New
York, SRGM 252, repr.; 276 (no cat.).

REFERENCES:

H. Read, H. G. Partens, K. Walsh, *Axis,* no. 5, Spring 1936, repr. p. 13; Grohmann, 1959,
p. 340 no. 623, repr. p. 309; J. Lassaigne, *Kandinsky,* Geneva, 1964, p. 106, repr. color p. 104.

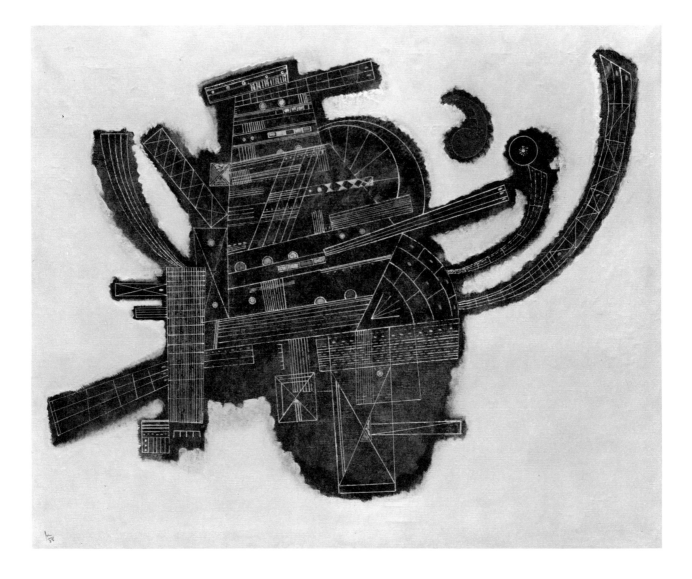

131 Dominant Curve. 1936.
(No. 631; Courbe dominante).

HL *1936, 631, Courbe dominante.*

45.989

Oil on canvas, 50⅞ x 76½ (129.4 x 194.2)

Signed and dated l.l.: *K / 36*; inscribed by
the artist on reverse: *K / Nº 63i / i936 /
«Courbe/dominante."*

PROVENANCE:

Purchased from the artist by Peggy Guggenheim, London, March 1938 (information
from HL); purchased from Peggy Guggenheim by Karl Nierendorf, New York, during
the war *(Confessions of an Art Addict,* p.
110); purchased from Nierendorf, 1945.

CONDITION:

In 1953 the surface was cleaned and a few
chips and scratches were inpainted.

All edges except the bottom are worn, with
some loss of paint and ground; the corners
also show loss of paint and ground. There
are 4 areas of very fine surface crackle, but
the condition is otherwise excellent.
(Nov. 1973.)

The elaborately executed preparatory drawing for this painting (fig. a) differs
in several details from the final work. However, the most striking difference
between the two is one of emphasis; the prominent yellow circle of the painting
and the smaller turquoise and violet circle that overlaps it are barely indicated
in the drawing by lightly traced dotted lines; the dominating effect of the black
forms is thus considerably greater.

Kandinsky himself, as well as subsequent writers, regarded the painting as
one of his most important works, and it hung in a prominent place in his
studio from its completion in 1936 until its sale to Peggy Guggenheim two
years later (Nina Kandinsky in conversation with the author, November 1972;
see also the photograph of Kandinsky seated in his studio with the painting
hanging behind him, *Concerning the Spiritual in Art,* New York, 1947,
frontispiece).

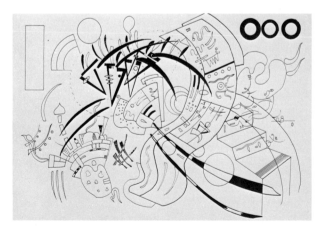

fig. a.
Kandinsky, drawing for *Dominant Curve,* 1936, ink on
paper, 12⅝ x 19¼ in., 32 x 49 cm., Galerie Karl Flinker,
Paris.

131

EXHIBITIONS:

Paris, Galerie Jeanne Bucher, *Kandinsky,* Dec. 3-19, 1936, no. 7; Kunsthalle Bern, *Kandinsky,* Feb.-Mar. 1937, no. 70; Paris, Jeu de Paume, *Origines et développement de l'art international indépendant,* July 30-Oct. 31, 1937, no. 150; London, Guggenheim Jeune, *Kandinsky,* Mar. 1938, no. 5, repr.; Chicago, SRGM 47-T, *Kandinsky,* no. 25; New York, SRGM 74, no. 92, 78 (checklist); Toronto, SRGM 85-T, no. 30; New York, SRGM 87 (checklist); 89 (no cat.); Montreal, SRGM 93-T, no. 21; New York, SRGM 95 (checklist); Brussels, SRGM 105-T, p. 41, repr.; Toronto, SRGM 117-T (no cat.); New York, SRGM 118 (checklist); New York, SRGM 147, *Kandinsky,* no. 74, repr. p. 96; 208, 212, 214, 226, 227 (no cats.); 232, 241, p. 212, repr. p. 213; 252 (withdrawn after New York showing), repr. color; 266, 276 (no cats.).

REFERENCES:

P. Guggenheim, *Art of this Century,* New York, 1942, repr. p. 42; Idem, *Out of this Century,* New York, 1946, repr. opp. p. 311 in photograph of "Abstract and Cubist gallery designed by Berenice Abbott;" M. Bill, *Kandinsky,* Paris, 1951, repr. p. 66; Grohmann, 1959, pp. 228, 340 no. 631, repr. color p. 231; P. Guggenheim, *Confessions of an Art Addict,* New York, 1960, p. 110; P. Overy, "Color and Sound," *Apollo,* vol. lxxix, May 1964, pp. 412-413; J. Elderfield, "Geometric Painting and Paris in the Thirties," *Artforum,* vol. viii, June 1970, p. 72.

132   Environment. 1936.
        (Surroundings; No. 633).

HL *1936, No. 633, Environnement.*

45.973

Oil on canvas, 39¼ x 32 (99.8 x 81.4)

Signed and dated l.l.: *K / 36;* inscribed by
the artist on reverse: *K / No 633 / 1936.*

PROVENANCE:

Purchased from the artist by Karl Nierendorf, New York, September 1938 (information from HL); purchased from Nierendorf,
1945.

CONDITION:

In 1953 the surface was cleaned and small
losses in the pale violet border were filled
and inpainted; the surface was coated with
PBM.

All edges are worn, showing some abrasion
and cracking in the paint film, especially at
the corners where there is also some loss of
paint and ground. There are a few scattered
areas of fine surface crackle, but the condition in general is excellent. (Nov. 1973.)

EXHIBITIONS:

Paris, Galerie Jeanne Bucher, *Kandinsky,* Dec. 3-19, 1936, no. 8; Kunsthalle Bern, W. *Kan-
dinsky: Französische Meister der Gegenwart,* Feb. 21-Mar. 29, 1937, no. 71 (for sale); London,
Guggenheim Jeune, *Kandinsky,* Mar. 1938, no. 2 (for sale); San Francisco Museum of Art,
Seven Additional Kandinsky Oils, July 20-Aug. 9, 1939; New York, Nierendorf Gallery, *Works
by Kandinsky: A Retrospective,* Dec. 1942-Jan. 1943 (checklist; *Surroundings);* New York,
SRGM 43, *Kandinsky,* no. 216; Milwaukee, SRGM 49-T (no cat.); Pittsburgh, SRGM 53-T,
Kandinsky, no. 40; New York, SRGM 147, *Kandinsky,* no. 75, repr. p. 97; 252, repr.

REFERENCE:

Grohmann, 1959, pp. 232, 340 no. 633, repr. color p. 233.

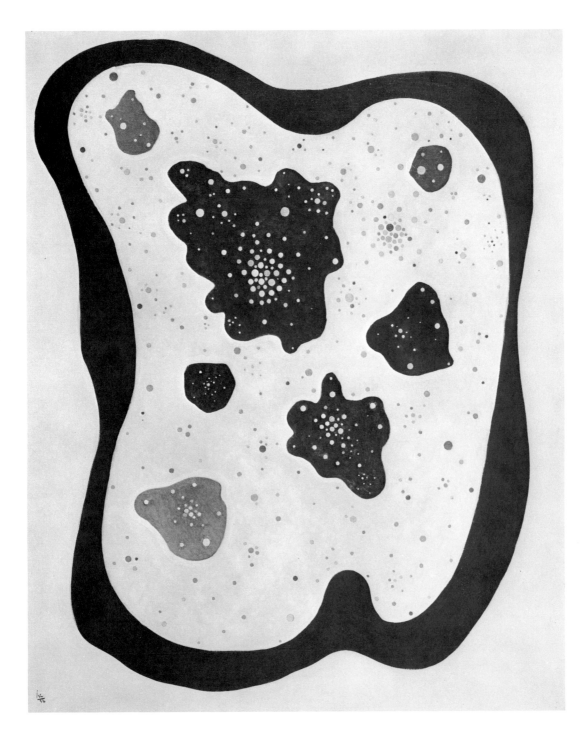

133 Capricious Forms. 1937.
(Formes capricieuses; No. 643).

HL *1937, No. 643, Formes capricieuses.*

45.977

Oil on canvas, 35 x 45¾ (88.9 x 116.3)

Signed and dated l.l.: *K / 37*; inscribed by
the artist on reverse: *K / Nº 643 / 1937.*

PROVENANCE:

Purchased from the artist by Karl Nierendorf, New York, September 1938 (information from HL); purchased from Nierendorf,
1945.

CONDITION:

In 1953 the painting was cleaned and surfaced with PBM.

All corners are slightly worn with minor
loss of paint and ground, and the edges are
in generally good condition. The right
margin has numerous rubs with some loss.
The condition in general is excellent. (Nov.
1973.)

EXHIBITIONS:

New York, Nierendorf Gallery, *Kandinsky,* Mar. 1941, no. 21; New York, SRGM 43, *Kandinsky,* no. 222; Chicago, SRGM 47-T, *Kandinsky,* no. 27; Pittsburgh, SRGM 53-T, *Kandinsky,* no. 38; New York, SRGM 147, *Kandinsky,* no. 77, repr. p. 99; Washington, D.C., Smithsonian Institution, *The Art of Organic Forms,* June 14-July 31, 1968, pl. 4; Staatliche Kunsthalle Baden-Baden, *Vasily Kandinsky: Gemälde 1900-1944,* July 10-Sept. 27, 1970, no. 147,
repr.; New York, SRGM 252, repr. color; New York, SRGM 266, 276 (no cats.).

REFERENCES:

Grohmann, 1959, pp. 234, 340 no. 643, repr. cc 463; P. Overy, *Kandinsky: The Language of
the Eye,* New York, 1969, pp. 46-47, 174, color pl. 57.

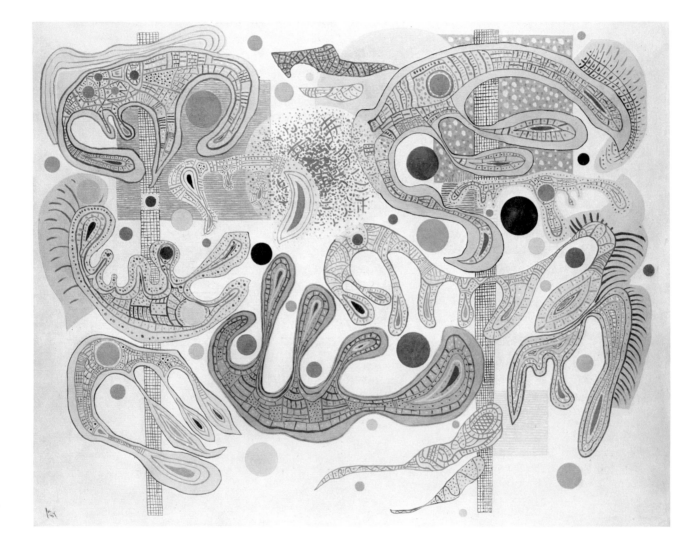

134   Yellow Canvas. 1938.
(La Toile jaune; Yellow Painting; No. 653).

HL *1938, No. 653, La Toile jaune.*

45.964

Oil and enamel (ripolin) on canvas, 45 ⅞ x 35 (116.4 x 88.8)

Signed and dated l.l.: *K / 38*; inscribed by the artist on reverse: *K / No 653 / 1938.*

PROVENANCE:
Purchased from the artist by Karl Nierendorf, New York, September 1938 (information from HL); purchased from Nierendorf, 1945.

CONDITION:
In 1953 the picture was cleaned and surfaced with PBM. 2 ¼ in. repaints are of uncertain date.

The edges and corners are abraded, with loss of paint and ground, especially in the corners. There is severe abrasion along the lower margin up to 4 inches from the bottom across the entire length. A very fine crackle in the paint film is visible in 4 different areas of the canvas, each instance approx. ½ to 1 in. in width. The overall condition is good. (Nov. 1973.)

EXHIBITIONS:
New York, Nierendorf Gallery, *Three Masters of the Bauhaus, Kandinsky, Klee, Feininger,* 1938 (no cat.); New York, Art of this Century, *15 Early, 15 Late,* Mar. 13-Apr. 10, 1943, no. 216; New York, SRGM 43, *Kandinsky,* no. 224; Milwaukee, SRGM 49-T (no cat.); Pittsburgh, SRGM 53-T, *Kandinsky,* no. 32; New York, SRGM 74, no. 97; 78 (checklist); Brussels, SRGM 105-T, p. 42, repr.; Baltimore, SRGM 113-T (no cat.); Toronto, SRGM 117-T (no cat.); Boston, SRGM 119-T, no. 23; Philadelphia, SRGM 134-T, no. 65; New York, SRGM 147, *Kandinsky,* no. 79, repr. p. 103; 195 (no cat.); 196 (checklist); 208 (no cat.); New York, M. Knoedler & Co., Inc., *Kandinsky: Parisian Period,* Oct. 21-Nov. 22, 1969, no. 19, repr.; Staatliche Kunsthalle Baden-Baden, *Kandinsky Gemälde 1900-1944,* July 10-Sept. 7, 1970, no. 150, repr. color; Dallas Museum of Fine Arts, *Geometric Abstraction: 1926-1942,* Oct. 7-Nov. 19, 1972, no. 32, repr. color; New York, SRGM 252 (withdrawn after New York showing), repr.

REFERENCES:
Grohmann, 1959, p. 341 no. 653, repr. cc 472; J. Lassaigne, *Kandinsky,* Geneva, 1964, repr. color, p. 100; R. C. Washton, "Vasily Kandinsky: A Space Odyssey," *Art News,* vol. 68, Oct. 1969, pp. 49, 56.

135   Little Accents. 1940.
       (Petits accents; No. 670).

HL *1940, No. 670, Petits accents.*

71.1936R 119

Oil on wood panel with mahogany veneer,
12⅝ x 16½ (32 x 42)

Signed and dated l.l.: *K / 40*; inscribed by
the artist on reverse: *Kandinky* [sic]-
«Petits Accents" / i940 / 32 x 42.

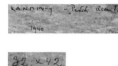

PROVENANCE:
Purchased from the artist by Galerie Jeanne
Bucher, Paris, April 1940 (information from
HL); purchased from Bucher by Hilla Rebay
at an unknown date; Estate of Hilla Rebay,
1967-71; acquired from the Estate of Hilla
Rebay, 1971.

CONDITION:
The work has received no treatment.

The overall pattern of pigment crackle is
caused by cracks in the veneer, due to
shrinkage in the panel. The condition is
otherwise excellent. (Apr. 1974.)

An extremely detailed pen and ink study for the painting is in the Guggenheim
Museum Collection (fig. a).

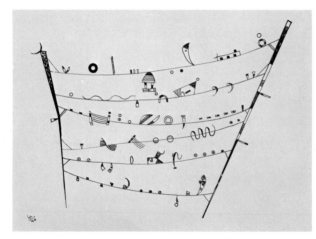

fig. a.
Kandinsky, study for *Little Accents,* 1940, ink on paper,
6¼ x 8½ in., 15.9 x 21.6 cm., The Solomon R. Guggenheim Museum, New York.

EXHIBITIONS:
New York, SRGM 74, no. 95; 241 (addenda); Bridgeport, Conn., Carlson Gallery, University
of Bridgeport, *Homage to Hilla Rebay,* Apr. 18-May 10, 1972, no. 71; New York, SRGM
252, repr. color; New York, SRGM 266, 276 (no cats.).

REFERENCE:
Grohmann, 1959, pp. 240, 341 no. 670, repr. cc. 486.

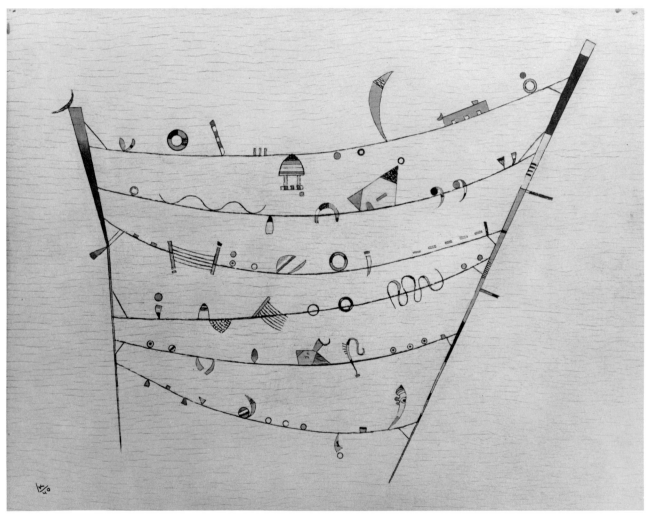

135

136   Around the Circle. 1940.
(Autour du cercle).

HL *1940, No. 677, Autour du cercle.*

49.1222

Oil and enamel (ripolin) on canvas,
38⅛ x 57½ (96.8 x 146)

Signed and dated l.l.: *K / 40*; inscribed by
the artist on reverse (photographed before
backing): *K / N⁰ 677 / 1940.*

PROVENANCE:
Nina Kandinsky, Paris, 1944-49; purchased
from Nina Kandinsky, 1949.

CONDITION:
In 1960 the work was backed with a new
board, but no other treatment has taken
place.

Apart from some minor wear at the edges,
and a few very fine scattered ground cracks,
the condition is excellent. (Dec. 1973.)

The final oil sketch for this work is with the Galerie Beyeler, Basel (fig. a). The
compositional differences between the study and the final work are extremely
minor and the colors in the two works are almost identical. Three exceptions
are the brown rectangle in the lower left corner and the pencil-shaped form
beside it, both of which are black in the study; the red square in the multi-
colored band in the upper left corner, which is black in the study; the white
area in which the orange-yellow snake form is placed in the upper right is a
slightly mottled pale blue/yellow in the study.

fig. a.
Kandinsky, *Around the Circle, No. 675*, 1940, oil on
wood, 15½ x 23⅝ in., 39.5 x 60 cm., Galerie Beyeler,
Basel.

136

EXHIBITIONS:

Kunsthaus Zürich, *Braque, Kandinsky, Picasso,* Sept. 21-Oct. 20, 1946, no. 93; Amsterdam, Stedelijk Museum, *Kandinsky,* Feb. 13-Mar. 14, 1948, no. 86; Paris, Galerie René Drouin, *Kandinsky: époque parisienne,* June 2-July 2, 1949 (no cat.);[1] Pasadena, SRGM 146-T, *Kandinsky,* no. 62, repr. color p. 88; New York, SRGM 212, 226 (no cats.); 252, repr.; 276 (no cat.).

REFERENCE:

Grohmann, 1959, pp. 237-238, 341 no. 677, repr. p. 317.

1. No catalogue of this exhibition has been located. Nina Kandinsky (in correspondence with D. Robbins, Feb. 1963) stated that the picture was purchased out of this exhibition.

137 Moderation. 1940.
     (*Modération; No. 678*).

HL *1940, No. 678, Moderation.*

46.1021

Oil and enamel (ripolin) on canvas,
39¼ x 25⅜ (99.7 x 64.6)

Signed and dated l.l.: *K / 40*; inscribed by
the artist on reverse (transcribed but not
photographed before lining): *K / N⁰ 678 /
1940.*

PROVENANCE:

Purchased from the artist by Madame
Fizine, Alsace, December 1945;[1] gift of
Madame Fizine to Ralph S. Beecher, New
York, 1945; purchased from Beecher, 1946.

CONDITION:

In 1953 the work was cleaned; in 1954 it was
lined with wax resin and surfaced with
PBM. 14 areas of inpainting, varying in size
from ¼ to 2 in., are scattered over the surface; these probably date from 1954 and
were presumably necessitated by cracking
and/or cleavage predating the lining
process. All are discolored and readily
visible to the naked eye.

The edges are somewhat soiled and show
some wear with loss of paint and ground,
especially at the corners. Visible cracks in
some areas are the result of cleavage which
was arrested by lining. Some flaking occurred in these areas, but this has now been
stabilized. The overall condition is fair.
(Dec. 1973.)

An extremely detailed watercolor study for the painting was formerly in a
private collection in France (fig. a, *XX Siècle*, vol. xxvii, December 1966, repr.
color p. 121). The forms in the watercolor are virtually identical to those of
the Guggenheim painting. The colors are difficult to compare, since the
present location of the watercolor is unknown and only the color reproduction
is available. Judging from the latter, the colors in the two works are in general
similar but not identical.

fig. a.
Kandinsky, study for *Moderation,* watercolor on paper,
dimensions and present whereabouts unknown.

1. The HL provides the cryptic information *"Dezembre* [sic] *1945 Alsace."* Ralph S. Beecher,
   in correspondence with Hilla Rebay, identified the purchaser as his mother-in-law, Madame
   Fizine, who then gave the painting to him and his wife as a wedding present.

137

EXHIBITIONS:

Boston, Institute of Contemporary Art, *Kandinsky,* Mar. 25-Apr. 18, 1952, no. 51, traveled to New York, M. Knoedler and Co., Inc., May 10-June 6, 1952, San Francisco Museum of Art, July 20-Aug. 26, 1952, Minneapolis, Walker Art Center, Sept. 14-Oct. 26, 1952; New York, The Museum of Modern Art, *German Art of the Twentieth Century,* Sept. 30-Dec. 1, 1957, no. 69, repr., traveled to City Art Museum of Saint Louis, Jan. 8-Feb. 24, 1958; Toronto, SRGM 117-T (no cat.); Boston, SRGM 119-T, no. 24; New York, SRGM 147, *Kandinsky,* no. 83, repr. p. 105; Boston, Museum of Fine Arts, *Surrealist & Fantastic Art from the Collections of the Museum of Modern Art and the Guggenheim Museum,* Feb. 14-Mar. 15, 1964, no. 32; New York, SRGM 208, 212, 226 (no cats.); Staatliche Kunsthalle Baden-Baden, *Kandinsky Gemälde 1900-1944,* July 10-Sept. 27, 1970, no. 162, repr.; New York, SRGM 241 (addenda); 252, repr. color; 266, 276 (no cats.).

REFERENCE:

Grohmann, 1959, p. 341 no. 678, repr. cc 491.

138   Various Actions. 1941.
(Actions variées; No. 683).

HL *1941, No. 683, Actions variées.*

47.1159

Oil and enamel (ripolin) on canvas,
35⅛ x 45¾ (89.2 x 116.1)

Signed and dated l.l.: *K / 41*; inscribed by
the artist on reverse: *K / N° 683 / 1941.*

PROVENANCE:

Purchased from the artist by Galerie René
Drouin, Paris, May 194?;[1] J. B. Neumann,
New York, by 1947; purchased from Neu-
mann, 1947.

CONDITION:

In 1953 the work was cleaned and surfaced
with PBM; in 1957 it was placed on a new
stretcher and the margins waxed. There are
4 small areas of inpainting (¼-½ in.).

The edges and corners show moderate wear,
and the condition is otherwise excellent.
(Dec. 1973.)

EXHIBITIONS:

New York, SRGM 74, no. 98; 147, *Kandinsky,* no. 85, repr. p. 106; 208, 212, 226 (no cats.);
252, repr.; 276 (no cat.).

REFERENCES:

Grohmann, 1959, pp. 237-238, 341 no. 683, repr. p. 319; F. Whitford, *Kandinsky,* London,
1967, color pl. 43.

1. The HL contains the note *"à R. Drouin en Mai 194 . . . ,"* the final digit being illegible.

139   Vertical Accents. 1942.
(Accents verticaux; No. 692).

HL *1942, No. 692, Accents verticaux.*

49.1192

Oil on plywood, 12⅝ x 16½ (32.1 x 42)

Signed and dated l.l.: *K / 42*; inscribed by
the artist on reverse: *K / No 692 / i942 /
42 x 32.*

PROVENANCE:

Nina Kandinsky, Paris, 1944-48; purchased
from Nina Kandinsky by Sidney Janis Gallery, New York, 1948; purchased from
Janis, 1948.

CONDITION:

The work has received no treatment.

It is painted directly onto the board with no
ground. All corners except the top right
show very slight wear and loss, but the condition is otherwise excellent. (Dec. 1973.)

EXHIBITIONS:

New York, Sidney Janis Gallery, *Kandinsky,* Nov. 9-27, 1948, no. 23; New York, SRGM 64
(no cat.); 74, no. 96; 252, repr.; 276 (no cat.).

REFERENCE:

Grohmann, 1959, p. 341 no. 692, repr. cc. 501.

140   White Figure. 1943.
     (*La Figure blanche; No. 705*).

HL *1943, No. 705, La Figure blanche.*

47.1140

Oil on board, 22⅝ x 16½ (57.3 x 41.8)

Signed and dated l.l.: *K / 43*; inscribed by
the artist on reverse (photographed before
mounting): *K / No 705 / 1943 / 42 x 58.*

EXHIBITIONS:

New York, SRGM 212, 226 (no cats.); 252, repr.

REFERENCES:

M. Bill, *Wassily Kandinsky,* Paris, 1951, repr. p. 80; Grohmann, 1959, pp. 240, 342 no. 705,
repr. p. 321; J. Lassaigne, *Kandinsky,* Geneva, 1964, repr. color p. 111.

PROVENANCE:

Purchased from the artist by M. Jonbert (or
Joubert?), Montreal, May 1945 (informa-
tion from HL); I. S. Jastro, New York, by
1947; purchased from Jastro by Solomon R.
Guggenheim, 1947; Gift of Solomon R.
Guggenheim, 1947.

CONDITION:

At an unrecorded date the work was
mounted on reinforced plywood, and some
extremely minor losses at the edges inpainted.

The lower right corner is crushed with loss
of support, and there are minor abrasions at
the edges, but the condition is otherwise
excellent. (May 1974.)

141   Fragments. 1943.
        (Fragments; No. 718).

HL *1943, No. 718, Fragments.*

49.1224

Oil and gouache on board, 16½ x 22¾
(41.9 x 57.7)

Signed and dated l.l.: *K / 43*; inscribed by
the artist on reverse (transcribed but not
photographed before mounting): *K / No
718 / 1943 / 58 x 42.*

PROVENANCE:
Purchased from Nina Kandinsky, 1949.

CONDITION:
In 1953 the work was mounted on Masonite
and reinforced with PVA emulsion; the surface was cleaned with 1% Soilax, some
minor losses at the edges filled with gesso
and inpainted with PVA, and the work surfaced with PBM.
The edges show some minor crushing and
loss and the corners are slightly rounded.
The central brown area shows some rubs
and a minor scratch, but the condition in
general is excellent. (Dec. 1973.)

The central motif of the tentacled amoeba-like form in *Fragments* recurs again
and again in Kandinsky's late work. S. Ringbom has suggested that it is
formally dependent on the Theosophical image for greed, while emphasizing
that the connection lacks iconographic significance. He sees it rather as an
illustration of Kandinsky's use of thought-forms as starting points for his own
abstract imagery, and an example, therefore, of Kandinsky's continuing preoccupation in the 1930's and 1940's with the Theosophical sources that had
influenced him before World War I. The thought-forms of the Theosophists
were "generated by and conducive to simple, specific feelings such as 'agony',
'joy', etc., whereas the abstract works [of Kandinsky] were generated by and
conducive to new, finer and as yet unnamed emotions characteristic of the
new era" *(The Sounding Cosmos,* Abo, 1970, p. 205). In drawing attention
to the Theosophical images that may lie behind some of Kandinsky's own
vocabulary, Ringbom stresses that these sources should be seen as something
of a dictionary, "a repertory of crude paradigms" from which Kandinsky
developed his own language to express what he felt was a new range of
hitherto undefined emotions.

EXHIBITIONS:
Amsterdam, Stedelijk Museum, *Kandinsky,* Feb. 13-Mar. 14, 1948, no. 94; Paris, Galerie René
Drouin, *Kandinsky: époque parisienne,* June 2-July 2, 1949 (no cat.);[1] Boston, Institute of
Contemporary Art, *Kandinsky,* Mar. 25-Apr. 18, 1952 (checklist), traveled to New York,
M. Knoedler & Co., Inc., May 10-June 6, 1952, San Francisco Museum of Art, July 20-Aug.
26, 1952, Minneapolis, Walker Art Center, Sept. 14-Oct. 26, 1952, Cleveland Museum of Art,
Nov. 6-Dec. 7, 1952, Coral Gables, Fla., University of Miami, Feb.-Mar. 1953; Brussels,
SRGM 105-T, p. 44; Toronto, SRGM 117-T (no cat.); New York, SRGM 132, 144 (checklists);
Pasadena, SRGM 146-T, *Kandinsky,* no. 64, repr. p. 90; New York, SRGM 208, 212, 214, 226
(no cats.); 232, 241, p. 214, repr.; 252, repr. color; 266, 276 (no cats.).

1. No catalogue of this exhibition has been located. Nina Kandinsky (in correspondence with
   D. Robbins, Feb. 1963) stated that the picture was purchased out of this exhibition.

REFERENCES:

M. Bill, *Kandinsky,* Paris, 1951, repr. p. 86; Grohmann, 1959, pp. 240, 342 no. 718, repr. p. 325;
H. Read, *Kandinsky,* London, 1959, repr. color opp. p. 22; L. P. Sihari, *Oriental Influences on
W. Kandinsky and P. Mondrian, 1909-1917,* unpublished Ph.D. dissertation, Institute of Fine
Arts, New York University, 1967, pp. 168-169.

142   Twilight. 1943.
       (Crépuscule; Dusk; No. 720).

HL *1943, No. 720, Crépuscule.*

49.1223

Oil on board, 22¾ x 16½ (41.8 x 57.6)

Signed and dated l.l.: *K / 43*; inscribed by the
artist on reverse (transcribed but not photographed before mounting): *K / N⁰ 720 /
1943 / 58 x 42.*

PROVENANCE:

Nina Kandinsky, Paris, 1944-49; purchased
from Nina Kandinsky, 1949.

CONDITION:

In 1953 the work was mounted on Masonite
with PVA. The surface was cleaned with 1%
Soilax, and scattered losses along the top
and bottom edges were inpainted with PVA;
the work was then surfaced with PBM. In
1956 some additional losses at the edges
were filled and inpainted.

There is slight wear at all edges; there is a
1 in. tear in the veneer of the board at the
upper left. The condition in general is good.
(May 1974.)

EXHIBITIONS:

Paris, Galerie René Drouin, *Kandinsky: époque parisienne,* June 2-July 2, 1949 (no cat.);[1]
Brussels, SRGM 105-T, p. 43, repr.; Toronto, SRGM 117-T (no cat.); New York, SRGM 144
(checklist); Pasadena, SRGM 146-T, *Kandinsky,* no. 65, repr. p. 91; New York, SRGM 195 (no
cat.); 196 (checklist); 208, 212, 214, 226 (no cats.); 232, 241, p. 215, repr.; 252, repr.; 276
(no cat.).

REFERENCES:

Grohmann, 1959, pp. 240, 342 no. 720, repr. cc 520 *(Dusk)*; K. Lindsay, "Les Thèmes de
l'inconscient," *XX Siècle,* vol. xxvii, Dec. 1966, pp. 49-50.

1. No catalogue of this exhibition has been located. Nina Kandinsky (in correspondence with
   D. Robbins, Feb. 1963) stated that the picture was purchased out of this exhibition.

143   Red Accent. 1943.
        (L'Accent rouge).

HL *1943, No. 722, L'Accent rouge.*

71.1936R 137

Oil on board mounted on mahogany plywood panel, 16½ x 22¾ (41.8 x 57.9)

Signed and dated l.l.: *K / 43*; inscribed on
reverse, possibly by the artist:[1] *K / N⁰ 722 /
1943 / 58 x 42*; not in the artist's hand:
Kandinsky / "Composition Marron."

PROVENANCE:

Probably purchased directly from the artist
by Hilla Rebay, Greens Farms, Connecticut;[2]
Estate of Hilla Rebay, 1967-71; acquired
from the Estate of Hilla Rebay, 1971.

CONDITION:

3 large tears in the lower center were repaired at an unrecorded date.

All edges and corners are slightly worn and
there are faint rabbet marks on all edges.
There is a 1 in. tear in the support, 1½ in.
from the top and 10 in. from the right; also
an area of minor paint losses 2½ in. from
the top and 2½ in. from the left. The condition is good. (May 1974.)

EXHIBITIONS:

Paris, Galerie Raspail, group exhibition, May 1944;[3] New York, SRGM 241 (addenda); 252,
repr.; 276 (no cat.).

REFERENCE:

Grohmann, 1959, p. 342 no. 722, repr. cc 521.

1. This inscription, although adhering to Kandinsky's style, does not seem entirely characteristic of his hand. It is possible that the inscription was copied by another hand from
   Kandinsky's original on the reverse of the board and transferred to the mahogany panel
   after mounting.

2. No record of this transaction has hitherto been found.

3. The HL entry reads *"Galerie Raspail V 44."* Nina Kandinsky (in conversation with the
   author, Nov. 1972) identified this as a group exhibition. No catalogue has hitherto been
   located.

144 Ribbon with Squares. 1944.
(Ruban aux carrés; No. 731).

HL *1944, No. 731, Ruban avec carrés.*

47.1141

Gouache and oil on board, 16½ x 22¾
(41.8 x 57.8)

Signed and dated l.l.: *K / 44*; inscribed by
the artist on reverse: *K / No 731 / 1944 /
58 x 42.*

PROVENANCE:

Nina Kandinsky, Paris, 1944-45; purchased
from Nina Kandinsky by Galerie René
Drouin, Paris, May 1945 (information from
HL); I. S. Jastro, New York, by 1947;
purchased from Jastro, 1947.

CONDITION:

In 1954 the work was mounted on Masonite, cleaned with 1% Soilax, and surfaced
with PBM. The edges were filled and
inpainted.

All edges and corners show very minor inpainting; heavier inpainting at the lower
right corner edge. There is a very fine
crackle in the orange/red circle and the
checkered area. There is a very light rabbet
impression on all margins. An area of high
gloss 1 x 3 in. in the lower right of the composition is due to heavy varnish. The overall
condition is excellent. (Dec. 1973.)

EXHIBITIONS:

Brussels, SRGM 105-T, p. 45, repr.; Baltimore, SRGM 113-T (no cat.); Toronto, SRGM
117-T (no cat.); New York, SRGM 195, 196 (no cats.); 202, p. 100, repr.; 208, 212 (no cats.);
226 (no cat.; added Jan. 19); 252, repr. color; New York, SRGM 266, 276 (no cats.).

REFERENCES:

Grohmann, 1959, pp. 240, 342 no. 731, repr. p. 328; J. Lassaigne, *Kandinsky,* Geneva, 1964,
repr. color p. 112.

4000 copies of this catalogue, designed by
Malcolm Grear Designers, typeset by
Dumar Typesetting, Inc., have been printed
by The Meriden Gravure Company in
April 1976 for the Trustees of The Solomon
R. Guggenheim Foundation.